Princeton Theological Monograph Series

Dikran Y. Hadidian

General Editor

13

THE EPIGONES

Giovanni Diodati

THE EPIGONES

*A Study of the theology of the Genevan Academy
at the time of the Synod of Dort, with special
reference to Giovanni Diodati.*

By

William A. McComish

PICKWICK PUBLICATIONS

ALLISON PARK, PENNSYLVANIA

Published by Pickwick Publications
4137 Timberlane Drive
Allison Park, PA 15101-2932

Library of Congress Cataloging-in-Publication Data

McComish, William A.
    The epigones.

        (Princeton Theological monograph series, 13)
        Bibliography: p.
        Includes index.
        1. Reformed Church--Doctrines--History--17th century. 2. Académie
de Genève. 3. Diodati Giovanni, 1576-1649. 4. Theology, Doctrinal--
Switzerland--Geneva--History--17th century.
    I. Title. II. Series
    BX9424.5.S9M33 1988   230'.42   87-11073
    ISBN 0-915138-62-X
    Rev.

Epigone, *rare. One of a succeeding (and less distinguished) generation.*

Oxford English Dictionary.

Contents

Introduction

This work is an attempt to undertake a study in the neglected field of early seventeenth century reformed orthodoxy, often called Calvinism. It is an attempt to study the theology of the Genevan Academy at a period only half a century after its foundation. Yet this half century had seen considerable changes in the world in which the Academy existed. Founded to propagate reformed ideas and to train protestant pastors, any optimism about a successful spread of reformed ideas throughout Europe must by now have faded. Under increasing threat from Lutheranism in the German states and Catholicism in Lithuania, Poland and France, with a developing Anglicanism beginning to assert its independence from continental ideas, it must have seemed to many, including perhaps the Genevans themselves, that they formed part of a group of churches that was on the defensive if not actually in a state of political and theological decline. The composition of the academic staff under discussion is itself an evidence of this, of the three epigones, two, Giovanni Diodati and Benedict Turrettini were born into families exiled from Lucca for religious reasons, and the third, Theodore Tronchin, came of exiled French Huguenot stock. Compared to the then contemporary strength and vitality of the Roman college founded by Ignatius Loyola, it is evident that the Genevan counterpart was in a less dynamic condition. Students still came from abroad, including members of distinguished families, a Hottinger from Zurich and a Primerose from Bordeaux, but less so after 1618 as the Thirty Years War gained momentum, disrupting travel and diverting finance from academic work.

It is a feature of Church history that some periods and individuals have received more attention than others. There are many reasons for this, availability of sources, romantic eclecticism with regard to distinguished personalities and the idea of progress in ecclesiastical history, or the interest of historians themselves. In this uneven spread of academic application, the period of orthodoxy in both Lutheran and reformed theology has received considerably less reputable attention than other periods, such as the reformations of the sixteenth century, or of other matters associated with the seventeenth century such as English puritanism or the thought of Pascal. Interest was more widespread about these matters in the nineteenth century, but the material produced is not often of much use to the history of ideas as it is understood in the late twentieth century, much of the work on reformed theologians being purely biographical in character. The relative abandonment of studies in reformed orthodoxy in the twentieth century must owe something to the climate of historical opinion about these matters. It would appear that they are considered either monotonous or distasteful. This is indeed something that will be noted below when the historiography of the Synod of Dort is considered. In the paucity of material produced on seventeenth century theology compared with the exhaustive attention devoted to major figures of the sixteenth century reformations, there might well be a suggestion that the later theologians are uninteresting or even unworthy of academic study. It is certainly true that with the establishing of the confessional and state churches, with the coming of the wars of religion, that the public statements of theologians are more easily predictable in terms of dogma if not theology than was the case in the mid sixteenth century.

Considerations of the relative merits of different eras in theology need not concern us here. In order to justify a study in reformed theology during the period of orthodoxy it is sufficient to state that the subject has been somewhat neglected. This is an attempt to define the theology of one important reformed academy at the time of the Synod of Dort - the very participation of these epigones in the Synod enables us to make a number of interesting comparisons with their contemporaries. Geneva is chosen because of its associations with Calvin and Beza. Yet such a study is in itself merely an introduction. It is but one point of entry into the vast subject of reformed orthodoxy which will require many other studies of the Genevan Academy before even the basic outlines are clear, let alone the study of other similar institutions - the academies of Sedan and Saumur, the universities at Glasgow and Zurich as well as the colleges in Holland and Hungary, the seminaries of the American colonies.

It is not thought to be possible in a thesis of this length to offer any definitive illustration of reformed orthodoxy or Calvinism, for it will be seen that the subject matter does not reveal a slavish imitation of theological predecessors nor any stifling unanimity of theological opinion among the orthodox themselves. Orthodoxy is not simple, but complex. The most definite conclusion of this thesis is that sweeping generalisations about orthodoxy should be abandoned.

The method employed in this thesis is to try to define the theology of the Genevan Academy around the years 1618-19 by reference to distinguished predecessors, notably Calvin and Beza, and to contemporaries, both sympathetic and antagonistic. Following sections on biography and bibliography, the thesis attempts to examine the Genevan theology on a number of important topics. Special attention is devoted to Giovanni Diodati and a decision was made to concentrate on his thought, in particular his exegesis. In moving to the realm of ideas, much difficulty was encountered because of the kinds of material available, statements from Dort, Biblical annotations, students' theses and anti-Catholic polemics. The intractible nature of the material limited discussion in many ways. There was a lack of evidence on some important points, but it has been possible to examine soteriological concerns in the chapter on Dort (chapter 2), attitudes to scripture as revealed in the Coton controversy (chapter 3) and the life of Giovanni Diodati (Chapter 6) and patristics (chapter 5) while a number of important topics could be raised through the study of students theses. The level of information is not always satisfactory but there is sufficient material on some matters to permit comparison of the epigones with their predecessors and contemporaries. The results will be noted at different points throughout chapters 2-6 and drawn together in the conclusion. The Genevan attitudes of this period are not always easily predictable.

This is not the kind of thesis that was originally planned, nor is it the thesis which I should like to write. It remains introductory in character, posing many problems and questions. In the hope that it might serve as a prolegomenon to future study, it has been provided with a bibliography of Dort and of the epigones. Also included as appendices are two unpublished Genevan documents relating to Dort, both written by Theodore Tronchin, a sermon delivered at Dort and a report to the Council of Geneva. Also included as an appendix are lists of the proof texts used at Dort. Some use of these has been possible in this thesis but much of the study of reformed orthodoxy will depend on incidence of texts and patterns in catenae and it is a possible aid to future study that they are included here.

The study of the theology of the Genevan Academy grew out of a suggestion by Dr. John M. Barkley, Principal of Union Theological College, Belfast, N. Ireland. Dr. Peter Fraenkel, Director of the Institute d'Histoire de la Reformation of the University of Geneva, suggested that I might examine the relationship of the theology of the Genevan Academy to that of the Synod of Dort. I wish to express my gratitude to these two scholars as well as to friends, librarians and academics in Europe and North America too numerous to mention but whose help has been indispensable. I also wish to thank my own family, the Foundation Schmidheiny and the Bourse Francaise of the University of Geneva for providing the financial support necessary for the completion of this task. Thanks are also due to the Home Mission of the Presbyterian Church in Ireland for generously providing me with the necessary time as well as a most agreeable environment in which to work at Kells in County Meath.

My most important debt is to my Father, the late Dr. William McComish, B.Com.,M.Sc. (Econ.), Ph.D. (Lond. Econ.), for his support and inspiration.

In offering this thesis to the Faculte Autonome de Theologie Protestante in the University of Geneva through the Institut d'Histoire de la Reformation, I find that my best recommendation for the work is not that it solves many issues, for it clears up very little, but that it poses many questions.

Wm. A. McComish

Geneva
August 1979

Chapter 1
Biographical and Bibliographical
Giovanni Diodati

Giovanni Diodati was born at Geneva during 1576. His family came from Lucca, where they had been converted to Protestantism during the time when Pietro Martire Vermigli was working there. The Diodati family had become exiles for religious reasons, and eventually settled in Geneva as did certain other Protestant branches of Luccan families such as the Turrettinis and the Calandrinis. The Diodatis were exiles of some substance and Giovanni's father had become a bourgeois of Geneva during 1572[1]. Giovanni studied theology at the Genevan Academy under Calvin's successors, men such as Theodore Beza and Isaac Casaubon. Giovanni showed himself to be a gifted linguist at an early age. He became a doctor of theology at the age of nineteen and was made professor of Hebrew at the Genevan Academy in 1597 at the age of twenty. In this post he was successor to Isaac Casaubon who had left Geneva to go to Montpellier[2]. Diodati was made rector in 1608 and retained the chair of Hebrew until 1618. He was also professor of theology at the Genevan Academy from 1599 until 1645, four years before his death[3]. Diodati left Geneva for short periods to go to Venice, to visit the French Reformed Churches and to act as a Genevan delegate to the Synod of Dort. Despite this lifelong connection with Geneva, Diodati seems to have considered himself as a Luccan exile living in Geneva. In his first complete annotated version of the Bible, published in 1607, he describes himself as being:- "di nation Lucchese"[4]. This identification with Lucca is not only typical of the young Diodati, since he also described himself as:- "di nation Lucchese" in the title of the 1640/41 *La Sacra Bibbia,* produced towards the end of his life. Diodati was essentially Italian despite his association with Geneva, and the best proof of this lies in the fact that his translation of the Scriptures has proved so useful that it is still being published, albeit in a modified form, more than three hundred years after its first appearance.

Three attempts have been made to write lives of Diodati. The earliest was Jean Diodati, in Dutch, written by G.D.G. Schotel and published at the Hague in 1844. This work is the unorthodox production of an eccentric scholar and is of little use to modern historians. An Italian life appeared at Turin during 1854, *Brevi introduzioni al libri Sacri dell' Antico e Nuovo Testamento per Giovanni Diodati traduttore della Bibbia proceduti dalla vita dell' Autore,* but the most widely circulated life of Giovanni Diodati was the *Vie de Jean Diodati, Theologien Genevois,* by E. de Budé (Lausanne 1869). This life is the most satisfactory account of Diodati's career, though it is intellectually unsatisfying, containing some factual errors and is more concerned with biographical and genealogical matters than with the academic or theological achievements of Giovanni Diodati. This life by E. de Budé was translated into Italian and published in 1870 as *Vita di Giovanni Diodati Teologo Ginevrino* and into English by Maria Betts in 1905 as *Life of Giovanni Diodati Genevese Theologian. Translator of the Italian Bible.* This is an abridgement as well as a translation and is quite unsatisfactory. Unfortunately, until now, it has been the only account of Diodati to be found in the English language.

Giovanni Diodati's career was that of a Reformed pastor in the academic service of the Church of Geneva. Diodati was, perhaps, more of a linguist than a theologian. It was of great interest to him that the Scriptures should be available to all men in readable form and with simple annotations. To this end, Diodati devoted all his academic gifts for the greater part of his life. Inevitably, this preoccupation of Diodati's was apparent in his interpretation of his academic appointment as professor of Hebrew at the Genevan Academy. Before his time, the chair of Hebrews had been a humanist creation, devoted to the study of Hebrew at a purely linguistic level. With Diodati, this was to change, and he brought a more theological approach to his section of the Genevan Academy. As Charles Borgeaud, the historian of the University of Geneva, has written:- "c'est a partir d'elle que la chaire d'Hébreu, perdant une independance scientifique relative et le charactere que lui avait imprime l'humanisme de ses fondateurs, commenca de graviter autour des chaires de théologie."[5] G. Diodati, with Theodore Tronchin and Benedict Turrettini, the distinguished son of another family of Luccan exiles, forms part of the group which Borgeaud calls "les Epigones", the successors of Theodore Beza, at the Genevan Academy. Diodati remained a faithful servant of the Genevan Church all his life, but, as will be seen later in the discussion of Diodati's struggle to publish his French translation of the Bible, his last years were disturbed by a number of protracted disputes within the Genevan Church. These would seem to have been of a largely personal nature.

Giovanni Diodati's main involvement in Italian affairs came when he was still young, and at a time when he had just completed his first annotated version of the Bible in the Italian tongue. He was part of a conspiracy at Venice which involved Paolo Sarpi, the official theologian of the Venetian Republic, two English ambassadors, Sir Henry Wotton (it was he who said that an ambassador is an honest man sent to lie abroad for the good of his country)[6], and Sir Dudley Carleton (who was the English ambassador at The Hague at the time of the Synod of Dort), George Bedell who later became an Anglican Bishop in Ireland, and the Huguenot leader Philippe du Plessis-Mornay. Diodati worked in this group with the object of weakening Papal power in Venice and visited that republic twice during 1605 and 1608. He wrote an account of this second visit which was published by E. de Budé in 1863 as *Briève relation de mon voyage a Venise en septembre 1608*. The conspiracy was revealed when one of Diodati's letters fell into the hands of the French Jesuit Pierre Coton[7], who at that time was confessor to the king of France and who later attacked the Genevan French Bible translations[8]. There are references to Diodati to be found in Sarpi's published correspondence, in *Paolo Sarpi lettere ai Gallicani (edizione critica, saggio introduttivo e note a cura)* by Boris Ulianich (Wiesbaden 1961) and in *Fra Paolo Sarpi - Lettere Ai Protestanti* (series - Scrittoria d'Italia) edited by Manlio Dirilo (Bari 1931, 2 vols.). Diodati's involvement with Sarpi led him to translate Sarpi's History of the Council of Trent into French, a work which had more success than any other work of Diodati's except the Italian Bible of 1640/41.

Diodati was sent, with Theodore Tronchin, to represent Geneva at the Synod of Dort in 1618/19. Diodati was ill during the Synod and we know that he was unable to attend some of the sessions in consequence[9]. This illness did not, however, prevent Diodati from taking a most active part in the affairs of the Synod. He addressed the Synod on the doctrine of *perseverantia sanctorum* and favourably impressed his audience, for the Scottish de legate Balcanqual wrote that Diodati did very sweetly just as he useth to preach, not as Doctors use to do in schools"[10]. This speech was also well-received by the Dutch Arminian historian G. Brandt, who was generally unsympathetic towards Diodati[11] In this instance Brandt praised Diodati's moderation. Diodati also gave advice to the Synod concerning Bible translation, but unfortunately, all trace of what he actually said would appear to have been lost[12]. Diodati also discussed the matter of censorship of the press, drawing on his experience at Venice[13], and explained that too much severity might be as harmful as too little control[14].

At the Synod of Dort, Diodati did not limit his theological contribution to the sessions of the Synod and he also preached elsewhere in Holland on a number of occasions. On his return to Geneva, Theodore Tronchin, Diodati's colleague, informed the Conseil de Geneve, that:-

"Pendant nostre seiour, outre le devoir quavons tache de rendre au Synode, Monsieur Diodati et moy avons presche fort souvent a Dordrech, Rotterdam, Delft, La Haye, Amsterdam, et en autres lieux, non sans fruit par la benediction de Dieu"[15]. These attempts met with varying success. Sir Dudley Carleton, then English ambassador at The Hague, wrote how Diodati preached before the court of Maurice of Nassau at Christmas 1618:- "Diodati, the minister of Geneva, had been at The Hague during the recess of the Synod, and preached in the court chapel both yesterday and to-day, in the presence of the prince of Orange and Count William, the princess dowager and Count Henry, and a great concourse of men and women of both factions which is a presage of a good agreement.[16]. However, not all Diodati's sermons were so well received. In accordance with his desire to promote Italian Protestantism, he decided to conduct Reformed Church services in Italian at Dort. Brandt, the Arminian historian, gives a malicious account of this:- "Te deser tijdt begost Deodatus, Professor te Geneven, alle Donderdaegen in't Italiaensch te prediken, om de Synode daer door to meer luister te geven. Dit duurde de geheele vasten Doch daer waeren soo weinige, die't Italiaens verstonden, dat men geen Leser, noch Voorsanger, noch medesingers kon vinden en de Predikatien sonder Lofsangen moest doen, regelrecht tagens den Geneefschen stijl; In d'eerste preeke waeren slechts ses of seven mannen, en eene vrouw, die hem hoorden"[17]. It is necessary to stress the importance of Diodati's preaching, especially his preaching in the Italian language, for none of his sermons have survived either in manuscript or in printed form.

Diodati also performed a diplomatic service for the Genevan state while at the Synod of Dort. With Tronchin, he was instructed to enter into negotiations with the government of Holland, with the purpose of trying to persuade the Dutch to cancel the considerable financial debt which Geneva had contracted towards the government of the Low Countries. Diodati was successful in this, for during April 1619, a letter from Diodati in Holland was reported to the Conseil de Geneve. He had written that:- "il a sonde quelques uns de Mrs. les Estats les plus confidents touschant les obligations qu'il a recogneu leur intention de ne nous en jamais rien demander"[18].

The Genevan delegates to the Synod of Dort took an active part in the theological discussions of that assembly. Diodati was elected to a committee which produced the Canons of Dort, the final statement of the Synod on the doctrines of salvation[19]. The Genevans also wrote their own account of the matters under consideration. In general, Giovanni Diodati and Theodore Tronchin express opinions which were generally similar to those of the other Reformed delegates at the Synod. Concerning the second article "De morte Christi et hominum per eam redemptione", however, the Genevans presented an interpretation that was somewhat dissimilar to those of the other delegations. In this instance, the Genevans refused to be bound by the Anselmian concept of redemption theory that was typical of the other delegations. The Genevan contributions were printed in the *Acta* of the Synod of Dort and are discussed in detail elsewhere in this thesis.

Giovanni Diodati's travels were very much curtailed after 1619 because of his constant ill-health. He had acted as a Genevan agent in France on two occasions during 1611 and 1617. In 1611, he had been sent to secure aid for Geneva among Huguenot elements[20].

Diodati was a relatively well-known figure in the Europe of his day. His correspondence reveals contact with numerous interesting figures in various countries the Huguenot leader Philippe Du Plessis-Mornay,[21] the expatriate Scottish theologian John Cameron[22], the, English diplomat Sir Dudley Carleton[23], the Prince of Orange[24], Cyril Lucaris, Patriarch of Constantinople[25], the famous ecumenist John Dury[26] and the French theologian Andre Rivet[27] as well as many letters associated with J.J. Breitinger, the redoubtable leader of the Reformed Church at Zurich[28] who maintained a vast correspondence with theologians and men of affairs all over Europe. Diodati's stature has already been revealed by his association with Paolo Sarpi, he not only knew Sarpi personally but translated his history of the Council of Trent. Diodati also translated Sir Edwin Sandys *Europae Speculum*. Both these works were published in a number of editions and they reveal Diodati's involvement with the intellectual concerns of his own day. His reputation was considerable in England, where the use of his name proved to be useful to Royalist propagandists at the time of the Civil War. Diodati's associations with England are discussed in detail later in this thesis[29].

The life of Diodati was far from being uniformly happy. He suffered from a brilliant early career which was followed by a period of twenty years, the years before his death, in which he declined in popularity within the Genevan Church and turned into an isolated and sometimes bitter old man. The courage, stubbornness and anger of Giovanni Diodati is revealed by the part which he played in the condemnation of N. Anthoine, a unitarian executed for Judaism at Geneva during the mid seventeenth century[30], and by his denunciation of the English regicides from the pulpit of the cathedral in Geneva (This incident is discussed later). One reason for this change in Diodati's circumstances was the effect of the ill-health which he had suffered throughout much of his life. The main reason,

4

however, certainly seems to have been the psychological effect of Diodati's protracted struggle to publish his French Bible, which is described in chapter V. This long and unhappy episode must have absorbed much of Diodati's energies, and it seems to be quite certain that this matter, combined with Diodati's ill-health to prevent either completion or publication of his proposed Latin translation of the Scriptures.

These misfortunes do not detract from the considerable nature of Giovanni Diodati's achievement as a translator of the Bible into the Italian language. The Diodati translation shares the distinction of the English Authorised or King James' version of the Bible as being a seventeenth century translation which is still in regular use well within the second half of the twentieth century. This bibliography lists only the earlier printings, for there are many nineteenth and twentieth century printings, over two hundred complete or partial editions of his Italian translation of the Bible have been traced. He created the standard Bible of Italian Protestantism. The only other part of his work which survived his death was the French translation that he made of Sarpi's history of the Council of Trent which was published a number of times after 1649. The Italian translation of the Bible by Giovanni Diodati has remained as a permanent memorial to its creator. It has survived on two levels. Firstly, it has retained academic respect because of the linguistic ability of Diodati. With, it must be admitted, a degree of editing, it has retained its place as a responsible and accurate translation, a fact which has led to its acceptance by major Protestant Churches and to its propagation by organisations such as the British and Foreign Bible Society and the Society for the Promotion of Christian Knowledge. This propagation of the Diodati Italian Bible was sometimes accompanied by a degree of criticism from various sources, mainly Catholic, but this did not prevent the Bible from retaining its position as the most influential Protestant version of the Scriptures in Italian. Secondly, Diodati's translation of the Bible has remained acceptable on a literary as well as on an academic level. In one sense, Diodati's Italian Bible has been a more remarkable achievement than the English Authorised version, in that the Authorised version was the product of a group of scholars while Diodati worked alone, though possibly with assistance from Benedict Turrettini, and produced a complete annotated version of the Bible in 1607 when he was only thirty-one years of age. His annotations reveal a pietistic and non-dogmatic emphasis that was at least fifty years ahead of the main intellectual development of the Reformed Churches. Although he could not live in Italy, the theologian "di nation Lucchese" could hardly have made a more notable contribution to Italian Protestantism and to Italian literature.

Bibliography of Giovanni Diodati

For ease of reference, this bibliography is divided into the following sections:-
Italian Bible
French Bible
Translations of the Annotations

> Diodati's translation of Sarpi
> Diodati's translation of Sandys
> Letter to the Westminster Assembly
> Letter to Lady Westmoreland
> Miscellaneous

It is intended that this bibliography should be read in conjunction with chapter V, "Giovanni Diodati", as well as with the preceding biographical note. The provenance of editions may be traced from the list of libraries on pp. 28-32.

Italian Bible

(1)

LA BIBBIA / CIOE, I LIBRI / DEL VECCHIO, / E DEL NVOVO / TESTAMENTO. / (scroll) / *Nuouamente traslati in lingua Itaaliana, / DA GIOVANNI DIODATI, / di nachion Lucchese. / (ornament)/ M.DC.VII. /*
Size x .

The ornament is that of a farmer broadcasting seed on a ploughed field, behind are a farmhouse and a city, above is a scroll in the sky bearing the legend:- "SON ART EN DIEU", all bounded by a design of two cherubs and four cornucopia, size 96 x 95 mm.

One volume, the folio signatures are:-(   )^2, A-B^8, C-Z^4, A-2Z^4,2A-3M^4, aA-yY^4, zZ^2, aAa-zZz^4, AaA-RrR^4.

(   )lr is the title page, (   )lv is blank, (   )2r has:- "LA TAVOLA DE'LIBRI CA- / NONICI DELLA SCRITTVRA / SACRA", (   )2v has the text of 2 Timothy 3/16, 17, in Italian, A1r(pl)-3M4r (p847) the Old Testament, 3M4v (unnumbered) is blank, aAlr has within a foliated ornament of 115 x 141 mm.:- "I LIBRI / APOCRIFI", aAlv has:- "LA TAVOLA DE' LI- / BRI APOCRIFI. / ", aA2r (p3) - zZlv (p178) the Apocrypha, aAalr has within a foliated ornament of 115 x 141 mm.:- "I LIBRI / DEL NVOVO / TESTA- MENTO. /", aAalv is blank, aAa2r - RrRlv the New Testament, the remainder blank.
The Old Testament is presented with introductions to the individual books, introductions to the chapters, and a combination of marginal notes and footnotes. The name of the book appears at the head of each page. The text is in two columns, each of 50 mm. Annotations are less copious than in no. 2. The Apocrypha has a half page introduction. The text of the Apocrypha has no chapter headings, neither has it been given marginal notes or footnotes. The name of the book is printed at the head of each page. The text is in two columns, each of 50 mm. The New Testament is treated in a similar manner to the Old Testament.

(2)

LA SACRA / BIBBIA, / tradotta / In lingua Italiana, e commentata / da / GIO-VANNI DIODATI, / DI NATION LVCCHESE. / Seconda EDITIONE, migliorata, ed accresciuta. / con l'aggiunta de' SACRI SALMI / in rime per lo medesimo. / (ornament) / Pet PTETRO CHOVET. / - / M.DC.XLI. /
Size 354 x 22 mm

The ornament is of a robed, bearded figure, standing under a tree, some of whose branches are falling and in whose remaining branches is entwined a scroll bearing the legend:- "NOLI ALTVM SAPERE". Size 11 x 74 mm. There is, in many copies, a second, engraved, title page, which reads:- (within an engraved portico, supported by four Corinthian pillars) LA / SACRA / BIBBIA / Tradotta / in lingua Italiana / da / Giovanni Diodati / M.DC.XL. / ABosse jn. et fecit.

The folio signatures are:- ( )^3, A-4A^6, A-2D^6, 2E^4, A-L^6, M^8, A-E^6, F^4.

( )1r is the engraved title page, ( )1v is blank, ( )2r is the title page, ( )2v is blank, ( )3r has:- "TAVOLA / DE' LIBRI CANONICI DELLA / SACRA SCRITTVRA", A1r (pl, unnumbered) - 4A5r (p 837) the Old Testament, 4A5v is blank, 4A6v are blank, A1r (pl) - 2E4r (p 331) the New Testament, 2E4v is blank, A1r has:- "I LIBRI / APOCRIFI.", A1v has "I SACRI / SALMI / MESSI IN RIME / volgari / da / GIOVANNI DIODATI", A1v is blank, A2r (p3) F4v (p 68) the Psalms.

The Old Testament text is in two columns, each of 63 mm. There is an introduction to each book, written by Diodati and there are introductions to the individual chapters. There are Scriptural cross references in the margins. There are copious footnotes, in smaller type then the Biblical text and greater in quantity than the text itself. The footnotes are contained in a single broad column of 151 mm. These notes are not the same as the annotations of the 1607 bible, list no. 1. There are page headings, these give the name of the book, but not the chapter number. Some words of the text are put in italic script. The New Testament is treated in a similar manner. The Apocrypha, pp 3-5(A2r-A3r) contain an:- "AVVERTIMENTO / sopra /I LIBRI / APOCRIFI", and there is an introduction to each book, but there are no marginal notes, chapter introductions or footnotes. The text is in two columns, each of 63 mm. The text of the metrical version of the Psalms is in two columns of varying width, and there are no annotations of any kind, but each Psalm is preceded by:- "SALMO-" and by its number in Roman numerals.

The four sections of this book are to be found bound in a number of different orders. There are a number of libraries which have copies of the metrical Psalms in this edition, but which do not have the other three sections. These are denoted as "2P" in the list of libraries. In the case of a separate copy of the Psalms, the title is:- "I / SACRI / SALMI, / MESSI IN RIME / volgari / Da / GIOVANNI DIODATI", and it is one volume of 68 pp, A-E^6, F^4. A1r is the title page, A1v is blank, A24-F4v have the metrical version of the Psalms.

(3)

LA / SACRO-SANTA / BIBLIA / IN / LINGUA ITALIANA. / Cioe / Il vecchio e nuovo Testamento nella purita della / Lingua volgare, moderna e corretta, corrispondente / per tutto al Testo fondamentale vero, distinta per Versetti a pro / della Gioventu, e stampata con lettere molti leggibili, / a pro di quei, che sono d'eta / avan- / zata: / VOLUME / A tutti i desiderosi della loro propria salute utilissimo, arrichi-

/ *tod'ardentissimi Sospirii a Dio, quasi per ogni* / *Capitolo.* / Da / MATTIA d' ERBERG, / cultore delle sacre Lettere. / (ornament) / - / NORIMBERGO, / *Alle Spese di quest'istesso* AUTORE, / Dimorante prossimo all' albergo dei tre Re, l'Anno / MDCCXII. /
Size 334 x 209.

Ornament is a representation of the head of Christ, within a halo, within a border bearing the words "CHRISTUS IESUS", within an ornament of leaves, size 85 x 108 mm.

Folio signatures, 1 engraved leaf, ( )^2, A-5I^4, 1 engraved leaf, A-2c^4.

The engraved leaf bears a replica of the tables of the law supported by cherubs and old Testament figures, it is marked "P: Decker Iun: delin: I: I: Wolff. fi:", the verso is blank, ( )1r is the title page, ( )2r has:- "A / QUELLI / Aiquali / L'Autore, o per Rispetto di dovuta Riverenza, o / per contrasegno di vera stima, o per Pegno di sincera / Amicizia consecra, dedica, e dona il / presente volume" by "*Humilissimo Servidore* / MATTIA d'Erberg, / cultore delle sacre Lettere.", ( )2v has:- "L'ORDINE / Dei Libri della Scrittura Sacra col numero dei capi / di quella.", A1r (p1)-5D4r (p767) the Old Testament, 5Dv (p 768)-5I4r (p 807) the Apocrypha (which is without separate title page), 5I4r (p 807)-5I4v (p 808) have: "TAVOLA / SOPRA IL / VECCHIO TESTAMENTO.", the engraved page has an engraving representing a sun, supported by figures of Christ, God the Father and the Holy Spirit (i.e., a dove) whose light is shining upon the four Gospels held by the four evangelists who are grouped around a table and supported by their symbols (the man, the lion, the eagle and the ox), the light from the four gospels then draws together on a single volume lying on the table. This leaf is marked:- "IL / NUOVO / TESTA / MENTO", the verso blank. A1r (p1)- 2C4r (p 207) the New Testament, 2C4r (p 207)-2C4v (p 208) is a:- " TAVOLA. / *Sopra il* / NUOVO TESTAMENTO.".

The text of the Old Testament is in two columns, each of 77 mm., with a central dividing line. Most books commence with an "ARGOMENTO", most chapters are followed by a few Scriptural cross references and close with a "SOSPIRIO". Each page is headed with the name of the book, not with the number of the relevant chapter or chapters, but with a brief description of the matter to be found on that page. Some words within the text appear in italics. The New Testament is treated in a similar manner to the Old Testament, but the paper used is of an inferior quality. The Aphocrypha is in two columns, each of 77 mm., with a central dividing line, the pages are headed but there are few cross references, few words in italics, through the chapters are begun and closed by a "SOSPIRIO".

(4)
LA SACRA / BIBBIA / CHE CONTIENE / IL VECCHIO, ED IL NUOVO / TESTAMENTO, / TRADOTTA / IN LINGVA ITALIANA / DA / GIOVANNI DIODATI, / DI NAZION LVCCHESE, / RIVEDUTA DI NVOVO / SOPRA DA / GIOVANNI DAVID MVLLER. / MAESTRO DELLE ARTI. / - / *IN LIPSIA* / AP-

PRESSO GIACOMO BORN, LIBRAIO. / 1744. /
Size 170 x 102 mm.

Folio signatures, ⁴, a-3P⁸, A-V⁸ lr is blank, lv is an extra engraved title page, signed:- *"Tobias Lobeck sculps. Aug. Vind."*, representing a portico supported by corinthian columns revealing:- *"LA / SACRA / BIBBIA / Tradotta / in lingua Ita- / liana / da / Giouanni Dio- / dati."*, the base of the portico has:- *"Lipsia MDCCXLIV"* and the arch of the portico bears an open book containing the words:- *"Urim et Tummim"*, there being a dove descending towards the arch of the portico, 2r is the title page, 2v is blank, 24-4r is an:- *"AVVISO ALLETTORE"*, 4v has a lost of:- *"I Libri del Vecchio Testamento"* and a list of:- *"I Libri Apocrifi"*, A1r-3P8v the Old Testament, a1r-P8r the Apocrypha, P8v is blank, A1r is the title page of the New Testament:- *"IL / NUOVO / TESTAMENTO / DEL / SIGNOR NOSTRO / IESU CHRISTO, / TRADOTTO / IN LINGUA ITALIANA / DA / GIOVANNI DIO-DATA / DINATION LUCCHESE. / RIVEDUTO DI NUOVO / SOPRA GLI ORIGINALI, / E CORRETTO / CON OGNI MAGGIOR DILIGENZA / DA GIO-VANNI DAVID MVLLER, / MAESTRO DELLE ARTI. / - / IN LIPSIA /APPRESSO GIACOMO NORN, LIBRAIO. / 1744."*, A1v has a list of:- *"I Libri del Nuovo Testamento."*, A2r-V8r the New Testament, V8v is blank.

The text is in two columns, each of 43 mm., with no central dividing line. There are no introductions to the books, but there are introductions to the chapters. There are no notes in the margin or at the foot of the page, but Scriptural cross references are included after many verses. The pages are headed with the name of the book in capitals and with the number of the chapter in Roman numerals. There are many words in italics.

(5)
LA SACRA / BIBBIA, / CHE CONTIENE / IL VECCHIO, ED IL NUOVO / TESTAMENTO, / TRADOTTA / IN LINGVA ITALIANA / DA / GIOVANNI DIODATI / (ornament) / - / IN DRESDA ED IN LIPSIA / APPRESSO GIORGIO CORRADO WALTHER, / LIBRAJO DELLA CORTE. / 1757./
Size 180 x 105 mm.

Ornament is of a baroque design supporting two birds and the head of a cherub while containing a bunch of flowers, size 31 x 42 mm.

Two volumes, (4), A-Z⁸, Aa-Zz⁸, Aaa-Ppp⁸, a-i⁸, K⁴, 1-p⁸ and A-V⁸. The New Testament has a separate title page:- *"IL / NUOVO / TESTAMENTO / DEL / SIGNOR NOSTRO / IESU CHRISTO, / TRADOTTO / IN LINGUA ITALIANA / DA / GIOVANNI DIODATI. / (ornament) / - / IN DRESDA ED IN LIPSIA / APPRESSO GIORGIO CORRADO WALTHER, / LIBRAJO DELLA CORTE / 1757."*, the ornament is of a baroque design supporting two birds and the head of cherub while containing a bunch of flowers, size 31 x 42 mm. Volume I has an index on pp 7-8 (unnumbered) and volume II has an index on pp 3-4 (unnumbered).

The text is in two columns, each of 43 mm., with a central dividing line. There are no introductions to the books, but there are brief introductions to the chapters. There are no notes in the margin or at the foot of the page, but there are Scriptural cross references at the close of many verses. The pages are headed with the name of the book in capitals and with the number of the chapter in Roman numerals. There are some words in italics.

(6)

(within a border of foliate ornaments) / SESSANTA / SALMI DI / DAVID, / (asterisk) / *tradotti in rime volgari Italia-* / *ne, secondo la verita del* / *testo Hebreo.* / Col cantico di Simeone, & i / dieci Comandamenti del- / ti della legge ogni cosa / insie- / me col canto. / APPRESSO / GIOVAN DI TORNES. / - M.DCVII. / Size, in 8o.

(7)

(within a border of human and foliate ornaments) / SESSANTA / SALMI DI / DAVID, / *TRADOTTI IN RI-* / *ma volgari Italiane, secon-* / *do la verita del testo* / *Hebreo.* / Col / Cantico di Simeone, & i/ dieci Comandamen- / ti della Legge ogni cosa / insieme col canto./ *APPRESSO* / *MATTEO BERJON.* / -/ *M.DC.XXI.* / *Size 119 x 70 mm.*

Folio signatures A-Z⁸, a-d⁸. A1r title page, a1v is blank, A2r-A6v has:- A TVTTI I CHRISTIANI, ET / *amatori della Parola di Dio",* A7r has:- *"La Domenica, al Catechismo.",* A7v has:- *"Il Giouendi alle preghiere.",* A8r has:- *"TAVOLA SECONDO L'OR* / *dine dell' alfabeto.",* B1r-M5r the Psalms, each with an introduction and with the first verse set to music, M5r has:- *"IL CANTICO DI SIMEONE"* with music, M5v has:- *"LI DIECI COMANDAMENTO* / *DI DIO"* with music, M7r has:- *"DEGLI ARTICOLO DEL-* / *LA FEDE"* with music, M8r has:- *"ORATIONE DEL NOSTRO* / *SIGNOR GIESV CHRISTO."* with music, M8v has:- *"SOPRA LE PAROLE DEL SI-* / *GNORE, Ego sum panis viuus, & c.* / *Gio 6",* with music, N1v has *"PREGO PER QVANDO DI* / *dee mangiare.",* N2r has:- *"RENDIMENTE DI GRATIE* / *poi che s'e mangiato",* N3r has:- *"LA FORMA DEL-* / *LE ORATIONI EC-* / *Clesiastiche",* O7r-P4r has:- *"LA FORMA D'AM-* / *MINISTRARE IL* / *BAT-TESIMO."* P4v-P8r has:- *"IL Modo DI CE-* / *LEBRARE LA SAN-* / *TA CENA",* P8v-Q3v has:- *"IL MODO DI CE-* / *LEBRARE IL SANTO* / *MATRIMONIO.",* Q3v-Q5r has:- *"DELLA VISITA-* / *TIONE DEGLI* / *AMMALATI",* Q5r-Q6v has:- *"ORATIONE PRI-* / *VATA, PER QVELLI* / *CHE SI TROVA-* / *no in cattiuita.",* Q7v-A8r has:- *"IL CATECHISMO,* / *CIOE,* / *FORMVLARIO PER* / *instruire & ammaestrare i fanciuilli nel-* / *la vera e pura dottrina Christiana, fatto* / *a modo di Dialogo, done il Ministro do-* / *manda, e il Fanciullo risponde",* a8v-b5r is:- *"ALCVNE PIE O-* / *RATIONI",* b5v-d4r is:- *"CONFESSIONE DI* / *fede fatta d'vn comune accordo da colora,* / *liquali in Francia Viuendo secondo la pu-* / *ra dottrina dell Euangelio del nostro Si-* / *gnore Giesu Christo.",* d4r-d7r is:- *"MEDITATIONE SOPRE* / *L'istesso Salmo.",* the rest is blank.

(8)(a)
I SACRI / SALMI / *Messi in rime Italiene* / da / GIOVANNI DIODATI. / (ornament)
/In Geneva, Appresso PIETRO AVBERT / - / M.DC.XXXI. /
Size 124 x 62 mm.
The ornament of of a dolphin entwined round an anchor, size 44 x 29 mm.
Folio signatures A-O^{12}, p^4.
The metrical Psalms without annotation of any kind.

(b)
I SACRI / SALMI / *Messi in rime Italiane* / da / GIOVANNI DIODATI. / (ornament)
/ - / M.DC.XXXI /
Size 117 x 64 mm.

The ornament is of a dolphin entwined round an anchor, size 44 x 29 mm.
Folio signatures A-O^{12}, p^4, Q.
The metrical Psalms without annotation of any kind. Leaf "Q" contains an:-
"Errori di stampa."

These are two impressions of the same edition, the addition of an *erratum* may
suggest that (b) is slightly later in date. There are two confusing features which
should not be allowed to conceal the fact that these books are of the same edition.
Firstly, the two books are of different format, and, secondly, (a) is located as
being printed in Geneva while (b) is *sine loco*. A comparison of the contents of
each page and of the situation of individual letters, reveals that these are invariably the same, and thus it is concluded that these are two impressions of the
same book. (a) is found in the Bibliotheque publique et universitaire, Geneva,
no. S 22876; (b) is found in the Musee historique de la reformation, Geneva, no.
6f(631).

A1r is the title page, a1v is blank, a2v-P4v the Psalms.

(9)
I SACRI / SALMI DI DAVID / MESSI IN RIME / VOLGARI ITALIANE. / DA
/GIOUANNI DIODATI / *di nation Lucchese*. / Et / Composti in Musica de A.G.
/(ornament) / In Haerlemme. / Appresso Jacob Albertz Libraro. / 1664. /
Size 160 x 94 mm.

The ornament is a figure playing a harp, size 36 x 39 mm.

Folio signatures ^{4}, A-Z^8, 2A^3. There is a colophon:- "Nella Stamperia di *Isaac
van Wesbusch*, addi 12 Marzo 1664." The metrical version of the Psalms with Latin
titles and with music, but no annotations. There is an introduction by the pub-
lisher to the reader.

(10)
CENTO / SALMI DI / DAVID, / *TRADOTTI* / IN RIME VOLGARI ITALIANE, /
SECONDO LA VERITA del testo Hebreo. / *Col Cantico di Simeone, et i dieci* /

The Epigones

Comandamenti della Legge: / Ogni cosa insieme col can / (ornament) / IN GINEVRA, /Appresso SAMVEL DE TOVRNES, / - / M.DC.LXXXIII / Size 136 x 75 mm.

The ornament is of an angel, holding a book, resting on a T cross standing on a skeleton, with an aureole behind, size 36 x 28 mm.

Folio signatures [12], A-O[12], P[10], 2r-8r has:- "A Tutti I Christiani, e Amatori della Parola di DIO", 8v-9v is "Tavola de Salmi secondo l'ordine del Canto", 10r-11v is a:- "Tavola Secondo l'Ordine dell'Alfabeto", 12r has an:- "Al Lettore", 12v has a verse, A1r-L8r:-"Salmi di David Tradotti in Rime volgari Italiane, accompagnati col canto", L8v has a:- "Prego per quando si dee mangiare", L9r-L9v has:- "Rendimento di Gratie poi che s'e mangiato", Ltor-M7r has:- "La forma delle orationi Ecclesiastiche", M7r-M11v has:- "La forma d'amministrare il Battesimo", M11v-N2v has:- "Il Mondo di celebrare la Santa Cena", N3r-N5v has:- "Il Modo di cebrareil santo Matrimonio", N6r-N6v has "Nella visitatione degli Ammalati", N7r-N8r has:- "oratione privata, per quelli che si trovano in cattivita", N8v-N10v has:- "Il Modo d'esaminare i Fanciulli che s'hanno a ricever alla Cena del nostro Signor Giesu Christo", N11r-O2v has:- "Alcune pi orationi", O3r has part of Psalms 3 and 4, O3v-O7v has:- "Preghira per prepararsi allaa Santa Cena", O8r-O8v has:- "Li dieci Comandamenti della legge diece Comandamenti della legge di Dio", O9r has:- :La summa di tutta la Legge", O9v is blank, O10r-P9v is a:- "Confessione di fede."

(11)
(ornament) / *IL* / *NVOVO TESTA-* / *MENTO* / del *Signor nostro* / *IESV CHRISTO* / (scroll) *Giovanni Dio-* / *DATI.* / 1608 / *P. Firens fecit.*/
Size 130 x 72 mm

The ornament, which contains the title, is of a classical portico supported by two corinthian columns, size 113 x 59 mm.
The scroll size is 4 x 17 mm.

The folio signatures are ( ), a-z[12], A-D[12], E[8]. ( ) 1r is the title page, ( ) 1v is blank, a1r and a1v have:- "LA TAVOLA DE' / LIBRI DEL NVO- / *uo Testamento.*", a24-E7r the New Testament, the rest blank.

The text is in a single column of 47 mm., and has marginal references to other passages of Scripture. There are no notes at the foot of the page. Each chapter has an introduction in italic type. Each page is headed with the name of the book but not with the number of the chapter.

(12)
IL / NUOVO / TESTAMENTO / DEL SIGNOR NOSTRO / JESU CHRISTO. / Tradotto / *In Lingua Italiana.* /Da / GIOVANNI DIODATI. / Di Nation Lucchese. / (ornament) / *In Haerlem,* / *Appresso Jacob ALBERTZ.* / *Librario.* /1665. /
Size 151 x 90 mm.

The ornament represents figures holding plumes seated around a table with, behind, the symbols of the four evangelists, size 35 x 43 mm.

Folio signatures, ( ), A-2H⁸, 2I⁶. There are three unnumbered leaves (alsounsigned) at the beginning which contain an engraved title page: "(within a portico with four corinthian columns) / *IL NVOVO / TESTAMENTO / del / Signor nostro / Jesus Christo / Tradotto / in lingua Italiana / da / Giovanni / Diodati di / nation Lucchese. / 1665.*", the title page, and a table of the books of the New Testament.

There are no introductions to the books or to the chapters. There are no notes at the foot of the page.

(13)
IL / NUOVO / TESTAMENTO / DI GIESU CRISTO / NOSTRO SIGNORE. / - / Consacrato / *A Sua Altezza Serenissima* / MONSIGNOR' IL PRENCIPE / CHRISTIANO / Duca di Sassonia. / &c. &c. &c. / *dal* / FERROMONTANO, / PER CHRISTIANO GOZZIO. / MDCCII.
Size 138 x 76 mm.

The ornament is a spiral, size 36 x 16 mm.

The text is in a single column of 62 mm. There are no introductions to the books or to the chapters. There are no notes in the margin or at the foot of the page. The pages are headed with the name of the book in capitals and with the number of the chapter in arabic numerals. There are a few words in italics.

(14)
IL / NUOVO / TESTAMENTO / *DI* / GIESU CRISTO / Nostro Signore e Salvatore. / Nuovamente revisto / *e* Con ogni diligenza corretto / *Accresciuto de' Sommarii,* / *e d'un / essatta divisione de' capitoli e versetti.* / (ornament) / - / In Zurigo,/ Presso di David Guessnero. / MDCCX. /
Size 148 x 76 mm.

The ornament is, within a rectangular design, an oval, revealing a man at work on a tree stump containing the words:- "INDVSTRIA HVMO SOLE", size 25 x 21 mm.

Folio signatures A-X¹².

The text is in two columns, each of 31 mm., with a central dividing line. There are no introductions to the books, but there are to the chapters. There are no notes in the margin or at the foot of the page. The pages are headed with the name of the book in capitals and with the number of the chapter in Arabic numerals. There are a few words in italics.

The French Bible

(15)
LA / SAINTE / BIBLE. / *INTERPRETEE* / PAR / IEAN DIODATI. / (ornament) /
Imprimee / *A GENEVE,* / Chez PIERRE AVBERT./ - / M.DC/XLIII. /
Size 420 x 280mm.

The ornament is of a cloaked and bearded figure under a tree, of which some
of the branches are seen to be falling and in the remaining branches of which is
entwined a scroll with the words:- "NOLI ALTVM SAPERE", size 102 x 74 mm.

Folio signatures ^{2}, ( ), A-5A^6, 5B^8, a-o^6, p^4, 2a-3l^6. 1r is the title page, 1v is
blank,( )lr is an engraved extra title page, ( )v is blank, 24 has a:- "TABLE DES
LIVRES / CANONIQUES DE LA / SAINTE ESCRIPTURE", 2v has:- "LES LIVRES
APOCORYPHES", a1r (unsigned)-5B7v the Old Testament, 5B8 is blank, 51r
has:- "LES LIVRES / APOCRYPHES". a1v has a:- "TABLE DES LIVRES / APOC-
RYPHES", a2r-p4v the Apocrypha 2a1r-315r the New Testament, 315v is blank,
the rest is blank.

The text is in two columns, each of 73 mm. There are introductions to the
chapters, notes in the margin and notes at the foot of the page. These are similar
to the annotations of the 1640/41 Italian Bible, list no. 2. The pages are headed
with the name of the book but not with the number of the chapter. There are
some words in italics. The Apocrypha is treated with less care than the Old and
New Testaments, there being no chapter headings, introductions to the books
nor words in italics. However a2 is an:- "AVERTISSEMENT / *SVR* / LES LIVRES
/ APOCRYPHES",

(16)
LE LIVRE DE / IOB/ *TRADVIT ET ANNOTE* / PAR / JEAN DIODATI/
Size 330 x 200 mm.

Folio signatures A-D^4, E^6. A1r appreviated title, A2r has:- "LE LIVRE DE IOB",
a3R-e6v the Book of Job, E6v also has a woodcut device.

(17)
LES LIVRES / DE / L'ECCLESIASTE, / *et DV* / CANTIQUE DES CANTIQVES.
/Traduits & expliques par Annotations perpetueles / Par / JEAN DIODATI. /
Size 330 X 198 MM.

One volume of 14 leaves. A single folding of ^{1}, A^3, C^2, D^2, E^2, F^2, G^2, P1
(unnumbered) is the title page, p2 (unnumbered) is blank, pp 3-15 Ecclesiastes,
pp 16-25 Song of Songs, the rest blank.

(18)
LES LIVRES / IOB / PSEAVMES. / PROVERBS. / ECCLESIASTE. / CANTIQVE

DES CANTIQVES. / *Expliques par brieves annotations* / par / IEAN DIODATI. / A GENEVE, / Ches IEAN DE TOVRNES . - c . c.xxxviii./
Size 212 x 155 mm

One volume of 8 466 (474) pages. Folio Signatures ⁴, A-3M⁴, 3N¹, p1 (unnumbered) the title page, p2 (unnumbered) blank, pp 3-8 the dedication, pp 1-466 the text.

This edition contains considerable annotations simila4 to those of list no. 17.

(19)
LES / PSEAVMES / *de* / DAVID / *en rime,* / Reueus par IEAN DIODATI. / (ornament) / A GENEVE. / Par PIERRE CHOVET. / - /M.DC.XLVI. /
Size 138 x 180 mm.

The ornament is of a tree, size 28 x 21 mm.

One volume of 373 pp. The text is in single column. There are no introductions to the Psalms. There are no notes in the margin or at the foot of the page. The pages are headed with the word "PSEAVME" and with the number of the Psalm in Roman numerals. The book contains the metrical Psalms in French with the first verse of each set to music.

(20)
SVITE DES / PSAVMES, / En vers Francois / PAR CL. MA. ' TH. DE BE. / *Et ceux quiont este retouchez* / Par feu M.V. CONRART Conseiller / & Secretaire du Roy, & c. / *Avec la prose mise a coste.* / Et les Arguments sur chaque Psaume / par feu M. Diodati. / (ornament) / A GENEVE / Chez IEAN PICTET. / - / *M.DC.LXXIX.* /
Size 82 x 143 mm.

Ornament is of an angel, holding a book, leaning on a cross, standing upon a skeleton and surrounded by an aureole, size 35 x 29 mm.

One volume, unpaginated, it is made up of 23 gatherings of 12 leaves. The text is preceded by 2 leaves and followed by thirteen blank leaves.

(21)
LES / EPISTRES / DES SAINTS / APOSTRES, / *Interpretez par* / JEAN DIODATI /(ornament) / A AMSTERDAM, / Chez PIERRE LE GRAND. /
Size 151 x 91 mm.

The ornament is a floreated pattern, size 50 x 61 mm.

Folio signatures ( ), A-R¹², S¹⁰. ( )1 is blank, ( )2r is the title page, ( )2v has 2 Timothy 1/13 in Greek, A1r-S10r the Epistles, Romans 1 & 2 Corinthians. Galatians, Ephesians, Philippians, Colossians. 1 & 2 Thessalonians, 1 & 2 Timothy, Titus, Philemon, Hebrews, James, 1 & 2 Peter, 1, 2 & 3 John and Jude.

Text in two columns, each of 27 mm. There are introductions to the books and to the chapters, which are very similar, but not identical to those in the 1644 complete Bible, list no. 15. There are notes in the margin and at the foot of the page, as in the 1644 complete Bible. The pages are headed with the name of the book but not with the number of the chapter.

(22)
LES / EPISTRES / DES SAINTS / APOSTRES, / *Interpretees par* / JEAN DIODATI / (ornament) / A AMSTERDAM, / Chez PIERRE LE GRAND. / MDCLXVII. / Size 153 x 94 mm.

The ornament is of a hand, appearing out of clouds, holding an orb, supported by the motto:- "SEMPER IN MOTU", size 48 x 52 mm.

Folio signatures A-S^{12}, A14 is the title page, A1v has 2 Timothy 1/13 in Greek, A2r-S11r the Epistles, the rest blank.

The text is in two columns, each of 28 mm. There are introductions to the books and the chapters, similar, but not identical to no. 15. There are notes in the margin and at the foot of the page. The pages are headed with the name of the book, but not with the chapter number.

Despite obvious similarity, this is not a re-impression of no. 21 but a re-edition. The layout of the text is very similar but the ornaments within the text are different and the text has been slightly changed in many places to modernise Diodati's French which was already somewhat archaic by this time.

Translations of the Annotations

(23)
Pious Annotations,/ UPON THE / HOLY BIBLE: / Expounding the difficult places thereof / Learnedly and Plainly: With other / things of great importance / - / By the Reverend, Learned and Godly Divine, / Mr IOHN DIODATI / Minister of the Gospell; / and now living in Geneva. / - / *It is ordered this* 11. *of January*, 1642, *by the Committee of the House* / *of* COMMONS *in* PARLIMENT, *concerning Printing, that this Exposition* / *of the Book of the Old and New Testament, be printed by* NICHOLAS / FUSSEL, *Stationer.* / IOHN WHITE. - / *LONDON,* / Printed by T.B. for NICHOLAS FUSSELL: and / are to be sold at the Green Dragon, in St *Pauls* / Church-yard. M.DC.XLIII./
Size 215 x 171 mm.

Folio signatures ( )^2, a^4, b^2, A-3B^4, A-Oo^4. ( )1v is a portrait of Diodati, ( )24 is an extra, engraved, title page, ( )2v is blank, a14 is the title page, a1v is blank, a24-b1v has:- "To the Reader", A-Oo^{4}v the annotations on the Bible translated into English with the introductions to the chapters. There is no Biblical text.

(24)

Pious and Learned / ANNOTATIONS / UPON / the Holy Bible: / PLAINLY / Expounding the most difficult / places thereof: / BY / That Godly and Famous DIVINE, / Mr JOHN DIODATI, Minister of the Gospell; / Now living in *GENEVA*. / - /The second Edition. / - / Corrected and much enlarged, with additional notes / of the same Author, throughout the whole worke. / ALSO, / A Methodicall Analysis upon each severall book of the Old and / New Testament, setting down the chiefe heads contain'd therein; / A Worke not before this extant in English. / - / *LONDON,* / Printed by *Miles Flesher,* for *Nicholas Fussell.* 1648. / Size 219 x 173 mm.

Folio signatures (   )^2, A-2Z^8, 3A^6, 3B^4, A-2G^8, 2H^4. (   )lr is blank, (   )lv has:- "THE PORTRAICTVRE OF THE REVEREND, Mr: / Iohn DIODATI, Minister of Gods Word in Geneva / AEtat ^{1s}L 70. Anno 1647", this is a copperplate engraving which is signed:- "W. Hollar fecit 1643", it is similar to the portrait in no. 23, (   ) 2r is an additional engraved title page, with a shortened version of the title:- "PIOVS / *Annotations* / *Vpon the Holy* / BIBLE / *Expounding the* / *difficult places* / *there of* / *Learnedly and Plainly* / *By the* / REVEREND LEARNED and Godly Diuine, M^1: Iohn/DIODATI, Minister of the / Gospell / *The Second Edition* / LONDON / Printed for NICO / las Fussell 1648", this is similar to the engraved title page of the first edition and is signed:- "W. Hollar fecit 1643", (   )2v is blank, A1r is the title page, A1v is blank, A2r-A2v has:- "TO THE KINGS / MOST EXCELLENT / MAJESTIE.", by Nicholas Fussell, A34-A5v has- "TO / THE READER" by R.G., A6r-A6v has:- "An Advertisement to the Reader concerning the ANALYSIS", A7r-3A6r the annotations on the Old Testament, 3A6v is blank, 3B1r-3B4v the annotations on the Apocrypha, A-2H4v the annotations on the Old Testament.

(25)

Pious and Learned / ANNOTATIONS / UPON / the Holy Bible: / PLAINLY / Expounding the most difficult / places thereof / BY / That Godly and Famous DIVINE, / Mr. JOHN DIODATI, late Minister of the Gospel / augmented, with additionall notes of / *the same Author, throughout the whole Work.* / AND / The Analysis upon each severall Book of the Old and New Testament, / setting down the chief heads contained therein, being very much en- / larged, is now fully compleated in this third Edition. / - / *LONDON,* / Printed by *James Flesher,* for *Nicholas Fussell.* 1651./ Size 286 x 85 mm.

Folio Signatures A-4L^4, 4M^2, A^2, B-3Y^4. A1r is blank, A2v has:- "THE POR-TRAICTVRE OF THE REVEREND Mr. / Iohn DIODATI Minister of Gods Word in Geneva / AEtat^{1s}: 70. Anno 1647, this is a copperplate engraving which is signed:-"W.Hollar fecit. 1643", it is similar to that in no. 23, also inserted, and not part of a folio gathering, is an additional engraved title page with a shortened version of the title:-"PIOVS / *Annotations* / *Vpon the Holy* / BIBLE / Expounding the *difficult places* / *there of* / *Learnedly & plainly* / By the / REVEREND, LEARNED / and Godly Diuine Mr: Iohn /DIODATI, Minister of the / Gospell / *The Third Edition* / LONDON / Printed for NICO / las Fussell 1651", this is similar to the engravings in nos. 23 and 24, it is signed:- "W. Hollar fecit 1643", the verso blank, A2r the title page, A2v blank, A3r-A3v:- "TO THE READER", not as in no. 24, A3v-A4r has:- *"An Advertisement to the Reader* concerning the *ANALYSIS"*, A4r-4L3r the annotations to the Old Testament, 4l3v-4M1v the annotations to the Apocrypha, A1r3Y3v the annotations to the New Testament, the remainder blank.

(26)

Pious and Learned / ANNOTATIONS / Upon the Holy / BIBLE. / Plainly Expounding the most difficult / Places thereof: / BY / That Godly and Famous DIVINE, / Mr John DIODATI, late Minister of / the Gospel in *GENEVA*. / - / *The Fourth Edition*. / - /Corrected, and much Augmented, with / Additional Notes of the same Authour, throughout / the Whole WORK. / AND / *The Analysis upon each several Book of the Old / and New Testament, setting down the chief Heads contained therein, being / very much enlarged, is now fully compleated in this Fourth Edition.* / - / *LONDON,* / Printed by *Tho.Roycroft,* for *Nicholas Fussell.* 1664. /

Size 292 x 190 mm.

Folio signatures ( )², A², B-4L⁴, A-3N⁴. ( )1r is blank, ( )1v portrait of Diodati, inset engraved title page with a shortened version of the title:- "PIOVS / *Annotations* / *Vpon the Holy* / BIBLE / *Expounding the* / *difficult places* / *thereof* / *Learnedly & plainly* / *By the* / REVEREND LEARNED / and Godly Diuine, Mr Iohn / DIODATI, Minister of the / Gospell / *The Fourth Edition* / LONDON / Printed for Nico. / las Fussell, 1664", ( )2v is blank, ( )3r is the title page, ( )3v is blank, A1r-A1v has:- "TO THE / READER", A1v-4L2r the notes on the Old Testament, 4L2r has:- "An Advertisement concerning the / Books, which are called *Apocrypha."*, *4L2v-4L4v introductions to the Apocryphal* books with no textual annotations, A1r has:- "Pious and Learned / ANNOTATIONS / UPON THE / NEW TESTAMENT, / Plainly expounding the most difficult Places thereof. / - / By that Godly and famous Divine Mr. JOHN DIODATI / late Minister of the Gospel in Geneva. / - / The Fourth Edition. / - /", A2r-3N3v the annotations on the New Testament, the rest blank.

(27)

BIBLIA, / *Das ist:* / *Die gantze* / *Heilige Schrifft* / *Durch* / *D. Martin Luther* / *verteutscht* /*Mit* / *D. Pauli Tossani hiebevor aussgegan-* / *genen Glossen und aussgegan-* / *genen Glossen und Ausslegungen:* / *Welche aber* / *In diesen neuen Edition auss vollt omlicher ubersetzung* / *der Niderlandischen und Herrn* Deodati: *So dann auch hie und da auss anderer* / Theologorum *besten* Annotationen, *auff vieler gottieligen Leuten offters Anhalten ansehnlich vermehret und* / *durch etliche der Hebreischen Griechischen Niderlandischen und ander Sprachen wolerfahrne Diener Gottlichen Worts aufs* / *neu ganz durchgangen von unzahlbaren Fehlern mercklich aussgebesssert und deutitcher gegebem wordem dadurch der zeyt wo er / etwas tunckel und schwer nusslich erlautert und erflaret: auch Dn. D.* Lutheri Version *(wo es die Noth durfft erfordert den ur / sprunglichen Sprachen und andern geleworten Dolmetschungen entgegen gehalten wird wie auss deer Theologischen / Facultat zu Hendelberg bengedrucften Censur zu erseben. / So sind sich weitlaufftigere Borreden Summarien. Concordantien und dem / Alten und Neuen Testament jedem seine absonderliche und zivar meist auss dem Niderlandischen verseztigte / neue uberauss nussliche Haupt- und verbesserte Namen - Register dergletchen in Teutscher Sprache noch nie geschen / sampt vielen nusslichen Land-Tafeln und Kupffer-Figuren jedes an seinen Drt / bengefuget / Mit Chur-Prfaltz Durchleucht als des Heil. Rom. / Reichs* Vicarii, und *Chur-Brandenburgischern* special. / *Privilegio und Begnadigung / (ornament) / Gedruckt zu Franckfurt am Mayn /In Verlegung Theodor Falfensens. / - / Im Jahr Christi MDCLXVJJJ /*

Size 390 x 220 mm.

The ornament is of a group of people praying near a castle on land while a ship full of people is sinking out at sea, all headed with the words:- "Si Deus pro nobis, quis contra nos", size 65 x 110 mm.

(28)

BIBLIA, / *Das ist: / Die gantze / Heilige Schrifft / Durch / D.* Martin Luther / *verteutscht: / Mit / D.Pauli Tossani hiebevor ausgegan- / genen Glossen und Ausslegungen: / Welche aber / In dieser neuen Edition aus vollvommlicher Ubersetzung / des Niderlandischen und Herrn* Diodati: *So dann auch hie und da aus anderer /* Theologorum besten Annotationen, *auff vieler gottseligen Leuten offters Anhalten ansehnlich ver- / mehret und durch etliche der Hebreischen Griechischen Niderlandischen und anderer Sprachen woler- / fahrne Diener Gottlichen Worts aufs neu gantz durchgangen von unzahlbaren Fahlern aussgebessert / und deutlicher gegeben worden dadurch der Text wo er etwas tuncfel und schwer nusslich erlautert und er- / flaret: auch Hn. D.* Lutheri Version *(wo es die Nothdurfft erfordert) den ursprunglichen Sprachen und andern / gelehrten Dolmetschungen entgegen gehalten wird wie aus der Theologischen Facultat zu Heidelberg / bengedruckter Censur zu ersehlen. / So sind auch weitlaufftigere Borreden Summarien Concordantien und dem / Alten und Neuen Testament jedem seine absonderliche und zwar meist aus dem Niderlandischen verfertigte / neue uberaus nusliche Haupt- und verbesserte Namen-Register (dergleichen in Teutscher Sprache noch nie / gesehen) sampt vielen nutslichen Land-Tafeln und Kupffer Figuren jedes an seinem Ortbengefdget. / Vormahlen / Mit Chur-Pfaltz Durchleucht als des Heil Romischen / Reichs* Vicarii, und *Chur-Brandenburgischen* Special / *Privilegio und Begnadigung / Durch Theodorum Falcensen; / Tesso zum zwenten mahl verlegt und zu finden / In Francfurt am Mayn Ben* Johann David Zunnern Buchhandlern / *Dructis Balthasar Christoph Bust / - / Im Jahr Christi MDCXCJJJ. /*

Size, 385 x 240 mm.

(29)

ISTEN AJANDEKAVAL VALO / KERESKEDES / Avagy / ENEKEK ENEKENEK / MAGYARAZATTYA, / az URTUL adatott ajandek- / nak merteke szerent. /

Melly nagyobb reszent / Az Isteni tudomanyban mel- / lyen forgott kegyes Ferfiu-nak, *DEODA-* / *TUS JANOSNAK,* a'Szent Konyv- / re Olasz nyelven tott ertelmes jedzesibol / vetetterett: es azon nyelvbol, kozonseges / haszonert Magyarra fordittatott, a'szokra / szabattatott; sok helyeken penig a'Ver- / sekre tott *Praxissal* meg-bovittetett: / DEBRECZENI K. JANOS, JESUS Christusnak / meltatlan SZOLGAJA es a' DEBRECZENI *TRACTUSBAN* / levo Sz. Tarsasagnak *SENIORA* altal. / *Luc.* 19.13. *Kereskedgyetek mig meg jobuk:* / (ornament) / DEBRECZENBEN, / - / Nyomtattatott, KASSAI PAL altal, MDC.XCIII. /

Size 155 x 90 mm.
The ornament is a scroll, size 7 x 32 mm.

Folio signatures a-b⁴, c⁸, d⁴, a-z⁸, Aa-Hh⁸.

Diodati's translation of Sarpi

(30)
HISTOIRE DV / CONCILE / DE TRENTE / *Traduite* / DE L'ITALIEN DE / PIERRE SOAVE / POLAN. / Par IEAN DIODATI / (ornament) / *A GENEVE,* / Par Estienne Gamonet. / - / M.DCXXI. /

Size 226 x 154 mm.

The ornament is of a fountain supported by female figures, bounded by a border bearing the words:- "EGO SITIENTI DABO DE FONTE AQVAE VIVAE GRATIS APOC. XXI.", with a foliate, baroque, design, size 62 x 55 mm.

Folio signatures   ², A-6G⁴, 6H². lr is the title page, lv is blank, 2 has an "AV LECTEVR", A1r-6G2r the text of the book, 6g2v has a list of:- ITA" > Fautes a corriger 6G3r-6H2v is a:-"TABLE DES MATIE- / RES PRINCIPALES."

(31)
HISTOIRE DV / CONCILE / DE TRENTE, / Traduite / DE L'ITALIEN DE / PIERRE SOAVE / POLAN. / (ornament) / A TROYES, / Par PIERRE DV RVAV, demeurant / en la rue nostre Dame. / M.DC.XXVII. /

Size 224 x 154 mm.
The ornament is of a head with extravagant ornaments, size 48 x 73 mm.

Folio signatures A⁴, A-6M⁴, 6N². A1r is the title page, A1v is blank, A2 has an:- "Au lecteur", A3 is incorrectly signed "Ai j", A2r-A4v is the:- "Au lecteur", eight concluding pages contain a table to the work.

(32)
HISTOIRE DV / CONCILE / DE TRENTE, / *Traduite* / DE L'ITALIEN DE / PIERRE SOAVE / POLAN. / *PAR JEAN DIODATI.* / (ornament) / - / Imprime l'an 1627./
Size 225 x 160 mm.

The ornament is a grotesque face interlaced with a foliate design, size 52 x 50 mm.

Folio signatures ^{2}, a^2, A-6M^4, N^2.

(33)

HISTOIRE DV / CONCILE / DE TRENTE. / *Traduite* / DE L'ITALIEN DE / PIERRE SOAVE / Polan / Par IEAN DIODATI. / *SECONDE EDITION,* / Exactement, ' fidelment conferee a l'original. / (ornament) / *A GENEVE,* / Imprime pour Pierre Chouet. / - / M.DC.XXXV. /

Size 235 x 160 mm.

The ornament is of a fountain supported by female figures, bounded by a border bearing the words:- "EGO SITIENTI DABO DE FONTE AQVAE VIVAE GRATIS APOC. XXI", within a foliate, baroque design, size 62 x 55 mm.

Folio signatures ^{4}, A-6I^4. 1r is the title page, 1v is blank, 2r-4r has an:- "Au lecteur", 4v is blank, A1r-6H3r the text, 6H4r-6I4v table of contents.

(34)

HISTOIRE / DV / CONCILE / DE / TRENTE / Traduite, / DE L'ITALIEN DE / PIERRE SOAVE POLAN. / *Par IEAN DIODATI.* / Seconde Edition. / *Exactement, & fidelement conferee a l'Original.* / (ornament) / A TROYES, / Chez NICOLAS OVDOTX, demeurant en / la rue N.Dame, au Chappon d'Or Couronne. / - /M.DC.L /

Size 375 x 222 mm.
The ornament is a vase filled with fruit, size 34 x 52 mm.

Folio signatures ^{2}, ^{4}, A-5D^{4,5}E^2

(35)

HISTOIRE / DV / CONCILE / DE / TRENTE / Traduite, / DE L'ITALIEN DE /PIERRE SOAVE POLAN. / *Par IEAN DIODATI.* / Seconde Edition. / *Exactement, & fidelement conferee a l'Original.* / (ornament) / A TROYES, / Chez NICOLAS OVDOT, demeurant en / la rue N.Dame, au Chappon d'Or Couronne. / - / M.DC.LV /

Size 375 x 222 mm.
The ornament is a vase filled with fruit, size 34 x 52 mm.

Folio Signatures ^{2}, ^{4}, A-5D^4, 5E^2.

(36)

HISTOIRE / DV / CONCILE / DE / TRENTE, / Traduite, / DE L'ITALIEN DE / PIERRE SOAVE POLAN. / *Par IEAN DIODATI.* / Quatriesme Edition. / *Exacte-*

ment, & fidelment conferee a l'Original. / (ornament) / *A Troyes, & se vendent* / A PARIS, / Chez Nicholas & Iean de la Coste, au mont S.Hilaire, & a la petite / porte du Palais deuant les Augustins. / - / M.DC.LV. /

Size 360 x 220 mm.
The ornament is by "Briot" and represents two angels supporting an heraldic device of ermine tails, size 110 x 132 mm.

Folio Signatures ^{2}, ^{4}, A-5D^4, 5E^2.

(37)

HISTOIRE / DV / CONCILE / DE / TRENTE, / Traduite, / DE L'ITALIEN DE / PIERRE SOAVE POLAN. / *Par IEAN DIODATI.* / Quatriesme Edition. / *Exactement, & fidelment conferee a l'Original.* / (ornament) / A PARIS, /Chez Nicholas & Iean de la Coste, au mont S. Hilaire, & a la petite / porte du Palais deuant les Augustins. / - / M.DC.LVI. /

Size 360 x 220 mm.
The ornament is by "Briot" and represents two angels supporting an heraldic device of ermine tails, size 110 x 132 mm.

(38a)

HISTOIRE / DV / CONCILE / DE / TRENTE. / TRADVITE DE L'ITALIEN / DE PIERRE SOAVE POLAN. / *Par IEAN DIODATI.* / QVATRIESME EDITION. / Exactment, & fidelement conferee a l'Original. / (ornament) / A PARIS, / Chez GERVAIS CLOVZIER, au Palais, sur les degrez en montant pour aller a la / Sainte Chappelle, a la seconde Boutique, a l'Enseigne du Voyageur. / - / M.DC.LXV. /*AVEC PERMISSION.* / In Folio.
The ornament is of a tub of flowers, size 87 x 90 mm.

(38b)

The same edition, only published by "OLIVIER DE VARENNES, au Palais en la Gallerie des Prisonniers, pres la Chancellerie, au Vase d'Or", and the ornament is of an urn surrounded by a ribbon with the legend "PETIT A PETIT" supported by cherubs and female figures, size 108 x 119 mm.

(38c)

The same edition, only published by "IEAN COCHART, au Palais, dans la Gallerie des Prisonniers, au Saint Esprit", and the ornament is a tub of flowers, size 98 x 104 mm.

(38d)

The same edition, only published by "F.MVGVET, Imprimeur-Libraire ordin. du Roy, & de Monseigneur l'Archeuesque, rue de la Harpe, a l'Adoration des trois Roys", and the ornament is similar to that of 38c.

(38e)

The same edition, only published by "CLAVDE BARBIN, au Palais, deuant la Sainte Chappelle, au Signe de la Croix", and the ornament is similar to that of 38c.

(38f)

The same edition, only published by "IEAN RIVOV, au Palais, sur les degrez de la Sainte Chappelle, a l'Image Saint Louis", and the ornament is similar to that of 38c.

(38g)

The same edition only published by "NICHOLAS DE LAVLNE, en la Place de Sorbonne, a l'Image Saint Nicholas.", and the ornament is similar to that of 38c.

(38h)

The same edition, only published by "HVGVES SENEVZE, Place de Sorbonne, a l'Enseigne de la Ville de Chaalons" and the ornament is similar to that of 38c.

(38i)

The same edition, only published by "IEAN DE LA CAILLE, Imprimeur du Roy, & Libraire Iure, rue Saint Iacques, aux trois Cailles" and the ornament is similar to that of 38c.

(38j)

The same edition, only published by "PIERRE PROME, au bout du Pont Saint Michel, a l'Enseigne de la Charite" and the ornament is similar to that of 38c.

(38k)

The same edition, only published by "DENIS DAVID, Marchand Libraire, au bout du Pont-Neuf, proche les grands Augustins, a la Ville de Londres" and the ornament is of a tub of flowers, size 98 x 104 mm.

(38l)

The same edition, only published by "PIERRE DE LAVLNE, le fils, Place de Sorbonne, proche le College du Cluny. / - / M.DC.LXV." and the ornament is similar to that of 38c.

(38m)

The same edition, only published by "SEBASTIEN MARTIN, Imprimeur-Libraire Iure, rue Saint Iean de Beauuais, a l'Enseigne Saint Iean l'Euangeliste" and the ornament is similar to that of 38c.

Folio signatures ^{2}, 4, A-4P^4, 4Q^3, P. 1r is the title page, 2 has an:- "Au lecteur", 1r-4v "TABLE DES MATIERES / PRINCIPALES", A1r-4Q3v the text, 4Q3v also has:-"De l'Imprimerie / De SEBASTIEN MARTIN, Imprimeur-Libraire Iure, rue S.Iean de Beauuais, / a l'Enseigne Sainct Iean l'Euangeliste." the rest blank.

Diodati's translation of Sandys.

(39)
RELATION / *de l'Estat* / DE LA RELIGION, / *ET* / PAR QUELS DESSEINS ET, / artifices elle a este forges, et gouuernes / en diuers Estats de ces parties Oc- / cindentales du Monde. / *Tires de l'Anglois, du* Cheualier EDWIN / SANDIS. / Auec des additions notables. / (ornament) / *A GENEVE,* / PAR PIERRE AVBERT. / - /M.DC.XXVI. /

Size 160 x 100 mm.
The ornament is of an anchor fouled with a dolphin, size 44 x 29 mm.

Folio signatures A^4, AB^8, CD8, EF^8, GH^8, I-$2A^8$, $2B^4$. A1r is the title page, A1v blank, A2r-A4v have an:- "Au lecteur", A2r-2B2r the text, 2B2v-2B4r a table of the chapters, the rest blank.

(40)
RELATION / *de l'Estat* / DE LA RELIGION, / *ET* / PAR QVELS DESSEINS, / & artifices, elle a este forges, & gou- / uernee en diuers Estats de ces par- / ties Occidentales du Monde. / *Tiree de l'Anglois, du Cheualier* / EDWIN SANDIS. / Auec des additions notables. / (ornament) / M.DC.XLI. /

Size 128 x 70 mm.
The ornament is of a stylised animal head interlaced with decoration, size 32 x 30 mm., the ornament of Louis Elzevir of Amsterdam.

Folio signatures a-S^{12}.

Letter to the Westminster Assembly

(41)
AN / ANSWER / *Sent to the* / ECCLESIASTICALL / ASSEMBLY AT / LONDON. /*By the* / Reverend, Noble, and Learned Man / *JOHN DEODATE* / *the Famous* / Professour of *Divinitys* and most / vigilant Pastour of GENEVAH. / - / Translated *out of the* Latine / *into* English. / (ornament) / *GENEVAH,* / Printed For the good of *Great Brittaine, MDCXXXXVI.* /

Size 178 x 135 mm.
The ornament is made up of three separate foliate designs, each 10 x 7 mm.

Folio signatures A-B^4, A1r the title page , A1v blank, A2r-B4v the text.

(42)
(within a border of acorns and oak leaves) / A / REPLY / TO A / LETTER / Printedat / NEWCASTLE / VNDER / The name of an Answer, sent to the Eccle-siasticall Assembly at LONDON , about / Matters concerning the KING, and the Government / of the CHURCH. / With the Copy of the said LETTER to the /

Assembly, in the name of JOHN DEODATE, D.D. / *ALSO,* / A Certificate from one of the Scribes of the / ASSEMBLY at LONDON. / - / (ornament) / - / LONDON, Printed by F.C. 1646. /

Size 188 x 136 mm.
The ornament is a foliate pattern, size 6 x 28 mm.

Folio signatures A-B⁴.

(43)

AN / ANSWER / SENT TO THE / Ecclesiasticall Assembly / AT / LONDON. / By the reverend, noble, and learned Man, / JOHN DEODATE. / The famous Professor of DIVINITY, and / most vigilant Pastour of / *GENEVAH.* / (ornament) /*NEWCASTLE.* / Printed by Stephen Bulkley. 1647 /

Size 185 x 138 mm.
The ornament is of the royal coat-of-arms of Great Britain of Charles I, with the motto:- "DIEV. ET MON. DROIT". size 68 x 62 mm.

(44)

THE / KINGS / POSSESSIONS: / WRITTEN / BY HIS MAGESTIES own Hand; annexed / by way of Notes, to a Letter sent to / the *Ecclesiasticall Assembly* at / LONDON: / *In Answer to a Letter* sent from / them. / (ornament) / - / NEW-CASTLE: /Printed by Stephen Bulkley, Printer to the / kings Majesty, 1647. /

Size 182 x 138 mm.
The ornament is of four crowns in a horizontal line, underneath each being a national symbol: from left to right there is the Tudor rose, the thistle, the fleur-delys and the harp, size 9 x 24 mm.

Folio signatures A², B², C². A1r is the title page, a1v-A2v:- "THE PREFACE", A2v-C2v the text of the work.

(45)

Een Antwoort / *Aen de* Kerckelijcke Vergaderinghe tot / LONDEN, / *Gosonden door* / Den Eerwaerdighen, Edelen ende Hooghgheleerden / *IOHANNES DEO-DATVS.* /PROFESSOOR *in de Theologij ende Dienaer des Godde- / lijcken Woorts, binnen* / GENEVA. / *Eerst uyt Latijn in't Engels, ende nu uyt't Engels / in't Nederlands getrouvvelick vertaelt.* / - / *Tot GENEVA,* / Gedrukt ten goede van Groot Britannien, 1647. /

Size 188 x 143 mm.

Single folding, signature A⁴.

(46)

THE / VERDICT / UPON THE / *Dissenters Plea,* / Occasioned by Their / *MELIUS*

INQUIRENDUM. / To which is added. / A LETTER from Geneva, to / the Assembly of Divines. / Printed by His late Majesties Special / Command; with some Notes upon the Mar / gent, under His own Royal and Sacred Hand. / ALSO / A POSTSCRIPT touching the / Union of Protestants. / - / *LONDON,* / Printed for *Robert Clavel,* at the *Peacock* in / St. Paul's Church-Yard, 1681. /

Size 178 x 107 mm.

(47)

(within a border) / MEMOIRS / OF THE / *Two last Years of the Reign* / of that unparallell'd PRINCE, / of ever Blessed Memory, / King *CHARLES* I. / BY / Sir THO. HERBERT, Col. EDW. COKE, and / Major HUNTINGTON, Mr. Hen. FIREBRACE. / - / With the CHARACTER of that / Blessed MARTYR, / BY / The Reverend Mr *John Diodati,* Mr *Alexander* / *Henderson,* and the Author of the *Pincely-Pelican./* - / To which is added. / The *Death-Bed Repentance* of MR. LENTHAL, / *Speaker of the Long Parliment;* /Extracted out of a letter written from *Oxford, Sept.* 1662. / - / - / LONDON. / Printed for *Robert Clavell,* at the *Peacock,* at the West- / End of S. Paul's. MDCCII. /

Size 185 x 113 mm.

(48)

(within a margin) MEMOIRS / OF THE / *Two last yeares of the Reign* / of that Unparallell'd PRINCE, / of ever Blessed Memory, / King *CHARLES* I. / - / BY / Sir THO. HERBERT - Mr. HEN. FIREBRACE: / With the CHARACTER OF THAT Blessed Martyr, / BY / The Reverend Mr. *John Diodati,* Mr *Alexander* / *Henderson,* and the Author of the Princely Pelican. / - / To which is added, / The *Death-Bed* Repentance of Mr. LENTHAL, / *Speaker of the* LONG PARLIMENT; / Extracted out of a letter written from OXFORD, Sep. 1662 / - / - / LONDON, Printed for *Tho. Baker,* at the / Bible and *Rose* in *Ludgate-street,* 1711. /

Size 193 x 115 mm.

(49)

Admodum reverendi, nobilissimi, & doctissimi / Viri, ac domini, / DOMINI / IOHANNIS DEODATI, / S.S. Theologiae apud Genevenses / Professoris clarissimi, & Pastoris / ibidem vigilantissimi, / Responsum / Ad conventum Ecclesiasticum LONDINI / congregatum. /
Size 191 x 141 mm.

Letter to Lady Westmoreland

(50)

LETTRE / DE CONSOLATION / A MADAME / La Contesse de WESTMORE-LAND. / *Sur la morte* / de / *Messire* ROGER DE TOWNSHEND, / *Cheualier Baronnet, son* / *fils aisne,* / Par IEAN DEODATI. / (ornament) / *A GENEVE.* / Par IEAN de TOVRNES, /*M.DC.XLVIII.* /

Size 125 x 78 mm.
The ornament is of the arms of the Republic of Geneva surrounded by a wreath, size 30 x 28 mm.

(51)
LETTERA / SCRITTA ALL' ILL^mo / S^re, il Sr Conte / DI VVESTMORLAND, / *in suggetto della morte del Signor* / *Caualiero* / RVGGIERO TOWNSHEND, *Figlio primogenito dell' Illma sua Consorte.* / (ornament) / M.DC.XLVIII. /

Size 125 x 78 mm.
The ornament is of the arms of the Republic of Geneva, surrounded by a wreath, size 30 x 28 mm.

Miscellaneous

(52)
ENCHIRIDION / THEOLOGICVM / APHORISTICA METHODO / COM-POSITVM EX DISPV- / TATIONIBUS / ANTONII FAYI ECLESIASTE / et Sacrarum literarum Professoris, / Geneuae. /
Pp 89-90 (Disputatio XX), "DE SACRA SCRIPTURA":- "Asserente Ioan Deodat Genuensi."

Printed at Geneva during 1605.

(53)
(below a border of type ornaments) / GRAND TROVBLE / ARRIVE DE NOVVEAV / A GENEVE, CONTRE GENEVE ET / Charenton, esmeu par DIO-DATI Ministre du lieu; / Ou; La Saincte Bible, traduite & interpretee de nouue au par /IEAN DIODATI, Ministre de Geneue, / Opposee & contraire en sa Traduction, & en ses Expositions, / a toutes les Bibles predesentes de Geneue & de Charenton, / & aux Expositions contenues en icelles, & en tous les / Liures & Presches des Ministres de toute la / France, iusques a la presente annee 1646. /

Size 200 x 140 mm.

Folio signatures A-C⁴, the text of the work begins on the lower half of the title page A1r, C4v has:- "*Par* FRANCOIS VERON *Docteur en Theologie,* & c."

Provenance list of pre-1800 Diodati editions.

ABERDEEN, University Library; 1, 9, 15, 23, 25, 42.
ABERYSTWYTH, National Library of Wales; 2P, 23, 24, 26, 47.
ABERYSTWYTH, University College Library; 23.
AIX -EN-PROVENCE, De Mejanes bibliotheque; 33, 38m.
ALBANY, New York State Library; 25.
ANN ARBOR, University of Michigan Library; 26
ARMAGH, Archbishop Robinson's Library; 23.

AVIGNON, Musee Calvet; 18.

BALTIMORE, Johns Hopkins University Library; 23, 24.

BASEL, Offentliche Bibliothek der Universitat Basel; 1, 2, 2P, 11, 12, 15.

BERKELEY, University of California Library; 23, 24.

BERLIN, Deutsche Staatsbibliothek; 1, 2, 7, 8, 11, 15, 21, 22, 39, 40.

BERLIN, Universitats-Bibliothek der Humbolt-Universitat; 2.

BERN, Stadt- und Universitatsbibliothek; 2, 11, 12, 15.

BIRMINGHAM, University Library; 1, 23, 24, 26.

BONN, Universitatsbibliothek; 1, 6, 15, 22.

BORDEAUX, Bibliotheque municipale: 1, 2, 15, 35, 38m.

BOURGES, Bibliotheque municipale; 2, 38g.

BRESCIA, Biblioteca Queriniana; 2, 5.

BRNO, Universitni Knihovna; 1.

BRUNSWICK, MAINE, Bowdoin College, 25, 26.

BRUSSELS, Bibliotheque Royale Albert ler.; 2, 9, 15, 21, 38e, 38f, 38l, 39.

BUCHAREST, Academia Republicii Socialiste Romania Biblioteca; 2.

BUDAPEST, Magyar Tudomanyos Akademia Konyvtara; 1, 11, 29.

BUDAPEST, Radoy Library; 2, 2P, 5, 12.

BUDAPEST, University Library; 1.

CAEN, Bibliotheque universitaire; 15, 31, 37.

CAGLIARI, Biblioteca Universitaria; 2.

CAMBRIDGE, Emmanuel College Library; 1, 2, 15, 25, 47.

CAMBRIDGE, King's College Library; 1, 2, 24.

CAMBRIDGE, St. John's College Library; 2, 12, 24, 25.

CAMBRIDGE, Trinity College Library; 1, 15, 25, 26.

CAMBRIDGE, University Library; 1, 2, 8, 10, 11, 24, 26, 34, 38m, 40, 41, 42, 43, 46.

CAMBRIDGE, MASS., Andover-Harvard Library; 2, 12.

CAMBRIDGE, MASS., ANDOVER-Harvard Divinity School Library; 23, 24.

CAMBRIDGE, MASS., Harvard University Library; 24.

CAMBRIDGE, MASS., Houghton Library Harvard; 1, 11, 43, 53.

CAMBRIDGE, MASS., Law School Library, Harvard; 38d.

CAMBRIDGE, MASS., Widener Library, Harvard; 25.

CANTERBURY, Cathedral Archives and Library; 25.

CASHEL, Diocesan Library; 2, 25.

CHANTILLY, Bibliotheque de la Compagnie de Jesus; 15, 30, 35.

La CHAUX de FONDS, Bibliotheque de la ville; 15.

CHICAGO, Newberry Library; 25, 41, 43.

CHICAGO, University of Chicago Library; 25.

COIMBRA, Biblioteca Geral da Universidade; 2.

COPENHAGEN, Det Kongelige Bibliotek; 1, 2, 11, 15, 25.

DEBRECEN, A Tisantuli Reformatus Egyhazkerulet Konyvtara; 1, 29.

DEVENTER, Athenaeum Bibliotheek; 15, 26.

DUBLIN, Archbishop Marsh's Library; 2, 8, 9, 15, 16, 26, 30, 43.

DUBLIN, Royal Irish Academy Library; 43.

DUBLIN, Trinity College Library; 2, 9, 21, 25, 38d, 41, 43.

DURHAM, University Library and Cathedral Library; 15, 24.

DURHAM, NORTH CAROLINA, Duke University Library; 26.

EDINBURGH, National Library of Scotland; 2, 10, 15, 22, 25, 33, 41, 43, 48.

EDINBURGH, New College Library; 1, 2, 22, 23, 24, 25, 26, 30.

EDINBURGH, University Library; 2, 25.

ERLANGEN-NUREMBERG, Universitatsbibliothek; 12.

EXETER, The Cathedral Library; 2, 25, 26.

FLORENCE, Biblioteca Marcelliana; 2.

FLORENCE, Biblioteca Nazionale Centrale; 1, 4, 5, 8, 9, 11, 15, 22, 25, 40.

FLORENCE, Biblioteca Riccardiana; 2.

GAINESVILLE, University of Florida Library; 25.

GDANSK, Bibl. Pan; 1, 2, 11, 15.

GENEVA, Bibliotheque de la compagnie des pasteur ; 1, 2, 22.

GENEVA, Bibliotheque publique et universitaire; 1, 2, 8, 9, 10, 11, 12, 15, 17, 18, 21, 22, 23, 26, 30, 38d, 38m, 39, 52.

GENEVA, Musee historique de la reformation; 1, 2, 7, 8, 11, 15, 18, 23, 30.

GENOA, Biblioteca Universitaria di Genova; 1, 2.

GHENT, Centrale Bibliotheek, Rijksuniversiteit; 12, 38k, 39, 45.

GLASGOW, University Library and Hunterian Museum; 1, 2, 11, 22, 23.

GOTTINGEN, Niedersachsische Staats- und Universitatsbibliothek, 2.

GOTTWEIG-FURTH, Gottweig Stiftsbibliothek; 39.

GRENOBLE, Bibliotheque de Grenoble; 6, 18, 30, 33, 39.

The HAGUE, Koninklijke Bibliotheek; 1, 32, 40, 45.

HALLE, Hauptbibliothek der Franckeschen Stiftungen; 2, 4.

HALLE, Marienbibliothek; 2P, 15.

HALLE, Universitats- und Landesbibliothek; 1, 8, 21, 22, 30, 33, 35.

HAMBURG, Staats und Universitatsbibliothek; 28.

HAWARDEN, St Deniol's Library; 1.

HEIDELBERG, Universitatsbibliothek; 1.

HELSINKI, University Library; 1, 4, 8.

HEVERLEE-Louvain, Bibliotheek S.J.; 8.

ITHACA, N.Y., Cornell University Library; 23, 24.

JENA, Universitatsbibliothek; 1, 2, 4.

KIEL, Universitatsbibliothek; 1, 28.

KREMSMUNSTER, Stiftsbibliothek; 2.

LAUSANNE, Bibliotheque cantonale et universitaire; 2, 2P, 10, 11, 12, 15, 18, 19, 21, 3, 33.

LEEDS, Public Library; 25.

LEIDEN, Bibliotheek der Rijksuniversiteit te Leiden; 49.

LIEGE, Bibliotheque generale de l'universite; 38j.

LISBON, Bibloiteca Nacional; 1.

LISMORE, Diocesan Library; 23.

LJUBLJANA, Narodna in Universititna Knjiznica; 4, 12.

LONDON, Bible House Library; 1, 2, 3, 4, 9, 11, 12, 14.

LONDON, British Museum; 1, 2, 4, 8, 9, 10, 11, 12, 13, 15, 19, 22, 23, 25, 26, 27, 38d, 39, 42, 43, 50, 51.

LONDON, The Congregational Library; 1, 2, 26.

LONDON, Dr Williams', Library; 1, 2, 9, 21, 23, 24, 25.

LONDON, Guildhall Library; 42.

LONDON, Lambeth Palace Library; 23, 25.

LONDON, London Library; 24, 25.

LONDON, St Paul's Cathedral Library; 24, 43.

LONDON, Sion College Library; 1, 24.

LONDON, University of London Library; 12, 22, 23, 24.

LONDON, Westminster Abbey, the Muniment Room; 2.

LONDON, Ont., University of Western Ontario Library; 23, 25.

LOS ANGELES, University of California at Los Angeles, William Andrews Clark
Memorial Library; 24, 25.

LUCERN, Zentralbibliothek; 1, 2.

LUND, Universitetsbiblioteket; 1, 2.

LUXEMBOURG, La bibliotheque du Grand Seminaire; 38e.

LYON, Bibliotheque de la ville; 2, 15, 30, 33, 38i.

MADISON, WISCONSIN, University of Wisconsin Library; 23.

MADRID, Biblioteca Nacional; 1, 2, 8, 32.

MADRID, Biblioteca del Palacio Real; 2.

MAINZ, Stadtbibliothek; 30.

MALINES, Stadsarchief; 38m.

MANCHESTER, John Rylands Library; 1, 8, 11, 12, 15, 24, 25, 26.

MARBURG, Universitatsbibliothek; 2.

MAYNOOTH, St Patrick's College Library; 2, 2P, 38k.

MILAN, Biblioteca Ambrosiana; 1, 10.

MILAN, Biblioteca Comunale; 1.

MILAN, Biblioteca Nazionale di Brera; 1, 2, 15.

MILAN, Societa Storica Lombarda; 2.

MILAN, Biblioteca Trivulziana; 2, 33.

MILAN, Biblioteca del Universitaria del Sacro Cuore; 1.

MONTPELLIER, Faculte de Theologie Protestante; 15, 22, 33.

MONTPELLIER, Bibliotheque universitaire; 15.

MONTPELLIER, Bibliotheque de la ville; 1, 12.

MONS, Bibliotheque centrale; 38e.

MONTREAL, Bibliotheque centrale de l'universite de Montreal; 25.

MONTREAL, McGill University Library; 1, 5, 22, 25.

MUNICH, Bayerische Staatsbibliothek; 1, 2, 4.

NAMUR, Bibliotheque Moretus, facultes universitaires de Notre Dame de
la Paix; 23.

NAPLES, Biblioteca, Nazionale; 1, 2.

NEUCHATEL, Bibliotheque de la ville; 8, 12, 15, 20.

NEW BRUNSWICK, N.J., New Brunswick Theological Seminary Library; 23.

NEWCASTLE UPON TYNE, University Library; 23, 25.

NEW HAVEN, Yale University Library; 23, 24, 25.

NEW OSCOTT, Sutton Coldfield, St Mary's Seminary Library; 24.

NEW YORK, Union Theological Seminary Library; 25, 26, 41.

NIMES, Bibliotheque Seguier; 1, 33.

NORMAL, ILL., University of Illinois Library; 24.

NORWICH, Public Library; 23.

OSLO, Universitetsbiblioteket; 11.

OXFORD, All Souls College Library, 2, 26.

OXFORD, Bodleian Library; 9, 11, 12, 18, 23, 24, 25, 39, 42, 43, 44, 45, 46, 47.
OXFORD, Brasenose College Library; 24.
OXFORD, Christ Church College Library; 1, 2, 8, 15, 25, 26.
OXFORD, Hertford College Library; 1, 24, 25.
OXFORD, Lincoln College Library; 2, 26, 43.
OXFORD, Merton College Library; 26.
OXFORD, Oriel College Library; 25.
OXFORD, The Queen's College Library; 2, 33, 47.
OXFORD, St Edmund Hall Library; 26.
OXFORD, Worcester College Library; 1, 2, 25.
PADUA, Biblioteca Universitaria di Padova; 2.
PARIS, Bibliotheque de l'Institute Catholique; 39.
PARIS, Bibliotheque nationale; 1, 2, 8, 11, 15, 19, 22, 30, 31, 32, 35, 38b, 38c,
         39, 40, 53.
PARIS, Bibliotheque de la societe de l'histoire du protestantisme francais; 32,
         39.
PARIS, Bibliotheque de l'universite de Paris, a la Sorbonne; 33, 38b.
PARMA, Biblioteca Palatina; 1, 2, 8, 12, 25.
PISA, Biblioteca Universitaria; 1.
POITIERS, Bibliotheque municipale; 1, 15.
PORRENTROY, Bibliotheque de l'ecole cantonale; 2.
PRAGUE, Stani Knihovna; 1, 15.
PRAGUE, Strahovska Knihovna; 1, 2.
RIPON, Cathedral Library; 24.
RODEZ, Bibliotheque de la ville; 14, 32.
ROME, Biblioteca Gregoriana; 25.
ROSTOCK, Universitatsbibliothek; 1, 2, 4, 28.
ROUEN, Bibliotheque municipale; 1, 12, 39.
St ANDREWS, University Library; 1, 2, 11, 12, 23.
St GALL, Vadianischen Oder Berger-bibliothek; 2.
San MARINO, CAL., Henry E. Huntington Library; 23.
St. PAUL, MIN., University of Minnesota Library; 25.
SALZBURG, Bibliothek der Erzabtei St Peter; 22.
SALZBURG, Universitatsbibliothek; 1.
SAROSPATAK, Tiszantuli Reformatus Egyhazkerulet; 25.
SCHAFFHAUSEN, Stadtbibliothek; 9, 12, 15.
SOLOTHURN, Zentralbibliothek; 39.
STOCKHOLM Kungligabiblioteket; 1, 2, 15, 45.
STRASBOURG, Bibliotheque nationale et universitaire; 1, 2, 15, 22.
TORONTO, Knox College Library; 24.
TORONTO, Trinity College Library; 24.
TORONTO, University Library; 10, 23.
TORUN, University Library; 2, 11.
TOULOUSE, Bibliotheque de la ville; 2, 15, 33, 36, 38e.
TRENTO, Biblioteca Comunale; 2, 33.
TROYES, Bibliotheque municipale et archives anciennes; 1, 11, 15, 32, 35, 38h.
TUBINGEN, Universitatsbibliothek; 4, 11, 22.
UPPSALA, Universitetsbiblioteket; 1, 2, 8, 22, 40.

VATICAN, La Biblioteca Apostolica Vaticana; 1, 2, 8, 11, 15, 38a.
VERONA, Biblioteca Civica; 2.
VERSAILLES, Bibliotheque municipale; 2, 39.
VIENNA, Osterreichische Nationalbibliothek; 2, 11.
WARSAW, National Library; 33.
WARSAW, University Library; 2.
WASHINGTON, D.C., Library of Congress; 25, 38d.
WINTERTHUR, Stadtbibliothek; 11, 22, 33.
WORCESTER, MASS., American Antiquarian Society Library; 23.
WROCLAW, University Library; 1, 8, 15, 39.
ZURICH, Zentralbibliothek; 2, 15, 18.

Theodore Tronchin

Theodore Tronchin, one of the two Genevan representatives at the Synod of Dort, was six years younger than Giovanni Diodati, being born at Geneva in 1582[31]. In some ways, his career was similar to that of Diodati, since he served as professor of Hebrew at the Genevan Academy after Diodati from 1606 until 1618 [32] and became rector after Diodati in 1610, a post which he held until 1615 [33]. A number of Tronchin's Latin discourses which he made in his capacity as rector are still in existence [34]. Tronchin also acted as a professor of theology for an even longer period than Diodati, from 1615 until 1656 [35]. Like Diodati, he was appointed to the teaching staff of the Academy at an early age, being twenty-four years old when he was made a professor of Hebrew. His training, however, was not entirely theological but also philosophical for there is a manuscript dated 1598:- "Loci communes, ethici, physici, logici, etc., ex variis autoribus decerpti" compiled by Theodore Tronchin, deposited in the Archives Tronchin of the Musee historiquede la Reformation in Geneva. This is a considerable work for a boy of sixteen, consisting of 413 folia of 27 x 17 cm. The writing is so small that sixty-five lines are, on folio 68, written in only 10 cm. Thus there is some evidence to suggest that Tronchin matured at an early age. However, when these things have been said, further similarity with Giovanni Diodati is much less easy to outline, for Tronchin, unlike Diodati, had no political or diplomatic experience prior to the time of the Synod of Dort. Neither was Tronchin a translator of note, his works bring written either in French or in Latin, and including no translations of the Scriptures or other works. Thus the reasons for Tronchin's selection as a Genevan representative at Dort must necessarily have been somewhat different from the reasons for the selection of Diodati.

It is in this rapid advancement, that one may find the first reason for the choice of Tronchin as a Genevan representative. He must have been a remarkable young man to be selected for a professorship at such an early age, and this appointment no doubt shows the confidence of the Genevan authorities in his ability. His career can hardly have been hindered by the fact that he married Theodora Rocca, the adopted daughter of Theodore Beza [36]. Despite his youthful academic success, Tronchin left few works that reveal his quality as a theologian. Two sets of theses published well before the Synod of Dort were:- *Theses philosophicae de mundo, quas . . . sub praesidio D.Esaiae Colladonis in . . . Genevensium Schola philospophiae, publice disputandis proponit Theodorus Tronchinus, . . . Ad Diem*

14 Junii [37] and *De peccato originali.* The first set was published at Geneva during 1600 and the second at Leyden in 1606. Tronchin also wrote a six page introduction to the 1614 two volume edition of the *Operum Omnium Quae Extant* of Bartholomew Keckermann that was published in Geneva. It is interesting to note that these works of Keckermann represent a strict Aristotelianism that would have been favoured by Beza in opposition to the then popular ideas of Ramus[38]. It should be stated that these early works of Tronchin give no very clear indication of any considerable theological distinction and in *La France Protestante,* his works are described as "ni nombreux ni importants"[39].

A second reason which may have influenced the decision of the Genevan authorities to send Tronchin to the Synod of Dort, is that he was widely travelled, more so than Diodati. Also, he had been a student in the Low Countries where he had met a number of theologians who were to play an important part in the Synod. Iselin states that he studied under Sibrandus Lubertus at Franeker in Friesland, and under Gomarus, Trelcatius and Arminius at Leyden[40]. The Album Amicorum of Tronchin is still to be found at Geneva. In this, there are entries by such distinguished Dutch theologians as Arminius, Grotius, Gomarus and Walaeus[41]. The inclusion of Arminius and Grotius is certain proof of the fact that Tronchin accepted opportunities of meeting with theologians who were not strictly orthodox. The dates of entries in this same volume show that Tronchin visited Oxford, Cambridge and London in 1605. This experience of Dutch theological training must have been most useful to Tronchin when he was a deputy at the Synod of Dort, since he had studied under a number of the most influential Dutch theologians who took part in the Synod which was, in the first instance, called to resolve an internal theological dispute within the churches of the United Provinces. Nor was Tronchin a passive listener, for he brought back to Geneva a manuscript copy in his own hand of the lecture notes of Arminius on Galatians[42]. The neat and legible condition of this manuscript, in comparison with other documents of Tronchin, probably indicates that it was not intended for his private use only. This early interest in Arminius indicates that if Tronchin acted as an orthodox theologian at the Synod of Dort who was antagonistic to Arminius' successors - the Remonstrants - that he did so with a sound basis of knowledge and experience for his opinion. However, to conclude, the previous experience of Theodore Tronchin in the Low Countries made him a particularly appropriate choice as a Genevan representative at the Synod of Dort.

Tronchin, like Diodati, may well have had preoccupations about other matters than the Synod of Dort during the period of the Synod. This suggestion is made because Tronchin's most distinguished work:- *Coton Plagiaire / OV / LA VERITE / DE DIEV ET LA / FIDELITE DE GENE / ue, maintenue / Contre les / DEPRIVATIONS ET AC- / cusations de P. Coton Iesuite contre de tradu- / ction de la S. Bible faite a Geneue, contenuesen / un liure intitule / GENEVE PLAGIAIRE / Par Theodore Tronchin Pasteur et Professeur / en Theologie a Geneue.* appeared in publication at Geneva in 1620, only a year after the Synod. The question of a reply to the Jesuit Pierre Coton - which is discussed in detail in another section of this work, had been considered by La Compagnie des Pasteurs of Geneva as early as 17th April 1618[43]. It would seem that if Tronchin's work appeared in 1620, that he may well have been working on it for some time previously, since such a book, with its large apparatus of Patristic and other quotations, would not have been quickly prepared. For this reason it is quite possible that Tronchin could have been working on it at the time of the Synod of Dort.

Thus Theodore Tronchin was a suitable theologian to be sent from Geneva to the Synod of Dort because of his reputation as a theologian and because of his knowledge of the Low Countries. Against this, it may be suggested that he may have been occupied with writing a work against the Jesuit Coton at the same time.

It is, perhaps, best to close this brief account of Theodore Tronchin by quoting part of the description of him that was written by Jean Senebier in his *Histoire Litteraire de Geneve* (Geneva, 1790) :- "Je ne suis point etonne (*sic*) des distinctions flatteuses que Tronchin recut continuellement de sa patrie; il s'etoit fait des idees de theologie beaucoup plus saines que celles qu'on avoit eues jusques a lui; il stoit savant en histoire ecclesiastique et profane; il connoissoit la jurisprudence; il endoit bein les langues savantes et sa tete lumineuse rendoit d'abord clairemont tout ce qu'il savoit a tous ceux qui venoient le consulter; il ne fut pas sealement considere par son savior; sa franchise, sa doceur, ses vertus le firent encore cherir de tous ses concitoyens, et il mourut generalement regrette an 1657"[44].

Bibliography of Theodore Tronchin

(1)

Coton Plagiaire ou La Verite de Dieu et la fidelite de Geneve, maintenue Contre les depravations et accusations de P. Coton Jesuite contre la traduction de la S. Bible faite a Geneve, Contenues en un livre intitule Geneve Plagiaire. Par Theodore Tronchin Pasteur et Professeuren Theologie a Geneve.
1620, Geneva, 80, 946 pp.

(2)

T. Tronchin Oratio funebris . . . S, Goulartii . . . Accesserunt epicedia variorum.
1628, Geneva, 40.

(3)

Oratio funebris qua Illustrissimo Celsissimoque Principi, Henrico Duci Rohanio, Franciae Pari, Principi Leonis, etc. Publice parentavit Th. Tronchinus.
1638, Geneva, 40, 24 pp.

(4)

Harangue Funebre Faite a l'Honneur De Tres-Haut et Tres Illustre Prince, Henry Duc de Rohan, Pair de France, Prince de Leon etc. Traduite du Latin de Th. Tronchin.
1638, Geneva, 40, 24 pp.

(5)

Nemo In Academia Panegyri Dictus a L.T.G.
1645, Geneva, 40, 16 pp.

Benedict Turrettini

Benedict Turrettini was the gifted child of a rich family. His father was one of the Protestant exiles from Lucca in the late sixteenth century who had lived at Antwerp, Frankfort, Basel and Zurich (where Benedict was born) before settling at Geneva in 1592 where he remained until his death[45]. Thus Benedict was brought up within the Genevan Church as were the other epigones. Benedict's father gradually amassed an immense fortune through having played a large part in the formation of the Genevan silk industry. The family lived in a mansion in the rue de l'Hotel de ville.

Benedict Turrettini was much travelled, and spent some time studying at Zurich[46] before entering on his career as a theologian. A life of this theologian was published in Geneva by a later member of his family, a certain Francois Turrettini, in 1871, entitled *Notice Biographique sur Benedict Turrettini*. This is a particularly rare work as it was privately printed and not sold to the public. It is not a work of great merit, except in as much as it includes the texts of a number of otherwise unpublished letters and manuscripts such as Benedict Turrettini's history of the Reformation. His reputation has been somewhat overshadowed by the reputations of his son Francois Turrettini (1623-87) and of his grandson Jean-Alphonse Turrettini (1671-1737) both of whom served the theological faculty of the Genevan Academy with distinction. Both of these had somewhat different theological positions from Benedict Turrettini, but Francois seems to have regarded him with respect, for in the preface to his *Institutio Theologiae Elencticae*, he write:- "Et *Benedictum Turrettinum*, Parentem meum dulcissimum, benedictae et desideratissime memoriae, quem immaturo et luctuosissimo praereptum obitu, accurati et solidi Theologi laudem obtinuisse, et fama, me tacente, loquitur, et scripta eius estantur"[47].

Before attempting to evaluate the character of Benedict Turrettini, it is obviously necessary to discuss his work. This may be considered under three headings, his work as a theologian, his work as a pastor, and, thirdly, his political activities.

Benedict Turrettini's career as a theologian was cut short by his untimely death. He was elected to a chair of theology in the Genevan Academy at the early age of twenty-three in 1612,[48] a position which he held until his death in 1631[49]. He was appointed rector for the years 1620-5,[50] but did not have a particularly easy tenure of office as it was during this period that there was trouble between the French and German speaking students of the Academy[51]. Unlike the other epigones, Diodati and Tronchin, Benedict Turrettini was not sent to the Synod of Dort, but he was sent as a representative to the French Synod of Alez in 1620 which made the canons of Dort binding upon the French Reformed Church,[52] a decision which he no doubt influenced. The greater part of his theological writings are composed of his works written against the attacks of Pierre Coton S.J., who had denounced the Genevan Bible translations. There are three books, *Defense de la fidelite des traductions de la S. Bible faites a Geneve* (1618), *Recheute de lesuite Plagiaire* (1620), and *Suite de la fidelite des traductions de la S. Bible faites a Geneve* (1626). A full bibliography of the works involved in the Coton controversy is included elsewhere, and the theological considerations of Turrettini's contribution will be discussed later in this thesis, for the moment it will suffice to state that his contribution to this affair was most distinguished.

A man with the outstanding academic ability of Benedict Turrettini was, inevitably, more the professor than the pastor. Yet he acted as pastor of the Reformed Church at Nimes for some time, a church which was then in difficulties[53]. An account of this episode has been published by C. Dardier, *Une page inedite de l'histoire de Nimes, Sejour a Nimes du pasteur et professeur genevois Benedict Turrettini* (Nimes, 1885). It is not a very useful work though it includes the texts of a number of manuscripts. Other material on his work at Nimes is to be found in the life by F. Turrettini[54]. Benedict Turrettini also worked in the Italian church at Geneva,[55] and a collection of his Italian sermons has been published, *Sei homelie sopra le parole di Gesu-Christo Luc XII, 5, 6,* (Geneva, 1623). A few French sermons were also published, *Profit des chatiments ou sept sermons sur Hebr XII 5-11,* (Geneva, 1630). His success as a pastor may be judged from the fact that Pierre du Moulin of the famous Reformed congregation of Charenton near Paris, and an opponent of Diodati[56], actually wanted the services of Turrettini as a pastor[57]. Thus, while primarily an academic, Turrettini's service as a pastor was not inconsiderable.

The third kind of matters which occupied Benedict Turrettini were of a political nature. Theodore Tronchin and Jean Diodati had certain financial matters to discuss with the Dutch authorities at the time of the Synod of Dort, but this did not end Genevan dependance on the liberality of the States General of the United Provinces. This was the period of the Thirty Years War, when the security of a tiny republic could not be very certain. Believing that they were threatened from Savoy, the Genevans felt they needed money to strengthen their fortifications. This time it was Benedict Turrettini who was sent to appeal for help. There is no doubt of his success, Senebier, in his *Histoire literaire de Geneve,* wrote that:- 'Il partit en 1621; il s'adressa aux Etats-Generaux, aux villes Anseatiques, et il remplit heureusement le but de sa commission."[58], while G. Fatio in his *Geneve et les Pays-Bas* wrote that on his return:- "Le Petit Conseil se montra fort satisfait du resultat obtenu par son depute"[59], yet it was not the kind of work that he performed most willingly since he wrote to the Compagnie des pasteurs that:- "Je ne desire rien tant que de voir la fin de ces poursuites, ou mon ame ne peut plua s'occuper, etant rappelee violement a ce qui est de notre vocation"[60]. A considerable number of documents concerning this mission were published by Francois Turrettini in his life of Benedict[61], while more material is to be found in H. de Vries de Heeckelingen, *Geneve, Pepiniere du Calvinisme Hollondias.* Benedict Turrettini's political activities were not only practical but also theoretical, for he wrote the only Genevan work of political theory dating from the period of the epigones, *Recueil de pieces concernant la doctrine et pratique de l'Eglise romaine sur la deposition des rois,* etc, (1627), a work whose subject unfortunately lies beyond the scope of this present thesis.

The previous paragraphs have shown Turrettini to have had a short, crowded and brilliant career. It is not, of course, easy to judge him in retrospect, but he may well have been the most theologically gifted of the epigones, since Diodati produced no theoretical works and Tronchin wrote only *Coton Plagiaire* which is inconsiderable compared with the three books which Turrettini wrote against Coton as will be discussed in another place. Turrettini is constantly less dogmatic and much more reasonable in his judgements, and a case in point is the matter of the Hebrew vowel pointing, where Tronchin claims them as canonical and which Diodati probably believed to be canonical[62], but which Turrettini saw as being of no great importance. He gives both opinions, for and against and tries to avoid taking a definite stand on a matter which he sees to be uncertain. This broad mindedness of Benedict Turrettini was not necessarily remarkable in his own day but it would seem that he had a very much more liberal and tolerant spirit than his son Francois. This tolerance of Benedict Turrettini's was even recognised by seventeenth century opponents such as the Arminian historian G. Brandt, who wrote:- "Te deser tijdt, of wat, vroegere, was Turretin Professor der Theologie te Geneven weegens die stadt naer Hollandt gesonden om hulp te vesocken tagens den Hartogh van Savoyen wiens groote toerusting haer in groote bekommering braght, vreesende dat het haer soude gelden. Dees, die in de Synode van Alez sijn yver tagens de Remonstranten hadt getoont, scheen nu andre insichten in't stuk der geschillen gekregen te hebben. Hy verhaelde in den Hage aen seker Heer, uit wiens aentekeninge ik dit schrijve, dat hy door Calis reisende met den gebannen Predikant Goulart, sich daer noch onthoudende, hadt gesprooken, en hem gebeden dat hy te Geneven sou koomen woonen, hem alle vriendtschap en broederschap aenbiedende, in't heimalijk en in't openbaer, gelijk onder Christenen betaemde, sonder naedeel van elks gevoelen, over't welk hy wenschte in't vriendelijk met hem in handeling te treden. Hy betuigde meer dan eens, dat hy de strengheit, die men hier te Lande tegens de Remonstranten gebruikte, miet kon goedtvinden, maer misprees"[63].

Thus, in conclusion it may be said that Benedict Turrettini was probably the best systematic theologian of the epigones, and it may not be too much to claim that his relatively early death robbed the Genevan Academy of the most promising Reformed theologian of the first half of the seventeenth century.

Bibliography of Benedict Turrettini

(1)

In Nuptias . . . Benedicti Turrettini . . . sponsi, et . . . Loysiae Michaeliae, sponsae. nubentium die 26 Maii anno M.DC.XVI 1616, Geneva, 4o.

(2)

Defense de la Fidelite des traductions de la S. Bible faites a Geneve. Opposee au livre de Pierre Coton Jesuite Intitule Geneve Plagiaire. Par Benedict Turrettini Pasteur et Professeur en l'Englise et Eschole de Geneve. 1618, Geneva, 4o, 700 pp.

(3)

Index Librorum et expurgatorum Illustrissimi ac R.D.D. Bernardi de Sandoval et Roxas Card et Archiep. Tolet Hispaniarum Primatis, Majori Castelliae Cancellarii, Generalis Inquisitoris, Regii status Consiliarii, auctoritate et jussu editus. De Consilio Supremi Senatus S. Generalis Inquisitionis Hispaniarum luxta exemplar excusum Madriti Apud Ludouicum Sanchez Typographum Regium, Anno 1612 cum appendice anni 1614. Actus

B. Turrett. Praefatione et Hispanie. Decret. Latina versione. Indicis huic libro nomen praefigitur apte: Nam proprio Sorices iudico pereunt. 1619, Geneva, 4o, 890 pp.

(4)

Recheute du Iesuite Plagiaire, ou examen des dialogues que P. Coton a opposes pour replique a la fidelite des traductions de la S. Bible faites a Geneve. Y jointe une briefve instruction touchant les Versions de l'Escriture S. et leurs qualites, contre les sophismes du Dialogiste. Par Benedict Turrettini, Pasteur et Professeur en l'Englise et Eschole de Geneve. 1620, Geneva 4o, 267 pp.

(5)

De la Communion a Jesus Christ, et refutation des erreurs de nostre temps sur ce sujet. Ou est respondu a ce qu'a dit contre icelle l'Illustriss. Cardinal du Perron en sa Replique au Serenissime Roy de la Grand Bretagne: et ou est refute son dernier escrit pour la Messe, intitule Examen du livre de Monsieur du Plessis contre la Messe.
1621, Geneva, 4o, 550 pp.

(6)

Sei Homile Sopra Le Parole di Iesu Christo, Luc XII v5.6 etc. Non Temiate coloro che poisono uccidere il corpo, etc. Fatte Hella chiesa Italiana raccolta in Geneva, da Benedetto Turrettini Ministro della Parola di Dio, nella detta Citta.
1623, Geneva, 8o, 432 pp.

(7)

Thomas JAMES, *Vindiciane Gregorianae, seu restitutus innumeris paene locis Gregorius M. ex variis Manuscriptis etc.*
1625, Geneva, 4o.
With a preface by Benedict Turrettini.

(8)

Suite de ala Fidelite des Traductions de la S. Bible faites a Geneve Contre La Plagiaire de P. Coton et autres escrits opposes aux Versions de l'Escriture Sainte. Avec briefve Refutation des obiections sur divers points de Controverse. Par Benedict Turretin, Pasteur et Professeur en l'Englise et Eschole de Geneve.
1626, Geneva,4o, 959 pp.

(9)

Daniel CHAMIER *Panstratiae Catholicae, sive Controversiarum de religione adversus Pontificos Corpus, tomis quatuor distributum. Cum indiciis necessarius.* (ed. A. Chamier)
1626-30, Geneva, in folio, 4 vols.
Included is the Disputatio theologica de Ecclesiae natura of Benedict Turrettini.

(10)

Recueil des pieces concernants La Doctrine et practique Romaine sur la desposition des Rois et subversion de leurs vies et Estats, qui s'en ensuit. Le tout tire d'Actes et Escrits authentiques.
1627, s.l., 8o, 543 pp.

(11)

Profit des Chastimens ou sept sermons sur l'exhortation contenue en l'Epit. aux Hebrieux chap XII v5.6.7.8.9.10.11. par Benedict Turretin Ministre de la Parole de Dieu en l'Eglise de Geneve, et Professeur en Theologie.
1630, Geneva, 8o, 624 pp.

(12)

Ioh. Henr. ALSTEDII *De Manducatione Spirituali, Transsubstantiatione, Sacrificio Missae Dissertatio. Eiusdem De Ecclesia eiusque partibus et proprietatibus tractatus adversus Bellarmini, et Becani, et aliorum Pontificiorum errores. Qui supplem. vice D. Chamieri Panstratiae in editione Germanica adiectus est. Accessit Joh. Pridaevxii Oxon. Acad. Theol. de Ecclesiae Visibilitate, doctissima lectio: et Ben. Tur. Prof. Gen. de Natura Ecclesiae Disputatio.*
1630, Geneva, in folio.

Notes

[1]E. de Bude, Vie de Jean Diodati (Lausanne 1869), pp. 22, 24.

[2]*ibid*, p. 26.

[3]C. Borgeaud, *Histoire de l'universite' de Geneve*, vol I, *L'Academie de Calvin*, p. 636.

[4]See p. 6.

[5]Borgeaud, *op. cit.*, p. 202.

[6]*Dictionary of National Biography*, vol CXIII, pp. 51-7.

[7]W. Bouwsma, *Venice and the Defense of Republican Liberty.*, p. 505.

[8]P. Coton *Geneve plagiaire ou verification des depravations de la parole de Dieu, qui se trouvent es Bibles de Geneve* (1618); *Recheute de Geneve Plagiaire* (1619).

[9]J. Hales, *Golden Remains of the ever Memorable Mr. Iohn Hales of Eton College* etc. (London 1659) part 2, pp. 12, 14.

[10]*ibid*, p. 20.

[11]G. Brandt *Historie der reformatie, en andre Kerkelyke geschiedenissen, in en ontrent de Nederlanden. Met eenige Aentekeningen en Aenmerkingen* (Amsterdam, 4 vols., 1671), vol 3, pp. 501-2.

[12]*Acta Synodi Nationalis, In nomine Domini nostri Iesu Christi, Authoritate Illustr. et Praepotentium DD. Ordinum Generalium Foederati Belgii Provinciarum, Dordrechti Habitae Anno 1618 et 1619 Accedunt Plenissime, de Quinque Articulis, Theologorum Iudicia* (Dordrecht, Isacci Ioannidis Canini, 1620), part I, p. 21.

[13]Brandt, *op. cit.*, Vol. III, p. 76:- "Deodatus van Geneven seide dat daer een bijsonder Collegie was opgericht van wereltrijke en geestelike persoonen, 't lelk de sorge over de drukkerijen was bevolen, en meinde, dat het dienstig sou sijn, dat men kier ook in ieder Provincie soodaenige Collegien stelde. Hij seide ook, *dat men de wijse des volks en des landts wat moest toegeven*, opdat het, sijnde een volk geneven tot vrijheit en vermaekelijkheit, door geen al te streng een jok beswaert wierde: Want daer was, sijns oordeels, niets dat de beste Reformatien kragtelooser maekte, als d'uiterste strengheit en een al te groote ijver om alles tevens te recht te brengen."

[14]*Actes du Syode National Tenu a Dordrecht, l'An 1618 et 19. Ensemble les Jugemens tant des Theologians Estrangers que de ceux des Provinces Unies des Pais Bas, sur les poincts de doctrine y debattus et controvers. Mis en Francois par Richard Iean de Neree* (Leyden 1624), part I, pp. 84-5:-
'T'Obmets tout ce que l'on pourroit dire des loix et de l'ordre lequel doibt estre garde en

l'Imprimerie d'autant que comme j'enten, il y a long temps qu'on en a baille loix, et qu'en ces Pays, cela appartient du tout a l'authorite des sages Magistrats.

Qu'on se garde seulement a l'advenir, du mal et du peril qu'apporte la licence inveteree, en ordonnant des Censeurs de livres, es Provinces ou il y a des Imprimeries, lesquels se prendront tant des politiques, gens d'Englise, que des Professeures des Academies.

Il faut conceder quelque chose a la coustume du Pays et de la nation, et ne fouler ou charger trop ce peuple et ce naturel enclin a liberte, et par fois a se recreer et passer doucement le temps: Car il n'y a rien qui tant gaste une bonne reformation, qu'une rigueur absolue et un trop grand desir d' amener ensemblement toutes choses a leur poinct."

J'approuve extremement tout ce qui a este mis en avant et exhibe, par les Freres, notammement ceux de Zuyt-Hollande."

The French text is used because the latin *Acta* here confuse the Swiss and Genevan statements.

[15]Geneva, Musee historique de la reformaiton, ms Archives Tronchin, vol XVII, report of Th. Tronchin to the Conseil de Geneve.

[16]Sir Dudley Carleton, *Letters from and to Sir Dudley Carleton, Knt. during his embassy in Hoolland. From January 1615/16 to December 1620. The second edition. With large Additions to The Historical Preface.* (London, 1775) pp. 319-20.

[17]Brandt, *op. cit.*, vol III, p. 448.

[18]Geneva, AEG, RC, 3 Jan 1619 - 1 Jan 1620, p. 75.

[19]*Acta* etc., part I, p. 2246.

[20]E. de Bude, *op. cit.*, pp. 85-109.

[21]Six letters traced. (a) 21.IX. 1607, From Diodati in Geneva Mornay. Ms in the Bibliotheek der Rijksuniversiteit, Leiden, ms Papenbrock 2. See *Bulletin de la Societe de l'histoire du protestantisme francais*, XXXI, 1882, pp. 350-2. (b) 8.I.1608, from Diodati. See A.D. de La Fontenelle de Vaudore and P.R. Auguis, *Memoires et correspondance de Duplessis-Mornay,* (Paris, 1824-5), X, p. 272. (c) 4.VI.1610, to Diodati. Ms in Bibliotheek der Rijksuniversiteit, Leiden, ms Papenbrock 2. See *Bulletin* as with "a" above, pp. 350-2. (d) 8.I.1611, from Diodati. Ms in Musee historique de la Reformation, Geneva, ms Ad. 2. (f) 26.XII.1614, from Diodati. Ms in Musee historique de la Reformation, Geneva, ms Ad.3.

[22]Two letters traced. (a) 19.IV.1610., to Diodati. Ms in Bibliotheek der Rijksuniversiteit, Leiden, ms Pappenbrock, 2. See *Bulletin de la Societe de l'histoire du protestantisme francais*, L (1901), pp. 159-61, and A.H. Swinne, *John Cameron Philosoph und Theologe (1579-1625),* (Marburg, 1968), p. 108. (b) 7.II.1612., to Diodati. Ms in Bibliotheek der Rijksuniversiteit, Leiden, ms Papenbrock 2. *Bulletin* and work by Swinne (p. 112) as above.

[23]Four letters traced. (a) 19.IV.1610., to Diodati. See Angilio Milli, *Giovanni Diodati il traduttore della Bibbia e la Societa Degli Esuli Protestanti Italiani a Ginevra* (Lausanne, 1908), appendix. (b) 3.I.1619., from Diodati. Ms in the Public Record Office, London, ms S.P. 84, vol 87, no. 178. (c) 18.I.1619., from Diodati. Ms in the Public Record Office, London, ms S.P. 84, vol. 88, no. 39. (d) 28.II.1619., from Diodati. Ms in the Public Record Office, London, ms S.P. 84, vol. 88, no. 197.

[24]Frederick Hendrik, Prins van Orange. One letter traced. 1626, to Diodati. Ms in Bibliotheek der Rijksuniversiteit, Leiden, ms Papenbrock 1b.

[25]Three letters traced. (a) 15.IV.1632, to Diodati. Ms in the Bibliothequede Mejanes, Aixen-Provence, ms 204 (1022). (b) 10.IX.1632., from Diodati. Ms in the Bibliotheque de Mejanes, Aix-en-Provence, ms 204 (1022). (c) Late 1632, to Diodati. Ms copy in the Bibliotheek der Rijksuniversiteit, Leiden, ms BPL 26 B.

[26]Three letters traced. (a) Late 1631, from Diodati. Ms in British Museum, London, ms Sloane 654 ff77. See E.J. Scott, *Index to the Sloane Manuscripts in the British Museum,* (London, 1904), p. 145. (b) 28.VIII.1633, from Diodati. Ms in Trinity College, Dublin, ms 293, C.3.8.,

no. 24. (c) Late 1633, from Diodati. Ms in British Museum, London, ms Sloane 654 ff 79. See E.J. Scott, *Index to the Sloane Manuscripts in the British Museum,* (London, 1904), p. 145.

[27]Seven letters traced. (a) 17.XII.1632, from Diodati. Ms in Bibliotheek der Rijksuniversiteit, Leiden, ms BPL 27 b. (b) 24.IX.1634, from Diodati. Ms in Bibliotheek der Rijksuniversiteit, Leiden, ms BPL 302. (c) 13.IV.1635, from Diodati. Ms in Bibliotheek der Rijksuniversiteit, Leiden, ms no. BPL302. (d) 6.X.1639, from Diodati. Ms in Bibliotheek der Rijksuniversiteit, Leiden, ms BPL302. (f) 24.VIII.1644, from Diodati. Ms in Bibliotheek der Rijksuniversiteit, Leiden, ms BPL 302. (g) 25.III.1645, from Diodati. Ms in Bibliotheek der Rijksuniversiteit, Leiden, ms BPL 302.

[28]Eighty-one letters traced, all in the Staatsarchiv, Zurich. They are:- 21.IX.1620, from Diodati, ms E II 390, 350; 21.II.1621, from Diodati, ms E II 390, 515; 11.V.1621, from Diodati, ms E II 390, 586; 20.XI.1621, from Diodati, ms E II 390, 750; 15.I.1622, from Diodati, ms E II 390, 830; 12.II.1622, from Diodati, ms E II 390, 864; 8.V.1622, from Diodati, ms E II 390, 878; 15.V.1622, from Diodati, ms E II 390, 926; 4.IX.1622, from Diodati, ms E II 390, 1072; 24.VII.1623, from Diodati, ms E II 390, 1264; 5.VIII.1623, from Diodati, ms E II 390, 1294; 10.X.1623, from Diodati, ms E II 390, 1320; 13.X.1623, from Diodati, ms E II 390, 1324; 18.XII.1623, from Diodati, ms E II 390, 1358; 19.I.1625 from Diodati, ms E II 393, 227; 23.III.1625, from Diodati, ms E II 393, 289; e.V.1625, from Diodati, ms E II 393, 309; 19.II.1627 from Diodati, ms E II 393, 723; all subsequent letters are from Diodati; 11.IX.1627, ms E II 374, 294-6; 14.II.1628, ms E II 393, 1o99; 13.IV.1628, ms E II 393, 935; 11.VIII.1628, ms E II 393, 1033; 17.IX.1628, me E II 393, LO61; 14.XI.1628, ms E II 393, 1139; 1.XII.1628, ms E II 393, 855; 13.XII.1628, ms E II 396, 288; c.1628, ma E II 396, 287; 16.II.1629, ms E II 395, 369; 10.III.1629, me E II 395, 815; 21.IV.1629, ms E II 395, 783; 15.XII.1629, ms E II 393, 1193; 15.II.1630, ms E II 395, 371; 16.III.1630, ms I II 395, 323; 20.IV.1630, ma W II 395, 301; 15.II.1630, ms E II 395, 189; 1.XI.1630, ms E II 395, 157; 7.III.1631, ms E II 396, 48; 14.III.1631, ms E II 396, 64; 12.VII.1631, ms E II 396, 120; 16.VIII.1631, ms E II 396, 150; 16.VIII.1631, ms E II 396, 120; 16.VIII.1631, ms E II 396,150; 16.VIII.1631, ms E II 396, 151; 20.IX.1631, ms E II 396, 190; ?.IX.1631, ms E II 396, 196; 18.X.1631, ms E II 396, 218; 8.I.1632, ms E II 399, 5; 23.II.1632, ms E II 399, 93; 4.III.1632, ms E II 399, 99; 22.IX.1632, ms E II 399, 393; 29.IX.1632, ms E II 399, 312; 2.I.1633, ms E II 400, 1: 17.I.1633, ms E II 400, 6; 11.II.1633, ms E II 400, 6; 26.II.1633, ms E II 400, 30; 26.II.1633, ms E II 397, 83; 10.III.1633, ms E II 400, 35, 23.V.1633, ms E II 400, 77; 27.VII.1633, ms E II 400, 89; 8.VII.1633, ms E II 400, 106; 12.VIII.1633, ms E II 400, 119; 23.IX.1633, ms E II 400, 142; 14.X.1633, ms E II 400, 165; 21.X.1633, ms E II 400, 158; 17.II.1634, ms E II 400, 14; 6.V.1634, ms E II 400, 289/91; 24.VI.1634, ms E II 400, 308; 6.XI.1634, ms E II 400, 339/40; 26.XI.1634, ms E II 400, 357; 15.IV.1635, ms E II 400, 401; 20.IV.1638, ms E II 401, 517;9.VI.1640, ms E II 404, 54; 29.VII.1640, ms E II 404, 72; 16.VIII.1640, ms E II 404, 83; 26.VII.1640, ms E II 404, 84; 9.IX.1640, ms E II 404, 84; 24.IX.1640, ms E II 404, 111; 1.XI.1640, ms E II 404, 111; 19.I.1641, ms E II 404, 161/5; 1.III.1641, ms E II 404, 178; 24.V.1641, ms E II 404, 242/4; 16.VI.1641, ms E II 404, 269; 8.IX.1642, ms E II 404, 777/8.

[29]See pp.

[30]B. Lescaze, "Nicholas Anthoine", thesis for the Faculte des Lettres, University of Geneva, 1969, passim.

[31]E. and E. Haag, *La France Protestante,* vol IX, p. 422.

[32]C. Borgeaud, *Histoire de l'université de Genève,* vol I, *L'Academie de Calvin,* p. 639.

[33]*ibid,* p. 636.

[34]Geneva, Musee historique de la Reformation, Archives Tronchin vol. 34.

[35]Borgeaud, *op. cit.,* p. 639.

[36]Haag, *op. cit.,* vol IX, p. 423.

[37]Printed catalogue of the Bibliotheque nationale de Paris, vol CXCIV, p. 886.

[38]*The New Schaff Herzog* vol VI, p. 304.

[39]Haag, *op. cit.*, vol IX, p. 422.

[40]*Historisches und Geographisches Lexicon,* vol IV, p. 685 (Basel 1727). Lubertus, Gomarus and Trelcatius all attended the Synod of Dort.

[41]Geneva, Musee historique de la Reformation, Archives Tronchin, vol 31, folia 72, 84, 31 and 114.

[42]*ibid,* vol 80.

[43]Geneva, Archives d'Etat, Registres de la Compagnie des Pasteurs, vol R6, fol 233.

[44]Senebier, *Hist. Litt. de Genève,* vol 2, p. 134, (Geneve 1790).

[45]*DHBS* vol 6, p.714.

[46]F. Turrettini, *Notice Biographique sur Benedict Turrettini*, pp. 20-4.

[47]F. Turrettini, *Institutio Theologiae Elencticae,* vol 1, p. 202b.

[48]C. Borgeaud, *Histoire de l'Universite de Geneve,* vol I, *L'Academie de Calvin,* p. 339.

[49]*ibid,* p. 640.

[50]*ibid,* p. 636.

[51]*ibid,* p. 451.

[52]Quick, *Synodicon in Gallia Reformata,* vol II, pp. 37-40; and F. Turrettini, *Notice Biographique* etc., pp. 104-26.

[53]F. Turrettini, *Notice Biographique sur Benedict Turrettini,* p. 87.

[54]*ibid,* pp. 86-103.

[55]*ibid,* p. 35.

[56]Geneva, Archives d'Etat, Registres du Conseil, RC 134, (1635) pp. 122-5:- "Quant a ce qu'on luy oppose et premierement le scandale respond que si on avoit esgard a cela il ne faudroit rien raire de bon; que pour ce regard les Papistes ont six versions et partant ne peuvent rien objecter: qu'il faut regarder quelle est leur objection c'est de n' avoir pas amende: que se scandaliseront davantage et diront qu'on a empesche chose utile a l'Eglise. Quant au scandale des foibles respond qu'il leur faut aider si ce sont gens qui ne lisent point il n'y faut pas avoir esgard: si'ils lisent ils seront aidez et consolez par le moyen d'une bonne version. Pour le gegarde su Synode d'Alais respond que ce furent des resolutions soudaines lesquelles ne sont gardees et ne peuvent avoir iuge sans avoir cognu l'oeuvre et oui l'auteur: que dupuis il a lettre du Ministre de Mets qui luy escrit que Monsieur Du Moulin a bien change d'avis." From this it would appear that DuMoulin, a most powerful man in the French Church and an opponent of Amyraut, had been known to be opposed ot Diodati's French Bible, the publication of which was the subject under debate. In the preface to his *Les Livres de Iob, Pseavmes, Proverbes, Ecclesiaste, Cantique des Cantiques* of 1638, p. 3, Diodati wrote:- "Je me trouve combatu en mon innocent dessein par un seul puissant ennemi, qui est la crainte: qui a de tout temps este reconue d'une transgrande estendue." There would seem to be little doubt that this powerful enemy could have been Du Moulin. Thus it is all the more interesting that he wanted a fellow epigone and Italian as a pastor at Charenton, unless, of course, the quarrel had not arisen at that time.

[57]F. Turrettini, *Notice Biographique sur Benedict Turrettini,* p. 29.

[58]Edition of 1786, vol. II, pp. 135-6.

[59]G. Fatio, *Geneve et les Pays-Bas,* p. 78.

[60]*ibid.,* p. 78.

[61]F. Turrettini, *Notice Biobraphique sur Benedict Turrettini*, pp. 127-270.

[62]F. Turrettini, *Institutio Theologiae Elencticae,* Vol. I, p. 119.

[63]G. Brandt, vol. IV, pp. 758-9. The English edition, *History of the Reformation,* vol. IV, p. 378, reads:- "About this time, or a little earlier, *Turretin,* Professor of Divinity at *Geneva,* was deputed from that city to *Holland,* in order to sue for the States assistance against the Duke of *Savoy,* at whose preparations they were alarmed, thinking that they were designed against them. This Gentleman, who had shown his zeal against the *Remonstrants* at *Alez,* seemed to have acquired other notions of the points in controversy. He said to a certain person at the *Hague,* from whose memoirs I write this, that travelling by Calais, he had

some discourse with *Simon Goulart*, one ofthe banished ministers who resided there, and had invited him to come to *Geneva*, where he offered him all manner of friendship and brotherhood, both publickly and privately, according to the rules of Christianity, without prejudice to his particular opinions, concerning which, he said, he should be glad to enter into an amicable debate with him. He declared more than once, that he could byno means approve, but rather blamed the severities put in practice against the *Remonstrants* in these provinces.

Chapter Two
The Synod of Dort
Historiography of the Synod of Dort

A discussion of the historiography of the Synod of Dort is an obvious preliminary investigation to any study of the Genevan contribution to the Synod.

For the modern church historian, the first discovery may well be that recent works of reference are strangely reticent about the Synod of Dort. The only synod in the seventeenth century that was attended by members who represented most of the reformed Protestant Churches, the Synod receives only brief mention in modern encyclopaedias such as the *Lexicon fur Theologie und Kirche* (Frieburg, 1957-67) and *Die Religion in Geschichte und Gegenwart* (Tubingen, 1957-65). This climate of silence extends even to modern manuals of Church history such as *Reformation Katholische Reform und Gegenreformation* by F. Iserloh, J. Glazik and H. Jedin (Frieburg Basel, Vienna, 1967), in which the Synod of Dort is mentioned only in passing. A modern classic such as *The history and Character of Calvinism* by John T. McNeill (1964, rp 1967), in which information concerning the Synod of Dort might be expected to be obtainable, only refers to the Synod some four or five times, and adds very little to theological evaluation of its work. However, the slight reference to Dort which McNeill makes does serve to illustrate its reputation. He writes:- "Its Dutch membership was prevailingly of the Gomarist or rigorous Calvinist persuasion, but theologians from the Churches of England and the Palatinate tempered the rigor of its decisions."[1] And again:- "The participation of his (i.e. James I of England) emmissaries in the Synod of Dort was featured by the assertion of episcopacy by one of them and the rejection of intolerant Calvinism by another."[2] In these lines, a clue may well be found as to the state of the reputation of the Synod of Dort among distinguished contemporary Church historians. McNeill is certainly sympathetic to Calvinism as is shown by his dedication of the work in question to his own father whom he describes as:- "an exemplar of Calvinist faith and virtues." Yet in these passages quoted above, McNeill's attitude to Dort is clearly revealed:- "rigorous Calvinist", "The rigor of its decisions" and "intolerant Calvinism." The Synod stands accused of intolerance. McNeill's approval of the charge is seen in the fact that he offers no defence. The synod would appear to be condemned.

The Bibliography of the Synod of Dort appended to this work (Appendix 2) reveals that a certain amount has been written about the Synod of Dort during the nineteenth and twentieth centuries. If a few of the best known secondary works are selected for consideration, it becomes obvious that the imputation of intolerance is repeated frequently. O. Chadwick in his *The Reformation* (The Pelican History of the Church, III) writes that:- "The Synod confronted the Arminians, now led by Simon Episcopius. In so large an assembly of the Reformed, including even an English bishop, it was impossible to canonise the extreme language of Gomar."[3] The presence of an English bishop being part of a defence against extremism would appear to be the imputation of intolerance in an otherwise lucid account. F.L. Cross in the first edition of the *Oxford Dictionary of the Christian Church* (London, O.U.P. 1958) is more blunt in his allegation of intolerance:- "The Synod . . . was biased against Arminianism from the start and its decisions were a forgone conclusion."[4] E.G. Leonard, in his *Histoire Generale du Protestantisme*, vol. II, (Paris 1961) goes so far as to write:- "Due a l'esprit de parti et soumise a l'esprit de violence, l'oeuvre de Dordrecht fut une des plus

45

ephemeres de l'histoire ecclesiastique".[5] Nor is the imputation of intolerance confined to church historians, since even a standard reference work such as the *Dictionary of National Biography* (London, 1885-1899 etc.) contains similar allusions in its articles on English representatives at the Synod:- "The work of the English divines at the Synod was to endeavour to soften the bitter narrowness of the Calvinistic deputies."[6] and "At this assembly, Hall, together with the other English deputies, did something to moderate the bitterness of the onslaughts of the Calvinists on the Arminians."[7] Reputable modern historical works also contain another accusation, which is that the Synod is responsible for then contemporary political crimes in the Low Countries such as the execution of the elderly van Olden Barneveld, or the arrest of the distinguished scholar Grotius who eventually had to flee the country. But contemporainety does not entail direct causation. The fact that Maurice of Nassau had an interest in the Synod, and the fact that Maurice of Nassau was responsible for the death of van Olden Barneveld, in no sense entails the conclusion that the Synod might be responsible for the death of van Olden Barneveld. Yet this is often what has been assumed. In 1874, the famous historian J.L. Motley wrote a bitter attack on the Synod of Dort that was included in his *The Life and Death of John of Barneveld:-* "Short work was made with the Arminians. They and their Five Points were soon thrust into outer darkness. It was established beyond all gainsaying that two forms of Divine worship in one country were forbidden by God's word, and that thenceforth by Netherland law there could be but one religion, namely, the Reformed or Calvinistic creed. It was settled that one portion of the Netherlanders and of the rest of the human race had been expressly created by the Deity to be forever damned, and another portion to be eternally blessed. But this history has little to do with that infallible council save in the political effect of its decrees on the fate of Barneveld. It was said that the canons of Dordrecht were likely to shoot off the head of the Advocate. There had been purposely a delay, before coming to a decision as to the fate of the state prisoners, until the work of the Synod should have approached completion. It was thought good that the condemnation of the opinions of the Arminians and the chastisement of their leaders should go hand-in-hand."[8] In this description, Motley does not state categorically that the Synod was responsible for the political crime of the execution of the prisoners, what he does mention is:- "the effect of its decrees on the fate of the Barneveld", and:- "It was thought good that the condemnation of the opinions of the Arminians and the chastizement of their leaders should go hand-in-hand." Thus forcefully instituted, this association of ideas has not lost ground during the nineteenth and twentieth centuries, for it is also to be found in the well known *Creeds of Christendom* of the American historian Philip Schaff which was published in 1877. Schaff writes that Motley:- "carictures the Synod of Dort in a manner unworthy of an impartial historian."[9] Schaff himself is unemotional in his treatment of the Synod, but his description of events tends to suggest an unfavourable value judgement. He quotes opinion both for and against the Synod, but the reader is left with the impression that it was an unpleasant incident. He states carefully that the political events were independent of the events at the Synod but writes of the two together:- "The victory of orthodoxy was obscured by the succeeding deposition of about two hundred Arminian clergymen, and by the preceding though independent arrest of the political leaders of the Remonstrants, at the instigation of Maurice. Grotius was condemned by the States-General to perpetual imprisonment, but escaped through the ingenuity of his wife (1621). Van Olden Barneveldt was unjustly condemned to death for alleged high-treason, and beheaded at the Hague (May 14, 1619). His sons took refuge in a fruitless attempt against the life of Prince Maurice."[10] This association of ideas - the Synod of Dort, the execution of van Olden Barneveld and the flight of Grotius - is also to be noted in the *Lectures on modern history* published by Lord Acton in 1906:- "It was during this truce that the best-known events of Dutch history occurred - the Synod of Dort, the suppression of the Republicans and Arminians by Maurice of Nassau, when he put Olden Barnevelt to death, and compelled the most illustrious of all Dutchmen, Grotius, to make his escape packed in a box of books."[11] It is to be noted that the contemporainety of the events is stated, but that Lord Acton does not state that the Synod was responsible for the political crimes, that particular perversion being the unfortunate privilege of the twentieth century. In *The Oxford Dictionary of the Christian Church* (ed. F.L. Cross), published in 1958 it is written:- "This victory for Calvinist principles led to some two hundred Arminian clergy being deprived, H. Grotius being sentenced by the States-General to perpetual imprisonment, and J. van Olden Barnevelt being beheaded on a false charge of high treason."[12] This dictionary quotes Schaff's book as a source, but includes mention of no seventeenth century source material.

Thus an unfavourable climate of opinion exists concerning the Synod of Dort, in so far, that is, as a climate of opinion exists at all - the references in the encyclopaedias and manuals of church history being so noticeably inadequate. No evaluation of these criticisms will be attempted here. It is, however, necessary to justify the inclusion in this present work of a study of the historiography of the Synod of Dort. The relationship is, however, quite simple. In this section of the present work, it will be related how two distinguished theologians from the Genevan Academy took a not completely unimportant part in the proceedings of the Synod of Dort. If the present academic climate of opinion that has been outlined above is seen as valid, then the Synod must be regarded as an event at which considerable intolerance was displayed by Reformed theologians and which led to the perpetuation of a number of grave political "crimes". If this judgement is accepted, and if it is shown that Genevan theologians did indeed play a considerable part in the proceedings - which in fact they did - then the suspicion would naturally arise that they too were guilty of intolerance and of the political crimes. Fortunately this can be discounted, since if true it might well question the desirability of this work as a whole. It can, in fact, be shown that the kind of modern discussion of the Synod of Dort that has been outlined above is somewhat inaccurate and, indeed, quite irrelevant. Thus it may be argued that the study of Genevan contributions to this Synod is indeed desirable, and due to the modern view of Dort, very necessary.

No climate of modern historical opinion exists without a valid basis. The works quoted above are all, without exception, competent scientific studies. If they had not been responsible works, their consideration would have been a barren exercise. But because they are generally reputable, it is obvious that they must have had some valid basis for their attitude to the Synod of Dort. In general, the most widely held views on the Synod come from works by G. Brandt and by Peter Heylyn. Brandt's *Historie der Reformatie, en andre Kerkelyke Geschiedenissen, in on ontrent de Nederlanden* was first published in 1671-1704, an English translation appearing in 1720 with a subscription list containing many distinguished names, and a very much abridged French edition in 1726.[13] Peter Heylyn wrote two accounts of the Synod, one in his *Aerius Redivivus or the History of the Presbyterians,* published in 1672 and another in the *Historia Quinquarticularis* of 1681. In these works may be seen the first hint of the foundation of a climate of historical opinion that is unfavourable to the Synod of Dort, or at least to the greater part of its orthodox members. Brandt (1626-85) was himself a remonstrant[14], while Peter Heylyn (1600-62) was an Anglican Laudian divine[15]. Thus it may be seen that two most influential historians of the Synod were men whose natural sympathies might be expected to be antagonistic to the Synod and its work. When the works of these two historians are considered, this is an impression that is confirmed. From this, it may be seen that modern histories of the Synod of Dort rely on source works, the authors of which were unsympathetic towards the Synod. Thus, to an extent, the modern attitude towards Dort may be explained, and may be seen to be incorrect.

The historical works of Brandt and Heylyn are very different in character. Brandt's is a detailed historical work based on a mass of evidence. His account of the Synod nearly fills a volume of 976 pages in Dutch. Heylyn's work is much more openly controversial, and some of the charges that he brought against the Synod members must be considered below. Yet Brandt's treatment of the theologically orthodox members of the Synod is constantly slightly detrimental. The Genevan representatives are included in this censure and one may use this evaluation of them as an instance of his method since it clearly reveals a certain bias.

Brandt describes Tronchin's speech to the Synod on the subject of perseverance as being, in the opinion of Poppius, "very confused" and as having very little to do with the subject.[16] Yet Brandt must have known the good opinion of this sermon that was written by the Scottish Anglican, Walter Balcanquall who wrote, in a letter to the English ambassador Sir Dudley Carleton:- "Deodatus was this session appointed to discuss the first Article; but because of his sickness, his colleague *Tronchinus* did perform that task for him, publickly all auditors being admitted, who with good commendation did establish *Sanctorum perseverantium.*"[17] The opinion of Balcanquall is all the more valuable since he is not an obviously similar theologian to Tronchin, since he had been converted to episcopacy from a rigidly anti-episcopalian background.[18]

In his *Historia Quinquarticularis,* Peter Heylyn accuses the Synod of Dort as being an intolerant assembly. This is not a vague, general statement, but a well defined imputation:- "A Synod much like *Trent,* in the Motives to it; as also in the managing and conduct of it. For as neither of them was Assembled till the Sword was drawn, the terrour whereof was able to effect more than all other arguments so neither of them was concerned to confute, but condemn their Opposites."[19] The idea that the orthodox theologians at the Synod could not refute the remonstrants is a favourite theme of Heylyn, to which he returns in *Aerius Redivivus:* "To put an end to those Disorders, a Conference was appointed between the Parties held at the *Hague,* before the General Assembly of the Estates of the *Belgick* Provinces, *Anno* 1610. The Controversie reduced to five Articles only, and the dispute managed by the ablest men who appeared in the Quarrel on either side. In which it was conceived, that the *Remonstrants* had the better of the day, and came off with Victory. But what the *Contra Remonstrants* wanted in the strength of Argument, they made good by Power."[20] and:- "they prosecuted their Opponents in their several Consistories, by Suspensions, Excommunications, and Deprivations, the highest Censures of the Church. This forced the *Remonstrant* Party to put themselves under the protection of *John Olden Barnevelt.*'[21] This belief in the strength of remonstrant argument leads Heylyn to write that the remonstrants could have saved themselves if the Synod had not been so antagonistic:- "the *Remonstrants* might have found a way to have saved themselves, either by fomenting the Contentions, or by finding some favours at their hands . . . but no such favour could be gained, not so much as hoped for."[22] and that the Synod:- "were resolved not to hear those Arguments which they could not answer."[23] Some of Heylyn's censures have a more general bearing, and reveal a knowledge of the theological background to the Synod:- "Some other differences there were amongst them, not reconcilable in this Synod; as namely, whether the Elect be loved out of Christ or not: whether Christ were the cause and *foundation of Election,* or only the Head of the Elect; And many others of like nature. Nor were these Differences managed with much sobriety as became the gravity of the persons, and weight of the business, but brake out many times into such open heats and violences, as are not to be parallel'd in the like Assemblies; the *Provincial* Divines banding against the Foreigners, and the Foreigners falling foul upon one another."[24] Thus in the writings of Peter Heylyn, a clearly defined attitude towards the Synod is to be observed. This is not to say that it is in the writings of Heylyn that one must seek the genesis of this attitude, it may well be that it had already been established, but it must be recognised that in the writings of Heylyn the idea of the Synod as an intolerant assembly finds eloquent and influential expression.

One feature of writings concerning the Synod of Dort is that, in general, apologies for the Synod are more common than writings which favour the Synod without reference to works of an antagonistic bias. No history that was sympathetic towards the Synod, and which was of a stature similar to the books of Brandt and Heylyn was written during the seventeenth century. Instead, "Calvinist" apologists such as Thomas Fuller in the seventeenth century and Augustus Montague Toplady in the eighteenth century are, in their discussion of the Synod, dominated by a desire to refute what they believed to be the calumnies written about the Synod. Therefore, it may be said, that in general, the "Calvinist" versions are primarily responses to works which criticise the Synod on various grounds.

Brandt and Heylyn's imputation of intolerance has been discussed, and it is not impossible that their judgement has played a significant part in the formation of the basic concepts from which the modern climate of opinion concerning the Synod has developed. The charge of intolerance, however, is only one criticism of the Synod. The charge of responsibility for political crimes has also been mentioned, and this must be considered as well as two other accusations, the accusations that the members of the Synod took an oath to condemn the Remonstrants, and finally the charge that the Synod acted as both party and judge in the dispute.

The charge that the Synod was responsible for then contemporary political crimes such as the execution of van Olden Barneveldt or the imprisonment of Grotius, as stated in the *Oxford dictionary of the Christian Church* is quite false. In the early years of the seventeenth century, two distinct internal struggles developed and became acute in the Low Countries. One was a political struggle between Maurice of Nassau and other figures - such as van Olden Barneveldt - within the state. The other, the struggle between orthodox and remonstrant, was at first completely religious in nature. In the years 1618 and 1619 the two struggles were both resolved; the Arminians were condemned by the Synod of Dort and van Olden Barneveldt was executed through the influence of Maurice of Nassau. Because these events were contemporary, it is easy for them to be confused. At first, the two conflicts were distinct, and it was only when the Arminians accepted the patronage of van Olden Barneveldt that the religious and secular struggles became interwoven, the religious struggle developing a political character. Maurice of Nassau became interested in the religious conflict only after this patronage had been accepted, since, in accepting it, the Arminians had become a faction, or at least part of a factional grouping, within the state. Maurice's lack of interest in theological matters is demonstrated by his often quoted remark that he did not know if predestination were blue or gray, but that he knew that Barneveldt's trumpets playing a different tune to his own.[25] Another reason why the political and religious struggles have been confounded may well be the general tendency of Church historians to overstate the importance of religious influence upon political events, not that this attitude is always confined to Ecclesiastical historians. Yet it must be clearly recognised that van Olden Barneveldt was executed because of the political danger that he posed to Maurice of Nassau, and not because of his religious affiliation, in which Maurice would not have been particularly interested if van Olden Barneveldt had not become a patron of the Arminians. Van Olden Barneveldt was executed because Maurice of Nassau found it politically expedient, and the Synod of Dort as such was not concerned in his condemnation, even if the private opinion of certain members - possibly including Diodati of Geneva - would have been favourable to this. It will be seen in considering the place of the Genevans at the Synod, that political considerations may well have had an influence upon their attitude. Dr. P. Itterzon has shown the considerable influence exerted upon the Synod of Dort by James I of England.[26] But these are quite separate considerations, no international Synod in the seventeenth century could be expected to live in a political vacuum without political pressures, but this is not to say that in contrast the Synod had any influence upon current political events, and any suggestion that the Synod was in any way responsible for the death of van Olden Barneveldt or the imprisonment of Grotius is certainly to be rejected. The kind of attitude represented by a competent twentieth century historian such as Henri Hauser:- "ce drame theologico-politique s'acheva le 13 par l'execution d'un veillard de soixante-douze and" i.e. van Olden Barneveldt, "dans la cour du chateau des comtes de La Haye",[27] must be rejected as being unacceptable.

The problem of the Synod as being both party to and judge of the Arminians can also be traced to Heylyn, though in fact the dispute originated at the Synod itself. Peter Heylyn in his *Aerius Redivivus* wrote:- "And finally they took such order with the rest that they (the orthodox) would not suffer them (the remonstrants) to sit as Judges in the present Controversies, but only appear before them as Parties Criminal. All which being condescended to, though against all reason, they were restrained to such a method in their disputation, as carried with it a betraying of their Cause and Interest; and for not yielding hereunto they were dismist by *Bogerman* (the president of the Synod) in a most bitter oration, uttered with fiery eyes, and most virulent language."[28] In his *The Historic Proof of the Doctrinal Calvinism of the Church of England* (1774), Agustus Montague Toplady attempted to defend the Synod with a certain amount of success. He asked why the remonstrants should complain about appearing as criminals and not as judges since they formed a faction in the state and had a responsibility to the public to state their case, and since they were being encouraged by the enemies of Holland, namely, France and Spain. Toplady states that Dort was both an ecclesiastical and a civil court, which was convened for the consideration of people whose "crimes" were of a mixed nature.[29] The question of the Synod acting as both party and judge has largely disappeared from more modern considerations of the Synod, though there is a hint of it in Schaff, when he writes:- "Thus the fate of the Arminians was decided beforehand. Episcopius and his friends - thirteen in all - were summoned before the Synod simply as dependants, and protested against unconditional submission."[30] Yet it is worth raising this point, for it is symptomatic of the kind of controversy that has plagued the historiography of the Synod, for it is virtually pointless of Heylyn to accuse in this way, and unnecessary of Toplady to defend the Synod. The basic fact of the situation was that the Synod had to give judgement, it was summoned by the States General to do so, and, inevitably, the members of the Synod would either reject or accept the doctrines of the remonstrants, and it is not surprising that their decision was unpopular among the remonstrants. To institute a dispute about such matters is an unworthy task for any serious historian. The problem of the authority of a council or a synod of the Church is not new, it must be considered by each assembly, and can be expected to be questioned by each group that are faced with what appears to be, for them, an unfavourable decision. What is truly relevant to any discussion of this problem with reference to the Synod of Dort, is that the Synod was itself aware of this as a problem and at one time actually debated synodical theory - a point that has been completely ignored by the various historians involved in the dispute. The synodical theory of the Synod of Dort, or rather the Genevan contribution to this, is discussed in another section of this chapter. Thus it may be seen that this controversy is archetypical of the historiography of the Synod of Dort. An important theological theme has been completely ignored and has been replaced in later works by controversies as to whether the Synod was being just or unjust in acting as both party and judge, when the Synod had no possibility of acting otherwise.

In a work called *Redemption Redeemed,* written by John Goodman in the seventeenth century, it was suggested that the members of the Synod of Dort took an oath to condemn the remonstrants before the Synod began. This is a very grave charge. In his *Church History of Britain,* first published in 1655, Thomas Fuller refuted this suggestion. Fuller was himself the nephew of one of the Anglican representatives at Dort, John Davenant[31] but Davenant had died in 1641[32], so Fuller had recourse to another English theologian who had been at the Synod, the then aged Joseph Hall, who informed him that:- "Truly, sir, as I hope to be saved, all the oath that was required of us was this . . . every person . . . calling the great God of heaven to witness, that he would impartially proceed in the judgement of these controversies, which should be laid before him, only out of and according to the written word of God, and no otherwise; so determining of them as he should find in his conscience most agreeable to the holy scriptures . . . and this was all the oath that was either taken or required."[33] The rejection of Goodman was repeated by Toplady and the accusation has passed out of controversy concerning the Synod. In point of fact, there is no reason why this should have been the end of this particular controversy. The members of the Synod were to accept no other authority but the word of God. However, if another authority had been considered, such authority would have most probably been the symbolic works accepted by Dort and the Dutch Reformed Churches, the Heidelberg Catechism and the Belgic Confession. It is to be noted that the remonstrants could not have been condemned because of anything written in either of these documents, and so the accepted limitation to judge the remonstrants on the word of God alone could have been interpreted as a hostile act on the part of the Synod.

One general criticism of the history of the Synod as it has been written, is that a bad use has been made of the good printed sources that are available. One honourable exception to this is Moréri who in his *Le Grand Dictionnaire* used Brandt, the *Acta* and various minor works to produce a well-informed and impartial article.[34] Bayle, odly enough, does not mention the Synod. The *Acta* of the Synod have been published in three languages, Dutch, French and Latin.[35] Two important series of letters have been published concerning the Synod. One series was written by the deputies of Hesse and was published by H. Heppe as "Historia Synodi nationalis Dordracenae, sive Literae delegatorum Hassiacorum de iis quae in synodo D. acta sunt ad Landgravium Mauritium missae." in *Zeitschrift fur di historische Theologie*, 1853, pp. 226-327. The second series of letters is formed of those written by the British delegation to the English ambassador in Holland, Sir Dudley Carleton. These were published in *Golden Remains of the ever Memorable Mr. Iohn Hales of Eton College etc.*, that was published at London in 1659, reprinted in English 1688, Latin 1724 and Dutch 1670. The letters of the British Delegates are most informative concerning the day-to-day events of the Synod, but these letters have also been misused by the historians for Heylyn, writing about Hales' duties, could write:- "(he) was suffered to be present at the hearing of it; so that it might be said of them . . . when the persecuting humour was upon them: *Audire nolunt, quod auditum damnare non possunt;* they were resolved not to hear those arguments which they could not answer, or to give ear unto the proving of those Points which they could not honestly condemn, if they had been proved."[36] On the other hand, Augustus Montague Toplady also uses these letters as a source for his defence of the orthodox and for his attack upon the remonstrants.[37] This kind of misuse of a good historical source reveals that it was used by writers whose judgements were already made, and who sought not truth but the justification of their own opinions. The view of Dort to which both these writers contribute has, unfortunately, apparently formed the basis of much modern writing concerning the Synod. It is typical of the general obscurity concerning the events of the Synod, that even when these letters have been used in a less polemical manner as, for instance, by A.W. Harrison in *The Beginnings of Arminianism to the Synod of Dort* (London, 1926) their faults, which include wrong numbering of the sessions of the Synod, are also included because Harrison did not use the *Acta* of the Synod. A proper use of the *Acta* has recently been demonstrated by W. Rex in *Essays on Pierre Bayle and religious controversy* (The Hague, 1965).[38] The letters of the Hessian delegates have rarely been used at all. Another important source which has been little used is the *Beitrage zur Kenntnis der Geschichte der Synode von Dordrecht* published at Basel in 1825 by Matthias Graff which contains accounts of visits to the Synod by Wolfgang Meyer of Basel and J.J. Breitinger of Zurich as well as an annotated *album amicorum* of Meyer. Graf seems to have been influenced by earlier prejudicial accounts of the Synod and finds little good to say of Diodati quoting the remark about the Dort canons beheading Barneveldt and quotes without reference an alleged remark of Diodati:- "die kirche wurde sein Ruhe habe, so lange dieses haupt der Arminianer lebte."[39]

Thus, without necessarily attempting to judge the value or validity of the criticisms discussed above, it might not be overstating the case to suggest that in the works discussed above (with the exception of Rex' book), though this discussion has been far from exhaustive, an attitude of antagonism towards Dort was created that has been a factor in the formation of the unfavourable modern climate of opinion concerning the Synod. It is suggested that the bad reputation of Dort is largely a result of hostile early works by remonstrant and Carolyne Anglican historians. This historiography would have founded a tradition that has lasted until the twentieth century. It is not surprising that the remonstrants were popular in the era of Protestant rationalism and liberalism because it was easy for them to be viewed - incorrectly viewed - as precursors. This is understandable, but what does require explanation is that this unfavourable tradition persisted beyond these phases and existed throughout the time of Protestant neo-orthodoxy. Obviously the strength of the unfavourable climate of opinion is a considerable factor in itself, and the reticense of an historian of Calvinism such as John T. McNeill might well be attributed to this, a survival of the unease created by the remonstrant historians. Another possible reason for the dearth of material concerning Dort that has been observed in the encyclopaediae and manuals of Church history, is that the newer understanding of Calvin which considers only Calvin's own doctrine and so far has revealed little even about Beza, has shown less interest in later orthodoxy.

No serious attempt has been made to consider the accuracy of the criticisms of the Synod that have been noted above. Was the Synod intolerant? It would be quite incorrect to deny that certain sessions degenerated into vicious verbal exchanges. Nor is their any truth in the assertion that the Remonstrants had no grounds for their belief that the Synod was prejudiced against them. It has not always been understood that there was a mutual intolerance between Arminian and Gomarist in the Dutch Churches. The Arminians desired, as has been shown by Lecler[40] not so much tolerance as freedom to express their opinions. They based this on a belief that they would be protected by Barneveldt - though they obviously failed to anticipate the relationship between religion and politics which was to develop after 1606. The orthodox members of the Synod were almost certainly no more intolerant than the bulk of mankind in their own day with regard to theological matters; the word "almost" could be omitted from this sentence were it not for want of an accurate standard of judgement. This is not an excuse for their conduct, since the members of a Synod of theologians might be expected to be above the attitudes and prejudices of their own day. Certainly, the Synod could never, be it ever so bigoted, have been more intolerant than some of the biased, inaccurate, or ill-informed value judgements that have been made against it. One attitude that has appeared from time to time, based on the view of the Synod as an intolerant body, is the idea that because of the Synod was intolerant, the Remonstrants might be viewed as persecuted liberals. There is considerable evidence to show that the Remonstrants behave in an irresponsible manner at the Synod, but this is not the place for this to be discussed, though it might reveal that the remonstrants had themselves presupposed the opinion of the Synod, thus alienated the sympathy of the Synod, and thus revealed themselves as having an intolerant attitude towards the Synod. It is, perhaps worth quoting the remarks of Sir Dudley Carleton, the English ambassador, when he thanked the States General of the United Provinces for their treatment of the British delegation, who had visited various places in the Low Countries, including the remonstrant stronghold of Leyden:- "he tendered the States public thanks for their great respects to the English divines, using words to this effect, that they had been entertained at Amsterdam, welcomed at the Hague, cheerfully received at Rotterdam, kindly embraced at Utrecht, etc., and that they had seen Leyden."[41] It is to be remembered that the British delegates are generally considered as the most liberal and tolerant of the foreign divines who attended the Synod of Dort.

Yet the question posed earlier in this section has not yet been adequately answered. If the Synod of Dort was an intolerant assembly, which is one of the most generally held attitudes as revealed by modern historians, it is desirable to proceed with a detailed study of two active orthodox members of that Synod. First the problem of intolerance must be considered. It might be possible to refute the allegations concerning the Synod in the manner outlined in the previous paragraph. Such, however, is not the object of the present study. The allegations of intolerance are not to be evaluated in the present work. They are not to be either accepted or refuted, for they are very largely irrelevant to the present study.

What this consideration of the historiography of the Synod of Dort has revealed is a great ignorance of the real significance of the Synod. The Synod was composed of the most distinguished reformed theologians in Europe, and they set out to resolve a theological problem, it is an example of the retarded development of studies in seventeenth century reformed protestantism that it is the theological aspect of Dort that has received least attention. The Synod of Dort was a Synod of theologians, and the importance of the Genevan contribution must be seen as having been primarily theological.

Such a study has not been attempted before. The Genevan representatives, Giovanni Diodati and Theodore Tronchin have been unjustly accused by Brandt as has been shown above From this it may be concluded that there is a necessity for a revaluation of the role of Diodati and Tronchin in the Synod of Dort. But it would be quite unhelpful merely to show that Brandt had a pro-remonstrant bias and that Tronchin and Diodati have been unjustly accused. What is surely necessary is an evaluation of the theology of the Genevans at the Synod of Dort.

In conclusion, any study of influence on political matters, any study of intolerance falls wide of the mark. These are not the aspects that should be emphasized in any study of the Synod, for they are beside the main point of the Synod which was the resolution of a theological problem that had become acute in the Low Countries. That the Genevan representatives should have been included in such disputes is unfortunate, but it has been shown that at least some of Brandt's accusations are unjust. Leaving such secondary matters aside, the study of the Genevan theological contribution may be begun. The doctrines of the Genevans will be considered in relation to those of other groups as contemporary opinions are revealed in contributions to the debates of the Synod. The Genevan statements on doctrine will be found to be clinical rather than emotional, for there is no hysteria to be found in the *Acta* despite the accusations of the remonstrant historians. At one point the Genevans, in their statement about the second article will be seen to be tolerant and accommodating to views that differ from their own . What the Genevans set out to do at Dort was to expound what they believed to be correct doctrine. It is to be regretted that the discussion of this doctrine that is included in the following pages should be the first study devoted to this topic since the Synod of Dort closed in 1619.

Financial Responsibilities
of the Genevan Delegates.

Before beginning any discussion of Genevan theological contributions, one practical observation must be made. The "orthodoxy" of the Genevans was virtually assured before the Synod, for a non-theological reason, quite apart from any personal views of Diodati and Tronchin. As has been said above, the struggle between orthodox and remonstrant in Holland had assumed a political aspect when the remonstrants became patronised by van Olden Barneveldt, and what had been a religious party became part of a faction within the state. Normally, Dutch politics would not have been a particularly important matter for the Genevans, but at this time they were of peculiar significance due to financial matters. Diodati and Tronchin had, in their visit to the Low Countries, not only the theological disputes to consider but also certain financial responsibilities.

The late sixteenth and early seventeenth centuries were a period of financial embarrassment for the Genevan authorities. As Guillaume Fatio has written:- "Les resources dont il pouvait disposer ne suffisaient pas a pourvoir a toutes les charges d'un petit etat qui, s'il n'etait pas en guerre continuelle avec un voisin puissant, le duc de Savoie, devait du moins se tenir sans cesse sur ces gardes.", and:- "Le tresor etant vide et les citoyens ruines, il semblait impossible de soutenir une couteuse academie.", therefore it was decided to send ambassadors:- "de collecter aupres des cours protestants des pays du nord, afin, disait-on, de 'rédresser les ecoles dela ville.'"[42] In order to rectify this unfavourable state of affairs, two appeals were made to various European governments. The first of these, headed by the jurist Jacques Lect, was successful in finding financial aid in England and also in the Low Countries. In November 1592, the Conseil was informed that:- "les seigneurs de la Chambre des Comptes ont rapporte le conte particulier dudict Sr. Lect de la teneur suyvante: . . . plus a receu de la collecte du Pays-Bas 14143 livres 16 solz 9 deniers, sans que la collecte de Franck-enthal y soyt comprise.[43] Despite this generous support, the financial condition of Geneva did not improve, and a second approach was made through Jacob Anjorrant, another jurist. There was certainly plenty of good will towards Geneva in the Low Countries. Louise de Coligny, princess of Orange, wrote to Theodore Beza in April 1593, that the States General of the United Provinces were considering support for Geneva. In July of the same year, a letter from Anjorrant was considered by the Conseil of Geneva:- "au lieu de faire une subvention liberale a ceste ville, comme on avoit cy-devant escrit, ilz nous fourniroient une bonne somme d'argent, sans la specifier, qu'on l'auroit en prest pour trois ans sans interestz et apres les dicts trois ans avec interestz et apres les dicts trois ans avec interestz au denier 16, qui est a 6 1/4 pour 100."[44] It would seem to be certain that this second offer of support fell short of expectations, for Louise de Coligny actually wrote to the Conseil of Geneva in the spring of 1594, expressing her regret that she had been unable to assist the negotiations.[45] However, by July 1594, a sum of more than 37,197 florins was in the hands of the Genevan authorities[46], and further financial negotiations took place between the two republics in 1598 and 1599.[47]

Thus Geneva had contracted considerable financial obligations toward the Low Countries. The debt was, of course, of a confessional nature. Holland was supporting the Genevan Academy and Genevan fortifications because of the importance of the city to the reformed churches. These financial considerations became part of the task of Diodati and Tronchin at the Synod of Dort. They were to enter into negotiations with the government of Holland as regards the cancellation of the debt. They may also have been entrusted with preparing the way for a further loan, the financial position of Geneva still remaining insecure. Since such matters could only be settled with the Dutch government, it was obvious that Diodati and Tronchin must do nothing to displease the administration of the United Provinces. But, as has been pointed out, the remonstrants were not just a theological but also a political faction that was opposed by Maurice of Nassau. Since it was Maurice of Nassau with whom the Genevans would have to discuss their financial affairs, Diodati and Tronchin were under an obligation to the government of Geneva to do nothing to displease him. For this reason they might be expected to display a strictly orthodox and anti-remonstrant attitude during the Synod of Dort. These financial considerations should be regarded as a pressure upon Diodati and Tronchin, and as proof of the fact that they were not free agents, but the conclusion cannot be drawn from it that they were thus forced to act as orthodox in the Synod of Dort.

The Genevan delegates began to negotiate with the Dutch authorities before the end of the Synod of Dort (May 1619), for in April 1619 the Conseil of Geneva was informed of a letter from Diodati:- "il... escrit qu'il a sonde quelques uns de Mrs les Estats les plus confidents touschant les obligations qu'ils leur sont dues par ceste seigneurie et qu'il a recogneu leur intention de ne nous en jamais rien demander et continue a poursuyvre cest affaire."[48] The Genevan delegates continued their enquiries about the financial matters for some time after the Synod was over, and when Tronchin, who arrived back in Geneva some time before Diodati who had gone to visit England, made report to the Conseil that despite various delays, a memorandum had been presented by them on request to Muis van Holy of the Dutch government. It was an indication that things were moving in favour of the Genevans.[49] The copy of the memorandum given to Muis van Holy is also included in the Archives Tronchin of the Musee historique de la reformation of Geneva.[50] It makes it clear that the debts which the Genevans were discussing were those which dated from 1594.

The best proof of the success of Diodati and Tronchin in dealing with these financial affairs is the fact that a short time afterwards, in 1621, Geneva was able to send Benedict Turrettini, the third epigone, the Low Countries to demand further support:- "on lui remit en partant des lettres pour Messieurs les Etats Generaux et pour le prince d'Orange. Il eut deux fois audience des Etats, auxquels il representa d'une maniere si touchante et si pathetique la situation ou l'on etait dans Geneve qu'il en obtint la somme de trente mille livres comptant, et dix mille libres par mois en cas de siege pour trois mois.[51]

Minor Contributions of the Genevan Delegates

Minor Genevan theological contributions to the Synod of Dort may be separated into eight classes.

1.   The first is the letter, sent to the Synod by four Genevan pastors and professors (Simon Goulart Sr., Pierre Prevost, Benedict Turrettini and Daniel Chabrey) on 7th October 1618 and read before the third session of the Synod. In this letter, they express their sadness at the state of contention which exists in the Dutch Church, state their pleasure at the formation of the Synod to resolve the problem, recommend Diodati and Tronchin to the assembly, denounce those who attack true doctrine, condemn those who recreate the ancient heresies of Arius and Pelagius, and urge the delegates to become formidable to their enemies by concord and unity. They assure the Synod of their prayers that it might be endowed with the grace of God to distinguish true from false so that the Church might be consoled and the reign of Christ advanced. From this letter it becomes obvious, although no distinct theological points are discussed, that in the eyes of Geneva, the Arminians are already condemned.[52]

The attitude of Geneva towards the remonstrants and towards Arminianism was to change little in the years that followed. What is interesting, however, is that orthodox Genevan theologians became increasingly conscious of the fact that the remonstrants are dangerous to them not because they draw different conclusions using the same methods of exegesis and systematic theology, but because they do not, in fact, accept the basis of orthodox reformed protestant systematic theology. Thus in his *Institutio Theologiae Elencticae* of 1680, Francois Turrettini wrote:- "quaestio non modo necessaria est ad intelligendam veram Theologiae naturam; sed etiam propter Controversias hujus temporis, maxime contra Socinianos et Remonstrantes, qui Theologiam ita stricte practicam dicunt, ut nihil in ea praecise ad salutem necessarium sit, nisi quod pertinet ad praecepta morum et promissiones, unde *Obedientia praeceptorum, et fiducis promissionum,* Religionem totam quoad fundamentalia absolvunt, seclusa mysteriorum notitia, Quo sine obscurum non est, ut elevent necessitatem cognitionis dogmatum de Trinitate, et Incarnatione etc., et sic viam facilius sternant ad Religionem communem, per quam omnes promiscue servari possint, id est ad Atheismum."[53] Whether or not the more profound reasons for the Genevan dislike of the remonstrants were already understood, this letter left the members of the Synod in no doubt as to the attitude of the Genevan Church. Brandt wrote:- "Mit dit schrijven van die van Geneven kon men genoegh merken, wat se van de Remonstranten alreeds oordeelden, en wat voor een ordeel dat hunne afgesendenen tagens hen souden vellen."[54] It is safe to presume that behind Genevan attitudes lies the idea that faith is a permanent reality and, since they had no great sense of historical progress, faith being older than heresies, all heresy must be a simple repetition of what had been postulated in patristic times and refuted by the faith of the Church. It is unnecessary to condemn the Arminians for taking away the idea of salvation from their doctrine of the Trinity since such ideas were already condemned in antiquity. This is an approach that is at least as old as Tertullian.

The Church of Geneva may have thought it advisible to send this letter to strengthen their position at the Synod since it is known from the correspondence of the English ambassador that:- "Geneva hath much stomached that they were so long forgotten[55], from which it may safely be assumed that the Genevans were invited rather later than the other delegations.

2.   One of the first questions discussed by the Synod of Dort, one of a series of problems that were discussed in the earlier part of the Synod before the arrival of the remonstrants, was the possibility of a new Dutch translation of the Bible. This was discussed in sessions VI, VII, VIII, IX, X, XI, XII and XIII[56] of the Synod. On one occasion, as was noted in chapter 1, Diodati presented written advice to the Synod concerning translation, but no trace of the text of this has been found[57]. Diodati was not alone in the Synod as an experienced Bible translator, since an English delegate - Samuel Ward - had been one of the translators of the English "King James" or "Authorised" version.[58]

The Dutch Bible, eventually produced because of the initiative of the Synod was the Dutch *Biblia* eventually published in 1637, the standard Bible of the Dutch Church and also, it might be added, of the remonstrants.[59]

3.   The third subject to which the Genevans gave consideration was the problem of catechetics, another subject discussed in the earlier part of the Synod. The Genevans produced, as did the other foreign delegations, a short statement concerning their system of instruction. They describe Genevan theory and practice of catechism - how the work proceeds in the villages, how uneducated people are to be taught, how difficult matters are to be avoided. Yet the picture that grows out of this description is far from idyllic, with the inclusion of certain

ideas such as catechetical questions being answered in public, that have since passed out of use. One of the most interesting pieces of information that is included is that the Genevan Catechism is taught to the children and simple folk, while the Heidelberg Catechism is reserved for the College. This Genevan acceptance of the Heidelberg Catechism - a document which does not mention predestination - may be, perhaps, not without importance for the Genevan contibution to the debate on predestination.[60]

4.   The fourth class of Genevan contribution to the Synod is also related to this early phase of the Synod and concerns the question of printing. The Synod was concerned about the fact that it was easy for seditious works to be printed - this preoccupation may have been caused by the fact that remonstrant writings had been regarded as a cause of much of the trouble that had arisen. Thus the debate concerned censorship. Diodati's contribution to this discussion is described by Hales who, in turn, is used as a source by Brandt. The latter does mention that Diodati said that "something must be allow'd to the humour of the People and Country" though he seems not to realise that Diodati was not speaking about the Genevan but about the Venetian republic.[61] Fortunately, there is another account of this speech by Hales that is probably more impartial in attitude and which makes it clear that Diodati was not talking about Geneva but about Venice:- *"Theodatus* of *Geneva* told us, that in his travails, at *Venice* he had observ'd that there was a Colledge of sundry persons, secular and spiritual, to whose care was committed all the business of Printing. He thought it fit there should be such Colledges here erected."[62] In fact, what Diodati would seem to have been trying to say is that too much severity is as harmful as too little control, and to point out that everything cannot be done at the same time:- "Il faut conceder quelque chose a la coustume du Pays et de la nation, et ne fouler ou charger trop ce peuple et ce naturel enclin a liberte, et par fois a se recreer et passer doucement le temps: Car il n'y a rien qui tant gaste une bonne reformation, qu'une rigueur absolue et un trop grand desir d'amener ensemblement toutes choses a leur poinct."[63]

5.   A fifth class of contribution may be defined as public addresses made to the Synod by the Genevan delegates. Diodati was to lecture on the 5th article in the 90th session.[64] A Scottish theologian, W. Balcanqual writes that:- *"Deodatus* was appointed to discourse of the first Article, but being sick, the five Belgick professors discussed it."[65] On this occasion Brandt gives us more information:- "Deodatus, Professor of Geneva, was appointed to treat about the Fifth Article in the XCth Session, which was publickly celebrated the same day in the afternoon; but he acquainted the President that he was indisposed; upon which he ordered the Five Netherland Professors to discuss each of them one or two of the Remonstrants arguments, which they had made use of at the Conference at the Hague."[66] Diodati was to speak once again during the 94th session, five days later, but was still too ill to do so. Theodore Tronchin took his place, and, according to Balcanqual:- *Deodatus* was this Session appointed to discuss the first Article: but because of the continuance of his sickness, his colleague *Tronchinus* did perform that task for him, publickly all auditors being admitted, who with good commendation did establish Sanctorum perseverantiam.[67] It is to be noted that Balcanqual has a good opinion of this address, for a very different account is to be found in Brandt.[68] The full text is to be found in the Archives Tronchin of the Musee historique de la reformation at Geneva. Some of the theological

aspects of this address will be discussed in the sections that follow. As usual, what Brandt says is not completely false. Tronchin does, for instance, mention the Book of Dreams, but what makes Brandt a biased source is his attitude and his choice of adjectives. On the hundredth session, time was once again to be devoted to the address of Diodati, but he was still ill and his place was taken by Martinius of Bremen. Eventually, Diodati was well enough to lecture during the 106th session on 8th March 1619. This address seems to have met with a generally good reception. It was on this occasion that Balcanqual wrote that Diodati:-"did very sweetly just as he useth to preach, not as doctors use to do in Schools."[69] Brandt certainly gives a much more favourable account of this address than he did of that of Tronchin, quoting Diodati as saying that many of the reprobate had excellent qualities, and writing that he spoke more moderately than was usual among the orthodox.[70]

It is much to be regretted that no written account of this address has been found, so that it cannot be discussed further in this thesis.

6.   We also know, that both Diodati, who was presumably limited by his ill-health, and Tronchin, used the occasion of the Synod to preach extensively in various places in Holland. In his report to Conseil, Tronchin, who had,presumably, numerous contacts dating from his student days, mentions that they preached at the Hague - where Diodati preached to the Court [71] - Amsterdam, Delft and Rotterdam as well as Dordrecht.[72] Diodati, as Brandt's malice informs us,[73] also tried to have an Italian service at Dordrecht. Perhaps we should be surprised that there were as many as nine adult Italian speaking protestants at that time in such a small place as Dordrecht.

7.   The Genevans contributed some remarks on the Belgic Confession which was discussed at the Synod.[74] There is a very brief manuscript of the Genevan suggestions in the Archives Tronchin, in the hand of Theodore Tronchin, but this list of suggestions cannot be related to the text of the Confession. In any case, they would seem to be of little theological importance.[75]

8.   An eighth class of Genevan contribution was Diodati's reading of a long letter to the Synod from the French theologian Pierre du Moulin, who, with the rest of the French delegation, had been refused permission to attend the Synod by the French government. This letter need not be considered here, since Diodati was not responsible for the contents,[76] and it is not known if there were any particular reason why Diodati was asked to read it.

Synodical Theory

In the section concerning historiography, mention was made of one criticism that has been made of the Synod of Dort, which is that it acted as both party and judge as regards the remonstrants. This question arose in the Synod itself and not simply as later interpretation of events. It was raised by the remonstrants in the Synod during the 27th session, when they claimed that the Synod was party and judge, and compared their position to that of the protestants at the Council of Trent. Indeed we are aware of opposition to the calling of councils by Paul III which rested on a similar argument to one used by the Arminians at Dort *viz* that the Pope would be both party and judge. [77] A dispute on the nature of conciliar and synodical ecclesiastical authority had already affected the reformed churches in France and Geneva when, in the 1560's, Jean Morely[78] published his *Traicte de la discipline et police chrestienne* (Lyons, 1561, 4°) which claimed that the Consistory of the Calvinists was undemocratic and unbiblical and that the reformed churches should adopt a more synodical if not congregational system. Both Beza and Chandieu[79] opposed this. Chandieu in particular gives an authoritarian view of reformed ecclesiology arguing in favour of the French consistorial system of government by pastors, deacons and elders and against what he obviously sees as the danger of anarchy in an ochlocratic community like those of the anabaptists.[80] The desire for order, authority and discipline was a common feature of the reformed churches - and of the type of delegate at the Synod of Dort.

In opposition to the remonstrant proposals, a statement was provided by each foreign delegation to decide on the method of procedure. The Genevan statement bears on the competence of the Synod to decide such matters. The problem of authority is one which has to be decided by any ecclesiastical council - because this is the basis of its power to make decisions. This poses the question of the concept of synodical theory. The contribution of the Synod of Dort to this kind of theory has never been adequately considered, and the fact that the Genevans at Dort made a contribution to synodical theory would appear to have been completely ignored since the close of the synod.

The Genevans begin by stating that in any political or ecclesiastical body there must be those who have competence to judge matters in order to maintain and conserve such a body. The authority of such judges must be recognised for the common good of the body. In the Church, the authority and right to judge resides in a legitimately assembled representative synod. The members of the churches which compose the synod have no right to counter its decisions, for such a synod is a sovereign judge. No exception to such synods can be taken on personal grounds since such synods are judges of dogma and not of persons. In matters of discipline within the Church, there are two recourses; one is to civil authority and the other is to such a synod, so that it may promote peace by publicly pronouncing upon such matters as are under debate. Nobody can justly complain about having to submit to the authority of such a synod, and they repudiate the comparison with Trent. Since the remonstrants are a new and small part of the Reformed Churches of the Low Countries, they must be prepared to submit their doctrine to the Synod. They have no right to divide the Church nor to imagine that they are faced by an adverse party. The remonstrants must submit to the doctrinal decisions of their brothers. The Genevans state that in secular matters there can be different classes of judgement, but not in the Church as regards doctrine. The Synod is composed of members of the universal Church, seeking correct doctrine for the whole Church. If the remonstrants refuse to recognise the decisions of the Synod, then they must forfeit their right to be members of the Dutch Reformed Churches. If they are no longer members of the Dutch Reformed Churches, then they are outside the control of the Synod and their treatment becomes a matter for the civil power.[81]

It is necessary to include this section, not just for interest, but in order to show that the Genevan delegates at the Synod of Dort had a clear and well defined synodical theory. They had no doubt of their competence to judge questions of doctrine. The question of the Synod being both party and judge is not even mentioned, since decisions of synods concerning doctrine are absolute the Synod must inevitably fulfil both functions. What is repudiated is the idea that there is any influence of personality on matters of doctrine. The reference to the civil power is a warning to the remonstrants of the possible consequences of intransigence. In considering the Genevans' contributions to orthodox discussion of the five articles, it must not be forgotten that they had already clearly defined the purpose, and the authority of the Synod of Dort.

The Genevan Biblical Catenae.

The problems concerning the Genevan Biblical catanae at the Synod of Dort fall naturally into two groups, those concerning the Latin text that was used, and those concerning the interpretation. This section will similarly be divided into two parts to consider separately the various problems which arise.

Text

This section again is simply and naturally divided into three groups of problems, those concerning the kind of Latin text of the Bible that was used by the Genevans at the Synod of Dort, those concerning textual comparisons of the Genevans and the other delegations that were present at the synod, and a consideration of the consistency of the Genevans themselves in their quotation of the Bible.

The Genevan Latin text

The text of James 1/17 is quoted by Tronchin and Diodati in thesis 4 of reprobation in article 1:- "Apud Deum non est mutatio, vel conversionis obumbratio."[82] When this text is considered in the Vulgate:- "Omne datum optimum et omne donum perfectum desursum est, descendens a Patre luminum, apud quem non est transmutatio, nec vicissitudinis obumbratio."[83] the Genevan text is seen as an abbreviation and a quite different text, for "apud quem non est transmutatio" has become "Apud Deum non est mutatio," and "nec vicissitudinis obumbratio" is "vel conversionis obumbratio". The 1567 Bezan text[84] is more similar to the Vulgate in that "apud quem non est transmutatio" is the Vulgate verbatim, but is also the source for the Genevan "vel conversionis "obumbratio." Diodati must have been aware that this Dort text was an abbreviation, for in his 1607 and 1640/41 Italian Bibles, he quoted translations of this text as did Beza and St Jerome:- "Ogni buona donatione, et ogni don perfetto, e da alto, discendendo dal Padre de'lumi, appo' ilquale non v'e mutamento ne obombratione di rivolgimento" (1607) and "Ofni buona donatione, ed ogni dono perfetto, e da alto, discendendo dal Padre de'lumi, appo' Lquale non v'e mutamento, ne obbombration" di rivolgimento." (1640/41)[85, 86] It is to be noted that there are minor differences in the two readings, e.g."obombratione" of 1607 becomes "obbombration" in 1640/41, but on the whole they are closer to Beza and the Vulgate than they are to the text quoted at the Synod of Dort.

From this, it may be concluded that the text of James 1/17 which was used by the Genevans at Dort was an abbreviation which conformed neither to Beza's nor to St Jerome's version of this text. It is also possible that the Dort text does not necessarily conform to Diodati's translations of the Bible into Italian.[87]

External Comparison.

The text James 1/17 was quoted by different delegations at the Synod of Dort. On six occasions, it was noted without the text being quoted, by Gomarus on Article I,[88] South Holland on Article I [89], North Holland on Articles III and IV[90],twice by Overijssel on Articles III and IV[91], and by Gueldres on Articles III and IV[92]. On four occasions, however, the text is quoted.

As has been noted above, the quotation of this text by the Genevans:- "Apud Deum non est mutatio, vel conversionis obumbratio"[93] is an abbreviation which conforms neither to the Bezan Latin Bible nor the Vulgate. However, the Gueldres representatives use of this text:- "Apud quem (patrem luminum) non est transmutatio, aut conversionis obumbratio[94] though abbreviated, is a verbatim quotation of the Bezan version:- "Omne munus bornū et omne donū est perfectū supernē, descendens a Patre luminū, apud quē nō est transmutatio, aut cōversionis obumbratio.[95] The Embden representatives also quote this text:- "Apud quem non est transmutatio et conversionis obumbratio."[96] in a very nearly verbatim copy of the Bezan text, the only change being an insertion which is necessary to the sense of the quotation, and the change of preposition from "aut" to "et". The representatives from Groningen and Omland also quote this text in a version only slightly different from that of Beza:- "Omne munus bonum, et omne donum perfectum superne est descendens a Patre luminum."[97] The Overijssel representatives quote an abbreviation of James 1/17 that does not owe a great deal to Beza:- "omnis donatio bona, et omne integrum donum est superne descendens a Patre luminum."[98]

From this discussion of James 1/17, the conclusion may be drawn that the Genevan representatives at the Synod of Dort quoted an abbreviation of James 1/17 that conformed neither to Beza nor to the Vulgate, and that while other delegations also supplied abbreviations, that their texts were different from the Genevans, and that a number of them were more clearly Bezan in their quotation of the text.

The study of Matthew 15/13 and Job 12/14 revealed that in both cases the Genevans were using a form of words that was not similar to the Bezan Latin text, to the Vulgate or to the Latin Bible of Junius and Tremellius. For the sake of brevity the analyses of the utilisation of these two texts have been relegated to Appendix II.

Matthew 24/24 is one of the more frequently quoted texts in the statements submitted to the Synod of Dort. It is a text that was used by the Genevans:- "Exurgent Pseudo-christi et Pseudo-prophetae, et facient signa et miracula magna, adeo ut seducturi essent, si fieri posset, ipsos electos."[99] This is a different translation from that of Beza:- "Sturgent enim pseudo-christi et pseudo-prophetas, et edent signa magna et miracula ita ut seducant (si fieri possit) etiam electos,"[100] and from the Vulgate:- "Surgent enim pseudochristi et pseudo-prophetae: et dabunt signa magna et prodigia ita ut in errorem inducantur (si fieri potest) etiam electi."[101] The Genevan text at Dort is, however, similar to the Italian translations of Diodati, and it is not an abbreviation:- "Percioche falsi Christi, e falsi profeti, surgannero, e faranno gran segni, e miracoli; tal che sedurrebero, le fosse possibile, etiando gli eletti."[102] (1607) and:- "Percioche falsi Christi, e falsi profeti, surgeranno, e farano gran segni, e miracoli: tal che soddurrebbero, se fosse possibile, etiando gli eletti."[103] (1640/41).

Matthew 24/24 was quoted thirty times by the other delegations at the Synod of Dort. On seventeen occasions, the text was noted but not quoted. The Hessian delegates:- "Excitabuntur Pseudochristi et Pseudo-prophetae, et edent signa magne et miracula; ita ut seducant (si fieri possit) etiam electos[104] quote this text in a translation that would be entirely Bezan were it not for the fact that they commence by "Excitabuntur" and not "Surgent enim". The British delegates quote an abbreviation:- "Ut in errorem jnducantur (sic) si fieri posset, etiam electi"[105] that is almost entirely drawn from the Vulgate. Needless to say, neither of these texts bears any considerable resemblance to that of the Genevans. The representatives from the Palatinate quote a text:- "Excitabuntur Pseudo -Christi et Pseudo-prophetae, et edent signa magna et prodigia, ita ut seducant (si fieri possit) etiam electos"[106] that resembles the Hessians in that it begins with "excitabuntur" and is otherwise Bezan, except that, like the Vulgate, it refers to "prodigia" and not to"miracula". The North Holland delegates quote an abbreviation:- "Fieri non potest, ut seducantur electi"[107] that is like no version already considered, though the word "seducantur" may suggest a Bezan origin. Zeeland representatives quoted this text twice in considering, Article 1, and their abbreviations are quite close to the Bezan text:- "Ut seducant, si fieti possit, etiam electos"[108] and:- "Seducerent electos, si fieri posset".[109] The delegates from Groningen and Omland also quote an abbreviation which could be based on Beza:- "Seducerent, si fieri posset, etiam electos",[110] as does the delegation from North Holland on Article V:- "Ita ut (si fieri possit) seducant etiam electos",[111] the delegation from Zeeland on Article V:-"Ita ut seducant, si fieri posset, etiam electos",[112] and the delegation from Overijssel on Article V:- "Ut seducant si fieri posset etiam electos"[113] and:- "Seducent (si fieri possit) etiam electos"[114] while a particularly Bezan text is offered by the delegates from Overijssel in their submission concerning the first article:- "Excitabuntur Pseudo-Christi et Pseudo-prophetae, et edent signa magna et miracula, ita ut seducant (si fieri possit) etiam electos".[115] As in the case "Excitabuntur." Of course, the recurrent use of "excitabuntur" suggests another common source, but a source which is closer to Beza than the Vulgate.

From this brief discussion of the use of Matthew 24/24 at the Synod of Dort, the conclusion may be drawn that the Genevan text is similar neither to the Vulgate nor to Beza, but that it does conform to the Italian Bibles of Diodati. It is to be noted that Geneva is not in accord with the versions of this text used by other delegations, some of which more closely resemble the Bezan version or the Vulgate. The Genevans are not the only delegation to quote abbreviated texts.

Two subsidiary problems arise from this discussion of Matthew 24/24. It has been noted that the English quote a text which closely resembles the Vulgate, while the Hessians appear to quote a Bezan text. As the Genevans approximate neither to a Bezan nor to a Vulgate text, this must be examined in order to discover whether the British or the Hessians do so in other cases.

Some tests appear to suggest that the British have been influenced by the Vulgate. The British use of Matthew 13/11:- Vobis datum est nosse mysteria regni coelorum"[115] has a distinct similarity to the Vulgate: - "Quia vobis datum est nosse mysteria regni caelorum".[116] Also the British text of Ephesians 1/11:- "Praedestinati secundum propositum ejus, qui omnia efficit secundum consilium voluntatis suae"[117] is similar, but not identical to the Vulgate: - "Praedestinati secundum propositum ejus, qui operatur omnia secundum consilium voluntatis suae"[118] The first half of the British text of John 6/39:- "Haec est voluntas ejus,qui misit me, ut nihil perdam ex eo, quod dedit mihi"[119] is also similar to the Vulgate. However, it cannot be accepted as a general rule or tendancy that the British are very much influenced by the Vulgate for there are texts such as Romans 9/11 where the British statement of the text:- "Nondum natis pueris, cum nihil fecissent boni aut mali, ut propositum Dei secundum electionem maneret",[120] is quite different to that of St Jerome:- "Cum enim nondum nati fuissent aut aliquid boni egissent aut mali (ut secundum electionem propositum Dei maneret".[121] Also there are texts such as Ephesians 1/4 where the Vulgate: - "sicut elegit nos in ipso ante mundi constitutionem, ut essemus sancti et immaculati in conspectu ejus in charitate",[122] and Bezan:- "Sicut elegit nos in piso antequam iaceretur fundamenta mundi, ut simus sancti et inculpati coram eo per charitatem"[123] versions are relatively similar to each other and differ from the British: - "Elegit nos ut Sanctissimus et immaculati".[124] There are also, it is to be noted, texts such as Romans 9/18 where the British:- "Cuius vult miseretur"[125] and the Bezan texts:- "Itaque cuius vult miseretur"[126] are remarkably similar. Other examples of this are to be found in a consideration of Romans 9/11 where the British text is: - "Nondum natis pueris, cum nihil fecissent boni aut mali, ut propositum Dei secundum electionem maneret."[127] and the Bezan: - "Nondū enim natis pueris, quū nihil fecissēt boni vel mali, ut propositū Dei qđ est secūdū ipsi electione, id est no ex opib, sed ex vocate, firmu maneret"[128] It is also shown by a consideration of Romans 9/23 where the British text is:- "Ut notas faceret divitias gloriae suae erga vasa misericordiae"[129] and the Bezan:- "Ex ut notas faceret divitias gloriae suae erga va sa misericordiae, quae praeparivit ad gloriam?"[130]

The Hessian theologians have been noted above as using a Bezan version of the text Matthew 24/24. It is very relevant to the subject of the Genevan catanae to discover if another delegation were under Bezan influence to a much greater extent than were Diodati and Tronchin, whose influence by Beza has already been seen to be slight. The Hessians quote John 3/36:- "Qui credit in filium, habet vitam aeternam; qui vero Filio non obtemperat, non videbit vitam, sed ira Dei manet super ipso."[131] and the Bezan text is clearly seen to be very closely related:- "Qui credit in Filiū, habet vitam aeternā: qui vero non credit Filio, non videbit vitam, sed ira Dei manet super eum."[132] The abbreviations of the Bezan text pose no problem to the similarity of the two texts, but the final word of the Hessian text is "ipso", while Beza had preferred "eum". The only major dissimilarity is that Beza writes "qui vero non credit Filio" while the representatives from Hesse prefer "qui vero Filio non obtempereat." When the text of 2 Timothy 2/19 is examined, there are more major divergences to be noted between the Bezan text:- "Solidum tamen fundamentum Dei stat, habes sigillum hoc, Nouit Dominus qui sint sui.",[133] and the Hessian:- "Firmum, inquit, stat fundamentum Dei, habens sigillium hoc: Deus novit, qui sint sui."[134] However, these differences largely depend upon style, upon word order rather than content, e.g. the Bezan "fundamantum Dei stat" becomes "stat fundamentum Dei". In fact, only three words have been changed; "Dominus" has become "Deus" and the Hessians preferred "Firmum, inquit" as a beginning, rather than the Bezan "Solidum tamen." These would not seem to be sufficient reasons for dismissing Bezan influence on this text. Very striking indeed is the similarity between the Bezan version of John 10/16:- "Alias etiam oves habeo quae non sunt ex hac caula, illas quoque oportet me adducere."[135] and that of the theologians of Hesse:- "Alias etiam oves habeo, quae non sunt ex hac caula, illus quoque me oportet adducere."[136] The only difference is of trivial importance, the fact that "oportet me" has been transposed. Thus it may be concluded, that as regards several texts, there is a considerable degree of similarity to be noted between the text of Beza and that of the Hessian representatives at the Synod of Dort. The limitations of this conclusion must be clearly understood, it cannot be suggested, on the basis of the above study, that the Hessians were strictly Bezan in the texts of their Biblical quotations, since all the Hessian texts would need to be considered before such a conclusion could be formulated, and this present work is not the correct place for such an enterprise. Yet, sufficient material has been examined above to enable the suggestion to be made that the Hessian delegation were more influenced by Beza's work than were the Genevans. From this, the conclusion may be drawn that the Genevans were less Bezan in their quotations of Biblical texts than was at least one other important foreign delegation at the Synod of Dort.

Internal Comparison.

The discussion of the Latin text used by the Genevans at Dort, was basically inconclusive, in so far as the conclusions were negative. The Genevans at Dort were not very much influenced by the Vulgate or by Beza's Latin version of the Bible, or by the edition of Tremellius. Their texts were seen to be different from those used by other delegations. Yet no attempt was made to define exactly what was the origin of the Genevan position. This omission must be explained. Before any attempt could be made to trace any original, from which the Genevan texts might have come, it was necessary to ensure that the Genevans did, in fact, quote the same text on each occasion that they quoted a particular verse of Scripture.

In thesis 1 of Article I the Genevans quote Ephesians 1/4: - "Elegit nos in ipso, ante iacta mundi fundamenta, ut essemus sancti et inculpati coram ipso in charitate. Postquam nos praedestinavit in adoptionem per Iesum Christum in sese, secundum beneplacitum voluntatis suae. In laudem gloriae gratiae ipsius, qua nobis gratiosus fuit in dilecto."[137] This verse is used by them again in Article II, thesis 1 and Article II, thesis 3. The quotation in Article II thesis 3 is a drastic abbreviation of the text:- "Elegit nos in ipso, etc. et nos reddidit gratiosos in dilecto".[138] This does, however, include a word - "reddidit" - which is not used in the longer version of this text that has already been quoted. The third Genevan use of this text is even shorter:- "Electi sumus in ipso"[139] but it serves to show that the Genevans are inconsistent with themselves in their quotations of Ephesians 1/4 for "Elegit nos in ipso" has been completely changed to "Electi sumus in ipso."

Another text, in the quotation of which the Genevans may be seen to be somewhat inconsistent is 2 Thessalonians 2/13. In thesis 1 of Article I this text is quoted as:- "Nos autem debemus perpetuo agere gratias de vobis, fratres dilecti in Domino, quod Deus vos elegit a principio as salutem, in sanctificatione Spiritus, et fide veritatis."[140] It is used again in thesis 5 of Article I, but in an abbreviated form:- "Vos elegit a principio in sanctificatione Spiritus, et fide in veritatem."[141] However the only textual change is from "veritas" to "veritatem" and it would be quite improper to base on so little evidence any theory of the Genevans being inconsistent.

The introduction of a third text, 1 Peter 1/20, however, will serve to show that the Genevans were capable of being seriously inconsistent in their quotation of Biblical texts at the Synod of Dort. 1 Peter 1/20 is quoted in thesis 1 of Article I:- "Christus praeordinatus ante iacta mundi fundamenta, et manifestus ultimis temporibus propter vos, qui per eum creditis in Deum."[142] It is quoted again, in an abbreviated form in thesis 4 of Article I:- "Christus manifestatus ultimis temporibus propter vos, qui per eum creditis in Deum."[143] but there are no textual changes apart from the abbreviation. There are obvious changes in the wording of this text, however, when it is quoted in thesis 1 of Article II:- "Agni immaculati pretioso sanguine redempti estis, praecogniti quidem ante jacta mundi fundamenta, manifestati autem ultimis temporibus, propter vos, qui per ipsum creditis in Deum."[144] There can be no doubt that in this case the Genevans are using a different text of this verse than the one which they chose to quote in their discussion of the first Article.

Thus, on the basis of the study of these three texts, the conclusion may be drawn that the Genevans may be seen to be inconsistent in the quotation of Biblical verses. They do not always use the same text. It is this inaccuracy which renders useless the search for a source for the Genevan Latin texts. The reason for the Genevan inconsistency is not immediately obvious. It is possible, but quite improbable, that the differences reveal quotation from memory. More possible is the suggestion that Diodati and Tronchin accepted a number of different translations of certain texts of the Bible, which they varied and employed depending upon the theological context of their quotation.

Thus the conclusion of this section must be that the Genevans were not bound by any one Latin translation of the Biblical text and that they were certainly not bound by the Latin translations of Jerome, Theodore Beza or Tremellius and Junius. Contrary to the natural supposition that Diodati and Tronchin would be Bezan in outlook since they were his pupils and taught in the Academy where he had served for so many years, it is to be seen that the Genevans of 1619 were not faithful to Beza's Latin translation of the Bible, but that a German delegation to the Synod of Dort could be very much influenced by Beza's work.

The Genevan Biblical catenae - Incidence.

It was decided that a study should be made of the Biblical catenae used by the Genevans, in order that the texts used by them might be compared with the texts used by other foreign delegations. A list was therefore compiled including all texts used by the British, Genevan, Hessian, Palatine, Bremener and Emodener delegations on all five articles. Dutch delegations were ignored except for the college formed by professors Polyander, Thysius and Wallaeus who were joined by Gomarus in the consideration of the second, third and fourth articles. It was felt that this would sufficiently represent the bulk of theological opinion at the Synod.

It was hoped that at the simplest level, the study of this list of texts might show whether or not the Genevans' usage of the Bible bore any considerable resemblance to that of the other delegations. Further considerations on the nature of the general usage of the Bible by seventeenth century reformed exegetes were also possible. It was decided that a simple comparison should be made, as a kind of control, with the Bezan catenae used in the *Tabula Praedestinationis* which was first published in 1555 and which had various reprints, the most widely disseminated being that in the *Tractationes* of 1572 - 80.

In all, 1123 texts were used at Dort, the list breaking up into the following:

Genesis	22 texts used on	36 occasions
Leviticus	2	2
Numbers	3	3
Deuteronomy	30	45
2 Samuel	9	10
1 Kings	3	3
2 Chronicles	2	2
Job	6	6
Psalms	52	74
Proverbs	7	10

Song of Songs	3	3
Isaiah	35	57
Jeremiah	30	62
Ezekiel	17	32
Daniel	1	1
Hosea	6	7
Joel	2	2
Jonah	1	1
Micah	1	1
Zachariah	4	9
Malachi	4	12
Matthew	95	178
Mark	10	15
Luke	28	54
John	114	166
Acts	58	116
Romans	157	533
1 Corinth.	58	105
2 Corinth.	30	62
Galations	29	44
Ephesians	60	253
Phillippians	14	71
Colossians	19	28
1 Thessal.	5	8
2 Thessal.	13	31
1 Timothy	8	8
2 Timothy	16	61
Titus	9	25
Hebrews	52	99
James	11	15
1 Peter	21	55
2 Peter	10	20
1 John	44	96
2 John	1	1
Jude	3	9
Revelation	16	26
Totals	1123	2465

Factor of 2.195

It is seen that the 1123 texts were used a total of 2465 times at Dort. This is a low of the Hessian theologians, the only divergence from the Bezan text is the use of majority of texts were only used once (681 instances) or twice (181 instances). Yet some texts were extremely popular. The list of the most often quoted texts, put in order of the number of citations is as follows:-

46 - Romans 8/30
39 - Ephesians 1/4
35 - Romans 8/29

```
32 - Ephesians 1/5
29 - Romans 9/11
26 - Philippians 2/13
22 - Romans 9/18
21 - Philippians 1/6
21 - 2 Timothy 2/19
20 - Acts 13/48
18 - 2 Timothy 1/9
17 - Jeremiah 32/40
16 - Ephesians 1/11
16 - 1 John 3/9
14 - Romans 9/22
14 - Hebrews 6/4
13 - Matthew 24/24
13 - Romans 11/7
12 - Romans 8/32
12 - Romans 9/23
12 - 1 Peter 1/5
11 - Matthew 13/11
11 - John 10/28
11 - 1 Peter 1/2
```

So these 24 texts were employed on a total of 481 occasions. These then, were in 1619 the heart of Reformed catanae concerning soteriological problems.

When the 24 most often used texts at Dort are compared with those used most often by Beza, there is a definite overall similarity:-

	Dort (total 1123)	Beza (total 467)
Romans 8/30	46	4
Ephesians 1/4	39	7
Romans 8/29	35	5
Ephesians 1/5	32	7
Romans 9/11	29	4
Philippians 2/13	26	1
Romans 9/18	22	4
Philippians 1/6	21	1
2 Timothy 2/19	21	x
Acts 13/48	20	4
2 Timothy 1/9	18	3
Jeremiah 32/40	17	x
Ephesians 1/11	16	3
1 John 3/9	16	x
Romans 9/22	14	3
Hebrews 6/4	14	1
Matthew 24/24	13	x
Romans 11/7	13	2
Romans 8/32	12	1
Romans 9/23	12	5
1 Peter 1/5	12	x
Matthew 13/11	11	3
John 10/28	11	2
1 Peter 1/2	11	2

Of the 24 texts from Dort, Beza used 19. Those which he did not use but which the Synod did use were 2 Timothy 2/19 (21), Jeremiah 32/40 (17), 1 John 3/9 (16), Matthew 24/24 (13) and 1 Peter 1/5 (12). This would certainly suggest that the members of the Synod were not copying the Bezan catenae in any slavish manner, even if their systematic theology were similar. Yet 15 of the 19 texts used by Beza were used more than once and there is a general similarity considering that there are only 467 Bezan usages against 1123 at Dort. There are only 8 Bezan texts used 5 or more times:-

Proverbs 16/4	5
John 12/40	5
Romans 9/23	5
1 Corinthians 2/10	5
Ephesians 1/4	7
Ephesians 1/5	7
Ephesians 1/9	5
Ephesians 2/3	6

of which only three are in the "most often used" list from Dort. There is a definite connexion, but it is perhaps best seen when a broader view is taken, rather than in detailed analysis.

The quantity of texts from different books and the number of quotations from particular books is also revealing. The catenae conform to a general Melanchthonian scheme which is typical of reformers such as Calvin who wrote that if the Epistle to the Romans were properly understood it would open a door to all the most profound treasures of the Bible.[146] The first and fourth Gospels take pride of place among the Gospels and Romans taking precedence over all other New Testament books, indeed of the whole Bible. One hundred and fourteen texts were used from the fourth Gospel, but the average usage is low despite exceptions such as John 10/28 and these were used on 166 instances. A smaller number of texts were used from Matthew, 95, but these were used on 178 instances and one text, Matthew 24/24:- "For false Christs and false prophets will arise and show great signs and wonders, so as to lead astray, if possible, even the elect." was used more often than any from John. Romans is used very extensively, 157 texts on no less than 533 instances, 21.6% of the total. Beza used a total of 467 texts some 670 times. This gives an even lower incidence of reusage, 1.43. Yet in Beza there is the same Melanchthonian scheme as is seen from the following tables:-

Old Testament		
Genesis	9 texts used	9 times
Exodus	11	14
Levit.	-	-
Numbers	1	1
Deuteron.	3	3
Joshua	4	5
Judges	-	-
Ruth	-	-
1 Sam.	2	2

The Epigones

2 Sam.	2	2
1 Kings	2	3
2 Kings	1	1
1 Chron.	-	-
2 Chron.	3	3
Ezra	-	-
Nehem.	2	2
Esther	-	-
Job	7	7
Psalms	13	14
Prov.	5	10
Eccl.	-	-
Canticles	-	-
Isaiah	13	17
Jeremiah	3	3
Ezekiel	3	3
Daniel	1	1
Hosea	1	1
Totals	86	101

Gospels

Matthew	23 texts used	28 times
Mark	-	-
Luke	14	14
John	43	71
Text Total	80	113

Other New Testament

Acts	19	26
Rom.	101	170
1 Cor.	24	35
2 Cor.	20	22
Gal.	8	11
Eph.	27	60
Philip.	7	7
Col.	13	14
1 Thes.	2	4
2 Thes.	6	10
1 Tim.	6	6
2 Tim.	9	15
Titus	2	3
Phil.	-	-
Hebrews	13	17
James	5	5
1 Peter	14	19
2 Peter	7	7
1 John	17	24
2 John	-	-
3 John	-	-
Jude	1	1
Rev.	-	-
Totals	301	456

Grand totals O.T.	86 texts used	101 times
Gospel	80	113
o.N.T.	301	456
	467	670 incidence 1.4346

The first and fourth Gospels are used far more often than the others, especially the fourth, the usages being Matthew 28, Mark 0, Luke 14 and John 71. Romans again takes precedence over all other New Testament books, 170 instances out of a total of 569. Yet the low incidence of re-usage is marked. The 170 instances are built up from 101 texts. Yet the percentage of texts from Romans is 29.5% of the total. Not so very different from the 21.6% of texts from Romans used at Dort. The largest number of Old Testament texts from a single book are 17 from Isaiah, but this is only 18% of the Old Testament total, and therefore only 2.5% of the total Bezan usage. Among the Dort texts the first and third most popular texts were Romans 8/30: - "And those whom he predestinated he also called; and those whom he called he also justified; and those whom he justified he also glorified." And Rom. 8/29: "For those whom he foreknew he also predestined to be conformed to the image of his Son, in order that he might be the first-born among many brethren." Next in order comes Ephesians, 60 texts used 253 times, the most popular being the much used Ephesians 1/4 (39 times): - "even as he chose us in him before the foundation of the world, that we should be holy and blameless before him," and Ephesians 1/5 (32 times). Yet it would appear that the reputations of texts mattered as did the authority of books, for while 58 texts from Acts were used on 116 instances, an average of only 2 usages per text, one verse, Acts 13/48 was used twenty times because of its relationship to the doctrine of election. Another example of a much used text is Jeremiah 32/4: - "I will make with them an everlasting covenant" etc., the most often used Old Testament text.

The Genevans used texts on occasions which may be summarized as follows. They used 337 texts 394 times.

Genesis	1 text used	1 times
Numbers	2	2
Deuteronomy	3	3
2 Chronicles	1	1
Job	2	2
Psalms	18	18
Isaiah	13	13
Jeremiah	8	9
Ezekiel	3	3
Hosea	4	4
Joel	1	1
Zechariah	3	3
Malachi	1	1
Matthew	24	24
Mark	1	1
Luke	6	6
John	44	49

Acts	5	5
Romans	52	66
1 Corinth	17	18
2 Corinth	10	13
Galatians	7	7
Ephesians	24	33
Philippians	6	8
Colossians	8	10
1 Thess.	2	2
2 Thess.	5	7
1 Timothy	3	3
2 Timothy	6	7
Titus	4	4
Hebrews	17	19
James	4	5
1 Peter	8	13
2 Peter	1	3
1 John	14	19
Jude	1	2
Revelation	8	9

It may be seen from this list that for the Genevans, the most authoritative books on these matters in the New Testament were Romans, John, Matthew, Ephesians and Hebrews, the most authoritative in the Old Testament were Isaiah, Psalms and Jeremiah. This testimony gives the Genevans a very considerable over all similarity to the pattern of usage employed by the delegations generally. The usage of particular books and the incidence of texts would seem to conform to a generally accepted pattern. On the matters of individual tests, however, the position is not so clear. The Genevans were not bound by any concensus of opinion regarding individual texts. They used 174 texts that were not used by other delegations. This is quite a high proportion of their total, 51.3%, but it is no higher than that of other foreign delegations considering the generally low usage of individual texts. Of these 174 texts 44 came from the Old Testament where there was little uniformity among the delegations though the Genevans used texts such as Psalm 147/19 and Psalm 51/12 that were used by a number of other delegations. The New Testament texts used by the Genevans alone included:

Matthew 8/11 11/23 13/38 15/12 15/13 17/10 17/20 21/19 22/32 24/31 25/3 25/30 28/19

Mark 11/14

Luke 2/24 10/21 15/18

John 1/15 3/27 5/38 8/21 8/31 8/35 9/39 9/44 10/17 10/20 10/37 11/26 12/14 12/32 13/10 15/2 15/5 16/8 17/10 17/16 17/25 17/32

Acts 9/5 14/6

Romans 1/5 3/14 4/6 4/7 4/16 6/1 6/4 6/8 7/4 7/17 8/23 8/27 11/9 11/12 11/16 11/21 11/22 12/2

1 Corinth. 1/3 5/5 5/7 6/17 10/2 10/3 12/3 13/11 14/24

2 Corinth. 3/18 4/5 4/6 5/4 7/1
Galatians 3/22 4/4 4/9
Ephesians 2/14 3/10 3/13 4/10 4/19 4/29 4/33 6/23
Philippians 3/12
Colossians 1/17 1/21 1/22 3/7 3/10
1 Thessalonians 3/12
1 Timothy 4/5 6/11 6/17
2 Timothy 3/8 4/17
Hebrews 3/12 3/13 3/14 3/20 6/11 11/9 11/16 12/23 13/20 13/21
James 1/2 1/21
1 Peter 1/4 1/21 2/9
1 John 2/20 3/12 3/29 4/4 4/6 4/14 5/5
Revelation 2/17 3/8 7/14 22/11[147]

The Genevans used a number of texts more than once, 45 texts were used twice and 6 texts were used three times. Most of these were also used by other delegations and a few were not; Ephesians 4/15, Colossians 2/12, 3/11, 2 Thessalonians 1/11, Hebrews 6/13 and Jude 12 were used twice by the Genevans but not by other delegations, while the Genevans alone used 1 Peter 1/22: - "Having purified your souls by your obedience to the truth for a sincere love of the brethren, love one another earnestly from the heart.", which they used three times, but which was not used by other delegations. Other variations from the norm of textual usage by the Genevans might be noted such as the fact that the Genevans alone used Numbers, or that they made less use of Hebrews, Acts, Luke and Mark than certain other foreign delegations, rather less use of Genesis and Hebrews than the Hessians in their treatment of the second article and less use of Acts than the Hessians employed in treating the first article, but these are variations which rely on too few instances to be quantified with any realistic degree of statistical reliability. Of the most popular texts listed above, the Genevans used 21 out of the 24. Thus on that level at least their acceptance of texts generally regarded as significant can be observed. The texts which they did not use were Ephesians 1/5, Romans 9/23 and John 10/28.

A consideration of the texts used more than once by the Genevans but not by other delegations reveals a certain shift of emphasis on the part of Diodati. If the texts discussions in the Italian annotations of the Bibles, are examined, it is to be noted that Diodati used all seven texts. He relates them all to spiritual experience, to what might crudely be called "pietism". This is particularly interesting because it is another revelation of a tendancy which can be noted elsewhere in Diodati's work. With regard to 1 Peter 1/22, Diodati suggests that both "obedience" and "purification of souls" are related to the work of the Holy Spirit[148], while Colossians 3/11 :- "Here there cannot be Greek and Jew, circumcised and uncircumcised, barbarian, Scythian, Slave, free man, but Christ is all, and in all", is used to suggest that Jesus Christ is the only basis and cause of all good and all salvation for believers, Christ living and working in them by his Spirit and so leading them to regeneration.[149] Diodati uses Colossians 2/12: - "and you were buried with him in baptism, in which you were also raised with him through faith in the working of God, who raised him from the dead.", to state that Christ works in us a spiritual resurrection from sin in the likeness of Christ's own resurrection.[150] In Ephesians 4/15:- "Rather, speaking the truth in love, we are to grow up in every way into him who is the head, into Christ.", Diodati sees Christ as the basis of spiritual subsistence and the beginnings of all spiritual life for men.[151] Diodati relates 2 Thessalonians 1/11 to the doctrine of perseverance and, in a more extensive treatment suggests that the "twice dead" mentioned in Jude 12:- "These are blemishes on your love feasts, as they boldly carouse together, looking after themselves; waterless clouds, carried along by winds; fruitless trees in late autumn, twice dead, uprooted." are people who have relapsed into a sinful life after making some attempt to live Christian lives.[152] None of these interpretations is really unorthodox, though the remarks on Jude 12 could lead to a conflict on election, but there is a pietistic feeling about them all. Diodati, it would seem, was already moving from a strict dogmatism to a more spiritual position, less intellectual and more concerned with internal, personal experience.

The Genevan theological contribution - Article I *De Divina Praedestinatione*.

The method which was used at the Synod of Dort to consider the remonstrant doctrines, was for each delegation, Dutch and foreign alike, to present a written statement to the Synod, concerning each of the five different points at issue. After all opinions had been heard, the orthodox Canons were formulated by a committee of which Diodati was a member.[153] For this reason, it may be unwise to separate the Canons from the Genevan statements, since Diodati was an influence on the formation of both.

The first article concerns predestination in its dual aspects of election and reprobation. The remonstrants had protested against the doctrine of reprobation which they found distasteful. They stated in the synod that they wanted this doctrine to be discussed before that of election. The foreign divines were asked for their opinion, and each delegation submitted a statement. The Genevan statement[154] is not one of the most theological documents. Diodati and Tronchin state that scripture deals with election more often than reprobation, and that no noted theologian ever dealt with reprobation before election. They stated that the doctrine of absolute grace was the heart of the reformed Church, and their insistence upon absolute grace was to be remembered in Geneva many years after, as a definitive exposition of that Doctrine.[155] They emphasized the authority of Scripture. This document also reveals the Genevan frustration with the tactics of the remonstrants in the Synod. They claim that the Synod wants to find the truth of the remonstrant position and so must question the remonstrants both sincerely and candidly. They reiterate the right of the remonstrants to defend their position and claim that in this the members of the Synod are themselves less privileged. They accuse the remonstrants of time-wasting and of frustrating the purpose of the Synod. They complain about the obstinacy of the remonstrants and say that if the remonstrants are determined continually to thwart and contradict the Synod, it would be better if they behaved as enemies.

Thus, even before the Synod had begun to consider this doctrine, it was already involved in controversy. In this case, it is perhaps best if the discussion of the first article is divided in two. In the first instance, the general background of the theology represented at the Synod - the theology, in effect, of Theodore Beza - will be considered. Then a more detailed discussion will be submitted in order to relate the Genevan statement to the others submitted at the Synod.

General considerations.

There would appear to be a fundamental resemblance between the Genevans and the other delegations to the Synod of Dort (e.g. from Switzerland, Hesse, Nassau and Emden) about this first article. It would seem that the contributions of these various delegations conform in a certain measure to a prototype that is the work of Beza rather than of Calvin.

In order to justify these statements, this section will incorporate discussion of the Bezan doctrine of predestination and a brief comparison with Calvin, a discussion of some of the orthodox statements, and finally, a brief consideration of the Canons of Dort.

Beza

In distinguishing the doctrine of predestination, Beza does not merely consider the doctrine of election as expressed in Ephesians 1/4ff. Rather, he discusses the whole salvation history of mankind from the first decree that God made until the final glorification - from fall to reconciliation. The best representation of the Bezan doctrine is the schema which he himself included in his *De Praedestinationis Doctrina et Vero usu tractatio absolutissima*[156] (Geneva 1583):

Dei summe misericordis et summo iusti aeterna, optima, et immutabilis quae et

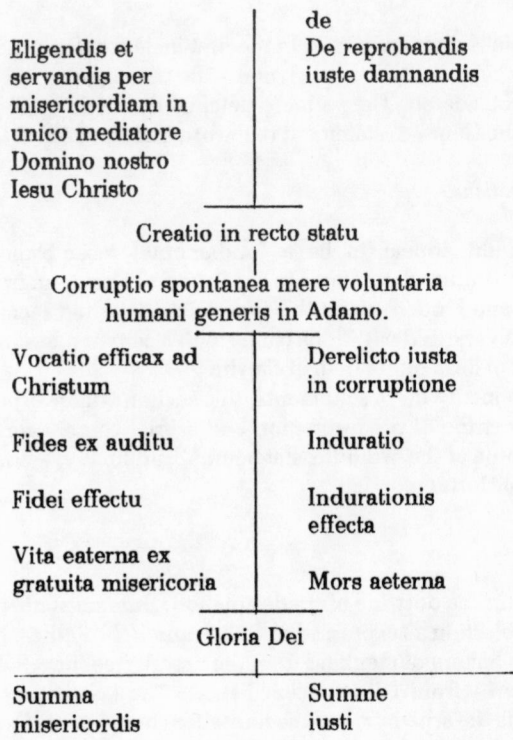

The first supposition of Beza's doctrine is that nothing is done outside the decree or the providence of God[157]:

> Praedestinationem vocamus primum in genere decretum illud Dei aetcrnum et immotum, quo, prout ipsi opt. maximo que libuit, cunctax, tum universalitor, tum singulariter decrevit, et per causas similiter ab ipso, prout libuit, creatas et directas ad gloriam suam patefaciendam, exequitur

and:-

> Ie t'accorde tout cela. Car il ne faut forclorre de la mutation du principal ouvrage de Dieu, ce decret eternal, lequel (comme nous avons monstre un peu auparavant) comprend toutes choses particulierement, sans nulle exception. [158]

This providence is the strength, or the force, by which God, from all eternity, did immutably decide when, how, and to what end he created all things. He explains this in *De Praedestinatione:* -

> Deus enim ab aeterno ex mera sua voluntate omnia, quod
> ad causarum etiam ordinem attinet, antecedente, ac Proinde
> nulla neque dignitatis neque indignitatis praevisae habita ra-
> tione, eos duntaxat, quos ipsi visum est, sive singulares
> homines, sive integros etiam populos, alios quidem amori et
> saluti, alios vero odio et exitio destinavit.[159]

The end to which God created all things was his own glory. God, according
to Beza, has decided from all eternity to do all things for his glory, his creation
of men, both elect and reprobate also tends to this end.

> Si enim architectus seu paterfamilias, quando cogitat aed-
> ificare domun aliquam, non ita desipit, quin priusquam aedi-
> ficet, de fine cogitet, ad quem domum aedificaturus sit; multo
> magis sic de Deo cogitandum est, qui cum sit infinita sapientia,
> certum finem in creando homine propositum habuisse, nullum
> dubitum est.[160]

Beza sees this election of certain men as the final cause of creation. By
symmetry, reprobation must also form part of the aim of creation. But this
symmetry does not signify that God creates some men in order to damn them.
Beza, in fact, believes that both election and reprobation are subordinated to a
higher purpose.

> La Predestination consideree en general n'est autre chose
> que cela mesmes que nous avons appele decret de Dieu, mais
> est ainsi appelee ayant esgard a la fin et au but de ce, decret.
> Car il n'y a chose que lo sage Createur de toutes choses n'ait
> destinee tant aux fins d'entre deux, que principalement a un
> dernier but: ce Createur (di-ie) qui n'a rien fait a la volee, et ne
> peut estre trompe ni changer de conseil.[161]

Beza sees this subordination of both election and reprobation to a higher
purpose as being part of the mercy of God. This purpose is more elevated than
creation, for it is the glory of God. This is one of the most significant concepts
in the doctrine of Beza - the ultimate end of the decree of God is the autoglorification of God.

> Dieu ayant delibere de toute eternite, comme on le peut
> cognoistre par les evenemens, de manifester sa gloire speciale-
> ment au genre humain, laquelle consiste partie en la manifes-
> tation da sa misercorde. partia en la demonstration de sa haine
> alencontre du peche.[162]

The final aim of the decrees of God is the glory of God himself[163]. God glorifies himself in maintaining his being which is both merciful and just;- "Ubi gloria Dei ex aeterno eius decreto summe misericordis et summe severi patefacta est."[164] Thus it must be that he created man and the world to manifest these two perfections and, in consequence, it must be that he has elected some and rejected others. Thus, among the elect, he manifests his bounty, and among the reprobate, his anger at their sin. The glory of God is that he is both merciful and just. This attitude may be seen both in the *Questions et Responses* of 1584[165] and in the confession of faith which Beza published in the year 1563.[166] The difference elect/reprobate reflects a difference in the being of God, and this entails its necessity.

Predestination to election is the demonstration of God's mercy;-

> Ex hac servitute Deus nemini debito, secundum aeternam suam in Christo praedestinatem electionem, quos ipsi libuit, ex mera sua misericordia religere, eadem sua misericordia, quando ipsi visum est, vocat, illuminat, fide donatos et regeneratos gratis in eodem Christo iustificat, in illis tandem glorificandis summam summae misericordiae gloriam suum petefacturus.[167]

This predestination to salvation has its source in the decree of God and is not in the foreknowledge of God about future human behaviour. Beza is, of course, supralapsarlan.

Reprobation also has its source in the decree of God, and demonstrates God's justice.[168] Beza is quite aware that this doctrine of reprobation is easily seen as imputing that God is the author of sin - a problem that also arose at the Synod of Dort, as will be seen below. Beza argues that the cause of evil is that the wills of the angels and the first men, which were good when created by God, voluntarily inclined to evil. God had created them good, but only mutably *(mutablement)* good and so they were capable of changing this state; to be immutably good is an attribute only of God himself.[169] This is a very brief introduction to Beza's doctrine of the decree of God and the doctrine of providence. The doctrine of predestination is, accurately, the realisation of this decree. Since the purpose of this section is not to discuss Beza's doctrine to any greater extent than that which is necessary for a clear understanding of the theology of the Synod of Dort, the Bezan doctrine of predestination properly so called need not concern us here, with the exception of one point.

To differentiate between the decree of election and reprobation, and election and reprobation in fact, Beza makes a scholastic - possibly Thomist - distinction between primary and secondary causes. The decree is the first cause and the realisation is the second cause. In the case of reprobation, for example, the secondary causes are corruption, infidelity and iniquity.

Nam aeternum Dei decretum, sic eventui a se determinato necessitate imponit, ut causa medias secundum ipsarum naturam moveri velit. Ex quo consequitur quod contingentiam humanae voluntatis minime tollat, sicut in disputatione de hominis natura plenius, Deo favente, disputabitur.[170]

Beza believed, in common with the Genevans at Dort and with Calvin, that the elect could be aware of their condition.[171] He approached the problem in a less Christocentric fashion than Calvin. Beza claims that faith can be seen both by God and by those in whom it is found. Beza - and this is a move in the direction of Dort - makes more of perseverance than Calvin.[172] It is impossible to know exactly who are reprobate and so the Gospel should be preached to all.[173]

From this brief introduction to the Bezan concept of the decree of God, three points may be isolated. Firstly, Beza, makes the auto-glorification of God the object of the world. Secondly, by making election and reprobation manifestations of Divine personality, Beza logically permits himself to derive all the processes of predestination from this concept of God. Finally, thanks to the division into first and second causes, Beza is enabled to create a system that embraces quite different ideas such as the grace of God and the sin of man.

Calvin

This is not the proper place for the study of Calvin's doctrine of predestination. That has already been quite competently considered in other works. But the statement has been made that Beza is the more obvious source of the theological climate of the Synod of Dort than is Calvin. The doctrine of Calvin must be studied so that this statement can be justified.[174]

Inevitably, since Beza became Calvin's successor in Geneva, there are considerable similarities between the doctrines propounded by the two men. Calvin also taught double predestination of election and reprobation. God rules all and controls all, down to the least detail. In the beginning, God made a decree by which he decided to create a part of mankind for eternal life, and another for damnation. This is the dominant theme of the twenty-first chapter of Book III of the *Institutes*. The action of God is a final action of which the object is his glory and his majesty. This goal is determined by his justice and his mercy. Predestination is here also founded in the decree of God and not in his foreknowledge. Like Beza, Calvin uses the distinction of first and second cause, God, the first cause, uses the secondary causes to realise his decree, as Calvin puts it: - "Therefore the Christian heart, since it has been thoroughly persuaded that all things happen by God's plan, and that nothing takes place by chance, will ever look to him as the principal cause of all things, yet will give attention to the secondary causes in their proper place."[175] Calvin teaches the necessity of the fall, which if it were not to be found in scripture, could be deduced from the omnipotence of God who directs all things by his secret council, and must therefore also direct the fall.[176]

Thus Beza has found, in Calvin, developed or in embryo, the ideas of the omnipotence of God, the double decree, the necessity of the fall, the carrying out of the decree by a chain of inferior causes, and the auto-glorification of God as the end of creation.

What, then, is the distinguishing feature of the Bezan position, since so much similarity is to be noted? It is the perspective of Calvin that is different. Calvin does not develop his concept of predestination into a scheme involving the whole salvation history of mankind, the "Tabula totius Christianisme" is the work of Beza. For instance, in Calvin's theology, there is no subordination of reconciliation and justification to a general scheme of predestination, and in the *Institutes,* Calvin considers justification (3.xi.-) before election (3.xx.-). For Calvin, the doctrine of election is an explanation of the doctrine of justification.

Another distinction between Calvin and Beza is that Calvin has a more general pastoral orientation in his theology, and, to him, predestination and the omnipotence of God are the foundation of the consolation of the elect. Assurance for the faithful is only rarely to be found as a dominant theme in the theology of Beza.[177]

As a general conclusion, it may be suggested that in the works of Calvin, predestination is not developed into a system embracing the whole salvation history of mankind. It will be seen below, that the features of the doctrines of providence and predestination that may be accorded to Beza rather than to Calvin are among those that are apparent in the theology presented as orthodox doctrine by the various delegations at the Synod of Dort. This will be examined in detail below.

Orthodox and Canons

When the statement of the Genevan delegation is considered in comparison with the theology of Beza that has been discussed above, it becomes obvious that they diminish the importance of the divine decree in favour of a doctrine of trinitarian providence. This doctrine is more explicit about the role of Christ.[178] The Genevans do not mention the final cause, the auto-glorification of God, and there is no mention of mercy and justice as being the qualities of divine personality that necessitate salvation and damnation. Thus certain ideas which are typical of Beza are not to be found in the expressions of the Genavans at Dort. However, they do maintain a total vision of salvation history which is realised in two ways and which is the work of the Trinity. This trinitarian vision is confirmed in the advice of the Genevans on the second article which will be discussed below.

The statement of the Swiss delegates on the first article is closer to the formulations of Beza than that of the Genevans. Christ is seen as the means of showing the richness of divine grace and mercy. The reprobate experience the power of God's wrath and justice.[179] They affirm the good pleasure of God as the only cause of predestination and reject election by forseen faith.[180]

The statement of the Nassau delegates is also close to the doctrine of Beza. They state that the object of election is the demonstration of the glory of the grace of God. They distinguish between the end and the means, or secondary causes, of which the first is Christ the mediator. Conversely, they differ from the Bezan scheme in that they do not allude to the roles of either justice or mercy.

The delegates from Bremen also produce the classic orthodox doctrine of salvation. They mention the auto-glorification of God and the showing forth of his mercy as salvation.[181] However, as a non-Bezan inclusion, it will be noted that they mention, as do the Genevans, the role of Christ and so would appear to have a more trinitarian insistence. Their interpretation of the decree responds to the perfections of God; to his liberty, in so far as He does what he wishes, to his justice and to his glory.[182] Thus Bremen could be said to be more Bezan than the Genevans, but their advice on the first article contrasts by its orthodox character with the more theological, almost Arminian perspective, with which Bremen responds to the second article.[183]

The Canons of Dort on the first article do not exactly follow the orthodox scheme of Beza. Nor, though certain articles do refute theses in order to contradict them, do the Canons follow the order of the remonstrant argument. Yet certain Bezan elements can be distinguished. The good pleasure of God appears as a cause of the decree, and in this God demonstrates his justice and mercy.[184]

Thus the environment of the Canons and the formulations of Beza would seem to be quite similar, both rely on an all-embracing salvation history. Thus it would appear that the Canons of Dort are an expression of thought that is more immediately derived from Beza than from Calvin. The orthodox theses of election mentioned briefly above and the Canons of Dort both contain a Bezan inclusive conception of theology. There are differences, which have been mentioned, such as the fact that there is an emphasis that is more noticeably trinitarian than the Bezan providentialist formulations. But the words and thoughts are very similar.

It is thus concluded, that the orthodox positions of the Synod of Dort are based on an inclusive conception of theology, a concept that involves the whole salvation history of mankind, and which is therefore more typical of Beza than of Calvin.

Particular considerations

In this section, there will be a discussion of Genevan theses concerning the first article that were presented to the Synod of Dort. These theses will be compared to statements submitted by certain other Dutch and foreign representatives so that the real theological position of the Genevans may be seen as relative to the climate of orthodox opinion. It will be seen that while there is one orthodox dogma, that it is capable of different interpretations that are in fact, different theologies.

The method which the Genevans use is very similar to that employed by Beza in the Tabula of predestination. First there is a brief statement of the point in question. Then there is a catena of relevant text . These catenae serve a dual function. Firstly, they support the meaning of the introduction statement. But there is more to it than this. The catenae have a common theme, an inner consistency based on the idea that each passage of scripture is somewhere in the Bible - expounded by another.

The first article had begun to cause controversy among the orthodox even before the statements of the various delegations had begun to be studied. Diodati and Tronchin were, at one point, worried that the British might attack the theology of Piscator, who they thought expressed himself in terms similar to those used by Beza.[185] This kind of side issue serves to illustrate the complexity of orthodox positions. Piscator was not Arminian at this time,[186] but had recently published *Disputatio Theologica De Praedestinatione Ac nominatim de tribus quaestionibus hodie controversus; videlicet* (Herborn 1595). This work has the various advantages of being relatively recent and quite short. In fact, the attack by the British delegates did not materialise, but it may have been for ecclesiological and political rather than doctrinal reasons since Piscator was the kind of writer favoured by the English puritans.

The Genevan method of work was to propose orthodox theses and to refute remonstrant opinion as heterodox and erroneous. This was normal reformed practice as used by Beza in the *Tabula*. Yet the Genevans' method was different from that of other delegations, for they quoted first a short, well expressed thesis, and then added a catena of Biblical texts as proof. The Genevan orthodox theses are all composed in this way; first theses and then scripture. It gives their opinions a clarity and a precision that is lacking in many of the other statements by Dutch and foreign delegations, not to mention their own theological students, as will be discussed later in this thesis. It was a method that favourably impressed other delegations to the Synod such as the British:- "their confirmation were nothing but places of Scripture, barely propounded in great number, and in a very fine contexture and frame."[187]

One difference between the Genevans and other important foreign delegations, is to be found in their rejection of doctrinal remonstrant errors. It was a principle of reformed controversy that it was insufficient merely to state true doctrine, unless that which was false was also rejected explicitly.[188] Thus a dialectic is set up between orthodox theses and heterodox antitheses. Some delegations devoted considerable attention to the rejection of errors. The British delegates quoted a large number of Patristic references - almost all Augustinian[189] and quoted directly rather than from Bradwardine - while the Dutch professors included many references to scripture.[190] In comparison, the Genavans produced a list of errors without any attempt at stating their authority for proclaiming this condemnation.[191] It must, however, be stated that this is neither an extreme nor a unique example, for the Swiss theologians at the Synod included no rejection of errors whatever. Some delegations such as the French Low Country Churches merely quoted remonstrant opinion and then included their authority for rejection in their orthodox counter-theses. Thus the Genevan position is not particularly unusual, since each delegation was at liberty to produce its own statements in its own way, but it must be asked why the Genevans were content with this short, unadorned statement, without any recourse to authority. The Genevans were far from being unable to quote authority when they wished to do so, as may be seen from the hundreds of Patristic references that Theodore Tronchin included in his defence of Genevan Bible translations against the Jesuit, Pierre Coton,[192]. Why was no authority quoted on this occasion? It is possible that at this time Genevan exegesis was unable to coincide exactly with Genevan systematic theology, since similarities have been noted between Diodati's later exegesis and that of the remonstrants, and an investigation of this is to be found later in this work.[193] There is another explanation, which is that the Genevans did not consider it necessary to quote authority when refuting erroneous doctrines. Another possibility is that this is part of a general tendency of Genevan theology in the seventeenth century, to devalue the use of the Fathers. In his *Institutio Theologiae Elenctiae* of 1679, Francois Turrettini stated categorically (2.21.1) that the Fathers cannot be used as a standard of judgment in matters of faith.

It is first of all necessary to compare the Genevan statement on predestination with the final text of the Canons of Dort. The Canons begin with a statement of original sin while the Genevan statement begins with a description of how God from all eternity selected some out of his own good pleasure; and the Canons 1/7 contain a similar idea that God's choice was made before the foundations of the world were laid down.[194]

The Genevans emphasize the role of Christ which is placed in thesis two of the Canons on the first article. Both statements emphasize the free will of God and the culpability of all men, the Genevans emphasize this culpability in thesis two.[195] Both the Genevan statement and the Canons accept that election, being from all eternity, is the same under the Old and New Testaments (Canons 1/8) while the Genevans refer specifically to the election of the Patriarchs.[196] Certain other key ideas also appear in the Canons and in the Genevan theses. The Genevans were concerned to state that no elect can become reprobate, nor any reprobate become elect, and they say this three times (article 1 thesis 5 of election, thesis 4 of reprobation and thesis 3 of the antitheses). It is also an idea which appears in thesis two of the Canons.[197]

The Genevans also believed that the elect are aware of their condition during their life on earth, and this is stated in thesis 6 of election. It is also an idea to be found in theses 12 and 13 of the Canons.[198]

Thus a broad similarity may be noticed between the Genevan statements and the final orthodox formulation of this doctrine in the Canons of Dort. However, there are a number of differences. The Canons represent a more pastoral approach, for they consider the election of the children of believers who die before becoming adult (thesis 17), and the case of those who do not yet believe they are among the elect (thesis 16). The Canons also devote some attention to the necessity of human faith and response (theses 2 and 3), in the salvation of men.[199] None of these things are discussed in the Genevan theses, but there are other distinctions which are not pastoral but theological. These are not questions on which the Genevan statements and the Canons are at variance, but where the Canons discuss questions that are ignored by the Genevans.[200] The Canons state categorically that election is not made from forseen faith and the Genevan articles are silent on this. The Canons assert that God is not the author of sin and that man is responsible for his own sins, it therefore being his own fault if he is reprobate. These are ideas that were ignored by the Genevans.

When the statements of other delegations about the first article are considered in relation to the Genevans, it becomes obvious that the Genevan doctrines were in no way abnormal, and that they were representative of then current orthodox reformed theology. The statements concerning the basic premises of God's election are generally uniform. The Bremen delegates stated that election was the decision of God, before the creation of the world, to save some of the corrupt mass of humanity. The Dutch professors, on this occasion Polyander, Physius and Walaeus, said that predestination was the immutable will of God by which He elected certain men to salvation, and that this was done from all eternity. The Swiss theologians, Breitingerus from Zurich, Rutimeirus from Bern, Beckius and Maierus from Basel as well as Koclius from Schaffhausen, claimed that God elected some to everlasting life to be delivered by Christ, and that the cause of predestination is the good pleasure of God.[201]

The British (thesis 2) and the Swiss (theses 4,7), like the Genevans, emphasized the role of Christ.[202] The British (thesis 4),the Swiss (thesis 10), the Dutch professors (thesis 4) and the delegates from the Walloon churches (theses 3,4) all stated explicitly or inherently, the idea included by the Genevans, that no elect can become reprobate, nor any reprobate become elect.[203]

The decree is immutable because it is the will of God from before the foundation of the world. A man may know himself to be elect, but it is not given to us to know or to be able to judge whether another person, at a particular moment has a faith which is in itself assurance of election. All men have periods of barrenness in their spiritual lives, but this no more means reprobation than that a tree is dead because it is without leaves in winter.[204] This kind of issue had already been debated in Geneva during the Jerome Bolsec affair of 1551.[205] The Swiss (thesis 11), the Bremen delegates (thesis 5) and the Walloons (thesis 6) also believed that the elect are aware of their condition in this life.[206]

The similarity of the Swiss and Genevan positions on so many important issues in 1619 is of considerable interest for the study of Swiss theology at a period that is intermediary between the foundation of the confessional reformed Churches and the *Formula Consensus Helvetica* of the later seventeenth century. Yet the Swiss make statements on issues that are ignored by the Genevans, such as the question of the election of the children of believers (Swiss thesis 8); this problem was also considered by the Bremen delegates (thesis 8) and by the three Dutch professors (thesis 3 of reprobation.).[207] The Bremen delegates also stated categorically that God is not the author of sin (thesis 2 of reprobation), and both they and the Swiss noted that man is responsible for his own sin (Swiss thesis 13, Bremen thesis 2 of reprobation).[208]

There are also other more significant differences between the Genevan theologians and the other delegations. The Swiss (thesis 12) state that they leave the exact formulation of divine decrees to the unknowable wisdom of God, and the concept of the divine decrees is a dominant feature of the Walloon's statement on Predestination (thesis 1), they also deny the order of these decrees posed by the remonstrants and state that it is erroneous to do this by human reasoning, rather than by the Word of God.[209]

The English, as has already been noted, include a most interesting apparatus of Augustinian proof texts while, on this occasion Diodati and Tronchin use no arguments supported by patristic authority. In this they were adhering strictly to the advice of Calvin in book three of the Institutes, for he states that the source of the doctrine of predestination is to be sought only in Scripture.[210] The only idea included in the Genevan statements that is not discussed by any of the other delegations considered here - the British, Swiss, Bremeners, Dutch professors and the Walloon delegates - is the idea of election under the Old Testament, which is discussed in the Genevan's seventh article of election.[211]

From this brief discussion, some tentative conclusion must be drawn concerning the relation of the Genevan sentiments to the opinion of the other delegations at the Synod of Dort. The question must be resolved as to whether the differences noted are sufficient to reveal a split between the Genevan theology and the other statements. In the consideration of the general matters, it has already been noted that there is a widespread acceptance of Bezan doctrine, though the Genevan statements could not be regarded as the most obvious example of this. Some ideas reveal a shift of emphasis rather than of doctrine, such as the suggestion that God is not the author of sin, but that man is responsible for his own sin. Other ideas reveal a difference in method rather than in theology such as the Patristics quoted by the British or the interest in the divine decrees displayed by the Swiss and Walloons. The idea of election under the Old Testament considered by the Genevans and ignored by the other delegations considered here - which surely represent the most influential groups at the Synod - but which is accepted by the Canons, is not really central to the doctrine. Similar is the exclusion by the Genevans of any discussion of the election of children who die before becoming adult, for this need not be indicative of any change in fundamental theology. Thus, in conclusion to this discussion of the Genevan theological contribution to the Synod concerning the first article of the Canons, it may not be unwise to consider the Genevan statements on election and reprobation as being of a series of different interpretations of the doctrines discussed at the Synod of Dort, which all nevertheless remain basically part of a largely uniform system of then contemporary reformed theology.

The Genevan theological contribution - Article *De morte Christi et hominum peream redemptione*

As was the case with the first article, discussion of this second article will be divided into two major parts, general considerations and particular considerations, a third section will also consider the Canons of Dort and the conclusions which may be drawn from this section. It will be shown that the orthodox deputies at the Synod of Dort supported the same dogmas as did the Genevans, but by the use of differing theologies. It is likewise in the discussion of this second article, that the Genevans may clearly be seen to have a different theological interpretation of the death of Christ than that which is accepted by the other delegations present at the Synod.

General considerations

It is perhaps best to begin this section by discussing the differences between the remonstrant position and those of the Palatines, the Swiss, the French as represented by Pierre du Noulin, and the Genevans. From this preliminary study it will be seen that the Genevans lack the Anselmianism that will be shown to be quite typical of the other delegations and that they do present two theses - with the usual Biblical catenae - which can be interpreted as being intended to imply a toleration of the Anselmian redemption theory that is propounded by the other delegations. Then, in chronological order, all the other statements about the second article will be briefly examined in relation to the tentative conclusions drawn from the first group.

The remonstrant position

The second remonstrant article of 1610 stated that Christ died for all men and has merited their salvation; yet only those who believe in him receive the benefit of their salvation.[212]

At the thirty-fourth session of the Synod of Dort on 17th December 1618, Bernard Dwinglo, a remonstrant, confonted on this doctrine in four theses.[213] He said that the *"pretium redemptionis"* that Christ offered to the Father is sufficient for all, and that none is *a priori,* that is by a decree, excluded from its benefits; that God can thus, without injury to his justice, offer man a new covenant; that according to the terms of this new covenant only believers benefit from the redemption bought (not wrought) by Christ, and that the people who actually benefit from the depth of Christ need believe that he died for them. If there were such a thing as *a priori* redemption, the reprobate could be taught unbelief.

This statement would seem to characterised by two things, both of them very much akin to some of the medieval methods of explaining the process of salvation.

Firstly, the salvation of man is conceived as an action within the Trinity. The Father, the representative of justice (to which, by the way, He is bound) is faced with the Anselmian dilemma *"aut satisfactio - aut poena."* The argument proceeds in Anselmian terms as revealed in the *Cur Deus Homo.* The Son then satisfies divine justice, paying the price for man, *pretium redemptionis sufficiens.*[214] Man, to Anselm, is by himself incapable of satisfying God:- *"Quod secundum mensuram pecati oporteat esse satisfactionem, nec homo eam per se facere possit."*[215] But man cannot be saved, unless God is satisfied. Man can, however, be saved by the intercession of a God-man, Jesus Christ.[216] The sacrifice of Christ acts as a substitute for all the sins of mankind, since his worth is so great that it far outweighs human depravity.[217] Christ's worth is infinite, yet he has sacrificed himself, so in order that divine justice may be satisfied, this sacrifice must receive some recompense. Yet, since He is perfect, He need receive nothing for himself. Thus it is possible for there to be a transfer of human retribution to Christ, so that divine justice can be fulfilled.[218] Christ pays man's debt to God. This transfer satisfies not only divine justice but also divine mercy.[219])

Secondly, and quite in harmony with what has gone before, salvation is conceived as being now ready, laid up, as it were, with the Godhead, so that the problem now arises as to how to deal it out to man. The remonstrants try to show that this, too, is to be thought of in non-nominalistic terms, God is now free within the bounds of justice to dictate terms for handing it out, and these terms are, simply, faith. This is reminiscent of much reformation thought, the idea of a pool of virtue which can be divided into sections small enough for human use. Another example of this kind of thinking is Eck's theory of the sacrifice of the Mass: Christ on the Cross has offered the Father a sacrifice of unlimited value, but the Mass has limited value and this is shared out to those who offer the sacrifice of the Mass, or to those for whom it is offered.[220] Both the image of God, implicit in the way salvation is conceived, and the image of the new covenant which provides the terms on which salvation is dealt out to men are strikingly parallel. It is interesting that so many delegations, as will be seen, refute the remonstrants in Anselmian terms. Anselmianism grew with the development of reformed protestantism and we find it in many authors including Calvin in his commentary of Romans [221] and Wm. Bucanus.[222] It is not universal - for instance we do not find *satisfactio* mentioned in Beza's *Tabula* on predestination, but the idea of Christ satisfying the justice of an outraged deity appealed to many. *Palatinate.*[223]

The Palatine theologians distinguish between the ordinance of preservation, where God shows his love for all creatures, and the ordinance of salvation, which is wrought by the merit of Christ. This latter is special, not general:- *"electorun propri, non communis."* They state that it is the will of the Father to reveal these things, such as the fact of Christ's gift of salvation being given to those who are simple and childlike, who are the faithful. They also quote New Testament passages where it is shown that the gift of salvation is a gift to the faithful. This does not limit the value of Christ's death, because it is included in the terms of the decree of election:- *"sic enim dilexit Deus electos suos. . . . ut ad demonstrationem istitiae suae voluit intervenir. . . electionis perfectam satisfactionem pro peccatis eorum."* The love of God for the sinner thus depends on Himself and not on any act of man.

The scriptures say clearly that God (i.e. the Father) has given some, but not all, men to his Son and supposes the identity of the saved with the faithful. They reject the distinction between remission in fact and as a theoretical remissibility, or the idea that there can be any other will in God than that which He reveals and puts into action. Hence they obviously go against not only the results of the remonstrants argument, but also its presupposition of a neutral, unactivated salvation, whereas in their first point they accepted the remonstrant view of Christ's work.

There is no real dispute about the sufficiency of the work of Christ, but interpreted in the way of the remonstrants, it would logically lead to the salvation of all men, even of the demons. The Palatine counter thesis, however, again accepts the remonstrant view of stored up salvation, since it says that Christ's merit is:- *"sufficiens. . .(et) etiam ad gratiae. . . communicationem in omnibus et solis electis."*

The Palatine theologians state that the remonstrant doctrine is similar to their own doctrine of a contingent salvation in their thesis 3 to the remonstrants. They opened a Biblical catena (e.g. Isaiah 53/11:- "righteous servant shall justify many" - but not all!), to show that salvation, and the application of salvation, are coterminous. They add an argument from analogy: what kind of medical value has a medicine that is not administered?, or, what value has an inheritance that is not transmitted to the heirs. There is no such thing as a salvation that lies unused.

The Palatines do contradict the remonstrants, but to some extent within the framework of reference that the remonstrants themselves provide. They quote remonstrant theses and provide orthodox counter theses. They argue on an exegetical basis, but also along systematic lines. They do accept and answer the questions of the remonstrants, such as, "what did the Son do for the Father?" and "Is there a decree that limits the value or application of the death of Christ or not?"

Switzerland[224]

To the first remonstrant thesis, the Swiss theologians state that by whatever name we choose to call salvation, Christ has obtained it for the elect. To the second point, they say that the sacrifice is of more than sufficient value, and that if it does not benefit all, it is because of the will of the Father. It is not up to man by a *liberalitas praepostera* to extend this to those who are *extra ecclesiam*, *extra corpus Christi* and so outside the number of human beings that are beloved by the Father. They deny that either the Father or the Holy Spirit did anything to save the damned. Here again there is used an argument from Analogy: the ransomed captive is not ransomed if the ransom is not given, i.e., they reject the remonstrant idea of a distinction between salvation and its application. They suggest that if Christ died for the damned, then conversely there might be elect who are saved without him. The work of Christ is seen as one. It is illicit to make some of it valid for all and some only for a few. Finally they reject the distinction between theoretical and effective salvation.

This follows the remonstrants rather less than did the Palatines, by treating salvation, not so much in Anselmian terms as in terms of a work of the whole Trinity, and rejects the distinction between salvation and the application of salvation, not at one point, but all along, as the main point of remonstrant doctrine. It treats less of value than of effectiveness and does not make use of the idea of the decree, but rather of salvation as actually received. It introduces the idea of the Church and sacraments, foreign concepts to the remonstrants and Palatine theologians alike. Yet at points they too accept the distinction between *impetrare* and *applicare* and they do echo another scholastic idea, namely, that the Holy Spirit is the love between the Father and the Son.[225]

Therefore this is an alternative complete view of the whole problem, rather than a refutation of the remonstrants in terms of their own theology. Yet obviously it accepts the same dogma as the Palatine theologians, but largely through an alternative theology.

Du Moulin[226]

Du Moulin begins with another problem - would it be just if all men were saved? The answer to this must be "no" with regard to those who persevere in disbelief. To say that Christ's death is sufficient to save those is to say that it is sufficient to do an injustice. Therefore it must be concluded that the proposition is correct only if by "all", one understands "all", the believers." If the others are not to be saved, the cause must be sought in their frailties, not in the insufficiency of the work of Christ.

The remonstrant doctrine is wrong in several ways, for it suggests that Christ died for Judas and it implies that the Father has accorded to the Son the salvation of those that He had from all eternity destined to be condemned. History teaches that only a part of the world receives the Gospel. Other remonstrant arguments are also quite wrong such as those which say that Christ died for all but was resurrected only for the elect. Du Moulin also rejects the distinction of the remonstrants between *impetratio* and *applicatio*. His main point[227] is that if Christ is dead for the damned, it does violence to divine justice. It is injustice if the damned will be punished by eternal death even though Christ died for them.

Again, this is a different theology, which involves the idea of justice, to which God is seen as being bound. Du Moulin turns it against the remonstrants. In a way, it is parellel to the procedure adopted by the Palatine theologians, but different in content. It is not at all Christological, though behind it obviously lies the same Anselmian view of salvation, though predestination and the justice of predestination are inherent themes.

The dogmatic framework is obviously common to Du Moulin and the other orthodox delegations at the Synod of Dort.

Geneva

The Genevans give expression to an idea that is only an afterthought for the Swiss and Du Moulin, and which was not mentioned at all by the Palatines: Christ is the head of the Church. Christ is, by God's good pleasure:- "datus mediator et caput certo hominum numero, corpus ipsius mysticum, ex Dei electione constituendum." This statement is followed by a Biblical catena, Isaiah 53/12, Ephesians 1/21, Romans 8/29, Ephesians 1/4, 1 Peter 1/20, Isaiah 53/12, John 17/6. Christ died for the elect alone. Christ is given as the *causa vocationis* and *cooptationis in ecclesiam*, the giving of all gifts. Again there are catenae, with quotations of Ephesians on the *caput/ecclesia* theme.

Faith is the *donum et effectum* of the Spirit given by Christ as head of the Church.

Faith is the condition of the new covenant. This is the common point of the remonstrants and the Palatine delegation, but it is so obvious that it needs no comment. It is to be noted that there has been, in this Genevan statement, no word about the Father having been satisfied by the Son's sacrifice, about the Father having instituted the new covenant, or of the new terms - faith - being perfectly just, thanks to the price paid to the Father by the Son. It is also very striking that the Genevans follow the arrangement and the wording of the remonstrants far less than the Palatines, who do so very much, the Swiss who do so rather less, and the Parisians represented by Du Moulin, who do so little. The Genevans do not do so at all.

The sixth Genevan thesis is a rule about universal propositions in scripture (of the kind: Christ died for all), which must be understood with reference to the Church either as reflecting on all its members or to the fact that the Church embraces all the nations. There is a very long catena of Biblical passages here which contains texts such as Ephesians 1/23, *Christus implevit omnia*, that sounds cosmic rather than universal, but which the Diodati *Bibbia* of 1607 interprets as in this case.

Equally striking are the last two theses which have no Biblical catenae, and are the only ones that specifically refer to the remonstrants position. One provides an orthodox acceptance of the distinction between *impetrario* and *applicatio*, while the other rejects the unorthodox interpretation:-

> Impetrationis et applicationis distinctionem hactenus recipimus, si cum carta personarum differentia intelligatur, nempe, ut propter Christum et eius satisfactionem, constet apud Deum certum decretum benevolendi et benefactiendi electis, priusquam actu illi vel existant, vel revers ille beneficia persentiscant; Deinde, ut impetratio causa ponatur efficax, perpetua, infallibilis ipsius applicationis actualis in electis.

> Si vero hac distinctione hoc spectatur et infertur, Deum per mortem Christi, erga omnes et singulos esse placatum, velle ipsorum salutem, mode ipsi velint, et voluntatem hominis illem universalitatem determinare, ut Pelagianum, rejicimus.[228]

This would be orthodox if understood of the two persons of the Trinity involved, i.e. if it means that because of Christ's satisfaction, the Father has made a certain decree before there was any actual saving to be done; but that the same death of Christ in fact saves the elect. Unothodox is equivalent to Pelagian if it means that Christ's death has reconciled God to all men, and that it is then their responsibility to accept this or not.

Tentative conclusion

It would seem to be safe to interpret this to mean that the Genevans are ready to accept a theology like that of the Palatines which argues in terms of the Son satisfying the Father, but not the resultant idea of a reservoir of grace that has to be dealt out either according to faith as it is found in individual men, or according to a decree conceived separately from factual salvation. Nevertheless, they do no more than accept such a theology. It is certainly not their own and it must have been in the course of the debates and consultations with other delegations that they made this concession.

Here it is to be clearly seen that there are several theologies and but one dogma. The Genevans do not think in Anselmian terms. Their theology is clearly distinguished from the Palatines, Swiss and French statements by its high-Church doctrine of salvation and almost complete absence of considerations like the idea that there is a justice to which God is bound, and that the decree is a sovereign act of God outside the work of Christ.

Thus the thesis - that there are different theologies in the framework of one dogma - is thrown into sharp relief.

What follows is an attempt to examine each statement concerning the second article with the ideas which we find in the Genevan statement with its emphasis on Christ as Head of the Church, and faith as gift, condition and effect of the new covenant. Various unsuccessful attempts were made to rationalise these statements with the somewhat untypical ideas of the Genevans. Attempts to group these arguments according to some typology fail because of the very richness of theological argument in the statements. Some delegations - from Hesse, Friesland, Drenthe, Walloon churches, Britain, the Palatinate and the Dutch professors give more emphasis to faith than some others, but this is in such a diverse way that to use it as a guide for some grouping of delegation statements as to their closeness to Genevan statements could be very misleading. The complexity of arguments will be noted in a section on the question as to for whom Christ died. If another idea is taken which or not typical of the Genevans, that of the Father's justice being satisfied by the sacrifice of Christ, a summary of its proponents - Britain, Hesse, Nassau-Wedderau, Martinius, Iselburg, Crocius, Emden, Gelderland, South and North Holland and the Dutch Professors - will reveal that it was used by delegations which on other grounds might be crudely regarded as being close to the Genevans. If the use of the Anselmian idea of *pretium redemptionis* is examined in the delegation statements, it gives an even less clear scheme of similarities and differences; it is not overt or covert in the Genevan statement but it is inherent in those coming from Du Moulin, Hesse, Nassau-Wedderau, Iselburg, Emden, Utrecht and Overijssel, while it is overt in those of Britain, Crocius, Gelderland, South and North Holland, Zeeland, Friesland, Drenthe, the Walloons - and the Remonstrants. This shows, as is mentioned elsewhere in this thesis, that reformed "orthodoxy" is by no means uniform or easy to define. The Genevan statement on the second article is dissimilar to the others, but the others do not reveal a uniform scheme. Discussion and argument among the reformed delegations to the Synod was real and necessary. If it is not surprising to us that the Genevans are untypical, it is because we do not know enough about them or the other delegations. A study of the theology of the Dort statements is three and a half centuries overdue.

Britain

The British delegates state firstly that Christ is dead because of the desire of his own will as well as that of the Father. He is dead for the elect, so that they might have remission of sins and salvation. The sureness of the remission and salvation shows the love of God. The promises of scripture - and this is very Anselmian - show us that the purpose of the sacrifice of Christ is that the elect might infallibly have their election.

> Ex speciali amore et intentione tum Dei Patris, tum Christi, mortuus est Christus pro electis, ut illis remissionem peccatorum et salutem aeternam reipsa obtineret, et infallibiliter conferret.[229]

Because of this divine love, the elect are given the gifts of faith and perseverance, and all other things necessary to accomplish the necessary conditions. By the grace of redemption, they understand that men are purchased - an Anselmian term - because God wishes it and not because of their own wishes.

God sent his Son as a ransom for mankind, because of his compassion.

Deus lapsi generis humani miseratus, misit Filium suum, qui seipsum dedit pretium Redemptionis, pro peccatis totius mundi.[230]

It is through the merit of Christ that the promises of God are made truly universal, that those who have faith obtain remission of sins and life eternal. The promise is universal, even though dissemination of it may be incomplete. The dissemination of the promises of salvation through the Church renders inexcusable those who hear them but do not repeat and continue to live in disbelief. Yet, despite this suggestion of human responsibility, the British clearly state the irrestistable nature that divine grace has for the elect. Despite the universality of the promises, God is not bound to communicate his grace to each and every man. If He chooses to leave some in ignorance, this will be in accordance with his justice and mercy.

Thus it may be seen that the British have a preoccupation with the universality of the promises of salvation. Yet their basic concept of the purpose of the sacrifice of Christ is completely Anselmian; its purpose was to pay a price so that the elect might surely have salvation. There is no explicit mention of the Genevan idea of Christ as head of the Church.

Hesse[231]

The delegates from Hesse began by describing the second article and by stating the remonstrant position. They then expressed their own opinion and expressed three propositions. Firstly, they stated that Jesus Christ must be the saviour of all men in general, and they accepted this as saying that in fact He saved the elect only. Secondly, they claimed that Jesus Christ has merited by his death and passion, the reconciliation of man with God, and the remission of sins. They state that the value of the sacrifice of Christ was so great that it could have merited the remission of all sin, but that it did not do so, and so they reject the point. Finally, the Hessian delegates expressed their belief that nobody is to be saved, except they have faith. They find this acceptable if it is understood that the ransom of Christ is paid for the faithful, who are already the elect. At this point the delegates from Hesse are clearly Anselmian;-

At Christi λυτρον in se est sufficientissimum ad omnium et singulorum hominum (si vel mille essent mundi) peccata expianda. Ergo, tale illud Deus Pater ab aeterno voluit esse.

Nassau-Wedderau [232]

The delegates from this Dutch dominated area were included among the foreign delegations and so their contribution must be considered in this action. They began by stating that Christ, by the merit of his death, has so reconciled the Father, that for love of him, the Father has promised the elect all saving gifts.

The will and intention of the Father in delivering his Son to death, and that of the Son in submitting to it, was to gain remission of sins and eternal life for those who had already been given to Christ by the Father.

> Voluntas et intentio Patris, Filium in mortem tradentis, et Filii eam subeuntis, fuit, ut Filius per λυτρον pretiosi sanguinis, iis quos Pater ipsi dedit, et impetraret et applicaret remissionem peccatorum et vitam aeternam. [233]

Christ is sufficient expiation for the sins of all the world, but is only dead for the elect. In dying for the elect alone, he has prayed for them, been resurrected for them, and is interceding for them.

The method of the Nassovian delegates was to quote a brief orthodox thesis as set against a heterodox- i.e. remonstrant - thesis, and to conclude each section by a discussion of the issues involved. They do not refer to the Genevan idea of Christ as head of the Church, but their second thesis is quite Anselmian in conception.

Bremen - I - Martinius [234]

The statement of Martinius on the death of Christ has been one of the most frequently discussed orthodox statements of the Synod of Dort. It will receive more detailed consideration later in this thesis. What needs to be mentioned here is that Martinius has no reference to Christ as head of the Church, but that he does refer to redemption in Anselmian terms:-

> Caeterum illa externa vocatio, cuius partesrecensui, neccessrio ante se requirit haec; premissionem et missionem Filii (futuram olim, nunc factam) et redemptionem, hoc est precii solutionem ad expianda peccata, et Deum ita placandam, ut ipse nullam aliam pro peccatis ullius hominis hostiam requirat, unica illa plenissima contentus; et ad homines reconciliandos, ut pro eis nulla alia satisfactione nulloque alio merito sit opus; modo (quod in remediis fieri oportet) illius communis et salutaris fiat applicatio. [235]

Bremen - II - Isselburg [236]

Iselburg is more concerned with defining the sufficiency of the death of Christ than he is with discussing the mechanism by which the death of Christ becomes sufficient, but he does reveal a belief, which would seem to show

Anselmian influence, that Christ has paid the debts to the Father that mankind
has incurred by sin.

> Sed tantum pro ovibus suis electis, sive fidelibus omnibus et
> singnlis (sic), eorumque loco et bono, animam posuit, sive
> mortuus est Christus; sensu, ut eorum sit salvisicus Sacerdos,
> propitiator et victima eos solos Patri suo actu ipso reconciliarit,
> eisque remissionem peccatorum, justitiam et vite aeterne
> hereditate impetrarit: non secus ac si ipsi pur eum Dei justitiae
> satisfecissent, ei qui debit, sua solvissent. Peccatorum autem
> omnium remissionem Christus fidelibus impetravit, ita ut non
> tantum satisfecerit pro illis que committunt, tanquam in com-
> muni peccati et lapsus sorte considerati, aut quae omnibus
> sunt communia, sed etiam pro illis que sunt singularia, queque
> committunt, posteaquam sunt ad participationem divine gra-
> tiae vocati, et per fidem Christo insiti, quecunque deum illa
> sint.[237]

> Ita destinavit Deus Christum in mediatorem cum peculiari
> intentione ac voluntate, certos quosdam ex genere humano
> redimenti, eosquo aeternum salvandi.[238]

Bremen - III - Crocius[239]

The statement of Crocius is shorter than that of Iselburg. He does mention
the ideas of the price paid by Christ, and the worth of Christ's death. Like
Iselburg, however: he does not mention Christ as head of the Church.

> Mortis Christi ea est dignitas; pretium, potentia, valor ac suffi-
> cientia, ut ad omnium ac singulorum hominum reconcilia-
> tionem cum Deo et peccatorum remissionem promerendam,
> acquirendam ac impetrandam ei prorsus nihil desit.[240]

Emden[241]

With regard to this second article, the delegates from Emden submit a long
series of twenty-one questions, all provided with orthodox antitheses as responses. In these antitheses, there is no reference to Christ as head of the
Church. However, there are traces of Anselmianism in the suggestion that Christ
paid a ransom to satisfy the sins of the elect.

> Christus sanguinis sui pretiosi effusione non tantum sictitiam
> illam et nullo Dei verbo munitem impetrationem remissionis
> peccatorum, hoc est, januae gratiae apertionem, vel potentiam
> et possibilitatem aperiendi januae gratiae nobis commeruit;
> sed reipsa plenissime pro omnium electorum peccatis satis-
> fecit, perfectissimum persolvit, *nosque redemit non auro nec ar-*

gento sed pretisio suo *sanguine* 1 Pet. 1.18.19. Et *magno pretio emit* 1.Cor.6.20. Catech. Heidelb. quaest. prima. contrarium Socinianismum plane abominamur.[242]

The Dutch Professors[243]

On this occasion the Dutch professors were Gomarus, Polyander, Thysius and Walaeus. They quote four main points.

They begin by stating that the value of the death of Christ is of such an inestimable worth that it could suffice to save the whole posterity of Adam.

Fatemur, meritum, et valorem mortis et satisfactionis Christi, tantum, tantique pretii esse, tum propter eius perfectionem, tum propter personae ipsius infinitam dignitatem ut non tantum sufficiat ad omnia hominum peccata, etiam maxima, expianda, sed otiam ad omnes Adami posteros, quamvis multo plures essent, servandos modo id vera fide amplecterentur.[244]

Christ died through his own will and that of the Father, his purpose in doing so was to pay a ransom to the Father for mankind.

Non est etiam dubitendum, quin haec fuarit Dei Patris, Filium suum tradentis, et Christi se ipsum offerentis, intentio; ut tale ac tantum λυτρον persolvet. Nam, quidquid Christus per mortem suam egit, hoc ex intentione Patris et sua egit.[245]

The Church has a duty to announce this ransom to the whole of mankind, yet the dispensation of this ransom is hidden in the secret purposes of the Father.

Christ is not dead for the reprobate but only for the elect. They add arguments to justify their orthodox position.

The attitude of the Dutch professors was obviously determined by the climate of controversy that had been present in the Low Countries before the Synod, for their theses are largely a defence or an apology for the orthodox position. What is particularly significant for the present study, is to note that their basic doctrine is completely Anselmian and that there is no mention of Genevan concept of Christ as head of the Church.

Gelderland[246]

The delegates from Gelderland begin by stating that Christ, the saviour of the world, is dead for us all in that he has obtained reconciliation and remission of sins by the death on the cross. They reject the remonstrant position.

They claim that the remonstrant position is not based on scripture, and quote Prosper to prove their point.

Christ is dead for those men that God calls to salvation. Christ is not dead for all men.

Christ is dead for all those whom God has commanded to believe in Jesus, and for whom he has been crucified.

It cannot be said that Christ is dead for sins that have not been forseen by the Father, which is to say that Christ is not dead for the sins of the non-elect.

If Christ, in dying had merited grace for all men, then all would have been given grace to believe, but all do not have this belief.

Those for whom Christ has satisfied divine justice need no further satisfaction for their sins.

Christ is the mediator of all those for whom he is dead.

The lengthy judgement of the Gelderland deputies is a particularly subjective document. They quote a number of their contemporary Dutch polemical works including those of Arminius as well as a moderately large Biblical catena. They are much concerned with the refutation of remonstrant positions. The preoccupation with their polemical situation leaves little room for really objective theological argument. The sixth point is inherently Anselmian, but there is no trace of the Genevan concept of Christ as head of the Church nor of the Palatines' suggestion of a reservoir of grace. It is interesting to note, however, that in explaining their first point, they do actually quote from a patristic source, the *De Vocatione Gentium,* which at that time was attributed to Prosper of Aquitaine.[247]

South Holland[248]

The delagates from South Holland state that God has decided from all eternity to save all men, but only some are effectively purchased by Christ as an attribute of God's glory;-

> Deum, uti ab aeterno decrevit, non omnes homines, sed certos quosdam ex genere humano selectos, ed laudem gloriosae suae gratiae servare, ita etiam simul statuisse, ut satisfactio, et meritum obedientiae et mortis Christi, quod in se quidem sufficaret omnibus et singulis hominibus redimentis, sit medium subordinatum et proprium, quo expiatis peccatis illorum, qui sibi a Patre dati sunt, afficaciter et infallibiliter, electi ad salutem satarnam tanquam ad finem absolute a Deo intentium perducerentur.[249]

The price - and this is a particularly Anselmian idea - that Christ has paid is for the elect alone: -

> Et quia media sapienter destinata, finem adaequatum non excedunt. Statuunt: Satisfactionem et meritum Christi, seu pretium redemtionis; quod Christus passione et morte sua Deo Patri persolvit, non esse efficax, sive ad impetrandum, sive ad applicandum finem illum adaequatum, nisi insolis Electis.[250]

They deny that God would have let his son die for the non-elect.

This statement by the deputed theologians from South Holland clearly reveals two archtypical attitudes of the orthodox as demonstrated at the Synod of Dort. The first thesis reveals an acceptance of the Bezan notion of the autoglorification of God, while the second thesis is explicitly Anselmian in that it represents Christ as paying a price for the salvation of men. The South Holland representatives also include further discussion and a rejection of remonstrant errors that need not be considered here. They do not mention the Genevan concept of Christ as head of the Church.

North Holland[251]

First of all the deputies from North Holland state the remonstrant article and then: deny that Christ is dead for each and every man, just as the apostles could cure all maladies but did not cure every sickness. Christ is dead for all, which is easy to say, all the elect. They then include a Biblical catena of texts such as Matthew 1/21. They include the Anselmian ideas that he died as a payment for our sins. The North Holland representatives conclude with a discussion of the errors of the remonstrants.

This delegation also chooses to deny that God has reconciled all men to himself, or that he has remitted all the sins of all men. In confirmation of these points they quote a long Biblical catena. They conclude by discussing remonstrant opinions and by a refusal to consider the order of the divine decrees.

Thus it may be seen that the statement of the deputies from North Holland was dominated by the refutation of the remonstrants and by the compilation of Biblical catenae. There is an inherent acceptance of the Anselmian theory that Christ paid a price to the Father for the redemption of mankind, but there is no hint of a concept of Christ as head of the Church.

Zeeland[252]

The Zeeland deputation stated that the price paid by the death of Christ is sufficient to expiate the sins of all men, but that this was the will of the Father who wished his Son to pay a price only for the elect. They quote a Biblical catena as proof:-

> Et si fateamur λυτρον mortis Christi sufficiens esse in sese, ad expiandum peccata omnium et singulorum hominum: absoluta tamen voluntas et intentio Patris, Filium unigenitum in mortem tradentis, et Filii eam subsuntis fuit, persolvere redemptionis pratium pro omnibus et solis Electis.[253]

They also produce a second set of justifications for their position.

The second of this set is relevant to our present purpose:-

Si Christus persolvit Redemptionis paetium pro omnibus et singulis, tum omnes et singuli debent salvari et nemo perire. Atqui non omnes et singuli servantur, quin imo multi parount. Ergo, etc. Maior est verissima, ex institia Dei, qui alias damnatos injuste puniret, pro damnatos injuste puniret, pro quibus Christus, ex sententia Remonstrantium, persolvit Redemptionis pretium.[254]

They conclude by refuting heterodox, i.e. remonstrant, opinion, and by quoting Augustine *Contra Julian.*

Thus it may be seen that in the statement of the Zeeland delegates, there are two major themes which we are attempting to trace throughout the contributions submitted to the Synod of Dort. They make an obviously Anselmian interpretation of the redemption and also include, in a manner denoting acceptance, an idea that is similar to that expressed by the Genevans, of Christ as saviour of his body, which is the Church. This is not very different from the Genevan concept of Christ as head of the Church.

Utrecht[255]

The delegation from Utrecht stated that the will and intention of God the Father in delivering his son to death was not to give salvation and eternal life to all. The intention of Christ in submitting to the death of the cross was not to save each and every man. Christ did not endure death for both Cain and Abel or for both Judas and St. Peter. There are those that perish and those who will be saved.

Christ has not satisfied divine justice for the sins of all men:-

Christus pro omnibus et singulis hominibus non est mortuus, reconciliationem cum Deo at remissionem peccatorum singulis non promeruit nec impetravit, justitiae Dei pro singulorum peccatis non satisfacit, sed quibus reconciliationem cum Deo et remissionem peccatorum promeruit, satisfactione sua plenissima, iis etiam omnibus et singulia applicat.[256]

God the Father, therefore, has not been reconciled to all mankind. God has not received in grace and is not reconciled to all mankind. Because of original sin, all children are worthy of condemnation.

These theses are followed by an extended discussion of the issues that have been raised. There is no suggestion the Christ is head of the Church, but some of these theses are clearly Anselmian.

Friesland[257]

The deputation from Friesland stated that Christ's death was for all, that is, all the elect. He is dead for each of the elect. In dying for each of the elect, he has purchased reconciliation with God for them. They then procede to state that faith is necessary for salvation. These are the bare outlines of what is one of the most verbose submissions on this second article. The Frisian deputies are at pains to contradict the remonstrants, but without stating the Genevan idea of Christ as head of the Church. There are some quite Anselmian passages in their discussion of how Christ has purchased reconciliation for the elect.

Overijssel[258]

The party from Overijssel state that God's purpose in delivering his son to death (and also the purpose of Christ) was to reconcile the elect with God and to remit the sins which they had committed and so give them eternal life. By his death and suffering on the cross, Christ has obtained the remission of sins, reconciliation with God and eternal life for all the elect. The obtaining of the remission of sins and reconciliation with God and the application of this reconciliation of it are all part of the redemption process of the elect.

In this short statement, the delegates from Overijssel obviously have a basic acceptance of the Anselmian position, though it is not very explicitly stated. There is no mention of the idea that Christ is head of the Church.

Groningen and Omland[259]

These delegates begin by stating that God the Father and Jesus Christ considered only the elect in their scheme of redemption. Secondly, they claim that the Son did not die simply to obtain remission of sins for men, but also to apply the benefits that follow to those for whom the remission was obtained. The third point is that the will of God the Father in applying to mankind the benefits that Christ has obtained by his death, saves us because of the ransome that the Son paid in dying. It is denied that the Son's death is conditional:-

> Tertium membrum theseos nostrae est; voluntatem, bona morte Christi impetrata, applicandi, et salutem propter mortis Filii pretium conferendi, non esse conditionatam, a conditione in homine latente dependentem.[260]

The deputies from Groningen and Omland arrange their doctrine around these three points and also include refutation of remonstrant theses. There is no mention of a concept of Christ as head of the Church. The third point would appear to be based on Anselmian theory.

Drenthe[261]

This delegation first of all denies that God ordained Christ as mediator before He had any intention of saving anyone in particular. They state that the necessity of Christ as mediator was the ransome which He paid to the Father. They see faith as an instrument by which we come to know the merits of Christ.

They state that God gave Christ to purchase mankind. The price of redemption that Christ has by his death offered to God to satisfy his justice was approved by the divine decree:-

> Pretium redemptionis, quod Christus per passionem et mortem suam Patri obtulit, eiusque justitiae satisfecit, fuit secundum voluntatem Decretum atque intentionem Dei efficax, ad reconciliationem pro electis suis solis, quorum Christua sacerdos est et propitiator, pro quibus etiam solis adaequate, cum intentione salvandi resurrexit, atque intercedit; Iohan. 17. Rom. 8.29. etc. testimonia multa alia sunt in praecedentibus, et in colloquio Hagiensi: quibus calculum subiumgimus.[262]

The alliance of grace is that by which God freely promises Christ to man if man receives Christ by faith.

The delegates from Drenthe follow the remonstrant order in propounding their theses. There is no mention of Christ as head of the Church and in the second and fourth points His purpose is seen interpreted in a particularly Anselmian fashion.

Walloon Churches[263]

They begin by stating that all mankind can be repurchased by the worth of the death of Christ, provided men have faith - this is Anselmian:-

> Pretium redemptionis, quod Christus Patri suo obtulit, in se et per se dignissimum est et sufficientissimum, ita ut omnes, valore et dignitate mortis Christi, redimi possent, si omnes et singuli crederent.[264]

Christ is dead only for the believers and has not only acquired reconciliation for believers, but has supplied them with sufficient grace for their salvation. The death, resurrection and intercession of Christ as well as the benefits that flow from this to the believers are such that reconciliation, justification, remission of sins, sanctification, redemption and the gift of eternal life must not be considered separately. God ordained Christ to be the propitiation of the sins of those men with faith in God, and of no others.

The Walloon delegates are obviously concerned that it should be clearly understood that Christ died only for the elect. Yet their basic premiss - expressed in the first thesis - concerning the mechanism and the purpose of this sacrifice is a completely Anselmian concept.

Particular considerations.

The second remonstrant doctrine discussed by the Synod of Dort concerned the death of Christ. If a doctrine of election from all eternity, such as that of the orthodox theologians, is accepted, then the role of Christ as saviour requires considerable clarification. Crudely, if God's choice had been made from all eternity; was Christ's coming really necessary? This obviously delicate point of reformed doctrine had been questioned by the remonstrants who denied that Christ was dead only for the elect and stated that Christ died for all men, that his sacrifice was sufficient for all men though not efficient for all, and that it does not save men, but rather makes them capable of being saved. They thus emphasized the utility of Christ's death and debased the doctrine of election. Man is to be saved, not because he is elect, but because his faith has been forseen with his repentance. In view of this faith and repentance, God, through the new covenant with man, offers salvation.

The orthodox reaction to this doctrine at the Synod of Dort is embodied in the Canons.[265] They state that man is sinful and subject to the justice and condemnation of God. Man cannot justify himself, he cannot satisfy this justice alone, but God, through his mercy, gave his Son, that he might make satisfaction for all the elect. Christ's sacrifice was sufficient to expiate the sins of the whole world and is of infinite value because Christ was not only man, but also God. Those who believe in this sacrifice are to be saved, and this is to be announced to all men. Many that are called do not repent, but this does not mean that Christ's death is insufficient. This benefit comes to believers through divine grace. God the Father ensures that all his elect receive faith to believe in this sacrifice so that they are cleansed from their sins and rendered capable of receiving the gift of salvation to eternal life. Thus the saving grace of Christ is sufficient for all the world but efficient only for the elect. Thus the remonstrant hope of a possible universal atonement is replaced by a doctrine of limited atonement.

The Genevan statement is in accord with this interpretation,[266] though it is shorter, more didactic and less argued. Diodati and Tronchin reject (article 8) any idea that by the death of Christ, God is appeased towards all in general, as being erroneous and Pelagian. They state that Christ was given by God to the elect, and that faith in Christ is itself a gift. The Genevans also state that Christ has taken all nations as his heritage and that the Gospel must therefore be preached to all people. They presumably believed that Christ's death, though efficient only for the elect, was sufficient for all, since this was stated in the Du Moulin letter that Diodati read to the Synod.

Some of the other delegations accepted very different interpretations of this doctrine. Martinius of Bremen,[267] for example, hinted that God wished to save all men and that He would willingly have done so, for He loved them. The redemption could have sufficed for all men:-

> Est communis quaedam Dei: φιλανθρωπια, qua dilexit totum genus humanum lapsum, et serio omnium salutem voluit. Neque hic satis erit, sufficientiam talem redemptionis ponere, quae satis esse posset: sed omnino talis est, quae sit satis, et quam Deus et Christus satis esse voluenint. Nam alioqui mandatum et promisso Evangelica convellentur.[268]

Yet this is not a means of redeeming the whole of mankind, for Christ did not make satisfaction for the sins of the impenitent and rebellious:-

> Exceptio ad res est, quod Christus non satisfecit, nec satisfac-
> ere voluit pro impoenitentia permanente, multo minus pro
> contumacia perseverante, qua beneficium illud contemnitur,
> aut benefactor contumelia afficitur; qualis est blaspheme mali-
> tiosa in iis, qui peccant in Spiritum Sanctum. Heb. 10.26.[269]

Martinius sees the advantage of this emphasis as being that it is obvious that the
death and damnation of the wicked is their own fault and is not because of
default of aid by which they might be saved. The scheme conforming to the
Bezan concepts of God as merciful and just.

> Rationes praecipuae, cur hanc sententiam sequar, sunt tres:
> 1 Ut Scripturae possint non contorte conciliari.
> 2 Ut maneat Deo gloria veritatis, misericordiae et justitiae in
> mandatis, promissionibus, et comminationibus Euangelicis: ne
> illis Deus secus aliquid velle vel agere judicetur; quam verba
> sonant.
> 3 Ut manifestum sit, culpam interitus impiorum esse in illis
> ipsis, non nutem in defectu remedii, per quod servari potuis-
> sent. Itaque sequor et retineo, quae in Explicationibus Cate-
> cheticis Ursini, pag. 256.257.258. leguntur; inter quae et illa:
> Christus est mortus pro omnibus merito et sufficientia λυτρον:
> pro solis credentibus applicatione et efficacia in quam eandem
> sententiam multa et Patrum et Scholasticorum, et racentium
> Ecclesiae doctorum testimonia citari possunt, ubi opus erit.
> Sed in Scripture simplice intelligentia hic acquiesco; in qua eam
> ipsam rem clarissime et creberrime tradi statuo.[270]

Thus it is easily seen that Martinius' attitude is very different to that of the
Genevans, though his reasoning is, perhaps, somewhat hazardous. Yet he does
belong to the same orthodox theological school as the Genevans, though he
could not so easily be accused by the Arminians of making God the author of sin,
for his doctrine of salvation is still conditional on man's faith. Martinius includes
a section of theses which describe how Christ is specially dead for the elect, and
in a rejection of statements by Huber and Puccius, he denies that Christ has
delivered from death, or justified, or sanctified those who are not saved.

Another statement from Bremen, that of Iselburg,[271] gives a somewhat
intermediary position between the Genevans and Martinius. Iselburg asks if God
wished to save all men, and states that Christ's death was sufficient to expiate
the sins of all men. This is offered to both elect and reprobate as well as the
unbelievers, those who reject it are justly condemned. Thus the reprobate are the
cause of their own death, and Christ is not responsible. Christ did not know the
wicked, and the Father never wished to have mercy on them - this would have
been a case of casting pearls before swine. Christ died only for the elect and there
are some whom Christ does not call.

These two statements from the delegation from Bremen seem to show the
lack of uniformity among the orthodox delegates, yet this dissimilarity is some-

what deceptive. They seem to suggest that Christ's mission was part of the divine desire to save all men, or to truly offer salvation to all men. This is an idea quite alien to the Genevans. It seems to allow more room for human response and thus may seem more "liberal" and less "rigidly Calvinist." Yet it is not so. For if there were a divine will to offer salvation to all men, then man's rejection of this offer makes him inexcusably culpable. But this does not really remove the responsibility for reprobation from God, for it would (according to the orthodox interpretation of the third and fourth articles - see below), according to the orthodox theologian, be within the power of God to enable all men to be endowed with irresistible grace. For as the Bremen theologians obviously believed, grace is essential to man's salvation and without this gift of God, man is helpless on his own. Also, if one gives credence to Martinius' idea of a divine desire to save all men, one is left in the position of having to attribute the thwarting of a divine wish to save the reprobate. Finally, the Bremeners are forced to admit that Christ died for the elect, and it is in this, the heart of this doctrine that one perceives their similarity to the Genevans. The Genevan statements, though very short, manage to avoid many difficulties encountered by the verbose Bremen delegates in their attempts to assert the responsibility of man for reprobation. The Genevans are more rigidly logical and it would have been, perhaps, more wise of the Bremeners to shelter behind Calvin's own idea that God's justice is not to be measured in mere human terms.

Yet Bremen obviously shared to some extent the Arminian idea that God's goodness can be equated with what we know as good. This is an idea which is found to some extent among other delegations such as those from Utrecht and the Palatinate.

Thus it is seen that the Genevans are similar in conclusion to one other foreign delegation, though not in method, attitude or in their range of theological ideas. Considerable differences having thus been noted, some comparison must be attempted between the Genevans and other delegations. The Dutch Professors,[272] Gomarus, Polyander, and Walaeus, state that the death of Christ was of sufficient worth to expiate all the sins of all men and so bring them to salvation, and that this must be preached to all men. Yet they emphasize that it must be left to God to disperse grace and that Christ is not dead for the reprobate, but only the elect. They support this by seven separate arguments (which are worthy of further examination) and conclude by rejecting remonstrant theses. A similar judgment comes from the Walloon Churches,[273] whose delegates stated that all men could be purchased through the sacrifice of Christ if only all believed, for Christ is dead only for the believers. Christ was ordained by God as propitiation for the sins, not of all men, but only of believers, and his merit is reconciliation and the remission of sins. They also include a list of rejected remonstrant doctrines. The Swiss[274] stated that by his death, Christ obtained benefits for the elect alone. None that perish, do so because of any insufficiency in Christ. The Father gave the elect to his Son to purchase, and the Son purchased the elect alone. Thus Christ died only for the elect, and not for the reprobate. They ask, as a metaphor, if anyone pays a ransome for a prisoner if it will do no good to the poor wretch, and thus they deny that Christ endured death for men who are never converted and whom He will never save. They deny the remonstrant idea that God predestined Christ as mediator before he had any intention of saving any particular people. They also seem to attack Martinius by stating that Christ's death cannot serve very many.

Conclusion and Canons

From these considerations, general and particular, of the second article, a number of simple conclusions can be drawn. From the general considerations it appears that the Genevans propounded a doctrine of the death of Christ that is quite different to the Anselmianism of the other delegations. The Genevans are not entirely alone in alluding to Christ as head of the Church as it is an idea that is known to the Swiss and to the Zeelanders, but these other delegations are also Anselmian. This is not to suggest that the Genevans disapprove of the Anselmianism of the other delegations, but they choose to use a different theology. Secondly, it is to be seen that the Genevans include an accommodating clause in their theses to ensure that there was no rift between their theses and those of the other delegations.

A further conclusion which can be drawn from the Genevan's failure to use the Anselmian doctrine of redemption, is that they are not only out of accord with all of reformed Protestantism as represented in the Synod of Dort, but also with seventeenth century Lutheran orthodoxy, for as G. Aulen has written in his

Christus Victor:-

> The doctrine of the Atonement in Lutheran Orthodoxy is not simply identical with that of Anselm; but the differences must not be exaggerated, and they do not in the least involve any departure from the essential Latin type. The strange thing is that the medieval doctrine of the Atonement remained, in a slightly modified form, while the penitential system and the idea of penance, on which it had originally been built up, had completely disappeared. The broad similarity of this doctrine with that of Anselm consists primarily in the fact that the whole conception is dominated by the idea of satisfaction; the satisfaction is treated as a rational necessity, the only possible method by which Atonement can be affected. Protestant Orthodoxy thus follows Anselm more closely than the usual medieval teaching.[275]

From the particular considerations, it becomes obvious that Genevan theology formed part of a curiously uniform climate of reformed theological opinion. The basic elements of each statement are very similar, there is emphasis on the sufficiency of Christ's death, but that Christ only truly died for the elect through the French Low Country delegates substitute "believers" for "elect".

The omnipotence of God and the helplessness of man is a constant underlying theme. One point where the Genevans seem to be a little different from other delegations, is that they do not explicitly mention sufficient grace, yet

Diodati read Du Moulin'a letter in which it is an idea that is accepted. It is as if the Genevans, believing that Christ died only for the elect, thought that it matters not at all if Christ had sufficient grace for all men. The Swiss, however, felt it necessary to state that the non-elect were not reprobate because of any insufficiency of Christ, an idea that was included in the canons. The Genevans are similar in conclusion to other delegations, but not in method, or range of theological ideas. It is clear that the orthodox have one dogma, but different theologies.

And what of the Canons of Dort? There is much in them that is not Genevan, for these too are inherently Anselmian as may be seen from thesis 1, where the problem of justice is seen as fundamental, and from the second, and third theses:-

> 1 Deus non tantum est summe misericors, sod etiam summe justus. Postulat autem eius justitiae (prout se in verbo revelavit) ut peccata nostra, adversis infinitam eius Majestatem commissa, non tantum temporalibus, sed etiam aeternis, tum animi, tum corporis poenis, puniatur: quas poenas effugere non possumus, nisi justitiae Die satisfiat.
>
> 2 Cum vero ipsi satisfacere, et ab ira Dei nos liberare non possimus, Deus ex immensa misericordia Filium suum unigenitum nobis sponsorem dedit, qui, ut pro nobis satisfaceret, peccatum et maledicto in cruce pro nobis, seu vice nostra, factus est.
>
> 3 Haec mors Filii Dei est unica et perfectissima pro peccatis victima et satisfactio, infiniti valoris et pretii, abunde sufficiens ad totius mundi peccata expianda.[276]

Thus it may be seen that the Canons are formed out of the kind of Anselmianist concept of redemption that has been discussed above. But this does not entail either a rejection or a condemnation of the Genevan position for there is, in the Canons, an acknowledgment of Christ as head of the Church.

> Hoc consilium, ex aeterno erga electos amore profectum ab initio mundi in praesens usque tempus, frustra obnitentibus inferorum portis, potenter impletum fuit, et deinceps, quoque implebitur: ita quidam ut electi suis temporibus in unum colligantur, et semper sit aliqua credentium Ecclesia in sanguine Christi fundata; quae illum Servatorem suum, qui pro ea, tanquam sponsus pro sponsa, animam suam in cruce exposuit, constanter diligat, perseveranter colat, atque hic et in omnem acternitatem celebrat.[277]

Thus, from this, the final conclusion may be drawn that there is a definite proof of Genevan influence in the Canons. It also serves to show that the other participants in the Synod of Dort were not prepared to ignore or criticise the position of the Genevan delegates, even when they accepted quite different theologies.

The Genevan theological contribution - Articles III & IV *De hominis corruptione et conversione ad Deum, eiusque modo.*

The third and fourth articles, concerning the effectiveness of grace and free will, were always discussed together. The Genevans[278] believed that man by himself could not hope for the kingdom of God without the aid of the Spirit. Man's turning to God is a latent effect of the grace of the Holy Spirit. Those who are regenerate have a change of heart, which is to say that conversion is followed by new life. The regeneration comes from true union with Christ. Yet, by its natural corruption, the will of the "old man" continues to resist, but this malice cannot resist effective grace and so the will cannot repudiate the Spirit. God himself works in conversion just as He engenders it. On the other hand, the natural malice is not weakened in those whom God does not regenerate.

> Genevan thesis 1 Homo animalis, id est, non habens Spiritum Dei, nullam habet vel in intellectu, vel in voluntate facultatem, dispositionem, vel aptitudinem ad ea quae sunt Regni Dei intelligenda, credenda, facienda, speranda; imo sicut mens ipsius morae sunt tenebrae, ita voluntas est inimicitia adversus Deum, qua perpetuo resistit, nequs unquam subiicitur Deo.
> Genevan thesis 8 Malitia cordis gratiae efficaci non potest resistere, quia per gratiae infusionem aufertur, debilitatur, mortificatur, et tandem plane aboletur: Et quod homo regenitus stat pro Spiritu contra carnem et peccatum suum proprium, est motus gratiae, et Spiritus ipsius; ubi infirmatur Spiritus, tum ad carnem proclivis sit etc labitur, sed nunquam spiritualis voluntas resistit Spiritui, sed gemit, si a voluntate carnali abripitur, et opprimitur.[279]

The Canons[280] contain all the ideas expressed by the Genevans, but their treatment includes many elements ignored by Tronchin and Diodati. They stress human responsibility, the fact that by his fall, man bereaved himself, and that corruption descended to Adam's posterity not by imitation (the Pelagian heresy), but by the propagation of a vicious nature. The Canons also include the idea of law, ignored by the Genevans, and point out (article 5) that the decalogue merely exposes the magnitude of sin, but does not disclose a remedy. The Canons claim that God revealed himself to fewer people under the Old Testament. The Canons point out that all are called by the Gospel but point out a fact ignored by the Genevans, that all do not come is the fault neither of the Gospel nor of Jesus Christ (article 9). The Canons (article 17) insist that the power of God does not set aside the use of the Gospel. There is thus a considerable difference between the Genevan theses and the Canons on the two articles. The Canons in no way contradict the Genevan doctrine, but they contain very many relevant ideas left out by the Genevans. The treatment in the Canons is much more comprehensive, but like the Genevan statements, they stress man's total depravity and the irresistible grace of God. The main theological difference is that the

Canons attempt to reconcile human responsibility with divine grace. The Genevans, with perhaps more logic, made no attempt to do so.

> Canons thesis 1: Homo ab initio ad imaginem Dei conditus, vera et salutari sui Creatoris et rerum spiritualium notitia in mente, et justitia in voluntate et corde, puritate in omnibus affectibus exornatus, adeoque totus sanctus fuit, sed diaboli instinctu, et libera sua voluntate a Deo desciscens, eximiis istis donis seipsum orbavit; atque a contrario eorum loco coecitatem, horribles tenebras, vanitatem ac perversitetam judicii in mente, malitiam, rebellionem, ac duritiem, in voluntate, et corde, imperitatem deinque in omnibus affectibus contraxit.[281]
>
> Canons thesis 3: Quae luminis naturae eadem hid Decalogi per Mosen a Deo Tudaeis peculiariter traditi est ratio. Cum enim is magnitudinem quidem peccati retegat, eiusque hominem megis ac magis reum peragat, sed nec remedium, sed nec remedium exhibeat, nec vires emergendi ex miseria conferat, adeoque per carnem infirmatus transgressorem in maledictione relinquat, non potest homo per cum salutarem gratiam obtinere.[282]

The Canons also include the Calvinist idea of how men might have a real, natural knowledge of God that is useless for salvation. The Canons are also concerned with the identity of both natural and revealed law while the Genevans refer in general terms only to the topic of revelation.

The Swiss theologians[283] also had their reasons as to why all men are not saved. They suggested (article 9) that all men are called, but that the means of salvation are not given to all men. Like the Genevans, the Swiss stated (article 7) that reprobate man naturally resists the promise of grace, and that the flesh perpetually fights against the Spirit. Unlike the Genevans, however, the Swiss (article 8) stated that the will of the elect can resist just as much as that of the unregenerate. The Swiss state other arguments ignored by the Genevans; that man lost all by the Fall and was despoiled of his ability to know the law of God (article 1), and that man is responsible for his own judgment even if it is harsh, for he has been given the law (article 3). Yet in spirit the Swiss are very similar to the Genevans, they state that the understanding is blind, so that it cannot recognise spiritual good, and that preaching is useless if not backed by the work of the Holy Spirit (article 4), that the will of man is not a cause of conversion (article 5) and that the will comes to seek good after conversion and begins to concur actively, even though God actually does all that is necessary (article 6).

> Swiss thesis 1: Homo ante lapsum integer fuit, liber ac bonus, ut intellectu suo, cum caeteras omnes, tum creatoris sui praecepta rectissimo nosse, voluntate sua bonum ab intellectu monstratum apprehendere, et affectus reliquos sibi, si vellet subjectos habere posset. Per lapsum vero his omnibus excidit, et qualis a lapsu factus est ipse, tales ex ipso sunt posteri

omnine omnes. Intellectus humanus Dei salutari cognitione
orbatus; arbitrium sua ad bonum supernaturale apprehendum
libertate spoliatum; affectus reliqui, cum Dei lege et recta ratione conformitate, privati; deinque omnia corrupta ac dapra-
vata sunt adeo, ut homo miser nihil salutaris vereque boni
cogitare vel velle, Deum non vere nosse, nec Deum aut prox-
imum diligare, aut quicquam aliud, quod scitu, creditu, factu,
speratu ad salutem est necessarium, viribus naturalibus capere
aut efficere vel velit, vel possit.[284]

Thus the Genevan theses are somewhat different to the Canons and to the
Swiss theses, but there is more dissimilarity between the theologians about these
two points than about the other articles, and the basic fact remains that in each
case the theological framework is essentially similar. The Swiss, here as elsewhere, use a more scholastic language than the other delegations.[285] Thus, the
third and fourth articles also serve to show that the orthodox theologians at the
Synod of Dort had one dogma, but that they supported this dogma by using
different theologies.

The Genevan theological contribution - Article V *De perseverante sanctorum.*

The subject matter of the fifth article under discussion was the matter of the
perseverance of the elect in faith. This was a traditional doctrine of the reformed
churches. It had been discussed by Calvin in the *Institutes*[286] and in other theological writings.[287] There had been various interpretations of *perseverantia sanctorum* in the past. An Englishman, William Tyndale, had interpreted 1 John 3/9 to
mean:- "they that are born of God cannot sin; for the seed of God keepeth
them."[288] This crude idea of perseverance had been declared anathema by the
Council of Trent, a decision of which John Calvin apparently approved.[289] Nor
was Calvin the only sixteenth century reformed theologian to note this doctrine,
for it is to be found in the writings of Amandus Polanus von Polandorf,
Wollebius[290] and Zanchius.[291]

As well as the discussion of *perseverantia sanctorum* to be found in the
Canons, another seventeenth century expression of this doctrine is to be found
in the Westminster Confession of Faith. Interestingly, it is not included in Archbishop Ussher's *Irish Articles* of 1615 on which the Westminster Confession was
so largely based.

Indeed, it might be suggested that this doctrine was most readily accepted
in the English speaking world. Another English puritan, Richard Baxter, defended the Synod of Dort's interpretation in his preface to a book written in
1658.[292] Even before Dort, the Aberdeen Assembly of the Church of Scotland had
a confession imposed on it by King James VI & I which stated in Bezan terms.

> We believe that the elect being renewed, or sealed with the
> Holie Spirit of promise in such sort, that albeit they beare about
> in their flesh the remnants of that originall corruption, and
> albeit they offend through infirmitie, and through the entise-
> ments thereof, sinne greivouslie, to the great offense of God,
> yit they cannot altogether fall from grace, but are raised againe
> through the mercie of God, and kepied to salvation.[293]

Yet despite this evidence of the acceptance of this doctrine by the reformed Churches, it does seem not to have been a particularly essential part of their theology. James VI & I, whose theologians defended this doctrine at Dort on his own orders, had himself opposed it at the Conference of Hampton Court in 1604.[294] Beza did discuss it, and perseverance is, for him, certainly one of the marks of a man who is truly elect. He does, however, approach the doctrine in a different way and links it to instructions to undertake good works[295] which are another important mark of election. But an orthodox theologian like William Ames, appointed to the University of Franeker in Friesland shortly after the Synod of Dort in 1622,[296] did not find it necessary to include it in his *Medulla Theologica* of 1641.[297] Even stranger than this is the fact that neither the Belgic Confession of 1561 [298] nor the Heidelberg Catechism of 1563 [299] both accepted as subordinate standards useful for teaching by the Dort assembly, makes mention of *perseverantia sanctorum*. There are two possible solutions. Firstly, this doctrine may have been considered as unfit for non-theological discussion and so not useful for teaching. The other possibility is that since there was a remonstrant statement, the members of the Synod believed it must be corrected by an ortho- dox statement, based largely on historical material. It is, after all, a problem debated since St Augustine, both before and after the reformation, though most notably by Gerson. The idea that such doctrine was not fit for all people seems to be accepted by the English delegation:- "Porro at illud monemus, inter ea, quae certa sunt, et in verbo divino solide fundata, esse tamen, quedam, quae non sunt omnibus promiscus inculcanda, sed suo loco et tempore prudentar attin- genda."[300] This is an idea that Joseph Hall also included in his farewell speech to the Synod.[301]

The Genevans state this doctrine in twelve theses, and the Canons in fifteen. In general there is little difference between these two statements, and there is a broad similarity in attitude and treatment.[302] The Genevans begin by stating that God's elect are unable to fail completely through sin. Man cannot persevere without God's help, and his perseverence follows election and justifi- cation, though the election is revealed by the perseverance. Those who fall away completely, who do not persevere, are therefore not elect, and must have imper- fect faith and regeneration. The really faithful persevere in grace with the aid of the Holy Spirit which is the cause of perseverance. Perseverance is the first stage in the process which leads to eternal life. The truly faithful can sin, but not in such a fashion as to destroy their union with Christ. When the faithful sin, they are conserved by the grace of God, and they are afterwards restored through penitence. The faithful know they are members of Christ by the working of the Holy Spirit within them, which protects them from the world and assures them of their perseverance. The Genevan statement concludes with the customary claims that perseverance is in accord with scripture, and that to contravene it is to rob the faithful of consolation and to deny the majesty of God.

The formulation of this doctrine in the Cannons of Dort is very similar, but a few differences may be noted. The Genevans note the unpleasant fate of the non-elect (theses 5) while the Canons do not. The Canons claim (thesis 9) that God will not tempt the elect beyond their strength to persevere, and while this may be implicit in the Genevan statement (theses 8), it is not explicit. Another difference is that the Canons (thesis 14) mention the means of grace, including preaching and the sacraments, in a more definite fashion than the Genevan theses. One interesting idea of the Genevans that does not appear in the Canons, is that while eternal life follows perseverance, this is in manner of order and not of cause, (thesis 7).

> Canons thesis 9: De hac electorum ad salutem custodia, vereque fidelium in fide perseverantia, ipsi fideles certi esse possunt, et sunt, pro mensura fidei, qua certo credunt se esse et perpetuo mansuros vera et viva Ecclesiae membra, habera remissionem peccatorum, et vitam aeternam.[303]
>
> Canons thesis 14: Quaemadomodum autem Deo placuit, opus hoc suum gratiae per praedicationem Evangelii in nobin inchoare, ita per ejusdem auditum, lectionem, meditationem, adhortationes, minas, promisea, nec non per usum Sacramentorum, illud conservat, continuat, et perficit.[304]
>
> Genevans thesis 7: Perseverantia est imago, imo principium vitae aeternae, et ista illem consequitur, ut adolescentia infantiam, virilitas adolescentiam, etc. per modum ordinis, non caussae. (sic)[305]
>
> Genevans thesis 8: Vera fideles cum succumbunt tentationibus, et a Diabolo et carne vel seducuntur vel abripiuntur, non propterea totaliter deficiunt a Christo, spiritu, fide, nec dona ejus omnia profundunt: quandoquidem peccatum, quantumvis atrox non statim abrumpit vinculum nostri cum Christo: quod sola impoenitentia finalis, delectatio et obdurantio intima, et gloriatio in malo, et peccatum in Spiritum sanctum praestarent, si in electos cadere possent.[306]

Despite these differences there is a broad similarity between the Genevan statement and the articles of the Synod of Dort on the fifth article. However, when the Genevan statement is compared with those of other delegations, more significant differences begin to appear. The Dutch theologian Lubbertus[307] notes that perseverance is not a habit but a gift of God. He quotes the Lord's prayer as evidence of Christ's recognition of our need to be delivered from evil. God gives it to the elect to persevere, but they retain the ability to sin and thus thwart God though not in such a manner as to lose the Grace of God. This doctrine consoles the faithful, for without God's help they would be unable to persevere. This statement of Lubbertus, was signed as being acceptable to the other Dutch professors who were present at the Synod of Dort. This is clearly a similar doctrine to that of the Genevans, but the method is very different.

> Perseverentia qua usque ad finem perseveratur in Christo,
> differt a perseveratione. Haec enim est actio, illa est habitus,
> vel instar habitus. Perseverantia est gratuim Dei donum.[308]

It might also be noted that the Canons do not avoid metaphysical terms such as *actio* and *habitus* which are foreign to the Genevans as has already been seen in the case of the third and fourth articles where the Swiss used more obviously scholastic language. This was also typical of Ursinius in considering the subject of Perseverance for the *Heidelberg Catechism*.

The method of the Swiss[309] is also different. As usual, they quote neither scripture nor patristics and include no rejection of errors, but their statement is written in *le patois de Canaan*. They state that those whom God has given to his Son cannot be lost, and they attribute perseverance to the virtue of the father, the guard of the Son and the observation of the Spirit. Thus the attributes of the Trinity are involved in a manner dissimilar to the other statements discussed above. The faithful persevere because they are upheld by God, whereas they would fail if left to themselves, yet they can sin, but, and this is the idea present in the Canons and not in the Genevan theses, God cannot let their temptation be too great for they will be upheld by Him and led to bliss. The elect can be certain of their perseverance. They also sin, but after assurance of perseverance they gradually die to sin. The Swiss expound more ideas ignored by the Genevans when they emphasize the means of grace which God uses to expedite this counsel, and when they stress the necessity of prayer.

> text of Swiss thesis 2; Est nempe Patris eligentis voluntas, ut
> quoscunque; dedit Filio, non pereant; sed novissimo die ad
> vitam aeternam resuscitentur. Est Filii Redemptoris voluntas,
> ut a Patre dati, sint secum, et secum vivant, spectenque; glo-
> riam suam in aeternum. Spiritus Sanctus quoque Paracletus
> cum electis manet in aeternum. Et revera, quos Deus Pater pro
> libera voluntate sua elegit misericorditer, quos Dei Filius san-
> guine pretioso suo redemit, quos Spiritus Sanctus illuminavit
> et sanctificavit, ii gratiose certo que servantur et perducuntur
> ad finem destinatum potenter.[310]

The English statement[311] is quite different to the Genevan for it is much longer and it contains discussion of ideas ignored by the other delegations such as whether those who are not elect can become sanctified and justified. They discuss other ideas such as the possibility of perseverance of the non-elect. They claim that if the elect died in a state of unrepentant sin, that they would not attain to eternal life, but they consider that God will not let any of his elect die before they have repented of any sins which might suspend their perseverance. The elect have a right to enter the kingdom of Heaven, this right cannot be lost, but the state of adoption can remain immobile. The leper who leaves home to be cured does not lose the right to enter his house, though he may not do so until he is cured. God does not adopt those as children that He will later have to reject, and sin cannot destroy grace. The British delegates attribute the perseverance of the faithful to the deliverance of Christ. They see it as a free gift of God which can be discovered and proved by the decree of election. They claim that each of the faithful might be certain of being guarded in true faith by the mercy of God and so led to eternal salvation and yet they will have periods in which they will be uncertain of this. If the Spirit becomes sufficiently weak, spiritual consolation can be withdrawn from us while God hides from us the light of his countenance as in Job. Yet, for the truly elect, the periods of despair will end and they will return to spiritual health and to growth in grace.

Thus it may be concluded that while the Genevans' contribution to the Dort discussion of this doctrine of *perseverantia sanctorum* was in broad accordance with the opinion of other delegations, there were a number of distinct dissimilarities in doctrine and more profound dissimilarities with regard to method. The general formulation of doctrine remains similar and Geneva is not noticeably at variance with the other interpretations presented to the Synod. This view is confirmed by the similarity of the Genevan statement to the text of the Canons.

However, when Calvin's doctrine of perseverance is examined and compared to that of the Genevans at Dort, notable dissimilarities at once become apparent. The basis of the doctrine remains the same; the true believer, the elect, cannot fall away.[312] Yet there are three distinct and significant ideas in Calvin's doctrine which are not in that of the Genevans at Dort. The first of these is the idea of human response. This idea is given in the *Institutes* 3.24.6; - "Let us therefore embrace Christ, who is graciously offered to us, and comes to meet us. He will reckon us in his flock and enclose us within his fold." The second idea is that of general and special calling, the idea that Christ calls the whole world, but that a special call is reserved for believers alone, that is, the elect. This idea shows a concern for the non-elect that was shared by the British as has been discussed above. The third doctrine that is found in Calvin and is ignored by the Genevans at Dort, is that the elect are capable of faithlessness and sin, except for the ultimate sin of unpardonable blasphemy, before they receive God's call.

There is, however, a longer Genevan contribution offered to the Synod of Dort concerning this doctrine. This is the address of Tronchin to the Synod, of which a manuscript is to be found in the Archives Tronchin of the Musee historique de la Reformation in Geneva. It has never been published. In this speech, Tronchin was aware of the possibility of sin by the elect, for he mentions Peter's denial of Christ and the flight of the disciples, but he does not discuss it with the same personal concern of Calvin, being happy to rest assured that Christ is stronger than Satan. Tronchin also briefly discusses the problem of response, but in a manner alien to Calvin. Those who do not vanquish the world, he says, are not born of God. Yet if they vanquish the world it is not their victory but God's. Tronchin betrays no obvious interest in those who do not believe. Neither does Tronchin mention preaching and the sacraments as do the Canons, though he does discuss the place of the pastoral ministry.

Thus the same theological differences are to be seen in a longer document. This is evidence that these were not ideas that were excluded merely because of space or for some other practical reason. Thus there is a real difference between

Calvin's own thoology and that of the Genevan representatives by the Synod of Dort.

Once again it has been demonstrated that the orthodox theologians of the reformed churches in the seventeenth century had different theologies by which they supported the same basic dogma.

Notes

[1]McNeill, *History and Character of Calvinism*, p. 221.

[2]McNeill, *op.cit.*, p. 321.

[3]O. Chadwick, *The Reformation*, p. 221.

[4]*The Oxford Dictionary of the Christian Church* p. 417.

[5]G. Leonard, *Histoire generale du Protestantisme*, vol. II, p. 221.

[6]*D.N.B.* vol. XIV, p. 101.

[7]*D.N.B.* vol. XXIV, p. 77.

[8]J.L. Motley, *The life and death of John of Barneveld*, p. 309, pp. 310-11.

[9]P. Schaff, *Creeds of Christendom*, p. 515n2.

[10]*ibid* pp. 513-4.

[11]Lord Acton, *Lectures on modern history*, (Fontana edition) 1960, pp. 170-1.

[12]*The Oxford dictionary of the Christian Church*, p. 417.

[13]See bibliography of Dort, Appendix 2, p. 422, Vols. III and IV were edited by his son.

[14]*Nieuw Nederlandsch Biografisch Woordenboek*, vol. VI, cols. 184-6.

[15]*D.N.B.*, vol. XXVI, pp. 319-23.

[16]Brandt, Dutch edition, vol. III, p. 469, English ed., III/236-7.

[17]Hales, *Golden Remains*, part 2, p. 14.

[18]*D.N.B.* vol. III, pp. 25-26.

[19]P. Heylyn, *Historia Quinquarticularis*, p. 529.

[20]P. Heylyn, *Aerius Redivivus*, p. 396.

[21]*ibid* p. 396.

[22]P. Heylyn, *Historia Quinquarticularis*, p. 532.

[23]*ibid*, p. 532.

[24]*ibid*, pp. 529-30.

[25]E. Lavisse, *Histoire de France*, vol. VII, part 2, pp. 214-5.

[26]P. Itterzon, "Koning Jacobus I an de Synode van Dordrecht", in *Nederlands Archief voor Kerkgeschiedenis*, 1932, vol. XXIV, pp. 187-204.

[27]H. Hauser, *La preponderance Espagnole 1559-1660*, Peuples et civilisations, p. 283.

[28]P. Heylyn, *Aerius Redivivus*, p. 397.

[29]A.M. Toplady, *The History of the Doctrinal Calvinism of the Church of England*, pp. 614-6.

[30]P. Schaff, *Creeds of Christendom*, p. 513.

[31]*D.N.B.* vol. XX, p. 315.

[32]*D.N.B.* vol. XIV, p. 101.

[33]Fuller, *Church History* etc., p. 318.

[34]*Le Grand Dictionnaire etc. . . . . Commence en 1674 par Mre Louis Moreri* 2nd edition, Basel, 1733, vol. 3, p. 594.

[35]See Appendix 2, Bibliography of the Synod of Dort, under 1620/4, 6, 8, 11 and 1624/1, 1668/1.

[36]P. Heylyn, *Historia Quinquarticularis*, p. 532.

[37]A.M. Toplady, *op. cit.*, pp. 626-7:- Mr. *Hales*, writing from Dort to Sir *D. Carleton*, who was then at the Hague, thus expressed himself, in relation to the Contumacy and Petulence of the Arminians: "The State of our Synod now suffers a great Crisis; and, one Way or

other, there must be an Alteration; Either the *Remonstrants* must yield, and submit himself to the Synod . . . or else, the Synod must vail to them: . . . . But the Arminian Fierceness was too harsh and stubborn to be moderated by any lenient Measures. And, hitherto none but softening Measures had been Tryed. For, those decrees of the Synod, extorted from the Synod by Dint of Insolence, and which carry'd any implication of seeming Severity, were, as Mr. *Hales* observes, "mere Powder and Shot, which gives a Clap, but does no harm:" Insomuch that, as the same unprejudiced Writer adds, "Some thought the Synod had been *too favorable* to the Remonstrants already; and that it were best now not to hold them, if they would be going: since, hitherto, they (the Remonstrants, or *Arminians*) had been, and, for any thing appeared to the contrary, meant hereafter to be, an Hinderance to all peaceable and orderly proceedings." And such they most undoubtedly were, in every Respect, and on every Occasion.

[38]The Acta are also used by G.P. van Itterzon in his "De Canones van Dordrecht, Dogmenhistorisch" in *Kerk en Theologie* no. 26, April 1975. This is a study of the dogmatic content of the Canon:- and a rather disappointing one at that. There is no mention of Anselmian redemption theory and only the Canons, not the delegation statements, are used. The best section is his note on Pelagianism, pp. 148-50.

[39]Graf, *op. cit.*, p. 205.

[40]J. Lecler, *Histoire de la tolerance au siecle de la Reforme*, vol. 2, pp. 263-72.

[41]Fuller, *op. cit.*, p. 314.

[42]G. Fatio, *Geneve et les Pays Bas* (Geneva, 1928) p. 41.

[43]H. de Vries de Heeckelingen, *Geneve Pepiniere du Calvinisme Hollondais* (The Hague, 1924) p. 344.

[44]H. de Vries de Heeckelingen, *op. cit., p. 353*.

[45]*ibid.* pp. 369-70.

[46]*ibid.* p. 385.

[47]*ibid.* pp. 386-406.

[48]Geneva, Archives d'Etat, Registres du Conseil de Geneve, 3 Jan 1619 au 1 Jan. 1620, p. 75.

[49]Report of Tronchin to Conseil, ms in Musee historique de la reformation, ms Archives Tronchin, vol. 17.

[50]Musee historique de la reformation, ms Archives Tronchin, vol. 17, fol. 164.

[51]J.-A. Gautier, *Histoire de Geneve*, (Geneva 1909), vol. VII, pp. 129-30.

[52]Acta 1/11-13. The full title of the edition of the Acta that is used here is:- "*Acta / Synodi / Nationalis, / In nomine Domini nostri / Iesu Christi, / Authoritate / Illustr. et Praepotentium DD. Ordinum / Generalium Foederati / Belgii Provinciarum, / Dordrechti / Habitae / Anno 1618 et 1619 / Accedunt Plenissima, de Quinque Articulis, / Theologorum Iudicia. /* Dordrechti, Typis Isacci Ioannidis Canini / et Sociorum, 1620," The Acta have a complex printing history, see bibliography in Appendix 3, and the various editions are perhaps best distinguished by the name of the printer rather than by the title.

[53]F. Turrettini, *Institutio Theologiae Elencticae* 1/20-1.

[54]Brandt, Dutch edition, III, p. 31.

[55]Sir Dudley Carleton, *Letters*, p. 303.

[56]Acta, 1/19-24. There is nothing useful for this in M. Graf *Beitrage* etc.

[57]Acta, 1/21.

[58]D.N.B. vol LIX, p. 335.

[59]T.H. Darlow and H. F. Moule, *Historical Catalogue of the Printed Editions of Holy Scripture* etc., vol. II, no. 3307, p. 309.

[60]*Acta* 1/33-4.

[61]Brandt, Dutch edition, 3/76. English ed. 3/38.

[62]Hales, *op. cit.*, part 1, p. 23.

[63]Actes 1/84-5. The French text has been used because the Latin text confounds the Swiss and Genevan statements.

[64]See pp. 2,3 above.

[65]Hales, *op. cit.*, 2/12.

[66]Brandt, Dutch edition, 3/457. English ed. III/231.

[67]Hales, *op. cit.*, 2/14.

[68]Brandt, Dutch edition, 3/469-70, English edition 3/236-7:- *Deodatus had taken it upon himself to proceed; but being prevented by sickness his Colleague Tronchinus would supply his place, and make an end as he had desired him:* and it is said in *Balcanqual's letters,* That he maintained with credit the doctrine of the *Perseverance* of the *Saints*. But in the brief Notes or Diary of *Poppius,* which I have lately seen, I find that he said little concerning the doctrine and that his discourse was very confused. And in the *Historical Account* of the *Remonstrants,* his argumentations are represented after the following manner: "He struck at the *Remonstrants,* in the Introduction of his discourse, by saying, *That these Provinces had been tormented with an Article sickness.* Then he went on, and, in treating of *Perseverance,* discoursed somewhat loosly of the promises, which are conditional, and of their certainty. In the confusion, he adjured the Government, that after so great victories, by which they had reduced their enemies to despair, they would depend and maintain this sweet and comfortable doctrine in their churches; further exhorting the Clergy to insinuate the same doctrine into the minds of their hearers, and always to maintain it, without scrupling the pains it might cost them; adding they were like sheep among wolves, but that God would give them the victory over their adversaries. He warned them to beware of Philosophy for the *Remonstrants,* he said, had borrowed all their arguments from *Aristotle's Morals,* against which they ought to be on their guard. 'The conclusion of his speech was: *That as* Hippocrates *said in his Book of Dreams, that those who dreamt that they saw the Sun flee from them and that they were for following it, discovered a certain symptom of an approaching deprivation of their senses: So they who were for giving up this comfortable doctrine, betrayed a sure sign of their being about to fall into desperation and madness.* As soon as he had made an end of speaking the President returned him hearty thanks, and then declared, that herewith an end was put to the publick discussion of the *Five Articles.*

[69]Hales, *op. cit.*, 2/20.

[70]Brandt, Dutch Edition, 3/501-2, English edition 3/252-3:- *'Deodatus* whose turn of haranguing in publick had been now superseded several times, on account of his indisposition, treated about the *Perseverance of the Saints.* He said, among other things, 'That some of those who were *Reprobated* received sometimes very great and extraordinary gifts, and thereby seemed to be true believers, and highly exalted in the knowledge of the will of God, appearing to take more pains, and to exert a greater zeal for religion than others; but their faith not being founded on eternal *Election,* they fell at last, and their punishment became the more severe. *On the other hand,* That the Elect might and did fall into great and grevious sins, and even shameful villanies, but nevertheless, did not totally fall from the grace of God; and therefore were at last converted and saved. *Solomon* might fall, as far as he could, thro' royal luxury and licentiousness, but his wisdom, or the seed of faith, remained in him, and never deserted him.

"He spoke of the doctrine of *Reprobation* in the milder terms than the *Contraremonstrants* were wont to do, denying *that sin was a fruit of* Reprobation. When he came to the *Remonstrants* arguments, relating to their opinion of *Perseverance,* he was heard to say 'That he was not prepared to answer the evasions and exceptions of those new Philosophers, who by their subtilties and niceities overturned all principles, and brought all things into doubt. As for him, he would keep to his good old ways." As soon as he had ended his speech, the President returned him thanks after an extraordinary manner, telling him, *That he had made this excellen't Oration, which was extracted from the quintessence of practical Divinity, by the inspiration of the Holy Ghost.*

[71]Sir Dudley Carleton, *Letters* etc., pp. 319-20.

[72]Geneva, Musee historique de la reformation, Archives Tronchin, vol. XVII.

[73]Brandt, Dutch edition 3/448; English edition 3/227.

[74]Brandt, English edition, III/287.

[75]Geneva, Musee historique de la reformation, Archives Tronchin Vol. XVII, fol. 146f, remarks by Tronchin on Belgic Confession.

[76]*Acta*, 1/289-300.

[77]H. Jedin, *Geschichte des Konzils von Trient* I/232-52 et passim.

[78]E. & E. Haag, *La France protestante* 7/505-6.

[79]There is an appendix of documents on the Morely affair in H. Meylan, A. Dufour & C. Chimelli *Correspondance de Theodore de Beze* 8/211-30 (Geneva 1976). See also T. Maruyama "The reform of the true Church. The Ecclesiology of Theodore Beza" chapter 5, a 1973 Princeton thesis to be published by Droz in Geneva.

[80]A. de la Roche Chandieu *La Confirmation de la discipline ecclesiastique* etc. p. 75, *et passim*.

[81]*Acta*, 1/102-4.

[82]*Acta*, 2/58.

[83]*Biblia Vulgata*, 2/250.

[84]Beza, *Iesu Christi D.N. Novu testamentu* etc., (Geneva 1567) leaf 353: Omne munus bornū et omne donū est perfectū supernē, descendens a Patre luminū, apud quē nō est transmutatio, aut cōversionis obumbratio.

[85]Diodati 1607 *Bibbia* 3/276.

[86]Diodati 1640/41 *Bibbia* 2/297.

[87]*Acta* 3/24.

[88]*Acta* 3/175.

[89]*Acta* 3/193.

[90]*Acta* 3/216 and 3/217.

[91]*Acta* 3/175.

[92]*Acta* 2/58.

[93]*Acta* 3/28.

[94]T. Beza, *Iesu Christi D.N. Novum testamentum* etc., 1567, leaf 393.

[95]*Acta* 2/78.

[96]*Acta* 3/224.

[97]*Acta* 3/294.

[98]*ibid.* 2/54.

[99]Beza, *op. cit.*, leaf 40.

[100]*Vulgate* 2/28.

[101]Diodati 1607 *Bibbia* 3/33.

[102]Diodati 1640/41 *Bibbia* 2/32.

[103]*Acta* 2/32.

[104]*Acta* 2/7.

[105]*Acta* 2/226.

[106]*Acta* 3/43.

[107]*Acta* 3/46-7.

[108]*Acta* 3/48.

[109]*Acta* 3/87.

[110]*Acta* 3/262.

[111]*Acta* 3/272.

[112]*Acta* 3/293.

[113]*Acta* 3/297.

[114]*Acta* 3/71.

[115]*Acta* 2/4.

[116]*Vulgate* 2/14.

[117]*Acta* 2/3.

[118]*Vulgate* 2/206.

[119]*Acta* 2/3.

[120]*Acta* 2/3.

[121]*Vulgate* 2/170.

[122]*Vulgate* 2/206.

[123]Beza *op. cit.*, leaf 298.

[124]*Acta* 2/4.

[125]*Acta* 2/3.

[126]Beza, *op. cit.* leaf 246.

[127]*Acta* 2/3.

[128]Beza, *op. cit.* leaf 245.

[129]*Acta* 2/3.

[130]Beza, *op. cit.* leaf 246.

[131]*Acta* 2/25.

[132]Beza, *op. cit.* leaf 142.

[133]*ibid.* leaf 330.

[134]*Acta* 2/27.

[135]Beza, *op. cit.* leaf 158

[136]*Acta* 2/29.

[137]*Acta* 2/50.

[138]*Acta* 2/111.

[139]*Acta* 2/110.

[140]*Acta* 2/51.

[141]*Acta* 2/53.

[142]*Acta* 2/51.

[143]*Acta* 2/53.

[144]*Acta* 2/110.

[145]J. Calvin, *The Epistles of Paul the Apostle to the Romans and to the Thessalonians*, tr R. Mackenzie, ed. T.F. & D.W. Torrance, p. 5.

[146]Beza himself is not the Genevan source here, for of the 122 texts, 122 were used by Beza while 110 were not.

[147]Diodati, 1640/41 *Bibbia* 2/295.

[148]*ibid.*, 2/247.

[149]Diodati, 1640/41 *Bibbia* 2/246.

[150]*ibid.*, 2/233.

[151]*ibid.*, 2/312.

[152]*Acta* 1/246.

[153]*Acta* 1/152-4.

[154]Geneva, Musee historique de la Reformation, Archives Tronchin, vol. 38, fol 44r, speech of Calandrini before Conseil of Geneva in 1669:- "le plus expres contre la grace universelle est tire en propres termes du sentiment que Monsieur Deodaty et Monsieur Tronchin ont porte au Synode de Dordrecht au nom de cette Eglise."

[155]T. Beza, *De Praedestinationis Doctrina et vero usu tractatio absolutissima* (Geneva, 1583) p. 8.

[156]*Theses Theologiae in Schola Genevensi* etc (1586), theses "De aeterna Dei praedestinatione," defended by Raphael Egline of Zurich under Beza. Beza dedicated his *De Praedestinationis* to Egline who later became professor at Marburg (see F. Gardy and A. Dufour, *Bibliographie des oeuvres theologiques, litteraires historiques et juridiques de Theodore de Beze*, Geneva 1960, p. 187).

[157]T. Beza *Questions et Responses Chrestiennes* (Geneva 1584) p. 108. Another relevant passage is on p. 112:- La somme donc de ce que tu as traitte de la prouidence, est: Que rien

n'advient Dieu ne le sachant ou ne le voulant: c'est a dire, rien n'auient a l'aventure, mais du tout ainsi que Dieu l'a ordonne en son conseil eternel, disposant puissamment et avec efficace les causes d'entredeux, a fin que necessairement pour le regard de ce dernier elles viennent a la fin ordonnee: et que toutefois Dieu n'est autheur de mal quelconque, et ne l'approuve nullement, pource qu'il besonge tresiustement, par quelques instrumens qu'ils execute son oeuvre.

[158]Beza,*De Praedestinatinationis* etc. p. 147.

[159]Beza, *Ad acta colloquii Montisbelgardensis Tubingae edita.* (Geneva 1578) p. 522. See also *Theses Theologiae* etc. p. 17;- Deinde specialiter hoc decretum ad humanorum genus applicantes, Praedestinatione vocamus aeternum illud, quod et quale diximus, decretum, quo immutabiliter et aeterno constituit, in aliis quidem summa misericordia servandis, in aliis vero instissima sua severitate damnandis, sese, qualis revera est, ab effectis, summe videlicet misericordem et summe iustum, Remonstrate.

[160]Beza, *Questions et Responses* p. 121. See also J.S. Bray *Theodore Beza's doctrine of predestination*, p. 87.

[161]*ibid*, p.137.

[162]*ibid.*, p. 121.

[163]Beza, *Ad acta colloquii montisbel gardensis* p. 532.

[164]Beza, *Questions et Responses*, p. 5:-

Question. Pour cognoistre cela, que consideres-tu premierement en Dieu?

Response. Vue parfaite iustice, et une parfaite misericorde.

[165]Beza, *Confessio Christianae fidei, et eiusdem collatio cum papisticis Haeresibus* s.1. (Geneva) 1563, pp. 41-2, Hominum alii batam vitam ac salutem, alii sempiternam mortem ac miseriam consequentur, idque propter Dei gloriam, ut passim literae sacrae testantur. Itaque quum neque fortuito quicquam accidat, neque Deus unquam consilium mutet, perspicuum est Duem non modo previdisse sed etiam ab aeterno decrevisse genus hominum demonstrandae suae gloriae causa creare, alios quidem gratis servando per misericordiam, alios vero iusto suo iudicio damnando. See also Bray, *op. cit. p. 95.*

[166]*Theses Theologiae* etc. p. 18.

[167]Beza, *Ad acta colloquii Montisbelgardensis* p. 531, Conspicitur ergo institia Dei, cum in salvatis, tum etiam in damnatis. Quicunque enim in Christo electi sunt, illi etiam salvantur. Nam vita aeterna coronatur obedientia Christi, etiam in membris eius, ipsis gratis imputate, passione et morte Christi acquista. Mortis autem aeternae iusta poena, peccatores in sua miseria, iusto Dei iudicio relicti, mulctantur.

[168]Beza, *Questions et responses* p. 106.

[169]Beza, *Theses Theologiae* etc., p. 17. See Bray *op. cit.* p. 93.

[170]Beza, *Tractationum Theologicarum* (Geneva, 1582) pp. 203 (193 *sic*)-204.

[171]Kickel, *Vernunit und Offenbarung bei Theodor Beza* (Neukirchen 1967) pp. 150-2.

[172]Beza, *Tractationem Theologicarum* (Geneva 1582) p. 204.

[173]For modern discussions of Calvin's theology, see "Petit supplement aux bibliographies calviniennes 1901-1963" par une equipe de l'institut d'Histoire de la Reformation in *Bibliotheque d'humanisme et renaissance travaux et documents*, vol. XXXIII, 1971, pp. 406-7.

[174]Calvin *Institutes* 1.xvii.6.

[175]*ibid.*, 1.xv.8., 2.i.4., 2.i.10.

[176]e.g. (Perkins), *A golden chaine or the description of theologie, containing the order of the causes of salvation and damnation, according to God's word. A viewe whereof is to be seene in the Table annexed . . . adioned to the order which H. Theodore Beza used comforting afflicted consciences,* 2ed (Cambridge 1597) pp. 213-7.

[177]*Acta* 2/50:- Deus ab aeterno, ex mero beneplacito voluntatis suae, certas personas, ex semine et posteris Adae, in, et cum eodem lapsas, reas et corruptas, decrevit in Christo per et propter Christum, ex eadem in hunc finem ipsis singulariter a Patre destinatum, gratiose et efficaciter vocare, fide donare, iustificare, per Spiritum regenerationis sanctificare, et

per haec, et post naec omnia, tandem in aeternum glorificare.

[178]*Acta* 2/41-2, Damnationis causam propriam igitur, et proximam, intra impios ipsos quaerere, ecclesias nostrae fidei commissas docemus, peccatum videlicet, sive haereditarium illud, sive adversus Legem, aut Evangelium praevarication sit. Quoties item de causis damnationis facienda est mentio, non tam ad causam supremam et arcanam, justamque Dei voluntatem, quam ad hominis impij peccatum et culpam attendum esse monemus, ut palam constet, nihil damnatis praeter meritum evenire. Deum autem ad peccandum quempiam cogere, vel peccati esse autorem plane horremus. Nam Deus noster non delectatur ulla iniustitia, et odit omnes, qui operam dant iniquitati.

[179]*Acta* 2/41, Reprobationem et damnationem ipsi quoque distinguimus. Cur hunc prae illo Deus reprobaverit, extra Dei ευδοκιαν illam, causem nullam admittimus. *Quem enim vult, indurat.* Cur vero hunc vel illum damnet, propter peccatum fieri, et peroffensas reatum in hominem at damnationem venisse, magistro Apostolo, didicimus. Et revera, ut Deus non damnat nisi propter peccatum, nic damnare non decrevit, nisi propter peccatum.

[180]*Acta* 2/59, Decretum Electionis divine proprie dicte, est illa Dei voluntas, qua ipse ante jectum mundi fundamentum, sive ad aeterno, non ex respectu ullius dignitatis, quae esset in homine, sed ex mero suo beneplacito, statuit, ad singularem misericordiae et gloriae suae demonstrationem, ex corrupta per lapsum primorum parentum nostrorum ad participationem gratiae suae efficaciter vocare, justificare, et glorificare: propter Christum, per Christum, et in eo. Atique hoc est decretum electionis definitum, completum, integrum atque unicum: ad Vetus et Novum Testamentum simul spectans.

[181]*Acta* 2/60, Praeterea, hoc decretum est liberrimum, quatenus Deus irae Dei placatore et hominum reconciliatore; benignissimum, ut simul dandae salutiferae gratiae et gloriae propositum.

[182]See p. 89.

[183]*Acta 1/250,* Est autem Electio immutabile Dei propositum, quo ante jacta mundi fundamenta e universo genere humano, ex primaeva integritae in peccatum et exitium sua culpa prolapso, secundum liberrimum voluntatis suae beneplacitum, ex mera gratia, certam quorundam hominum multitudinem, aliis nec meliorum, nec digniorum, sed in communi miseria cul aliis jacentium, ad salutem elegit in Christo, quem etiam ab aeterno Mediatorem et omnium Electorum Caput, salutisque fundamentum constituit, atque ita eos ipsi salvandos dare et ad ejus communionem per verbum et Spiritum suum efficaciter vocare ac trahere, seu vera in ipsum fide donare, justificare, sanctificare, et potenter in Filii sui communione custoditos tandem glorificare decrevit, ad demonstrationem suae misericordiae, et laudem divitiarum gloriosae suae gratiae: sicut scriptum est, *Elegit nos Deus in Christo, ante jactamundi fundamenta, ut essemus sancti et inculpati in conspectu ejus, cum charitate; qui praedestinavit fundamenta, ut essemus sancti et inculpati in conspectu ejus, cum charitate; qui praedestinavit nos quos adoptaret in filios, per Iesum Christum, in sese, pro beneplacito voluntatis suae, ad laude gloriosae suae gratiae, qua nos gratis sibi acceptos fecit in illo Dilecto* Ephes 1.4.5.6. Et alibi, *Quos praedestinavit, eos etiam vocavit, et quos vocavit, eos etiam justificavit, quos autem justificavit, eos etiam glorificavit.* Rom. 8.30. and,

Acta 1/257, Deus non tantum est summe misericors, sed etiam summe justus. Postulat autem ejus justitia (prout se in verbo revelavit) ut peccata nostra, adversus infinitam ejus Majestaxtem commissa, non tantum temporalibus, sed etiam aeternis, tum animi, tum corporis poenis, effugere non possumus, nisi justitiae Dei satisfiat.

[184]Geneva, Archives d'Etat, Megistres de la Compagnie des Pasteurs 10 Jan 1612 jusqu' au 31 Dec 1619, p. 280.

[185]*The New Schaff Herzog* 9/73 etc. This view has not been modified by recent research.

[186]Hales, *Golden Remains*, 2/19.

[187]Schaff, *Creeds of Christendom*, p. 519a.

[188]On the first article the British used forty-five patristic references.

[189]*Acta* 3/3-11.

[190]*Acta* 2/50-59.

[191]Th. Tronchin, *Coton Plagiaire,* etc. See p. 44.

[192]See Chapter 6.

[193]*Acta* 1/250, already quoted as note 183 on p. 119.

[194]Text of the thesis two of the Canons, *Acta* 1/249, Verum in hoc manifesta est charitas Dei, quod Filium suum unigenitum in mundum misit, ut omnis qui credit in eum, non pereat, sed habeat vitam aeternam. 1. Johan.4.9. Johan.3.16. Text of thesis two of the Genevan statement, *Acta* 2/51, Et eadem mera ευδοκιαν, et voluntatis in sese propositio, discrevit istas personas ab aliis, in eadem massa, et sub eodem reatu existentes, nec ulla dignitate, qualitate, disposnitione aliis praecellentes.

[195]*Acta* 1/250, text of Canons thesis 8, Haec Electio non est multiplex, sed una et eadem omnium salvandorum in Vetere et Novo Testamento, quandoquidem. Scriptura unicum praedicat beneplacitum, propositum et consilium voluntatis Dei, quo nos ab aeterno elegit et ad gratiam, et ad gloriam; et ad salutem, et ad viam salutis, quam praeparavit, ut in ea ambulemus.

and *Acta* 2/55, Electio Patrum sub Vetero Testamento fuit ab eodem fonte, ad eundem finem, per eadem media principalia, atque in Novo; Id est, ex mero Beneplacito Dei, in Christo, per fidem ad salutem aeternam fuerunt ordinati.

[196]*Acta* 2/53, text of Genevan thesis 5 of election, Decretum hoc Apud Deum stat firmum et immotum, adeo ut quicunque electus est, semper ad finem gloriae, sed non nisi per media a Deo instituta et inviolabilia, perveniat; nec unquam electus fieri potest reprobus.

and *Acta* 2/57, text of Genevan thesis 4 of reprobation, Hoc decretum praeteritionibus habet etiam suam immutabilitatem et infallibilitatem: adeo ut nullus reprobus fieri possit.

and *Acta* 2/58, text of Genevan antithesis three, Electus stricte acceptus, potest fieri reprobus, et contra.

and *Acta* 1/250-51, text of Canons thesis eleven, Atque ut Deus ipse est sapientissimus, immutabilis, omniscius et omnipotentes ita Electio ab ipso facta, nec interrumpi, nec mutari, revocari, aut abrumpi, nec Electi abiici, nec numerus eorum minui potest.

[197]*Acta* 2/54, Genevan thesis six of election, Notitiam, sensum, certitudinem istius decreti Deus electis in hac vita largitur, modo, mensura, tempore, quo ipsi placet. Nec ullus est ecectus, qui aetate rationis capace, non ante mortem, certissimam istius decreti persuasionem per Spiritum Sanctum accipiat.

and *Acta* 1/251, De hac aeterna et immutabili sui ad salutem Electione, Electi suo tempore, variis licet gradibus et dispari mensura, certiores redduntur, non quidem arcana et profunditates Dei curiose scrutando, sed fructus Electionis infallibiles, in Verbo Dei designatos, ut sunt vera in Christum fides, filialis Dei timor, dolor de peccatis secundum Deum, esuries et sitis justitiae, etc. in sese cum spirituali gaudio et sancta voluptate observando.

and *Acta* 1/251, Canons thesis thirteen, Ex hujus Electionis sensu et certitudine, filii Dei majorem indies sese coram Deo humiliandi, abyssum misericordiarum ejus adorandi, seipsos purificandi, et eum, qui ipsos prior tantopere dilexit, vicissim ardenter diligendi, materiam desumunt: tantum abest, ut hac Electionis doctrina atque ejus meditatione in mandatorum divinorum observatione segniores, aut carnaliter securi, reddantur. Quod iis justo Dei judicio solet accidere, qui de Electionis gratia, vel temere praesumentes, vel otiose et proterve fabulantes, in viis electorum ambulare nolunt.

[198]*Acta* 1/249, text of Canons thesis two, Verum in hoc manifesta est charitas Dei, quod Filium suum unigenitum in mundum misit, ut omnis qui credit in eum, non pereat, sed habeat vitam aeternam.1.Johan.4.9.Johan.3.16.

and *Acta* 1/249, text of Canons thesis three, Ut autem homines ad fidem adducantur, Deus clementer laetissimi huius nuntii praecones mittit, ad quos vult et quando vult, quorum ministerio homines ad resipicentiam, et fidem in Christum crucifixum vocantur. Quomodo enim credent in eum de quo non audierint? quomodo autem audient absque praedicante? quomodo praedicabunt, nisi fuerint misse? Rom.10.14.15.

and *Acta* 1/252, text of Canons thesis seventeen, Quandoquidem de voluntate Dei ex verbo ipsius nobis est judicandum, quod testatur liberos fidelium esse sanctos, non quidem nature, sed beneficio foederis gratuiti, in quo illi cum parentibus comprehenduntur, pii parentes de Electione et salute suorum liberorum, quos Deus in infantia ex hac vita evocat, dubitare non debent.

[199]These are very current orthodox ideas and their omission need not be of great significance.

[201]See text of Bremen thesis 1. And *Acta* 3/3, 5, text of Dutch professors theses 1 and 2, Praedestinatio ad salutem est aeternam, libertimum et immutabile Dei decretum, quo pro gratuito voluntatis suae beneplacito quosdam homines ex universo genere humano in peccatum prolapso ac perdito ad salutem in Christo elegit, eosdemque secundum suam electionem per verbum ac spiritum suum efficaciter vocare, per fidem in Christum justificare, sanctificare, in fide ac sanctitate conservare, et tandem glorificare construit, ad divitis suae gratiae ac misericordiae demonstrationem. Atque hoc est, de certis quibusdam hominibus in Christo et per Christum salvandis, verum, unicum et totum Electionis decretum.

Electio illa quorundam hominum ad salutem, tam ratione Veteris, quam Novi Testamenti, est unica, uno eodemque actu divino ab aeterno peracta, definita, completa, et absoluta: tametsi ex nostro concipiendi modo, ac finis diversorumque mediorum respectu, per quae electi ad finem illum sunt destinati, ac suo tempore perducuntur, distincti in eo gradus considerari possint, atque in sacris literis proponantur.

and *Acta* 2/38-9, text of the Swiss theologians on article 1, theses 1 and 2, Deus aeterno et immutabili decreto, secundum liberrimum, merum et gratuitum voluntatis suae beneplacitum, certos quosdam homines e communi miseria per Christum liberandos, ad vitam aeternam elegit, reliquosin exitio sponte attracto relinquere, et judicio propter peccata damnare statuit, ut notas faceret superemintes illas opes gratiae suae erga vasa misericordiae suae, quae praeparavit ad gloriam; potentiae item atque justissimae irae suae erga vasa ire, quae coagmentata sunt ad interitum.

Tametsi verissimum sit, Deum fideles perseverantes salvare, infideles contra et converti nescios in peccatis relinquere velle, tamen his verbis exprimi Praedestinationis decretum totum et plene, negamus. Omittitur enim causa praedestinationis suprema et unica, videlicet, sive Dei liberrima illa voluntas; personas item electas certas et per fidem certo salvandas non attingit. Deinque, quia verba haec; fideles et infideles, credentes et non credentes, sunt ambigua; Etenim modo, de fide praevisa, ut conditione electionis antecedanea; modo, de fide, ut fructu electionem consequante, explicantur.

[201]*Acta* 2/3, text of British thesis 2, Christus est caput et fundamentum Electorum: adeoque omnia beneficia salutifera in Decreto Electionis praeparata, non nisi propter Christum et in Christo, conferuntur electis. and *Acta* 2/40, text of Swiss thesis 7, Quemadmodum fuit praecognitus ante jacta mundi fundamenta Mediator, non indefinitus aliquis, qui forte fortuna occurreret, sed singularis et certus, Dominus noster Iesus Christus; ita Deum certos et singulares homines, hunc videlicet et illum, elegisse credimus. Dilexit utique nominatim Iacobum, segregavit ab utero Paulum. Et ut quisque fidelium vere dicere potest; Vivo ego per fidem Filii Dei, qui dilexit me, et semetipsum tradidit pro me, sic quoque vere dicere potest, Deus elegit me.

[202]*Acta* 2/5, text of British thesis 4, Electionis decretum est definitum, inconditionatum, completum, irrevocabile, immutabile: ita ut electorum numerus nec augeri possit, nec minui. and *Acta* 3/93-4, text of French Low Country Churches, theses 3 and 4, Electio ad salutem unica tantum est, eaque certa et immutabilis, a qua vere credentes dimoveri non possunt: non variabilis, vel ab hominis actione suspensa, sed firma, et quae sola Dei gratuita in Caristo nititur. Electi peremptorie sunt omnes vere credentes, quos Deus gratiose et efficaciter vocavit, justificarvit, et per Spiritum suum in diem redemtionis obsignavit, quesque seduci non parmittit. Unde etiam num viventes et ante peractum vitae

cuirsum absolute et simpliciter Electi vocantur.

[203]Th. Beza *Tractationum Theologicarum I/16-17 etc.*

[204]J. Calvin *opera* in *Corpus Reformatorum* (ed Baum, Cunitz and Reuss) XXVI/160.

[205]*Acta* 2/61, text of Bremen thesis 5, Haec electio nobis patefit in tempore, quum per Verbum et Spiritum Dei regenaramur, seu efficaciter vocamur, ut in Christum credamus, sancte vivamus, et spem aeternae glorie certam concipiamus.

and*Acta* 3/94, test of French Low Country Churches, thesis 6, Fideles in hac vita de aeterno Dei amore, suique electione, et de vita aeterna, ex fide fideique fructibus, atque interno Spiritus Sancti testimonio certi sunt. Et ex huis rei scientia atqué tum in vita, tum in morte, solidam et immotam consolationem animo percipiunt.

[206]*Acta* 2/63, text of Bremen thesis 8, De solis fidelium infantibus qui ante aetatem doctrinae capacem, demoriuntur, statuimus eos a Deo diligi et servari ex eodem Dei beneplacito, propter Cristum, per Christum, et in Christo, quo adulti: unde ex relatione foederis sancti sunt. Cuius rei confirmandae gratia, baptismo sacro initiantur et Christum induunt.

and *Acta* 3/10-11, text of the Dutch professors thesis 3 of reprobation, Longe diversa est conditio feorum infantium, qui ex foederatis parentibus et aliorum qui ex non foederatis nascuntut, queniam Scriptura hos impuros, atque a Christo et foedere gratiae alienos pronunciat.

[207]*Acta* 2/64, text of Bremen thesis 2 of reprobation, Ideoque quicunque damnatur, illi omnes justissime propter peccata damnatur. *rejicimus*. Quod culpa, cur plurimi homines pereant, fit in deo.

and *Acta* 2/41, text of Swiss thesis 13, Reprobationem et damnationem ipsi quoque distinguimus. Cur hunc prae illo Deus reprobaverit, extra Dei οθδοχιαν illam, causam nullam admittimus. *Quem enim vult, indurat.* Cur vero hunc vel illum damnet, propter peccatum fieri, et per offensas reatum in hominem ad damnationem venisse, magistro Apostolo, didicimus. Et revera, ut Deus non damnat nisi propter peccatum, sic damnare non decrevit,nisi propter peccatum.

[208]*Acta* 2/41, text of Swiss thesis 12, Quis decretorum divinorum sit ordo et numerus quandoquidem viae Dei non sunt sicut nostrae, et cogitationes Dei non aunt, sicut cogitationes nostrae, nec quisquam ipsi a consilio fuit, nos ista ei uni et soli permittimus, cujus intelligentiae, tete Psalmista, non est numerus. Quia tamen praedestinare includit et finem et media ad finem, nos hominem uno eodemque actu primum ad gloriam, deinde ad gratiam; ad salutem nempe et ad vocationem, fidem, justificationem et sanctificationem esse destinatum credimus, Crediderunt enim quotquot ordinati erant ad vitam aeternam.

and *Acta* 3/93, text of French Low Country Churches thesis 1, Decretum Electionis, suis quidem membris distinctum, numero tamen unicum est; complectens totum ordinem gratiae et gloriae: adeoque ipsas, personas singulares, quas Deo visum fuit eligere. etc.

[209]*Institutes* 3.xxi.2.

[210]The idea of election under the Old Testament is typical of Calvin and Bucer and forms part of a general tendancy to minimize differences between the two covenants - except, of course, for the *modus administrationis*. There was also a Melanchthonian school where the diversity was stressed. These were differing emphases rather than disputes.

[211]H. Bettenson (ed), *Documents of the Christian Church,* 2nd 3d., pp. 268-9.

[212]*Acta* 1/115-6.

[213]*Acta* 1/115, Dwinglo thesis 1.

[214]Anselm, *Cur Deus Homo,* title of part 1, chapter 19. For a modern treatment see G. Aulen, *Christus Victor.*

[215]*Acta* 2/6.

[216]*ibid.,* 2/14.

[217]*ibid.,* 2/18.

[218]*ibid.,* 2/20.

[219]Discussions of this subject will be found in E. Iserloh, *Die Eucharistie in der darstellung des Johannes Eck*. (Reformationsgeschichtliche Studien und Texte.) Munster 1950.

[220]J. Calvin *opera* in *Corpus Reformatorum* (ed Baum, Cunitz & Reuss) XLIX/94.

[221]H. Heppe, ed E. Bizer *Die Dogmatik der evangelische-reformierten Kirche* p. 374.

[222]*Acta* 2/91ff.

[223]*Acta* 2/103ff.

[224]See, for example, Peter Lombard, *Sentences* 1/9.

[225]*Acta* 1/239ff.

[226]*Acta* 1/296.

[227]*Acta* 2/113.

[228]*Acta* 2/85.

[229]*Acta* 2/86. The phrase "pretium Redemptionis" used here is of particular interest since it is only Beza who translates λυτρον αντι πολλων in this way. (Iesu Christi D.N. Novum Testamentum ed Th. Beza, Geneva, 1565, p. 190). It is not a translation used by Erasmus or the Vulgate and certainly seems to be an Anselmian echo.

[230]*Acta* 2/97-103.

[231]*Acta* 2/105-10.

[232]*Acta* 2/106.

[233]*Acta* 2/113ff. The three delegates from Bremen all submitted separate statements on this article.

[234]*Acta* 2/114.

[235]*Acta* 2/118-26.

[236]*Acta* 2/121-2.

[237]*Acta* 2/126.

[238]*Acta* 2/127-8.

[239]*Acta* 2/127.

[240]*Acta* 2/128-38.

[241]*Acta* 2/134.

[242]*Acta* 3/96-100.

[243]*Acta* 3/96.

[244]*Acta* 3/96.

[245]*Acta* 3/100-10.

[246]*The New Schaff Herzog* 9/282, as it is today - see B. Altaner & A. Stuiber, *Patrologie* p. 451.

[247]*Acta* 3/110-16.

[248]*Acta* 3/110-11.

[249]*Acta* 3/111.

[250]*Acta* 3/116-22.

[251]*Acta* 3/122-6.

[252]*Acta* 3/122.

[252]*Acta* 3/123.

[254]*Acta* 3/127-35.

[255]*Acta* 3/128.

[256]*Acta* 3/135-46.

[257]*Acta* 3/147-51.

[258]*Acta* 3/152-7.

[259]*Acta* 3/155.

[260]*Acta* 3/157-65.

[261]*Acta* 3/163.

[262]*Acta* 3/165-7.

[263]*Acta* 3/165.

[264]*Acta* 1/257-60.

[265]*Acta* 2/110-3.

[266]*Acta* 2/113-8.

[267]*Acta* 2/113-4.

[268]*Acta* 2/115.

[269]*Acta* 2/116-7.

[270]*Acta* 2/118-26.

[271]*Acta* 3/96-100.

[272]*Acta* 3/165-7.

[273]*Acta* 2/103-5.

[274]G. Aulen, *Christus Victor* (London 1970), pp. 128-9.

[275]*Acta* 1/257-8.

[276]*Acta* 1/258.

[277]*Acta* 2/170-6.

[278]*Acta* 2/170, 174.

[279]*Acta* 1/263-8.

[280]*Acta* 1/263.

[281]*Acta* 1/263-4.

[282]*Acta* 2/161-4.

[283]*Acta* 2/161-2.

[284]A phrase such as "bonum supernaturale." See Altenstaig, *Lexicon* E4v etc.

[285]*Institutes* 3.24.6- 3.24.11. *Calvini opera* 4/513-21.

[286]Notably in *De aeterna Praedestinatione Dei.*

[287]Wm. Tyndale, *The Exposition of the Fyrste Epistle of Seynt Jhon,* 1531, r/p *English Reformers,* ed. T.H.L. Parker, "The Library of Christian Classics," vol. 26, (Philadelphia and London, 1966), p. 142.

[288]*Corpus Reformatorum* vol.7, col. 481.

[289]H. Heppe, *Die Dogmatik der evangelisch-reformierten Kirche,* p. 461:- "Perseverantia Sanctorum est donum Dei, quo electis iustificatis et sanctificatis Christi gratia per Spiritum S. obsignatur, ut nunquam ea penitus excidant (Wolleb). Perseverantiae donum est beneficium Dei, quo salvificam gratiam Christi per Spiritum sanctum in electis regenitis obsignat, ut finaliter in ea permanent nec ea unquam penitus excidere possint (Polan)."

[290]Zanchius, *Opera,* tom. 4, col. 158:- Renati sicut sine speciali Spiritus sancti gratia, qua illos regat et agat, non possunt in fide, pietate ac sanctitate proficere sic etiam in ea perseverare non possunt, nisi qua tenus fidem et pietatem in eis conservat Spiritus sanctus, et eos regendo efficit ut perseverent ita ut sicut initum et progressus salutis, sic etiam finis, qui est finalis perseverantia, a sola Dei misericordia pendeat, merumque sit Dei donum. Zanchius discussed the thesis of which this was the title. His interest in this doctrine may be seen in his *De Perseverentia Sanctorum,* in the Opera Omnia, vol. 7, cols. 91-387.

[291]R. Baxter, *Grotian Religion,* etc.

[292]Calderwood, *History of the Kirk,* vol. 7, p. 238.

[293]P. van Itterzoon, "Koning Jacobus I en de Synode van Dordrecht" in *Nederlands Archief voor Kerkgeschiedenis,* 1932.

[294]W. Kickel, *Vernunft und Offenbarung bei Theodor Beza,* pp. 150-3.

[295]*Dictionary of National Biography* 1/356.

[296]A list of editions of the *Medulla* will be found in the bibliography.

[297]P. Schaff, *Creeds of Christendom,* 1/356.

[298]*The New Schaff Herzog,* etc. 5/204.

[299]*Acta* 2/225.

[300]*Acta* 1.38-43, see also the *Life of Hall* by Jones, pp. 477-92.

[301]*Acta* 1/271-6 and 2/247-54.

[302]*Acta* 1/272.

[303]*Acta* 1/273.
[304]*Acta* 2/250.
[305]*Acta* 2/250.
[306]*Acta* 3/250-1.
[307]*Acta* 3/250.
[308]G. Herlyn, "Die Lehre von der Pradestination in Genfer und Heidelberger Katechismus" in *Reformierte Kirchenzeitung* vol. 88, 1938, cols. 460-4.
[309]*Acta* 2/240-3.
[310]*Acta* 2/240.
[311]*Acta* 2/207-25.
[312]*Institutes* 3.24.7., *Calvini Opera* 4/514-6.

Chapter 3
The Coton Controversy
The background to the Coton controversy.

The subject of early seventeenth century French language controversy between Reformed and Jesuit polemicists is much too large to be considered at length in this present thesis, but an understanding of certain aspects is vital to a comprehension of the Coton controversy.

The first half of the seventeenth century was a period of relative political calm for the French Reformed Church which had become well established and, to an extent, institutionalised after the Edict of Nantes. It was a period of flowering for the Reformed academies such as that of Saumur. The existence of these latter led to a decline in importance of the Genevan Academy which had become less unique and less necessary after their foundation. Thus the French public was exposed to the French Bibles, French writings and, above all, the French preaching of the Reformed Church in France. This was the time of celebrated preachers such as Jean Daille, Pierre du Moulin and the other pastors of the great protestant Church at Charenton which was just outside Paris. Inevitably, the availability of so much protestant propaganda led to considerable efforts to counteract its influence on the part of the authorities of the Catholic Church, and to this work the Jesuits made a significant contribution.

There was a considerable amount of literary material put out by both sides which helped to add to the great numbers of works written by the polemicists as Pierre du Moulin on the Reformed side and Francois Véron S.J.[1] on that of the Catholic Church. An examination of the works of Véron will help to outline the state of the controversy at this time. Véron became a French Jesuit but left the order in 1620 so that he might have more freedom to engage in polemics and who finally became curé at Charenton, his dates are 1575-1649 A.D.[2] Hurter described him as:- "Theologus erat eruditus, disputator sagax et promptus, orator vehemens, qui stilo utebatur subinde acri".[3] The catalogue of the Bibliothèque nationale in Paris lists some two hundred items under his name.

Véron's attacks upon the Reformed Church covered a wide field. He wrote against Reformed confessions in works such as *La Discipline des eglises pretendues reformees...avec la refutation d'icelle par la discipline contenue en l'escriture sainte* (Paris 1643), and also wrote a number of tracts on the doctrine of the eucharist such as *Actes de la conference sur le Sainct Sacrement de l'autel par l'Escriture saincte addressez aux ministres de Charenton* etc. (Caen 1629), *De la Communion soubs les deux especes selon l'Escriture saincte* etc. (Rouen s.a.) and *Preuve de la S^{cte} Messe par textes de l'Escriture, saincte* etc, (Paris 1623). In each case, it is to be noted, the Bible is given an important place in the title. This is not the case with all of Véron's works, but it is found to occur so frequently that it would seem that the Bible was the source of Véron's authority. In this he is following the instructions of Bellarmine, under whom he had studied in Rome.[4] Bellarmine had taught that disputations could only be carried out where there was a common basis for discussion which, for theological matters, he took to be Scripture. He had created scandal in Rome by saying this in his opening lecture in the Gregoriana. It also appears in the preface to his *Controversies:-* "Neque enim disputari potest, nisi prius in aliquo communi principio cum adversariis conveniamus: convenit autem inter nos, et omnes omnino haereticos, verbum Dei esse regulam fidei." Thus, Véron was using the Bible as a standard of judgment in his anti-protestant polemics. The appeal to Scripture was certainly in response to current French climates of opinion, and thus is revealed the fact that the French Bible enjoyed a central position in inter-confessional disputes of the period. The public accepts the Bible as a standard, and when Véron wishes to discredit the Reformed clergy, he can do no better than to destroy the public's faith in the protestants' fidelity to Scripture. Thus Véron attacks individuals, *L'Escriture saincte et toute la religion chrestienne combatue par Mestrezat. ministre de Charenton et deffendue par Francois Véron* etc (Paris 1633), groups, *La Saincte Bible abandonnee par les ministres du Languedoc et des Sevenes* etc (Paris 1625) or even the ministry of the Reformed Church as a whole, *Tous les ministres de France convaincus d'estre faussaires de l'escriture saincte* etc (Paris 1623).

Inevitably, this basing of the controversy on the Bible led to Catholic criticism of French protestant versions of the Bible which had come from Geneva. Thus the subject of Genevan responses to such attacks is relevant to this thesis and will be considered as a type of source which reveals Genevan theology. It is a study of the case of Pierre Coton S.J. rather than of Francois Véron, since the epigones responded to the attacks of Coton while they ignored those of Véron.

For Véron, the controversy seems to have been French in a political as well as a linguistic sense. His writings do mention Genevan translations of the Bible, but usually in the context of a French situation such as the *Adrian Hucher ministre d'Amyens, mis a l'inquisition des passages de la Bible de Geneve* etc (La Fleche, 1615), or the conference which he had with Samuel Bochart on the subject of the eucharist and the "falsifications" of the Genevan Bibles which was held at Caen in 1628.[6] Véron did criticise the Genevan Bibles, but this was usually not aimed at Geneva but at French targets, such as the Synod of Castres in 1626. There was the undated *Falsifications des Bibles de Geneve en tous les principaux textes produicts par les ministres pour fondements de tous les articles plus remarquables de leur reformation* etc, a work which, despite its pretentious title, was only a pamphlet of twenty-four pages.[7] More dangerous was another short tract of 1646, *Grand trouble arrive de nouveau a Geneve contre Geneve et Charenton. esmeu par Diodati, ministre du lieu, ou la Saincte Bible traduite et interpretee de nouveau par Jean Diodati, ministre de Geneve, opposee et contraire en sa traduction et en ses expositions a toutes les Bibles precedentes de Geneve et de Charenton* etc (s.l., s.a.). Thus Véron was trying to sow dissention among the Reformed, between the translators and theologians of Geneva and the ministers of Charenton. Given the possibility of du Moulin's opposition to Diodati this was a particularly shrewd move of *divide et impera*, to underline the differences among the Reformed and to render French protestants suspicious of Genevan Bible translations. Véron was well informed for he wrote;- "Long temps y a que i'attendois ce gros Volume de Diodati,[8] a la publication duquel on tenoit cy-devant que les Ministres de Geneve s'opposoient,"[9] and such opposition had, in fact been in evidence as will be shown below.

Thus it may be seen that in the seventeenth century, Catholic propagandists writing in France in the vernacular language often kept the Bible well to the fore when justifying their positions. Genevan versions of the Bible were sometimes criticised, but within a French context. It is against this background that we must see the Coton controversy.

Now that the Catholic interest in Scripture as a component of polemics has been revealed to some extent, it is necessary to see if this method of attack affected the protestants, and to what extent they responded to the provocation that was offered. The controversy may have been in a French context, but it became a matter of urgent concern for the Genevans when Coton published his *Geneve plagiaire*. Geneva was not in the centre of events either before or after the Coton affair, but there would seem to be little doubt that Geneva's relations with the French Reformed Church were badly damaged as a result of this atmosphere of Reformed and Catholic controversy concerning Scripture.

It has been noted above that Francois Véron attacked the Reformed Churches at a number of levels with the charge of infidelity to the true meaning of Scripture. The Reformed polemicists had not been idle in defending their cause, and chief among those who did so was Pierre du Moulin of Charenton. He published considerable amounts of material on the subject of the fidelity of the Reformed and the errors of the Catholic interpretation such as *Du Juge des controverses, traitte aucuel est defendus l'autorite et la perfection de la saincte Escriture contre les usurpations et accusations de l'Eglise romaine* etc (Sedan 1630), *Oppositions de la parole de Dieu avec la doctrine de l'Eglise romaine* (Geneva 1637) and *Des Traditions et de la perfection et suffisance de l'Escriture saincte...avec un catalogue ou denombrement des traditions romaines* etc (Sedan 1631). Thus the Reformed had not been idle, and such an output shows a considerable confidence. And yet there would appear to have been uneasiness among the Reformed as is shown by the trouble which arose when Diodati, after the success of his 1607 Italian translation of the Bible, decided to follow this up with a French Version. In 1620 the French Reformed Synod of Alez was informed of this. The Synod of Alez, it is to be remembered, was that at which Benedict Turrettini upheld orthodox theology and which made the Canons of Dort binding on the French Church (see pp. 32-33). The French response, written by du Moulin, has never been published, but contains the following passage:- "la diversite des editions de la Bible, qui se trouvent differentes en plusieurs passages, est un achoppement a plusieurs infirmes, et que les Jesuites... produisans en leurs sermons et es conferences plusieurs Bibles differentes, ont trouble plusieurs consciences debiles."[10] From this it is abundantly clear that the French protestants were badly affected by the attacks of the Jesuits, and that members of the French Reformed Church were being convinced by the arguments of the Catholics such as Véron. Again, the Bible is to be seen as the heart of the inter-confessional controversy. Opposition to Diodati's publication of his French Bible prevented him from doing so for twenty-four years after this, and the opposition helped to turn him into a bitter and intransigent old man before his death in 1649. The opposition to his work came from various sources, and was justified in a variety of ways, but the idea is always present that a new translation, any new translation, will harm the Reformed cause in France. Diodati tried to counteract this attitude when writing to the Synod of Aloncon during 1637, which is a sure sign that it was still a widely accepted opinion,[11] and he also wrote about it in the preface to his 1638 *Les Livres de Iob Pseavmes Proverbes Ecclesiaste Cantiqve des Cantiqves*.[12] Even when his work had finally been published in 1644, Diodati, writing to the French Church noted that the main reason for the refusals to allow his French Bible to be published were the:- "scandales des infirmes, et des reproches des Adversaires."[13] He had published his French Bible in 1644 after having been encouraged by the warm reception accorded to the new edition of his Italian Bible in 1641. The difference was, of course, that there was no great Italian protestant Church constantly challenging Catholicism in the Italian peninsula and playing the role of the Huguenots in France

It is natural for any Christian Church to take great care over the translation of the Scriptures, but the attitude of the French Reformed Church was based on a fear of external criticism rather than a natural and responsible desire to have a good translation of the Bible. The national Synod did not take any decision on the matter of a new Bible until 1659,[14] nearly forty years after Diodati, not even a native French speaking man, had noted the crudeness and archaisms of existing translations. This uncertainty and timidity is the sign of a Church which is coping badly with its polemical situation.

It is against this background that the Coton controversy is to be seen in perspective. The French Reformed Church was being attacked by Catholic polemicists who were using Scripture to further their cause, and the French Reformed Church was losing an amount of its self assurance in Polemics as a result of these attacks, a point demonstrated by the objections to the publishing of the Diodati Bible. Into this milieu of debate and uncertainty came Coton's work, *Geneve plagiaire,* the result of nearly twenty years effort. Coton questioned not only Genevan translations, but even the text of the Old Testament itself, to the horror of the Reformed. With this direct and powerful attack, Geneva, which had ignored the jibes of Véron, had to become involved. Benedict Turrettini and Theodore Tronchin, two of the epigones, were chosen to uphold the accuracy, and the honour, of Genevan scholarship.

Pierre Coton S.J., and the Genevan Academy.

Pierre Coton was born during 1564, the child of a notable family, at the chateau of Chenevoux near Neronde (Loire). His family was anti-Jesuit and he entered the Society of Jesus against their advice.[15] He was a man of considerable intellectual eminence, having been educated under Bellarmine at Rome as well as at Paris, Bourges, Turin and Milan.

Pierre Coton S.J. was a man who was much disliked by the French protestant community. He was theologian with much influence at court with Henry IV, being "Predicateur ordinaire du roi" from 1603 and being made confessor to the king in 1608.[16] From this position of influence he managed to do considerable harm to protestant aspirations, and not only in France, for it was he who had helped to reveal the conspiracy involving Giovanni Diodati and Fra Paolo Sarpi at Venice, a conspiracy of which the object had been the conversion of the Venetian Republic to protestantism:- "A letter, supposedly from the Protestant pastor Giovanni Diodati in Geneva to a French correspondent, had fallen into the hands of the nuncio in Paris; and after strategic editing by Ubaldini, Coton, and perhaps the king himself, it was transmitted to the government in Venice by the French ambassador. This communication purported to describe a recent visit to Venice undertaken to promote the religious subversion of the Republic ."[17] Coton also engaged in religious controversy as had Véron, and had written polemical works against the French protestants before his first book appeared in which he criticised Geneva. Thus, in 1600, he had published *Cinquante et quatre demands...aux sieurs Du Moulin...et autres ministres de la Religion pretendue reformee* to which du Moulin replied with *Trente-deux demandes proposees par le P.Cotton, avec les solutions adjoustees au bout de chasque demande. Item soixante-quatre demands proposes en contre-eschange* (La Rochelle 1607). The other main polemical work of Coton had been the *Institution catholique* of 1610,[18] an attempt to produce a Catholic response to the *Institutes* of Calvin.

Thus on a polemical as well as a political level, Coton was known as an able opponent of the French Reformed Church in the early seventeenth century. However, the protestants were far from incapable of intellectual self-defence. Du Moulin's readiness to attack Coton has been noted above. Yet there were other less dignified methods, as is revealed by the following poem of Agrippa d'Aubigne:-

Si le Pere Cotton pretende a l'advenir
Effacer de Chastel du tout le souvenir,
Rasant la Pyramide et l'arrest qui la touche,
Qu'il vous remette aussi vostre dent dans la bouche

* * * * *

On abbat ce bel ouvrage,
Sire, puisqu'il vous plaist.

C'est par un cruel outrage
A nous et a nostre arrest
Vos confesseurs Cottonnes
En ont une joye extreme;
Si furent-ils condamnez
Et par vostre bouche mesme.

* * * *

Les courtisans a l'ame tendre
Trouvans Dieu trop rude pour eux
Ne veulent plus luy aller rendre
Ny leurs prieres ny leurs voeux.
Ils n'en veulent ny la painture
En pierre, boys, ny en lotton,
Mais, plus commode a leur nature,
Ils en ont fait un en Cotton.

* * * *

Le Roy n'aime point la figure
D'un saint de marbre ou de lotton;
Car la trouvant un peu trop dure:
Il en a fait un de Cotton.[19]

Other satirical poems are to be found in manuscript in the Achives Tronchin of the Musee historique de la Reformation of Geneva.[20]

Two events had made Coton particularly well-known in France. One was the assassination of Henry IV when the Jesuits were suspected of complicity by French public opinion. Coton tried to defend the Society of Jesus against such accusations[21] but the protestants were ready to take advantage of any such matter and du Moulin wrote *Anticoton, ou Refutation de la Lettre du P.Cotton, livre ou est prouve que les jesuites sont coulpables et autheurs du parricide execrable commis en la personne du roy tres-chrestien Henri IV d'heureuse memoire*. When Coton turned to attack Geneva, these matters were not forgotten. Tronchin, in his *Coton Plagiaire,* wrote of this affair:- "La France en a senti les maux, les bons Francois en ont reconu les auteurs, et deplore les causes: apres l'Auguste Parlement, les pierres en ont parle, et quand on leur a impose silence, on a veu les tristes effects les couteaux dans les dents et dans la coeur du Roy l'ont verifiee."[22]

Another happening which made Coton the talk of Paris was in 1605 and 1609 when he was supposedly found to be having contact with the Devil by asking him a series of questions. Whether true or not, it made excellent propaganda of which an amusing account has already been published.[23] Theodore Tronchin was also able to make capital out of this when he came to reply to Coton:- "Toute la France a veu des questions sur lesquelles Coton desiroit d'estre instruict du malin esprit l'an 1604 a Paris, apres avoir estudie les livres qui enseignent comment il se faut conduire en tels affaires, selon que en ses discours de la Messe il avoit voulu faire conoistre qu'il est entendu et verse en Magie: et le Iesuitte Del-rio a fait un gros volume pour monstrer que les Iesuites savent tout ce qui est de la Magie. Coton coucha par escrit de sa main des questions, touchant la Personne du feu Roy, sa sante et ses affaires."[24]

During the year 1599, at Grenoble, Pierre Coton first publicly attacked the Genevan translations of the Bible into French. Thursday the 25th February:- "Fut le premier jour de son Caresme qu'il fit promesse d'alleguer tous les jours a l'heure de son prosne, un passage qui auroit, disoit-il, este deprave en la Bible imprimee par lesdits de Geneve,"[25] Despite the hope of Benjamin Cresson, the protestant minister who wrote those words that:- "Dieu qui se moque de la vanite des hommes, a rendu ses intentions toutes inutiles," Coton does not appear to have been discouraged. He had, in fact, just begun a controversy that was, intermittently, to remain active until the time of his death many years later, during 1626.

Despite the fact that his first attack on the Genevan translations of the Bible took place in 1599, Coton's first book on the subject did not appear until 1618, the year of the beginning of the Synod of Dort, when Coton had finally lost his place at court following the murder of Henry IV. This first work was *Geneve plagiaire ou verification des depravations de la parole de Dieu, qui se trouvent es Bibles de Geneve,* a considerable work in folio of 1174 pages. In this book, Coton uses the idea of plagiarism not in the modern sense of taking and using another's writings as one's own, but in the more ancient sense of a turning away of the true meaning of a literary passage. Coton provides the reader with some two hundred passages where he accuses the Genevan translators of turning away the sense of Scripture to suit their own purposes. This work was written for a French audience, but it was a specific attack on Geneva and it was for the doctors of the Genevan Academy to reply to this, though a number of French protestant writers came to the support of Geneva. These included the *Response aux allegations de P. Cotton* by B. Cresson, 1599, which has already been mentioned although it was an answer to verbal rather than written criticisms and pre-dates *Geneve plagiaire* by nearly twenty years; *Plagiatius vapulans* by Jacques Cappel, 1620, in which he criticises Coton's linguistic knowledge and notes faults in Hebrew, Greek and Latin that were committed by Coton in his *Geneve plagiaire;* *Jerusalem et Rome au secours de Geneve* by Moyse Blondel, 1621, and finally, *Traitez des originaux et des versions, servant de reponse a la Geneve Plagiaire du P. Cotton* of Matthieu Cottiere, 1619. It is of some interest to note that B. Turrettini, in his *Defense de la fidelite,* mentioned the work by Cresson and wrote that some of Coton's accusations had not changed over the years and that:- "le sieur Cresson avoit par un livret des lors refutees a Grenoble."[26] Thus Cresson's work met with Genevan approuval.

As early as 30 January 1618, the jurisconsulte Anjorrant had advised the Compagnie des pasteurs to reply to this book by Coton, but no decision was then taken as no copy of the book was to be found in Geneva.[27] Two weeks later, however, on the 13th February, the Compagnie had received the book, and Theodore Tronchin and Benedict Turrettini were deputed to work on responses to Coton with the instruction that they were to show their work to the Compagnie before printing or publication. Even the titles of the books were to be considered.[28] By April, the Compagnie was ensuring that the two professors were not writing works that were too similar.[29] It is clear that the task was regarded as urgent, for the Compagnie was concerned that the two theologians would arrange their work:- "ensemble le plus souvent qu'il leur sera possible, pour parachever au plus tost le dit oeuvre pour le mettre en lumiere." By the end of May the Compagnie had decided to allow a part of the work to be published so that it might appear in time for the Frankfort book fair.[30] Turrettini had more usable material than had Tronchin, and his work was considered by three members of the Compagnie including Diodati.[31] This book of Turrettini's was the *Defense de la fidelite des traductions de la S.Bible faites a Geneve* which was a response to Coton's preface and to the first fifty-two texts which Coton alleged were falsely translated. It is a considerable work and in his dedication Turrettini mentions that he had made:- "en quatre mois, la response a la principale partie d'un livre forme en dixhuict ans".[32] Turrettini himself proposed to the Compagnie that he should dedicate his book to the king of France as had Coton.[33] The Compagnie approved the text of this decision on 14th August 1618[34] as did the Conseil on the 15th of August.[35] Despite these intentions of rendering the book acceptable to the court of France, Anjorrant found that he had difficulties in making it available to the king.[36]

The next stage in the controversy was that while Benedict Turrettini was still working on the completion of his response to Coton, a task which occupied much of his time in the autumn of 1619[37] when Coton's answer to Turrettini's first book, *Defense de la fidelite* suddenly appeared. Coton entitled his book *Recheute de Geneve Plagiaire,* and it was known in Geneva by December 1619. It is indicative of the gravity with which Geneva regarded Coton's attacks that Turrettini was encouraged to reply to this new attack not by the Compagnie but by the Conseil. It had been reported to the Conseil that Coton's new work had been:- "compose avec beaucoup d'artifice"[38] The compagnie des pasteurs added its encouragement to that of the Conseil.[39] Turrettini then published *Recheute du Iesuite Plagiaire* in 1620. Soon afterwards, Theodore Tronchin's reply to *Geneve Plagiaire* was also published, and it was reported to the Compagnie in February of 1620 that this book:- "ne pouvoit estre que de grande edification et apporter beaucoup de fruict."[40] Coton did not reply to these books before he died during 1626, the year in which Benedict Turrettini published the last part of his refutation of Coton's *Geneve plagiaire.* This was entitled *Suite de la fidelite des traductions de la S.Bible faites a Geneve,* and Turrettini himself informed the Compagnie that:- "il avoit este prie par lettres de divers amis de continuer en la refutation du livre de Cotton."[41] This was the last of the polemical works that concerned the Coton controversy which was published.

The number of Genevan replies, and the sheer volume of material produced by Tronchin and Turrettini demonstrates just how seriously the Genevan Church, state and Academy considered Coton's attack to be. It produced a profound effect on Geneva, for years after in 1637, when writing to the Synod of Alencon, Diodati felt himself obliged to state that his French translation and annotations of the Bible did not affect the passages discussed by Coton, which the;- "Jesuit had so *Calumniously* impugned, and accused of falshood, and were so worthily defended by our late Reverend Brother, Mr *Turretin* of Blessed Memory."[42] Thus the influence of the Coton affair had still to be evaluated eleven years after Coton's death.

It remains necessary to explain why a consideration of this controversy is necessary to a study of the theology of the Genevan Academy at the time of the Synod of Dort. Obviously the two events are more or less contemporary, but there is a much more important reason than this. In his *Geneve plagiaire,* Pierre Coton listed the two hundred Biblical texts in the translations of which the Genevans, he claimed, were not faithful to the sense of the original. Thus, one objective was, as with Veron, to destroy public confidence in the Genevan translations of the Bible. But there is another, and probably more important reason for Coton's book. He wanted to criticise protestant orthodox Reformed systematic theology. To this end, his book is divided into ten sections concerning ;-

a- the eucharist
b- Christology
c- the sacraments

d- the Trinity and the saints
e- authority
f- faith
g- free will
h-justification
i- good works
j- the Apocrypha.

Coton's work can, in fact, be divided roughly into three sections. One part (section j, the first part of e and the preface) on Scripture, another part (sections a and c) on the sacraments and the third and longest part on the various aspects of the doctrines of salvation (sections b,f,g,h,i, and the first part of d).

The structure of the Genevan doctrine of Scripture as revealed by the Coton controversy.

The study of the Genevan concept of Scripture at the period of the Synod of Dort is a large and complex subject. There is not a vast volume of evidence, the students' theses, Diodati's annotations and prefaces to the books of the Bible, and the works of Theodore Tronchin and Benedict Turrettini written against Pierre Coton. These latter are of considerable interest since they contain refutations of Coton's criticism of the Biblical text. Yet none of this literature was written expressly to explain the Genevan doctrine of Scripture and such doctrine must therefore be sought carefully within the text of these works. Once again we are faced with the intractible nature of the available evidence.

The definition of scripture.

The most basic point which must be raised is to discover what books the epigones believed to have canonical authority. Turrettini writes in his Defense that the Bible, as we have it, is complete and that no canonical books have been lost:-

> Que si on persiste a croire des livres perdus, qui nous asseure, Qu'ils estoyent Canoniques, car a que faire dans le Canon de l'Escriture, toute la Physique escrite par Salomon? Est-il necessaire au salut et pour reigle de l'Eglise, avoir toutes les histoires, que personnes sainctes pourroient escrire de leur temps.[43]

The point is that it is not authorship which makes books canonical, but rather their usefulness for salvation. The fact that one book by a particular author is canonical would have little bearing on his other works. This is stated in both Belgic and Gallican confessions. There is also the usual protestant rejection of the Old Testament Apocryphia though Diodati does write notes on each apocryphal book in his complete annotated Bibles and one student quotes a text from the Apocrypha when presenting a series of theses for disputation.[45]

The epigones also believed in the essential purity of the Greek and Hebrew texts as they were then known to themselves:-

> Puis que tous les Peres Grecs de l'ancienne Eglise, ont leu le
> texte Grec comme nous l'avons auiourd'huy: et tous sont
> d'accord qu'ils l'avoyent tres-entier: il appert clairement, que
> nous l'avons eu son integrite, aussi bien qu'eux. Il n'est done
> point besoin pour authoriser le texte Grec, auquel Dieu a
> voulu que les Apostres escrivissent le Nouveau Testament in-
> spires par son esprit, que l'autorite de l'Eglise survienne: puis
> qu'il a son autorite de Dieu.[46]

The purity of the Hebrew text is, in this instance, a more complex and controversial question than the Greek as will be discussed elsewhere, but the purity of
the available versions and the completeness of their texts were points that were
asserted on many occasions by the epigones. A subsidiary point arising out of
these statements is the refusal to accept as canonical early manuscripts written
in other languages:-

> Nous sommes d'accord donc ensemble que les paraphrases
> Chaldaique du Vieil Testament, et Syriaque du Nouveau sont
> utiles, mais ne font point la loy a l'Eglise.[47]

Translations of Scripture.

It is banal to state that the production of Bibles in the vernacular had been
a principle of reformation of the Church, yet the controversies concerning the
uses and authority of Biblical translation had assumed very considerable proportions during the seventeenth century. The controversy between Coton and
Geneva forms only part of this large subject. Automatically, Tronchin establishes
the authority of the original Greek or Hebrew over that of any translation, Latin
or otherwise.[48] Turrettini is of a similar opinion.[49]

Yet, for the epigones, this does not in any sense question the necessity of
translating the Bible, far from it. Turrettini believes firmly in the necessity of
translations, it is doing God's work to translate the scriptures. The Genevan
belief in this is underlined by the life and work of Diodati more than by any
statement of Turrettini.[50] In support of this idea of the need to translate scripture,
Turrettini produces the analogy of the different translations of the Bible being as
different clothing only, the essential Spirit remaining present in all forms of the
text. Despite this spirit of dedication, however, it is to be noted that the
Genevans had no inflated conception of the worth of their translations. Turrettini is quite prepared to admit that they are imperfect.[51]

Diodati was clearly dissatisfied with previous Protestant translations, and
spent much of his life translating and trying to have published his own French
version of the Bible[52] accompanied by a translation into French of the annotations
to his own Italian version of the Bible. Despite this confidence in their ability to

translate and re-translate the Scriptures, the Genevans took criticism very seriously indeed, and there was considerable opposition to Diodati's new translation, one reason constantly being given against its publication was that it would arouse antagonistic Catholic criticism. This fear of new translations came to be a feature of the French Reformed Church during the seventeenth century. There were a number of elements in this, there was the fear of Catholic critics using a number of different translations to confuse and upset protestant lay people in the many public disputes that were held throughout France between Catholic and reformed clergy, and there was also the dispute concerning the Hebrew vowel pointing which made many uncertain about the authority of the Old Testament. It was, of course, feared in reformed circles, that Catholic, or more specifically Jesuit, criticism was not merely an attempt to cast doubt on Genevan translations, but to question the authority of the Bible as a whole.

> Mais le but de Coton n'est ni d'honorer S.Hierosme, ni de defendre *la Latine,* et la preferer aux autres: mais son intention est de nous arracher les mains l'usage de l'Escriture Saincte, nous ramener au siecle d'ignorance.[53]

This, according to Tronchin, was an attempt to undo the work of the Reformation:-

> En la reformation on a restabli ce que l'Apostasie Romaine avoit difforme; on l'a fait selon la parole de Dieu et la plus pure et saine antiquite: et d'avoir rendu les Pseaumes au peuple de Dieu, les leur avoir mis en bouche.[54]

The purity of the Hebrew text.

To Tronchin, the chief end of the reading of Scripture was the learning of the word of God in order to comprehend the doctrine of salvation:-

> nostro siecle a veu ce comble d'impiete, que en l'Eglise Romaine, le premier boulevart de leurs disputes a este de taxer l'Escriture S. d'insuffisance a nous instruire en la connoissance de salut; et ce pour attribuer tout suffisance au Pape de Rome sous le nom de l'Eglise.[55]

Therefore, in order to substitute the authority of the Church for that of scripture, which Tronchin sees as the aim of the Jesuits, it becomes necessary for them to question the purity of the Biblical text. Thus they attack the reformed:-

> Ce qu'il pretend en dire, est, qu'ils ne sont ni pure ni entiers ni certains et partant n'ont point d'autorite. Quelle religion de Jesuite? Dire clairement qu'il ne peut la defendre ni escrire contre nous, sinon qu'il oste premierement toute creance et tout autorite aux Originaux de la verite de Dieu?[56]

Coton had indeed questioned the completeness, purity and definitive character of the Hebrew text in his *Geneve plagiaire*.[57] This attitude was criticised by Tronchin in blunt terms, mainly on the usual grounds that the Old Testament has been established by God.[58] To counter the arguments of Coton and to establish the early date of the Hebrew pointing, Tronchin claims that Jerome was aware of the pointing,[59] and that the Massoretes had not corrupted the text.[60]

Hebraeos vera et germana antiquitate (1623) really began the controversy on this within reformed protestantism by attacking the canonicity of the pointing, by arguing that Jewish scholars such as the Rabbi Aben-Ezra (floruit c1150 A.D.), in general recognised the newness of the Hebrew pointing, and by noting that the marginal notes, the q'ri, are always on consonantal problems and never concern vowels.[61] Yet Cappel's work was only published in 1624 when the Coton controversy had lost much of its momentum, and so this work is later than the books of Tronchin and Turrettini that are being considered in this section. There were earlier attempts to canonise the Hebrew pointing such as that of Amandus Polanus von Polansdorf in his *Syntagma theologiae christianae*, published in 1610, but this was before the controversy became acute. Buxtorf's son, another Johannes Buxtorf of Basel, replied to Cappel in *Tractatus de punctorum origine, antiquitate et auotoritate oppositus arcano punctationis revelato* (Basel 1648) but since this is very much later, the Coton affair clearly antedates the dispute within reformed protestantism. It is not impossible, of course, that the Coton controversy played a role in stimulating discussion of the question of Hebrew pointing, but there appears to be no factual evidence to show that it did.

Turrettini's conclusion of the matter may be regarded as the epigones' definitive resolution of this problem. His answer is quite undogmatic and much less assured than that of Tronchin.[62] The best method, according to Turrettini, is to follow the advice of Jerome, that it matters little if one transcribes "Salem" or "Salim" so long as no odd or extravagant word is derived from the unpointed text. He may oppose to this opinion the fact that St Jerome and other fathers of the Church are silent on these points and that St Jerome and the Septuagint do give different readings from those known in the seventeenth century, suggesting that the pointing was not standardised in their day.[64] It is to be noted that Turrettini's claim that Jerome does not mention the Hebrew vowel points contradicts what Tronchin said.

The problem of Hebrew pointing, and of its authority, became a controversy within the reformed churches, and positions became increasingly intransigent throughout the century until the *Formula Consensus Helvetica* of 1675 declared the pointing to be canonical. The first important post-renaissance scholar to question the pointing's contemporaneity with the unpointed Hebrew text was a sixteenth century German Jew, Elias Levita, who stated that the pointing was introduced into the Masoretic texts about 500 A.D.[65] Levita's ideas were attacked by Johannes Buxtorf, senior, of Basel, but even Buxtorf did not claim the pointing to be original but to have been introduced about the time of Ezra, after the return from the Captivity. His ideas were contained in *Tiberias sui commentarius massorethicus*, (Basel 1620). Yet the canonicity of the pointing never became a considerable problem during the sixteenth century, and it was not until the seventeenth century that Louis Cappel's work *Arcanum punctuationis revelatum, sive diatriba de punctis vocalium et accentuum apud* Turrettini also opposes Coton's arguments, but by a quite different method. Firstly, he states that even if the Hebrew text were corrupt, it would still have more authority than any other.[66] He defines three accusations of Coton who said that the Masoretes invented the pointing, that having done so they corrupted the Old Testament at will and made an agreement that no other Bible should be used.[67] As is typical of Turrettini's reasoned approach to controversy, he begins by stating that the question of the canonicity of the Hebrew pointing is debatable[68] and continues to ask if, on the one hand, God would have given these writings in an unsatisfactory form[69] while he informs us that we then continue to discuss specific charges of Coton and claims that we are mature enough to note the errors committed by the Massoretes:-

> Mais l'ignorance et la malice n'ont, ni discretion pour juger, ni
> volonte pour approuver le bien, et connoistre la verite, la ou
> elle est.[70]

One most interesting point is that one of Turrettini's arguments seems also to be found in the work of Louis Cappel which might indicate some communication between them. This is the idea that comparison of ancient Greek translations and paraphrases of the Old Testament shows that these were made from unpointed texts.[71] However, Turrettini's ideas are not identical with those of Cappel and it would be unwise to stress this point on such slight evidence.

So, in conclusion, it may be noted that the epigones were not prepared to decide publicly on the canonicity or non-canonicity of the Hebrew vowel points, possibly because of some knowledge of Cappel's forthcoming work. Turrettini does not appear to find it a major issue, possibly wishing to avert further controversy by not adopting an intransigent position. What does seem to be quite clear, however, is that neither Tronchin nor Turrettini consider the question of the pointing to alter the authenticity of the Biblical text nor its authority, for Turrettini asks:-

> Car quand, ni le Grec ni l'Hebrieu, n'auroient ni clairte ni
> certitude, la trouveroit - on en son Eglise? La verite de la
> Doctrine celeste, y est elle plus pure, plus forte, qu'en
> l'Escriture, en quelle langue, qu'elle soit?[72]

and Tronchin writes:-

> Car ce fondement est certain que *tout homme est menteur,* quand
> il parle des choses du Royaume de Dieu, sinon quand il en
> parle selon que Dieu nous l'Enseigne en sa parole.[73]

The purpose of scripture.

The Genevans are on more traditional problems at this point. They re-iterate the sense and sometimes even the language of their confessions. There is little exceptional about their statements on these matters. They do not deviate from well established orthodox positions and while their defense of these is fluent and forthright, it is not particularly distinguished. Scripture, according to Turrettini, is the word of God, and was given to man as part of the working of Divine providence.[74] It is the work of God and not of man, being written by men under the inspiration and guidance of the Holy Spirit,[75] and in it is revealed the will of God for men according to Tronchin's statements:[76] yet these Genevan attitudes are far from naive, and both Tronchin and Turrettini are aware of the problems involved, since Tronchin points out that what is obscure in one part of Scripture, admitting that some points are obscure, is always clarified by another.[77] Turrettini[78, 79] is more concerned with textual problems and believes that the main purpose of scripture is to transmit the word of God to man and thus to reveal doctrine, which is contained within it, there being an interaction between the credo of Church and the biblical text. It would seem that at this time, so close to Dort, the doctrines, which had the most importance for the epigones were those relating to salvation. This is perhaps best expressed by Tronchin:-

> Toute l'Escriture Saincte est comme une lettre que Dieu escrit
> a tous ses enfans, comme a dit Gregoire Evesque de Rome,
> lises donc tout ce que Dieu vous escrit pour vostre salut.[80]

He also gave other instances of the seventeenth century preoccupation with salvation which he shared with all contemporary theologians and with most contemporary laymen.[81]

Thus, in conclusion, it may be seen that the Genevan concept of Scripture was that the Bible was the word of God, not of man, given to man by God's providence to reveal His will, and that it contained the materials necessary for the formulation of dogmatic propositions. There are various problems of interpretation, but these can be overcome, and man can clearly see God's doctrines revealed in scripture, and thus find his way to salvation.

This brief discussion of the Coton controversy does lead on to a number of interesting matters. It is a revelation of the importance which Geneva and the French Reformed Church gave to the attacks of Jesuit polemicists. These controversies, often passed over as an unpleasant aspect of seventeenth century Church history, unworthy of serious historical study, a kind of boring game played out between theologians, must now be seen as a matter of real importance. The reactions noted above, the fear of the French Reformed Church about Diodiati's new translation of the Bible, and the replies of Geneva ordered by the Conseil all reveal the seriousness with which European protestants regarded Jesuit polemics. It is not for us to question their judgment. The polemics, written in an age when fear of damnation was an aspect of everyday life, must have had a real effect on people - or the protestants would hardly have been so worried. This unease is an instance of protestant defensiveness, if not defeatism, in the seventeenth century. It was not merely theoretical but practical, as the Genevan attempts to export their reformation were checked in Venice and, later, in Constantinople.

The controversy itself is of interest in that, as with so many other matters in this thesis, it leads us to a consideration of important matters that have been insufficiently explored; the matter of the Hebrew vowel points where even Tronchin and Turrettini seem to differ; the authority of the Bible the authority of a book depending on usefulness for salvation rather than authorship; the Genevan idea of the need to translate and retranslate the Bible and the idea of the essential meaning of a text coming across through different translations.

NOTES

[1] A & A de Backer & C Sommervogel S.J., *Bibliothèque de la Compagnie de Jesus* vol VIII, cols 603-10 and *Catalogue des livres de la bibliothèque nationale* vol CCVI cols 1019-83.

[2] *Dictionnaire de théologie catholique* vol XV,2, cols 2699-700.

[3] H. Hurter S.J. *Nomenclator Literarius Theologiae Catholicae*, vol III, col 987.

[4] *Dictionnaire de biographie francaise*, vol IX, pp. 830-1.

[5] R.Bellarmine, *Disputationes de controversiis Christianae fidei, Adversus huius temporis haereticos*. vol I, p-6v.

[6] *Catalogue de la bibliothèque nationale* vol CCVI, col 1031, Haag, *La France Protestante* vol II, p319.

[7] *Catalogue de la bibliotheque nationale* vol CCVI, col 1046.

[8] The 1644 French translation of the Bible by Diodati, see Diodati bibliography p. 22, no. 15.

[9] F.Veron, *Grand trouble arrive de nouveau etc.* p. 1.

[10] Geneva, Bibliotheque publique et universitaire, manuscript Ami Bullin 53, folia 77-80.

[11] Quick, *Synodicon in Gallia Reformata*, vol II, p. 421.

[12] Diodati, *Les Livres de Iob* etc, p. 4.

[13] Geneva, Bibliotheque publique et universitaire, manuscrit francais 427, Correspondence Ecclesiastique 1637-44, folia 183-5.

[14] Quick, *Synodicon in Gallia Reformata*, vol II, p. 552.

[15] *Dictionnaire de biographie francaise*, vol IX, pp. 830-1.

[16] *Ibid*, vol IX, p. 831.

[17] W. Bouwsma, *Venice and the Defense of Republican Liberty*, p. 505.

[18] *Catalogue de la bibliotheque nationale*, vol XXXII, col. 1123.

[19] Pierre-Paul Plan, *Pages Inedites de Theodore-Agrippa D'Aubigne* (Geneva 1945) pp 133-4.

[20] Geneva, Musee historique de la Reformation, Archives Tronchin vol LXXIII.

[21] *Dictionnaire de biographie francaise*, vol IX, col 831.

[22] Th. Tronchin, *Coton plagiaire*, 2 5b.

[23] Charles Read, "Le Grimoire du R. P. Coton" in *Bulletin de la societe de l'histoire du protestantisme francais*, vol XXXIX, (1890) pp. 200-22.

[24] Th. Tronchin, *Coton plagiaire* 2 5a.

[25] B. Cresson, *Response aux allegations*, pp. 6, 13.

[26] B. Turrettini, *Defense de la fidelite*, p. 2 4b.

[27] Geneva, Archives d'Etat, RCP E copy p. 286, 30 Jan 1618.

[28] *Ibid*, p. 287, 13 Feb 1618:-"Estant question de respondre au livre de Cotton, intitule Geneve Plagiaire, auquel il condamne la version de la Bible, et en outre traite de divers articles qui sont en controverse entre les orthodoxes et ceux de l'Eglise romaine. Advise que deux de la Compagnie facent la response, pour plus exactement recercher tout ce qui sera necessaire de coucher en une response de telle importance. Et a cest effect nos deux freres, Messieurs Tronchin et Turretin Professeurs en Theologie ont este nemmes pour y travailler et communiquer aux particuliers de la Compagnie leurs cayers devant que mettre

au net de ce qu'ils auront fait: et ne mettront rien sur la presse que tout l'oeuvre ne soit parachevee, et lors sera advise du tiltre du livre."

[29]Geneva, Archives d'Etat, RCP copy pp. 295-6, 10 April 1618;-"Sur le propos entrejette de la response a Cotton par deux de nos freres. A este advise que nos dits freres communiquent ensemble de leurs labeurs de peur que tous deux ne facent une mesme chose. Et cependant sera rapporte vendredi prochain ce qu'ils en ont desja fait par ceux qui ont pris charge de conferer les pieces l'une avec l'autre. Messieurs Goulart, Prevost, Diodati, Gervais et la Roche les feront."

Ibid, pp. 296-7, 17 April 1618:- "Nos freres qui ont eu charge de voir ce qui a este, fait de la response a Cotton, Jesuite, ayans rapporte ce qu'ils en ont recognu, assavoir beaucoup de labeur et addresse a la refutation des faussetes alleguees par le dit Cotton en son livre. La Compagnie louant Dieu des dons et de l'adresse de nos dits freres, les a exhortes de continuer au dit oeuvre, avec toute la prudence: qu'il sera possible tant pour restreindre le dit oeuvre le plus succinctement qu'ils pourront, et communiquer ensemble le plus souvent qu'il leur sera possible, pour parachever au plus tost le dit oeuvre pour le mettre an lumiere."

[30]*Ibid*, p. 302, 29 May 1618:- "Propose qu'il seroit bon de mettre en lumiere une partie de la response qui se fait au livre de Coton par nos freres Messieurs Tronchin et Turretin tant pour donner quelque contentement aux esprits les plus prompts, des la foire prochaine de Francfort que aussi pour procurer un peu de relasche a nes dits freres qui autrement seront trop presses a poursuivre une prompte response a tout la livre, ou bien icelle tarderoit trop longtemps a estre produite. Advise que nos dits freres en conferent ensemble pour s'accorder dy moyen de ce faire: soit tous deux ensemble, soit un seul: mesmes estant laisse a la liberte de notre frere Monsieur Tronchin de faire se refutation en Latin."

[31]*Ibid*, p. 303, 19 June 1618.

[32]B.Turrottini, *Defense de la fidelite*, 3b.

[33]Geneva, Archives d'Etat, RCP copy p. 308, 31 July 1618.

[34]*Ibid*, p. 310, 14 August 1618.

[35]Geneva, Archives d'Etat, RC t 117 f 173v, 15 August 1618:- "A este leue l'epistre luminaire de Sp Benedick Turretin sur la response par luy contre le livre de Pierre Cotton intitule Geneve, plagiaire, laquelle il a dediee au Roy, et a este arreste qu'elle soit laissee et dediee et dediee comme elle est."

[36]*Ibid*, f 204v, 16 Sept 1618:- "Rapport de Monsieur Anjorrant. Se proposa lors le livre du Capucin Cotton Intitule Geneve plagiaire, surquoy il eust advis que messieurs les ministres de cest Eglise debvoyent faire response, a laquelle Sp. Benedic Turrcttin a travaille, et laquelle il a veue, et estime qu'on ne trouvera de quoy y contrerooller. Il estoit desja parti quand on luy envoya la response pour la presenter au Roy, en quoy il se fust trouve bien empesche, bien l'eust il peu faire remettre en la bibliotheque du Roy comme fut la harangue de feu Monsieur Lect sur la mort du feu Roy, laquelle on n'a jamais voulu permettre luy estre presentee ny a a la Royne."

[37]Geneva, Archives d'Etat, RCP copy p. 368, 22 Oct 1619.

[38]Geneva, Archives d'Etat, RC t 118 f 238r, 15 Dec 1619:- "Messieurs de Chasteauneuf et Sarrazin Rapportent qu'ils ont veu ledit livre Intitule, Recheute de Geneva plagiaire, lequel ils trouvent avoir este compose avec beaucoup d'artifice, et que Monsieur Turetin doit estre exhorte d'y respondre par form de duplique. Arreste d'exhorter ledit Seignoir Turetin a ce faire, et a cest effect qu'il soit descharge des lecons publiques pour quelque temps.

[39]Geneva, Archives d'Etat, RCP copy p. 376, 17 Dec 1619.

[40]*Ibid*, p. 9, 4 Feb 1620.

[41]Geneva, Archives d'Etat, RCP copy pp. 9-10, 25 March 1625.

[42]Quick, *Synodicon in Gallia Reformata*, vol II, p. 414.

[43]B. Turrettini, *Defense de la fidelite*, p. 24.

[44]See W. Niesel, *Bekenmni chriften und Kirchenordnungen*, 66-7, 120-1.

[45]I. Pollin, *Theses theologicae de Dei providentia. Quas, cum bona Dei providentia*, A3v, thesis XIV. The text was Wisdom 8/1.

[46]T. Tronchin, *Coton Plagiaire ou la verite de Dieu* etc., pp. 44-5.

[47]*Ibid.* p. 38.

[48]Tronchin, *Coton plagiaire*, p. 63, S'il y a des cas ou il faille, esclaircir la Bible Latine par le texte Hebrieu et Grec, elle n'est pas authentique, elle n'a pas absolue et souveraine authorite: car il y a d'autres textes plus clairs, et moins corrompus qu'elle, sinon qu' on voulust dire qu'il la faut esclaircir et corrige par exemplaires plus obscurs et plus corrompus qu'elle, ce qui seroit absurde. Il y peut donc avoir des erreurs.

[49]Turrettini *Defense de la fidelite*, p9, ils ont iuge plus expedient qu l'on ne s'estudiast plus a corriger la copie par l'original, et a refondre les types usez, et a les iustifier sur les matrices Royales et Divines du Grec et de l'Hebrieu, mais que *Latinae fidei redderentur Graecae:* et que le Grec fust corrige par le Latin: comme fit Accius Navius Magicien: on coupast la queux avec le rasoir, et qu'on reforme auiourd'huy l'Hebrieu par le Grec, le Grec par le Latin, et le Latin par le Romain, l'Eglise par la Cour, les commandemens du Maistre, par la desreiglee praticque des serviteurs? A quoy servent donc en la Preface, tant de baisemains a la Iesuitique, et reverences faites a l'Escriture, en l' honorant de beaux tiltres et feignant d'estre jaloux de son zele, si le but est tout contraire?

and

Ibid. pp. 63-4, Dire, qu'il faut corriger les Originaux par la Vulgaire, c'est le faiste de l'impudence, qui renverse de fonds en comble, et toute la raison, l'Escriture, et la Foy, et l'Antiquite, et particulierement S. Hierome, S. Augustin: brief, qui frappe toute l'Eglise. Mais a certain audace, il y a, Dieu merci, nombre de doctes, dans le parti des Adversaires, qui s'y opposent.....desquels il valoit mieux apprendre, que destruire et leur nom et leurs oeuvres d'un revers.

[50]Turrettini, *Defense de la fidelite*, pp. 14-5, On vouloit debattre contre Geneve, mais il a fallu ouvrir la bouche contre Dieu, devant que de mouvoir la langue contre nous. On se prenoit a nos versions, qui sont copies, mais il a fallu combattre les Notaires et les Protocolles du Sainct Esprit. La cause de Dieu nous servira de rempart, il est invincible. Pour nous defendre, il nous faut maintenir sa verite. Pour estre maintenus en nostre innocence, il nous faut declarer sa Justice. Et qui ne s'asseureroit ou la partie est si bien faite? Car si nous nous employons pour sa cause, certes il garantira la nostre, et si nous respondons pour sa parolle, douterons-nout (*sic*) qu'il ne nous assiste?

[51]*Ibid*, p. 2 + i b, Et quand il y auroit en nos traductions quelque defaut; si est-ce que ce n'est ni faussete, ni falsification. Car nous ne faisons point de nos versions un texte Authentique pour leur donner le cours au prix de l'original. Il nous suffit qu' elles servent aux fideles, sans vouloir qu'ils soyent assuiettes a autre parole qu'a celle de Dieu. Aussi ne pretendons-nous en maintenir que la fidelite; car l'autorite, nous la laissons toute entiere a l'Autheur et au Souverain, qui domine sur les consciences.

[52]See chapter 5.

[53]Turrettini, *Defense de la fidelite*, p. 7.

[54]Tronchin, *Coton plagiaire*, p. 100.

[55]*Ibid.* p. 2 + 3b.

[56]*Ibid.* p. 2 + 7a.

[57]Le 3. aage, se doit considerer depuis la mort de S. Hierome, iusques au temps que les Iuifs composerent leur Talmud. Car en cet interstice, la variete des examplaires Hebrieux fut si grande, que si les Rabbins n'y eussent apporte quelque ordre etc. Coton, *Geneve Plagiaire*, p. 27.

[58]Tronchin, *Coton Plagiaire*, p. 19, Des preuves que dessus appert, que Dieu par sa providence a establi sa parole et l'a conservee a son Eglise; que les Juifs qui aujourd'huy sont ennemis de l'Evangile de Jesus-Christ, n'ont jamais attente contre l'Escriture Saincte pour la corrompre, ne l'ont peu a cause de la fidelite des Chrestiens qui avoyent des livres aussi

bien qu'eux; ne l'ont voulu jamais, n'ayans tousiours monstre qu'une grande integrite de conscience en ce fait: et partant qua le texte que Dieu a inspire a ses Prophetes pour escrire en Hebrieu, comme il a este jadis, aussi l'est encores., l'original, pur, entier et certain de la verite de Dieu.

[59]Tronchin, *op.cit.*, p. 30, La verite donc es tres-pures fontaines de l'Hebreu. Sainct Hierome fait mention des poincts Hebrieux.

[60]Tronchin, *op. cit.*, pp. 37-8, Ainsi par l'autorite de tant d'hommes doctes qui ont approuve le jugement d'Arias Montanus, Coton et ses semblables qui disent l'Escriture Saincte avoir este corrompue par les Massorets, sont appelles iniques, et condamnes comme ignorans qui ne scavent ce qu'ils disent, et comme ennuyeux calomniateurs.

[61]Salvetat, *Essai sur Louis Cappel*, pp. 8-11.

[62]A. Polanus von Polansdorf, *Syntagma theologiae christianae* (Hanau 1625), vol I, p. 75. See also a short note on this subject in O. Ritschl, *Dogmengeschichte des Protestantismus,* vol I, pp 191-2.

[63]Turrettini, *Defense de la fidelitè*, pp. 54-5. Je ne veux contester sur cet article, qui ne fait rien au fonds: car tousiours seront les Adversaires trop empruntes, a verifier l'accusation, que par ces points ils ayent espanche le poison de leurs falsifications. Toutesfois, pour en dire en passant ce que ie remarque, le nom de Massoreth nous advertit, que c'est tradition, et non nouvelle introduction: mais practique qui a desia precede.

[64]Turrettini, *Defense de la fidelite*, p. 54.

[65]E-A.Salvetat, *Essai sur Louis Cappel* (Thése presentèe a la faculté de theologie protestante de Strasbourg, 1870), pp. 5-6.

[66]vous avez presuppose, que l'original est corrumpu. Est-ce par vostre vulgaire? mais ce n'est qu'une traduction. Et si elle a des atteintes a vostre dire, et souvent ne peut estre bien entendue sans retourner a l'Hebreu, sera-elle juge des autres?...Qui croiraon? ou la Regle, l'esquierre, le compas, ou le mur qui panche, fait ventre, se desprent, et menace ruine? Turrettini, *Defense de la fidelite*, pp. 12-3.

[67]Turrettini, *op.cit.*, p. 53, Quant aus Points, qui servent aux Hebrieux comme les voyelles...si les Massorets, en sont les auteurs, ou seulement les collocateurs: entre les doctes, il y a de la controverse, raisons et allegations; que je n'ay que faire d' entrelacer toutes.

[68]Turrettini, *op.clt.*, p. 53.

[69]*Ibid.*, pp. 53-4, Quelle confusion, quelle difficulte, s'il n'y eust eu aucunes voyelles? Est il a presumer que Dieu ait donne sa Loy, ses commandemens, en sorte qu'une partie y defaillist? Partant, plusieurs estiment que les poincts estoient devant les Massorets, mais que, comme encore aujourd'huy parmi les Orientaux, l'ordinaire escriture, et la lettre courante se passe de voyelles, ainsi qu' alors fort peu d'exemplaires avoient les poincts adioustez; et que la dissipation des Juifs leur apportant une ignorance de leur langue originelle, et un danger d'oubliance totale: les Massorets, pour retenlr l'usage de la lecture, et de la vraye prononciation des mots, mirent peine, en recueillant fort exactement des exemplair punctues qu'ils trouverent, et des observations anciennes tout ce qui servoit a leur dessein; de laissera la posterite une asseurance garantie, et forte barriere, contre toutes les corruptions, qui se fussent peu glisser dans l'enclos de l'Escriture.

[70]Turrettini, *Defense de la fidelite,* p. 59.

[71]Salvetat, *Essai sur Louis Cappel,* pp. 10-11.

[72]*Turrettini, Defense de la fidelite, p. 95.*

[73]*Tronchin, Coton plagiaire, p. 3-19.*

[74]Turrettini, *Defense de la fidelite,* pp. 74-5, En quoi est notable la merveilleuse Providence de Dieu, qui a voulu a l'homme material, lui donner sa verite, sa *parole de vie,* palpable et visible, comme en un corps, et dans ses membres. La mesme Providence, qui a voulu rendre sa verite ainsi perceptible, le fait en second lieu, par le don des langues, qui nous donnent acces et facilite a toucher ce en quoy Dieu s'est voulu manifester a nous.

[75]Turrettini, *op.cit.*, p. 4b, Et Dieu l'avoit baillee pour semence incorruptible, quelque corruption qui survint au monde, pour lumiere et enseigne opposee aux confusions. Que la Parole de Dieu soit douteuse, et celle des hommes Canonique et Catholique! Sire, ce sont des dogmes ou il nous meine, autant estran ges a la piete, qu'incognus a la pure Antiquite, bastis pour asservir les ames, les hommes, les Royaumes a la dictature de Rome.

[76]Tronchin, *Coton Plagiaire*, pp. 21-2, Entre les hommes le Testament est declaration de derniere volonte, pour regler les heritiers: au dire de ces gens, Dieu es Sainctes Escritures, (appellees Testament entre autres raisons pour celle la que c'est la derniere et totale declaration de sa volonte pour nostre salut, que nous en avons en ceste vie) aura fait un Testament ou il n'a pas suffisamment declare sa volonte? Ils crieront qu'il est corrompu? blasphemes, qui font auiourd'huy neantmoins des principaux points de nos differents.

[77]Tronchin, *Coton plagiaire*, p. 49, La difficulte qui y est ne doit pas estre une barriere pour chasser les hommes de la lecture de la parole de Dieu, mais un esguillon a la surmonter. Ce qui est obscur en un lieu est esclairci par l'autre; l 'assiduite, la diligence pour se la rendre familiere, l'invocation de Dieu pour obtenir sa grace et le don de son Esprit pour estre esclaire en la cognoissance de sa verite, sont les moyens par lesquels les choses nous sont rendues claires.

[78] Turrettini, *Defense de la fidelita*, p. 8, Ne nous trompons pas, on ne comdamne point nostre version, pour nous en donner une meilleure: ou l'original, pour nous esclaircir les difficultez qui y sont: car nous viendrons desireux de profiter, prests a corriger, disposez a escouter raison en tout chose. Mais a travers nostre version, on taxe le Texte mesmes, et dans le texte hebrieu, et Grec; la vulgaire, leur Authentique, est enveloppee en mesme faisseau, par les brouillesments dont elle est obscurcie; et dans les textes quels qu'ils soyent, l'Escriture; et en l'Escriture la parole de vie, la patente du Ciel, et en icelle finalement, on se prend a l'authorite de nostre Seigneur. Voila iusques ou passent les traicts, qui se lancent contre l'Escriture Saincte.

[79]Turrettini, *Defense de la fidelite*, p. 75, C'est pourquoy, comme pour Canon de nostre foy, nous ne voulons que la doctrine celeste; aussi pour reigle de ceste doctrine et corps, dans lequel il la faut cercher, nous ne voulons que le Canon des Sainctes Escritures, et la perfection des sentences y contenues; et pour reigle et fondement des sens particuliers de chasque passage, qui conservent la doctrine et analogie de la foy, il faut que pour indubitable et derniere certitude des interpretations, on vienne a l'Original; ou les mesmes sont de l'Esprit de Dieu mesmes, ni estrecies par ignorance ou malice, ni aggrandies et eslargies par l'audace, ou negligence des hommes.

[80]Tronchin, *Coton plagiere*, p. 91.

[81]Tronchin, *op.cit.*, p. 110, En l'Eglise Romaine ils demandent obeissance aveugle et de beste, dont ils tirent profit: pourtant ils sont marris qu'on ait mis en lumiere l'Escriture sainte. Car c'est-elle seule qu'il faut suivre par necessite: mais de tous les escrits des hommes il en faut juger avec liberte…c'est elle qui rend les hommes sages a salut, les fait sortir de Babylon, et establissment en leurs coeurs le regne de Jesus Christ, destruit celui de l'Antechrist: leur apprenant a discerner le bien d'avec le mal, le vray d'avec le faux; cela se fait par la lumiere de la parole de Dieu, qui seule en est la pierre de touche, et la reigle de discretion; qui sont les hommes de la servitude de Satan et de la superstition des hommes et les met en la liberte des enfans de Dieu, comme estant la puissance de Dieu en salut a tout croyant.

Chapter Four
Students' work.

One of the most interesting studies undertaken in this pattern of attempts to define the theology of the Genevan Academy at the time of the Synod of Dort involved not only the staff but also the students of the Academy. Theses written by students of the Genevan Academies are to be found in a number of libraries in Switzerland and elsewhere, the best collections being at the Zentralbibliothek in Zurich, the Stadtbibliothek in Winterthur and, of course, the Bibliotheque publique et universitaire in Geneva. There is, in fact, no complete collection of these theses and it is perhaps time that more work was undertaken on this important and revealing aspect of the work of the Genevan Academy.

The theses were all printed in Geneva by the usual series of university printers, Pierre de la Rouviere, Jean de Tournes, and Pierre Aubert. The theses were thus capable of wide dissemination and so were a public as well as an internal exercise. Wider interest in these theses would also have been generated by the dedications which they all contain. Many are the work of Genevan students who dedicated their work to their parents or to Genevan pastors, but there were many students from abroad, and we find a student from Saintonge, David Primerose, dedicating his theses to John Cameron and Louis Cappel, while a student from Picardy, Charles Des Champs, dedicated his theses to the Charenton pastors,Pierre Du Moulin, Samuel Durand and Jean Mestrezat. These distinguished men would all have received copies of such theses. The theses which concern us here date from an earlier period than Diodati's dispute with Du Moulin or the dispute concerning the Hebrew vowel points that concerned Cappel, but it is interesting to note that such dedications were made only a short time before such controversies developed.

The theses are interesting in a number of ways. They were, theoretically at any rate, written by the students themselves under the supervision of their professors. The Statutes of the Genevan Academy state that this is to be the case, though we need not expect many opinions to be expressed which would differ radically from those of the epigones. This very   dependence, inevitable in the climate of early seventeenth century Geneva is,of course, one sound reason for making some effort to study this large corpus of material. The theses will, we may be sure, express a great deal of the epigones' attitude to many subjects. It would, however, be wrong to regard these theses only as mere surrogate expressions of the epigones opinions, for, if this were so, then we should expect not only a similarity in doctrine but in method when looking at theses written under the direction of particular epigones. As will be seen below, this was by no means the case, theses defended under Diodati or Tronchin show a wide variation in methodology and in the use of exegesis. This does not contradict the point made previously that these theses are useful in determining the general doctrinal attitude of the Genevan Academy, though it is a necessary caution. The theses from this period are of particular relevance to this present study in that they consider subjects, such as the sacraments, which are not found discussed at

The Epigones

length in the epigones' own writings. The theses are academically difficult and
uniformly well prepared. Since the Academy did not award doctorates these are
all "undergraduate" theses and represent a high level of work not found among
theological undergraduates in twentieth century universities. The length of the
theses varies considerably, but they have an average length of some two to three
thousand words, and represent a considerable amount of work. The academic
level was a matter of great interest to the staff of the Academy since disputations
were conducted in public, and frequently held,in the case of non-Genevan students in the presence of representatives of other reformed churches. These
public disputations must have been of importance in preserving the status of the
Academy.

These theses are what Dibon [1] has called "Disputationes exercitii causa" or
"Disputationes sub praeside" when writing of seventeenth century Leyden, and
relate more to final theses for university degrees than to regular exercises. Little
work except for that of Petit [2], has been undertaken on this aspect of reformed
theological education.

The subjects covered in the themes chosen for theses around the time of
Dort, from 1618 to 1621 certainly reveal a considerable interest in the doctrines
discussed at that synod. This is quite natural, the group of soteriologoical doctrines which had aroused such heated argument in the Low Countries and elsewhere formed on the main interests of then contemporary reformed theologians
and would have been of consuming interest to both students and staff. It was the
kind of subject which students would have been required to explore. In the years
under Beza, theses were public exegetical exercises carried out by students, in
general accord with Melanchthonian teaching practice. These were based on the
largely Biblical lectures as a find of excursus. There is no reason to suppose that
the system had changed by the time of the Epigones.[3] Also, due to the necessity
of Genevan commitment on these matters at Dort, it was obvious that statements
on such controversial matters would have to be carefully formulated since these
would be public statements both at the disputation and by being published.
There are theses on divine providence by two different students Petrus Eilshemius and Isaacus Pollinus, two sets on predestination by Carolus Des
Champs and by Spanheim who was the most distinguished student of the
Genevan Academy at this time, two more series of theses were on perseverance
by Jacobus Stephanus and Jean Le Bachelle. Further subjects relevant to Dort
were theses *De Aeterna Dei Electione* by Jacques Michaeli and on justification by
Nicolas Vignier. As well as an interest in "Dordrechanist" subjects there was a
considerable interest in the sacraments, there being theses *De Sacra Domini Coena*
by Melchior Locherus and Abraham Brunus. There is a set on the sacraments in
general by Jacques d'Orville and a series on baptism by Rodolph Hottinger.
There are also a number of theses which are basically anti-Catholic in interest.
These include sets of theses on Purgatory by David Roverus, on the idolatry of
the Roman Church by Henry Hamers, on saving faith by Joannes Poumereau
and on Antichrist by Jean Le Bachelle. The only mainly anti-Lutheran series of
theses was *De Exanitione* by Jacques Duchat, though there is anti-Lutheran material in Locherus' theses on the eucharist. The preponderance of anti-Catholic
over anti-Lutheran polemics has been noted elsewhere in this thesis when con-

sidering the contents of the library.[4] This would seem to be further proof that the Genevan Academy was much more concerned with Catholicism than with Lutheranism, the reasons being largely geographical. Various other subjects of doctrinal interest were also explored, such as theses on sin by Samuel Jacquered and David Primerose, the theses on angels by J.J. Purrius, *De Verbo Dei* by Isaac Cohvaeus, *De Natura Dei* by Charles De'Andreas and *De Foedere Dei* by Daniel Pain.

Most of the students[5] who presented theses lived out their lives in relative obscurity. Only one, Friedrich Spanheim (1600-49), attained any considerable academic distinction. He returned to teach at the Genevan Academy in 1626 as professor of philosophy, later becoming professor of theology and rector. In 1642 he went to Leyden where he remained professor of theology until his death. Distinguished families were still sending their sons to the Academy, a sure indication of its good standing at the time. David Primerose was a son of Gilbert (1580-1641), one of the distinguished Scots like Alexander More, John Sharp and John Cameron who worked in the French speaking reformed churches about this time. Rodolph Hottinger was a member of the distinguished family of theologians from Zurich, later members including the very learned Johann Heinrich (1620-67) and Johann Jakob (1652-1735). Jacques Michaeli represented one of the rich Genevan families with Italian origins. Two students who presented sets of theses later fell into disrepute, Samuel Jacquerod of Lausanne who became a pastor in Vaud and was deposed in 1632 [6] and Jacques Duchat who later renounced protestantism. [7] Some of the students remain quite obscure despite the very thorough work of Suzanne Stelling-Michaud, including Isaac de Cohaua or Cohue of Orleans [8] and Abraham Brun of Geneva [9]. These young men may of course, have come to untimely deaths, but their very obscurity makes the high quality of their work even more interesting. The great majority of students who presented these sets of theses became pastors in one or other of the reformed churches and in this we see the Academy at its best, continuing the designs of Calvin who saw his creation as an institution for training theological ordinands for the reformed churches to a high standard. Heinrich Hamers from Frankfort-am-Main (1594-1653) later became a pastor in Holland [10], Melchior Locher from St Gall (1603-49) returned to his native canton as a pastor [11], Peter Eilshemius (1595-1649) from Emden became a pastor in Friesland[12], Nicolas Vignier from Blois (1600/1-25) later studied at Exeter College Oxford and was pastor at Blois for a short time before his untimely death, Isaac Pollin of Begnins (d1638) returned to his native canton where he served as pastor in different parishes, Jean-Jacques Pury (d1662) from Neuchatel also went to Vaud as a pastor, Daniel Pain from Poitiers (d1660) studied at Glasgow and served the French reformed Church, Hottinger became pastor at Wetzikon from 1628 until his death in 1670 [13] and Jean Le Bachelle (1588-c1665) from Metz, who like Hottinger presented more than one set of theses, later ministered to congregations in the Saar, Upper Rhine and the Palatinate [14]. The bulk of these students fulfilled the purpose of their training at the Genevan Academy. For the most part they were competent, responsible ministers of the reformed churches. It can therefore be stated from the evidence of the work contained in the thesis and from the lives of the men who studied in Geneva that at this time the Academy was still operating successfully as a training centre for reformed pastors in different reformed churches. Doubts are expressed elsewhere in this thesis about the quality of the epigones' work in other fields, but from the evidence here there would seem to be little question that the Academy under their care was operating successfully as a teaching institution. It would appear that the intention to make Geneva a centre of humanist as well as protestant studies was in decline at this period as is discussed in the chapter on the library, though there was an interest in the new astronomy, but any decline in the quality of the teaching staff is not easily to be seen reflected in the quality of students, the students work, or the careers followed by the alumni of the Academy. It would appear from other data that the area from which the Academy was drawing its students was shrinking, but this was due to external factors over which the epigones could not be expected to have any control, the growth of reformed academies in France, Hungary and the Low Countries, the overall shrinkage of the areas of reformed worship in Europe in the early seventeenth century, and the massive upheavals of the series of conflicts known as the Thirty Years War. If it were necessary or desirable to make over-simple comparisons of the academic quality of different reformed academies, then it might be suggested that Geneva at this period was less interesting intellectually than Saumur, Leyden or Heidelberg. Yet even if such was the assertion, it could not be supported by the evidence of the success of Geneva as a teaching institution. Nor, from the evidence presented here, would it be possible to suggest that the financial stringency experienced at Geneva between 1608 and 1628 had much or any effect on the kind of students who came to study, or on the quality of their training.

All three epigones were involved in this aspect of the Academy's work. They all presided over disputations and presumably helped to draw the theses up for presentation. There does not appear to have been any specialisation among the professors with regard to the subjects of the theses and all three presided over theses on matters pertaining to the soteriological controversies, anti-Catholic subjects and sacramental problems as well as other matters. Thus we find that Tronchin presided over theses *De Angelis* (Pury), *De Sacra Domini Coena* (Brun), *De Verbe Dei* (Cohvaeus), and *De Dei Providentia* (Pollin), while Diodati presided over theses *De Antechristo* (Bachelle) *De Natura Dei* (D'Andreas), *De Peccato* (Primerose), *De Praedestinatione* (Des Champs) and *De Foedere Dei* (Pain) as well as others. It would not seem to be the subject of the theses that was the deciding factor. It was probably settled by simple rotation or by a system of students selecting the theses subject based on the loci comunes drawn by one of the epigones from Academy lectures based, most probably, on exegesis. The professors themselves taught *a tour de rôle* as directed in Calvin's *Statutes*.

The methodology of the theses is by no means uniform, as has been mentioned above. It would appear that at this period the epigones tolerated various methods of presenting material. These may be grouped into four categories. It is not the case that particular categories are reserved for particular subjects, nor do individual epigones seem to prefer particular forms. The theses all have individual characteristics which does suggest that Calvin's original intention of the students being allowed to write their own theses was being adhered to by the epigones. But a suggested methodological grouping would be into the four following categories:-

type a -   characteristics:- theses frequently short;
                                    no explicit exegesis
                                    no patristic or other references
        Examples would include the theses *De Natura Dei* by
        D'Andreas (564 words) and the theses *De Sacra Domini Coena*
        by Brun (c2,200 words). The D'Andreas theses were presided
        by Diodati and the Brun theses by Tronchin.

type b - characteristics:-theses of different lengths, frequently long;
                                    - catenae important
                                    - no patristic or other references

        Examples would include theses presided over by Diodati such as
        the *De Peccato* by Primerose (c4,000 words), *De Praedestinatione* by
        Des Champs (2,500 words) and *De Antechristo* by Bachelle (c600
        words) as well as theses presided by Tronchin such as *De Verbo
        Dei* by Cohvaeus (c2,500 words) and *De Dei Providentia* by Pollin
        (c1,500 words).

type c - characteristics - theses of different lengths, often long catenae
                                    important
                                    patristic and other references included

        Examples would include the theses *De Baptismo* by Hot-
        tinger(c2,300 words) and *De Justificatione* by Vignier (c3,200
        words) both presided over by Turrettini and the Pain theses *De
        Foedere Dei* by Diodati (c3,000 words).

type d - characteristics - theses of different lengths
                                    catenae important
                                    patristic and other references include
                                    many theses provided with a "consectarium"

        Examples would include the Pury theses *De Angelis* (c2,000
        words) presided by Tronchin.

It must also be noted that certain theses such as Michaeli's 1622 discussion *De
vocatione hominis ad salutem*, type b theses without patristic references, have a
very definite scholastic form. Theses 1 - 14 form a table with strict subdivision of
each dogmatic point. Thus "vocatio" is "aut legalis" (again subdivided) or "aut
evangelica" which in turn is "aut externa" or "aut interna" and so on. The effective
cause is the philantropy of God, the foundation is Christ the mediator, the
instrument is external (word and sacrament) or internal (work of Holy Spirit). In
the theses 15 - 20 there is a less formally structured discussion of universality
where dogmatics are closely linked to exegesis, leading to a final section, theses
21 - 25, where the tabular methods are reintroduced. There are echoes of this
kind of rhetorical system in many of the theses, but it was not, it would seem,

obligatory. All students appear to have made attempts to ensure the logical sequence of the ideas they express throughout their sets of theses.

An interesting aspect of all the sets of theses under consideration is that they each reveal some interest in philology. This is inherent rather than explicit, but a concern for the etymological and semasiological aspects of dogmatic terms is most typical of these students. It appears in so many theses that it does not form an element in the criteria for classification of theses into the four groups noted above. Yet the way in which this philological concern is expressed does vary. Explicitly philological theses are perhaps more typical of the work prepared under Diodati than of those theses developed under the guidance of the other epigones - but this is not an absolute criterion for Bachelle's theses on the Antichrist, presided by Diodati do not have a theses devoted solely to etymology and semantics as is the case with Vignier on justification:-

> Iustificare non significat in hac disputatione, ut statum quaestionis conturbant Pontificii, vim Latinae compositionis inepte sequui, novae qualitatis collationem seu transitium ab justitiam inherentem vel actualem efficere sed ex more tum Hebraioi tum Greci sermonis, significatione forensi et iudicali, in hac controversis עשרה δικαιουν simitur pro *Absolvera, Justum promuntiare, et adea quae iustis adscribi solent, ius potestatemque tribuere*, ut contra *condemnare* כ ר עה non est *Malum facere* sed *poenae addicore*.[15]

This is also evident in Hottinger on baptism:-[16]

or Des Champs on predestination:-

> Praedestinare Latinis, Graecis προ ὁριζω duo significat; Primum, animo aliquid definire antequam agas; deinde, unumquodque antequam fiat ad certum usum & finem dirigere & deputare, atque sic ab aliis rebus seligere ac segregare. Hebraeis verbum ר אנ ח *Levit.* 20 *Num.* 16. significat
>
> electionem populi Israelitici a reliquarum nationum promiscua multitudine. Israelitici a reliquarum nationum promiscua multitudine. Igitur Praedestinatio seu ὁριφω nihil aliud esse vide

tur quam cuisusque rei ad certum suum finem ordinatio.[17]

This kind of philological method is frequently to be encountered in Diodati's annotations and in this we may see part of his influence on the teaching methods of the Academy. This kind of philological interest is not by any means peculiar to Diodati - the etymology and semantics of words used in the Old and New Testaments was a preoccupation of the seventeenth rather than the sixteenth century as is seen by the development of related polemics such as the controversy on the Hebrew vowel points which grew around the academy of Saumur and the university of Basel. Doubt about the Massoretic pointing had been expressed by Levita in the sixteenth century but Louis Cappel's Arcanum was not published until 1624. In this we see, as in the Coton controversy, [18] the teachers at the Genevan Academy in line with the interests of contemporary scholarship.

It is also to be noticed in passing that Hottinger is using a vocabulary that relates very much to late medieval scholastlicism in, for example, the *Lexicon* of Altenstaig who discussed baptism under the three headings *flaminis*, *sanguinis* and *flaminus* following Biel on the Sentences. This is yet another example of the rediscovery of medieval authors discussed elsewhere in this thesis [19]. The practice of linking their modern philology to these older ideas becomes increasingly typical of reformed theologians in the seventeenth century.

The exegetical interest of the theses is, of course, very considerable, but, as has been noted in the remarks on the suggested classification, the actual number of texts used in different theses varies very considerably as may be seen from the following table;-

Usage of the Bible by Genevan students in theses 1618-21

title and author	presided by	O.T.	Gospels	N.T. except Gospels	Totals
A - De Angelis (Pury)	Tronchin	30	23	33	86
B - De Antechristo (Bachelle)	Diodati	-	-	10	10
C - De Justificatione (Vignier)	Turrettini	5	5	35	45
D - De Sacra Domini Coena (Brun)	Tronchin	-	1	-	1
E - De Natura Dei (D'Andreas)	Diodati	-	-	-	0
F - De Verbo Dei (Cohvaeus)	Tronchin	6	6	17	29
G - De Peccato (Primrose)	Diodati	22	9	39	70
H - De Praedestinatione (Des Champs)	Diodati	16	17	52	85

title and author	presided by	O.T.	Gospels	N.T. except Gospels	Totals
I - De Baptismo					
(Hottinger)	Turrettini	1	15	24	40
J - De Dei Providentia					
(Pollin)	Tronchin	5(1)	2	7	15
K - De Foedere Dei					
(Pain)	Diodati	33	14	61	108

The number of texts used varies considerably. It is difficult to see what this relates to other than the individual wishes of the students concerned. Certainly it bears no simple relationship to individual professsors. Diodati's theses use a wide number of texts:- 0, 10, 70, 85 and 108; as do those of Tronchin:- 1, 15, 29 and 86. Nor does there seem to be any relationship between the type of subject and the number of texts used. Theses on the eucharist require only one proof text while those on baptism require forty. Among the Dort subjects, justification requires 45 proof texts, predestination 85 and providence only 15. Nor is there much apparent similarity between the proportions of the different parts of the Bible that are used when the percentages are reduced to the nearest whole percentage. The letters relate to the same theses as in the previous table above.

Usage of the Bible, numbers and percentages, by Genevan students in theses 1618-21

theses	O.T.	%O.T.	G	%G	other N.T.	%oN.T.	totals
A	30	35%	23	27%	33	38%	86
B	-	-	-	-	10	100%	10
C	5	11%	5	11%	35	78%	45
D	-	-	1	100%	-	-	1
E	-	-	-	-	-	-	-
F	6	21%	6	21%	17	58%	29
G	22	30%	9	13%	39	56%	70
H	16	19%	17	20%	52	61%	85
I	1	3%	15	38%	24	60%	40
J	5(1)	33%	2	13%	7	47%	15
K	33	31%	14	13%	61	57%	108

Even the three subjects C, H and J, most closely connected with Dort have quite different proportions. What this list does prove beyond doubt is that the Genevans of this period had a great respect for the New Testament and for the epistles rather than the Gospels. With the exception of D, which may be discounted because of its low reading, there is no case where the N.T. does not form the highest percentage, and in a clear majority of cases, a percentage so high that it is greater than the sum of the O.T. and G proof texts. To make a more detailed examination of the texts favoured by the Genevan students, it was found necessary to draw up a list of the individual books with the numbers of times these were cited by the students. The letters relate to those in the penultimate table with regard to the identification of sets of theses.

Usage of Biblical books by Genevan students in theses 1618-21

Book	total	A	B	C	D	F	G	H	I	J	K
Genesis	21	7	-	1	-	-	7	1	1	1	3
Exodus	5	-	-	-	-	1	-	-	-	-	4
Leviticus	3	-	-	-	-	-	-	1	-	-	2
Numbers	1	-	-	-	-	-	-	1	-	-	-
Deuteronomy	3	-	-	-	-	1	2	-	-	-	-
1 Samuel	3	1	-	-	-	-	-	1	-	-	1
2 Samuel	2	1	-	-	-	1	-	-	-	-	-
1 Kings	1	1	-	-	-	-	-	-	-	-	-
2 Kings	1	1	-	-	-	-	-	-	-	-	-
Job	7	5	-	-	-	-	1	-	-	-	1
Psalms	23	7	-	3	-	2	5	1	-	3	2
Proverbs	3	-	-	-	-	-	-	-	-	-	3
Ecclesiastes	1	-	-	-	-	-	1	-	-	-	-
Isaiah	16	4	-	1	-	1	3	3	-	1	3
Jeremiah	9	-	-	-	-	-	1	2	-	-	6
Ezekiel	4	-	-	-	-	-	1	2	-	-	1
Daniel	7	3	-	-	-	-	-	1	-	-	3
Hosea	5	-	-	-	-	-	1	2	-	-	2
Amos	1	-	-	-	-	-	-	1	-	-	-
Malachi	2	-	-	-	-	-	-	-	-	-	2
Wisdom	1	-	-	-	-	-	-	-	-	1	-
Matthew	33	11	-	1	-	1	3	8	4	1	4
Mark	14	4	-	2	-	1	1	-	6	-	-
Luke	18	5	-	1	1	-	2	2	2	-	5
John	27	3	-	1	-	4	3	7	3	1	5
Acts	30	2	-	-	-	1	-	12	9	1	5
Romans	76	1	-	22	-	2	14	16	1	3	17
1 Corinthians	17	1	-	2	-	5	1	2	2	-	4
2 Corinthians	14	4	-	-	-	-	3	3	2	-	2
Galatians	14	-	-	2	-	1	3	-	1	-	7
Ephesians	35	3	-	1	-	1	9	11	1	-	9
Philippians	5	-	-	1	-	1	-	3	-	-	-
Colossians	6	3	-	-	-	-	2	-	1	-	-
1 Thessalonians	1	-	-	-	-	-	1	-	-	-	-
2 Thessalonians	6	1	4	-	-	-	1	-	-	-	-
1 Timothy	5	1	-	-	-	-	1	-	1	1	1
2 Timothy	6	-	-	1	-	4	-	1	-	-	-
Titus	3	-	-	1	-	-	-	1	1	-	-
Hebrews	18	3	-	1	-	-	-	-	3	2	9
James	7	2	-	-	-	-	3	1	-	-	1
1 Peter	8	3	-	1	-	-	-	1	2	-	1
2 Peter	3	1	-	-	-	1	-	-	-	-	1
1 John	7	1	1	1	-	-	1	1	-	-	-
Jude	2	2	-	-	-	-	-	-	-	-	-
Revelation	13	5	5	2	-	1	-	-	-	-	-

From this table it becomes obvious that there were a small number of particularly favoured books. In the Old Testament the Psalms (23) and Genesis (21) were most popular. There are more references to Matthew (33) than to the fourth Gospel (27), but the most popular books are Romans (76) and Ephesians(35). It is not impossible because of the exegesis-lecture-commonplaces-thesis relationship that some of these were books which the epigones were lecturing on about this time. However, this cannot be stated categorically because there is no evidence available to inform us definitely that this was the case, and also because it does not fit in with the order of priorities of the Genevans at Dort, where the most popular Old Testament books were the Psalms and Isaiah, with only 1 text out of 59 being taken from Genesis. The Genevans at Dort used nearly twice the number of texts from John (51) that they did from Matthew (26). Romans (60 out of 252) and Ephesians (33) were again the more frequently quoted of the epistles. What is most similar to the material used at Dort is the proportion of usage of the different parts of the Bible. Here we have a proportion of O.T.- G - N.T.

of 44 - 92 - 276

or roughly 1 - 2 - 6

while the epigones at Dort had figures of:- 59 - 84 - 252

giving a rough proportion of 1 - 1-1/2 - 5.

Thus, they might not have been using the books of the Bible in the same order of priority, but they would seem to have been using the Bible in the same way with similar proportions and with the number of texts from the Old Testament and Gospels being roughly half the number from the rest of the New Testament. It is to be noted that even in the instances of popular books, there does not seem to be a consistency of interest on the part of one professor. A and G give the greatest number of texts from Genesis, yet A was presided by Tronchin and G by Diodati. Similarly the greatest number of texts from Matthew occur in A and H, but A was presided by Tronchin and H by Diodati. There seems to be little consistency. Yet the usage of the various parts of the Bible is similar with the dominance of the N.T. texts. This might all call into question the direction given by the epigones in the preparation of theses while reinforcing the picture of the overall consistency of Genevan work at this period. With regard to the large number of texts on Genesis it is to be noted that at this time Pareus' commentary on Genesis (1614) was added to the Academy library. [20]

The use of non-Biblical evidence is a much simpler problem in the study of these theses than their exegetical interest. It is a smaller problem not only in virtue of the fact that there is a smaller number of incidences, but beause only a minority of theses include explicit reference to non-Biblical sources. Implicit evidence has been ignored as being too untrustworthy - such as a vague allusion to Origen in Mitchaeli's theses *De Vocatione hominis ad salutem* from 1622. Explicit references to non-Biblical material occur in perhaps a third of the theses. Because of the spread of non-Biblical references throughout particular sets of theses, a decision to include or exclude such material must have been a definite methodological decision and so has been included as one element in the suggested classification mentioned above. There are non-Biblical references in the theses *De*

Foedere Dei (Pain) *De Baptismo* (Hottinger), *De Justificatione* (Vignier) and *De Angelis* (Pury); but against this there are many theses which quote no non-Biblical authority and these would include *De Natura Dei* (D'Andreas) *De Peccato* (Primerose) *De Verbo Dei* (Cohvaeus) *De Sacra Domini Coena* (Brun) *De Dei Providentia* (Pollin) *De Antechristo* (Bachelle) and *De Praedestinatione* (Des Champs).

The non-Biblical evidence used by the Genevan students comes from a wide range of material, classical, patristic, medieval and reformation authors are noted. As in the works written by Tronchin and Turrettini against Coton, there is an absense of orthodox reformed writers. This depends on a listing of the explicit references, for, as will be noted later, there is plenty of implicit calvinist thought. The listing of non-Biblical references does not reveal the students theology in any simple manner. This suggests another important aspect of the education which theological students received at the Genevan Academy about this time. The theses are polemical. They are based on the epigones own lectures or on Calvin or on a combination of both sources of authority, but this is never explicit. This is typical of then contemporary polemics such as those used in the dispute with Coton. The students were, it is concluded, being trained in polemical method for a ministry in which polemics would plan an important part.

References to classical authors are given by Pury and Pain, but not by Vignier or Hottinger. Pury mentions Plutarch's *De Oraculis* but Pain gives a much longer list involving Pliny, Aristotle, Pythagoras, Homer and Livy. Pain had obviously made use of the non-theological sections of the library. Augustine is by far the most often quoted patristic writer. He is quoted by Pury and Vignier as well as three times by Hottinger who also quotes Jerome and mentions the Donatist controversy. Pain mentions pelagianism and quotes the only Syriac father mentioned - Ephrem Syrus. Pury, who has the longest list of patristic references also mentions Basil, Tertullian, Damasus and Eusebius. The growing reformed interest in medieval and recent scholarship is also to be noted here, for Pury mentions Olaus Magnusson of Uppsala and the *Libri Carolini*. Hottinger uses Bernard and Pain the *Decretum Gratiani*. More contemporary authors quoted only include one author whose theology was at all similar to that of Geneva, Sebastian Münster, whose *Cosmographia Universalis* is mentioned twice by Pury. Vignier mentions Osiander only to refute his view of justification as had Calvin in the *Institutes*.[21] Hottinger mentions the Council of Trent while Pain twice notes Bellarmine and also Nicholas Sanders. As will be noted elsewhere in the discussion of the Academy library [22] at this time, a number of these works relate to recent book acquisitions. What must be clearly understood is that all these sources are used in an illustrative or polemical fashion, but never in such a way as to supercede the authority of scripture. This also applies to the text from the Apocrypha (Wisdom 8/1) used by Pollin.

The polemical nature of some students' theses may be seen in its anti-Catholic aspect in Bachelle's fifteen theses *De Antechristo* from 1620, presided by Diodati. As was noted above, these are type 'b' theses - containing proof-texts but no non-Biblical material. Bachelle begins by noting that the concept of Antichrist is scriptural, supporting this by references to 2 Thessalonians 2/- and to Revelation 13/ and 17/-. This Antichrist defiles and corrupts the church as is said in Revelation 13/11:- "it had two horns like a lamb and it spoke like a dragon."

Bachelle then notes that Antichrist works through heretics and has a variety of titles, "man of sin", "son of perdition", "Apostate", "false prophet" and "Whore of Babylon." This Antichrist was first seen as a promoter of heretics in Apostolic times as part of the Church but is not a single man but a succession. This last assertion is supported by 1 John 4/3, 2 Thessalonians 2/8, Revelation 18/7 and by a mention of Daniel. A second beast, the successor to the first is evidenced by Revelation 13/17. This Antichrist is involved in the ruin of the Roman empire through which he establishes his power, leading to heresy and general apostasy. God, however, (2 Thes 2/4) did not let this reign become absolute, though it was accompanied by many natural and false miracles which deceived many whose names were not in the lamb's book of life (2 Thes 2/9). In Revelation, John refers to Rome as "Babylon" (Rev 17/9.8) and the papacy is clearly the Antechrist, the pope in Rome. Until the second coming of Christ, the faithful are sustained by his Spirit.

In terms of doctrine, this is an unexceptional statement. The recognition of the pope as Antichrist was far from new, indeed it was an attribution first made by the Fraticelli about John XXII around 1317.[23] This attribution was adopted by Luther and appears more than once in the *Institutes* where Calvin also used the idea that it is the institution of the papacy which is Antichrist rather than any particular pope.[24] Calvin also makes another point emphasized by Bachelle, which is that Antichrist is associated with heresy.[25] The association of the Roman Empire with Antichrist is included in the notes of the Geneva Bible[26] and inspired Hobbes' to write that the papacy was the:-"ghost of the deceased Roman Empire sitting crowned on the grave thereof."[27] There was a great spate of books on the subject of Antichrist in the years 1590-1630[26] and these theses certainly stick to what were by now traditional protestant positions rather than succumbing to more fantastic notions that were then rapidly proliferating. One aspect of the problem which Bachelle omits is any reference to the chronology of the eschatological events which led to a great interest in Chronology throughout much of the seventeenth century.[29] If the Genevan collection of material on the new astronomy[30] had been gathered to help this kind of research there is no sign of it here.

Bachelle uses only ten texts in this set of theses, 2 Thes 2/-, 2/4, 2/7, 2/8, 1 John 4/3, Rev 13/17 (twice), 17/9, 17/18 and 18/7. Calvin does not use all these texts in the same way as Bachelle. 1 John 4/3 is mentioned only in the *Institutes* at 4.17.32 while the three texts from Revelations are not mentioned at all. Bachelle is only in accordance with Calvin when he considers the texts from 2 Thessalonians. 2 Thes 2/8 is used in 3.20.42, 2/7 in 4.7.25, while 2 Thes 2/4 is mentioned five times in 4.7.29, 4.7.25 (twice), and, more importantly in 4.2.12 and 4.9.4. All these usages in the *Institutes* relate to Antichrist. Bachelle is also in accordance with Diodati in his interpretation of antichrist in 2 Thessalonians, for this is the main interest of Diodati in that book. Diodati also relates Rev 13/17 and 17/8,9 to Rome though not specifically to Antichrist. 1 John 4/3 has no reference to Antichrist in the 1640/41 Sacra Bibbia and Rev 18/7 is not mentioned at all. Thus, Diodati is not to be seen forcing students to adhere to his own interpretations of scripture. What must not be overlooked, however, is that a number of texts relevant to the "problem" of Antichrist are not included here, notably 1 John 2/18,22 and 4/3 but especially 2 John 7, the only scriptural texts where the term "Antichrist" is used. This omission is even stranger because Diodati discusses Antichrist at each of these four texts in the 1640/41 annotations. Therefore the omission cannot be based on Diodati. Nor can the omission be based on Calvin's own commentary on 1 John, published in 1551 in both French and Latin[31] for on each point Calvin notes the purpose and work of Antichrist. However, when we look at the *Institutes*, we find that neither 2 John 7 nor 1 John 2/22 are used at all and that when 1 John 4/3 is used in 4.17.32 and 1 John 2/18 in 4.8.7 and 4.18.20 their interpretation is at no point related to Antichrist. The conclusion would seem to be that Bachelle's theses were a study based on the *Institutes* rather than on Diodati's or Calvin's Biblical annotations. Yet, with the inclusion of texts not used in the *Institutes*, Bachelle would seem either to have found another source or to be asserting his independence.

Further enquiries into the academic background of these theses based mainly on exegetical history may be undertaken by a consideration of three sets of theses on the problems that confronted the Synod of Dort - providence, predestination and justification. The theses selected were by Vignier, Pollin and Des Champs, with special attention paid to the last of the three. Pollin used only 15 texts Vignier 45 and Des Champs 85. These broke down into the following proportions:-

	O.T.	G	oN.T.
providence	5(1)	2	7
justification	5	5	35
predestination	16	17	52

the totals then obtained from the sum of these three are:-

26	24	96

as has already been noticed, the proportions of the Genevans at[32] Dort were:-

59	84	252.

Dividing the Dort proportions by the theses proportions we get a surprisingly uniform set of figures:-

2.3	3.4	2.7

The students use somewhat fewer texts from the Gospels and slightly more from the Old Testament, but there is an appreciable similarity. At Dort, as has been discussed in Chapter II[33] the six main foreign and the main Dutch colleges submitted a total of 1,123 proof texts used on a number of 2,465 occasions. The 2,465 instances break down into the following groups:-

379	413	1673.

Again, the oN.T. figure is greater than the sum of the other two and there is a considerable similarity in proportions to those of the students. If the Dort figures are divided by those of the students, we get:-

$$14.6 \qquad\qquad 17.2 \qquad\qquad 17.8.$$

The students are using a rather higher proportion of Old Testament texts than do their more distinguished contemporaries but since the number of texts is small (26), it would be wrong to read too much into this. The similarity of the New Testament figures, however, is quite startling and would seem to indicate that the students are using their Bibles in a pattern familiar to the staff of a number of the most distinguished reformed academies. It is now necessary to see whether this established general similarity extends to individual texts. In the following table, Column 1 indicates the texts used by Pollin, Column 2 contains those used by Vignier, 3 contains Des Champs proof texts, 4 indicates whether they are used by the Genevans at Dort, 5 indicates the number of times they were used by any of the seven main delegations at Dort including the Genevans and Column 6 indicates whether or not Diodati wrote annotations on them in his 1640/41 Bible:

	1	2	3	4	5	6
Genesis 6/5	-	-	1	0	4	yes
15/-	-	1	-	-	-	no
22/8	1	-	-	0	0	no
Leviticus 20/-	-	-	1	0	0	no
Numbers 16/-	-	-	1	0	0	no
1 Samuel 7/10	-	-	1	0	0	yes
Psalm 1/3	-	-	1	0	2	no
32/-	-	2	-	0	0	no
44/22	1	-	-	0	0	no
94/9	1	-	-	0	0	yes
143/-	-	1	-	0	0	no
Isaiah 9/6	-	-	1	0	0	yes
11/16	-	-	1	0	0	no
42/16	-	-	1	0	0	yes
43/25	-	1	-	0	0	yes
47/7	1	-	-	0	0	no
Jeremiah 32/39	-	-	1	1	2	yes
32/40	-	-	1	2	17	no
Ezekiel 36/26	-	-	1	0	6	yes
47/-	-	-	1	0	0	no
Daniel 2/-	-	-	1	0	0	no
Hosea 2/19	-	-	1	0	1	yes
2/20	-	-	1	0	0	yes
Amos 9/15	-	-	1	0	0	no

Matthew 7/17	-	-	1	0	0	no
7/18	-	1	-	0	5	no
10/-	1	-	-	0	0	no
11/21	-	-	1	1	2	yes
11/24	-	-	1	0	0	no
11/26	-	-	1	0	8	yes
11/27	-	-	1	0	1	yes
13/11	-	-	1	1	11	yes
15/-	-	-	1	0	0	no
16/-	-	-	1	0	0	no
Mark 2/7	-	1	-	0	0	no
9/24	-	1	-	0	0	yes
Luke 14/23	-	-	1	0	0	yes
17/5	-	-	1	0	2	yes
17/10	-	1	-	0	0	yes
John 4/-	-	-	1	0	0	no
5/-	1	-	-	0	0	no
6/-	-	-	1	0	0	no
6/29	-	-	1	0	2	no
6/44	-	-	1	0	7	yes
6/46	-	-	1	0	0	yes
10/-	-	-	1	0	0	no
10/15	-	-	1	0	4	yes
17/-	-	1	-	0	0	no
Acts 2/23	1	-	-	0	0	no
4/12	-	-	1	0	0	no
4/28	-	-	1	0	0	yes
9/3	-	-	1	0	0	no
9/4	-	-	1	0	0	no
9/5	-	-	1	1	1	yes
13/48	-	-	1	1	20	yes
16/6	-	-	1	0	3	yes
16/7	-	-	1	0	3	yes
16/14	-	-	1	0	5	yes
18/9	-	-	1	0	1	no
18/10	-	-	1	1	3	no
20/28	-	-	1	0	1	yes
Romans 1/-	1	-	-	0	0	no
1/16	-	1	-	0	2	yes
2/-	1	1	-	0	0	no
2/13	-	1	-	0	0	yes
3/-	-	1	-	0	0	no
3/23	-	-	1	0	4	yes
3/24	-	1	-	0	7	yes
3/26	-	1	-	0	0	yes

4/-	-	2	-	0	0	no
4/2	-	1	-	0	0	yes
4/4	-	1	-	0	1	yes
4/16	-	1	-	1	1	yes
4/23	-	1	-	0	0	yes
4/24	-	1	-	0	0	yes
5/-	-	1	-	0	0	no
5/1	-	1	-	0	7	yes
6/-	-	1	-	0	0	no
6/20	-	-	1	0	0	yes
8/-	1	2	-	0	0	no
8/2	-	1	-	1	2	yes
8/7	-	-	1	1	4	yes
8/27	-	-	1	1	1	yes
8/28	-	-	1	1	6	yes
8/29	-	-	1	3	35	yes
8/30	-	-	1	2	46	yes
8/38	-	-	1	1	5	yes
8/39	-	-	1	2	8	yes
9/-	-	-	2	0	0	no
9/6	-	1	-	1	4	yes
9/16	-	-	1	0	9	yes
9/26	-	1	-	0	1	no
10/-	-	-	2	0	0	no
11/-	-	-	2	0	0	no
14/23	-	1	-	0	1	yes
1 Corinthians 1/-	-	1	-	0	0	no
1/31	-	1	-	0	0	yes
2/24	-	-	1	0	0	yes
7/25	-	-	1	0	0	yes
2 Corinthians 3/5	-	-	2	2	6	no
10/5	-	-	1	0	0	yes
Galatians 3/-	-	1	-	0	0	no
4/9	-	1	-	1	1	yes
Ephesians 1/4	-	-	1	3	39	yes
1/6	-	1	-	0	9	yes
1/11	-	-	1	2	16	yes
1/19	-	-	1	1	3	yes
2/1	-	-	1	0	8	yes
2/5	-	-	2	0	3	no
2/8	-	-	1	1	9	yes
2/10	-	-	2	2	7	yes
5/25	-	-	1	0	3	no
6/23	-	-	1	1	1	no
Philippians 1/29	-	-	2	2	7	no
2/13	-	-	1	2	26	yes
3/12	-	1	-	1	1	yes
1 Timothy 4/10	1	-	-	0	1	yes

2 Timothy 1/9	-	1	-	2	18	yes
2/26	-	-	1	0	1	yes
Titus 1/1	-	-	1	1	8	yes
3/7	-	1	-	0	0	yes
Hebrews 1/3	1	-	-	0	0	yes
4/16	-	1	-	0	0	yes
11/-	1	-	-	0	0	no
James 4/12	-	-	1	0	0	no
1 Peter 1/9	-	-	1	0	1	yes
2/9	-	1	-	1	1	yes
1 John 1/18	-	1	-	0	0	no
2/19	-	-	1	2	9	yes
Revelation 1/5	-	1	-	0	0	no
1/6	-	1	-	0	0	yes

From this table it may be seen that these Genevan students were bound neither to follow the Genevan proof texts used at Dort nor the contents of the catenae of the other main delegations. Of 103 individual texts (i.e. excluding references to whole chapters) used by these students, no less than 71 had not been used by the Genevans at Dort and 40 had not been used by any delegation. To assert that these students were not bound to follow the Dort catenae is not to state that they rejected the exegetical traditions followed by the orthodox members of that Synod, for it is to be noted that a majority of their texts were used in the synod and these included 9 of the 24 most frequently used texts; Rom 8/30, Eph 1/4, Rom 8/29, Phil 2/13, Acts 13/48, 2 Tim 1/9, Jer 32/40, Eph 1/11 and Mat 13/11. However, the failure to include 15 of the most widely used texts would tend to suggest at least a change of emphasis.[34] The 9 texts mentioned above were not new to soteriological controversy at Dort and their inclusion need have little to do with the catenae of the synod. While the students use 31 texts used by delegations other than the Genevans at Dort, they do not seem to be following any particularly non-Genevan delegation. Nor does the fact that Des Marets dedicates his theses to Du Moulin help to establish his exegetical antecedents, for the dissimilarity between his lists and those of Du Moulin is much more clearly marked than between Des Marets and the Genevans at Dort. In Du Moulin's long statement sent to the Synod of Dort[35] in lieu of his attendance which had been forbidden by the French government[36], there are some 69 proof texts, a high proportion being Johannine, Des Marets used only five;- Ezech 36/26, Rom 8/28, Eph 1/4, Eph 5/25 and Titus 1/1. These are all texts used by different delegations at Dort and it would be unwise to suggest that they might come from Du Moulin. One point which might be noticed is that the students are using some of the texts used only by the Genevans at Dort. These include Acts 9/5, Rom 4/16, Rom 8/27, Gal 4/9, Eph 6/23, Phil 3/12 and 1 Peter 2/9. However, this list of seven texts does not form a considerable proportion of the 174 used solely by Diodati and Tronchin at Dort. A comparison was also made with the catenae of the chapters 21, 22 and 23 of book 3 of the *Institutes*, which also deals with election, its scriptural proofs and the refutation of criticisms. This proved to be another unconvincing exercise. Calvin used a total of 183 texts in these three chapters, the fact that Des Marets used only 10 of them would seem to indicate that he was not basing this set of theses on Calvin's work. It was then decided to examine Diodati's interpretation of the texts used by these three students. It was found that there was a very considerable similarity of interpretation. Of the 103 texts listed here, Diodati wrote notes on 77. Only a few of Diodati's interpretations were not germane to the subjects under discussion. The relationship thus clearly established is particularly striking on texts such as Galatians 4/9 where there is a strong relationship between Diodati's annotations and Vignier's theses, but where this interpretation is not explicitly found in Calvin nor in the catenae of any important delegation to Dort except Geneva. The conclusion is that for the three sets of theses discussed here, the source of exegetical knowledge was more frequently found in Diodati than elsewhere.

There are few simple answers to the problems involved in the study of these theses. As has been seen, there can be a dependance on either Diodati or Calvin. Bachelle was closer to the *Institutes* and Des Marets, Vignier and Pollin all closer to Diodati. Further dependance on the *Institutes* is to be seen in Hottinger's theses on baptism where the student from Zurich uses texts such as Gen 17/7 which are included in Calvin's chapter on baptism,[37] but which are not interpreted by Diodati in such a way as to relate to this sacrament. Calvinist influence is to be seen not only in exegesis but in dogmatic writing. Pury's theses on angels relate very much to the *Institutes* and his 2nd and 4th theses may be seen to relate to 1.14.9 while the 5th and 9th theses relate to 1.14.4. At least some of these theses must have been prepared as an exercise in Calvinist orthodoxy on the part of the students. There are no explicit references to be found, but the implicit evidence is very strong.

Notes

[1] P.Dibon *La philisophie neerlandaise au siecle d'or*, vol 1 (Amsterdam etc 1954) pp. 38ff.

[2] L.D.Petit, *Bibliographische Lijst der werken van de Leidsche Hoogleeraren (1575-1619)*, Leyden 1894.

[3] P.Fraenkel, *De l'Ecriture a la dispute*, p. 9 etc.

[4] Chapter VI, pp

[5] Some of the research on the students has been undertaken by myself, but at this point I must thank Madame Suzanne Stelling-Michaud for the great help which she has given me on these matters. Her careful scholarship is of a very high level, but it is matched by her generosity. I thank her for letting me use material prior to publication.

[6] S.Stelling-Michaud, *Le Livre du Recteur de l'Academie de Geneva (1559-1878)* (Geneva 1959 etc.), vol 4, p. 131.

[7] *Ibid*. 3/148-9.

[8] S.Stelling-Michaud, *Livre du Recteur*, 2/529.

[9] *Ibid*. 2/350.

[10] *Ibid*. 4/12.

[11] *Ibid*. 3/350.

[12] *Ibid*. 3/231.

[13] *Ibid*. 4/89.

[14] *Ibid*. 4/285.

[15] N.Vignier, *Theses Theologicae de Justificatione peccatoris coram Deo*, (Geneva 1620), A2r.

[16] J.H.Hottinger *Theses Theologicae de Baptismo*, (Geneva 1620), p. 3.

[17] C. Des Champs, *Theses Theologicae De Praedestinatione Sanctorum et eius effectis, Quas Christo duce et auspice Christo*, (Geneva 1619) p. 3. The texts are Leviticus 20/25 and Numbers 16/9.

[18] See Chapter III, The Coton Controversy, pp.

[19] J.Altenstaig *Lexicon Theologicum complectens vocabulorum* etc. (Antwerp 1576) p. D4v. "Baptismus est triplex, scilicet flaminis, sanguinis et fluminis." Altenstaig also used Scotus and Gerson in his sources here. The reference he gives to Biel is for the *Sentences* distinction 4, question 2, note 2, book 4.

[20] See Chapter VI, p.

[21] *Institutes* 3.11.5 - 3.11.12.

[22] See Chapter VI, pp.

[23] J.M.Barkley, *The antichrist a historical survey*, (Belfast 1967) p. 14.

[24] *Institutes* 4.7.25., 4.18.1.

[25] *Institutes* 4.7.25.

[26] *The Bible and Holy Scriptures* first printed at Geneva in 1560, Darlow and Moule mention (1/61 no.77) that some 140 editions had been printed by 1640, giving some measure of its importance.

[27] T.Hobbes, *Leviathan* (Penguin Books) p. 712.

[28] C.Hill, *Antichrist in Seventeenth-Century England*, p. 19.

[29] *Ibid*., pp. 25-33.

[30] See Chapter VI, pp.

[31] J.Calvin, *The Gospel according to St John 11-21 and The First Epistle of John* (Calvin's Commentaries, tr T.H.L.Parker, ed D.W.Torrance and T.F.Torrance, Edinburgh and London 1961) pp. 255-7, 259-61 and 286-7. J Calvin, opera in *Corpus Reformatorum* (ed Baum, Cunitz and Reuss) LV/324-6, 320-22 and 349. Calvin seems to have avoided using the Apocalypse whenever possible. This is not, however, typicle of all sixteenth century reformed theologians, note the anti-papal work of N.Colladon *Methodus...ad explicationem...Apocalypseos* (Morges, 1584). The real flowering of interest in this field came in the mid seventeenth century. It might be added that Colladon is not the source for Bachelle's ideas.

[32] See Chapter II, pp. 68-74.

[33] Nor are the texts which are included always used in the same sense.

[34] *Acta* 2/286-97.

[35] C.Read, *Daniel Chamier*, p. 348; and *Acta* pp. 1-8.

[36] *Institutes*, 4.15.1-22.

Chapter Five
Giovanni Diodati

The Italian translation of the Bible

Diodati's first complete, quarto, edition of the Bible in Italian with annotations was published in 1607 as *La Bibbia cioe, I libri del Vecchio e del Nuovo Testamento Nuovamente traslati in lingua Italiana, da Giovanni Diodati, di nation Lucchese* and a New Testament, without annotations appeared during 1608, *Il Nuovo Testamento del Signor nostro Iesu Christo tradotto da Giovanni Diodati*. These were followed over thirty years later by the great 1640/41 *La Sacra Bibbia* etc., (see p 16). Various editions of the Psalms in Diodati's versions were also published during the translator's lifetime. This monumental work has furnished Italian protestantism with its standard version of the Bible. Diodati's achievement was to produce, single handed, one of the main Bibles of European protestantism. His work stands on a level with that of the Luther Bible in German and the Authorised King James' Bible in English. The bibliography reveals the number of editions of this Italian Bible produced before the end of the eighteenth century. However, in more recent time the Diodati translation has been used very extensively by various Bible societies.

The most important aspect of Diodati's life work was approched by him in a spirit of humility and thankfulness to God. Diodati attributed any good in his work to God alone and frequently stated that the Lord had helped him in his task. In this, Diodati was in a Melanchthonian tradition of making a close connexion between Divine guidance and human effort in the matter of Bible translation.[1] This is well illustrated in Diodati's letter to J.A. de Thou, written during 1607:

> *"La fauorable jugement, qu'il vous pleast faire de l'eschantillon de ma translation de la Bible Italienne, que j'avoye donne a Mr de La Noue, ainsi que mon cousin l'Advocat me l'a signifie, m'a servi d'un grand esguillon, et confort, en la poursuite de ce grand labeur, que j'avoye entrepris en ma premiere jeunesse....J'ai tasche de tout mon pouvoir, es en la plus grande conscience, que j'ay peu, ouvrir la porte a nos Italiens a la connissance de la verite celeste. Nostre Seigneur qui m'a miraculeusement adresse, et fortifie en cest oeuvre, la fortifier par sa benefiction, a laquelle seule comme je rapette la perfection de mon ouvrage, aussi d'icelle seule espere je de sa gloire, et du salut des siens, qui est, et sera tousjours l'unique bas, ou, moyennant sa grace, i'adresseray toutes mes actions."[2]*

The immediate stimulus of Diodati's work was the situation in Venice during the early seventeenth century when there were high hopes among the protestants of Europe that the republic might be converted to the reformed faith. There was a great desire for protestant books among the Venetian aristocracy and Diodati himself wrote to the Huguenot leader, du Plessis Mornay in 1609 that:- "Nombre infini de livres y sont entres et y entrent a flots tous les jours, et sont avidement recueillis qu'ils se les arrache des mains les ungs aulx autres."[3] Diodati translated the Bible into Italian to meet this need, just as for similar reasons he later translated the works of Fra Paolo Sarpi and Sir Edwin Sandys into French. Diodati's *La Bibbia* was distributed by the English ambassador at Venice, Sir Henry Wotton, who also had the 1608 New Testament issued in a smaller format on this paper to make it more easy to disseminate.[4] Wotton was criticised at the highest level for distributing Diodati's Bible and wrote to the Earl of Salisbury during 1609:- "The Pope hath renewed his complaint personally, to the new Venetian resident with him, about the Bible introduced into this state by me."[5]

Diodati himself was particularly sensitive about reaction to his Italian Bible. In 1635 he assured the Genevan Compagnie des pasteurs that it:- "avoit si heureusement reussi et produit tant de fruict et dont il avoit tesmoignage et approbation de plusieurs grands personnages et notamment de Mons. Scaliger."[6] In his letter to the Synod of Alencon of May 1637, he said that:-"I shall therefore tell you, That the Providence of God having inclined me in the first years of my Theological Profession, yea, and almost from my Youth upward, to Translate and Explain the Italian Bible, I was therein so successful...and the greatest Persons of this our Age, had my Poor Labours in singular recommendation, which I mention not without blushing; it is the truth which I publish to the Glory of God only."[7]

Once again, Diodati reaffirms his assurance of Divine support and his belief that his work was done only for the glory of God. In 1641, Diodati assured the Conseil of Geneva that his Italian Bible:- "a bien este receue partout."[8] The introduction to the English translation of Diodati's Biblical annotations provides yet another source of contemporary reaction to the work. This quotes Vedelius as writing:- "Planius autem & distinctius, C1. vir Joh: Diodati in aureis suis Annotationibus, quas versioni suae Italicae (Operi nunquam satis laudano) Bibliorum annexuit,"[9] The writer of the introduction - presumably Robert Gentili - decided not to quote any Anglican testimonials as he was:- "unwilling to burden the Book" and since:- "the Author being so well approved of."[10] This ommission is to be regretted, but he does quote:- "a most *Reverend and famous Prelate*, now living in our Church" as saying that theological students should:- "study the Italian tongue, assigning no other reason, but this for their endeavours: The extraordinary great benefit, Divines might reap from these learned Annotations of Mr. Diodati."[11] The prelate is not named, but the reimpression and wide circulation of the English version of the annotations bears witness to the high esteem in which they were held. The German and Hungarian translations are further evidence of this. In 1644 Diodati again wrote to the French Reformed Church that his 1640/41 Italian Bible, which he had produced with great labour and at considerable cost to himself was very similar to the 1644 French version, at which he had been working many years. The Italian version, he wrote, had received:- "une approbation universelle mesme des Juifs, Jesuites Cardinaux des plus celebres, et autres principaux ministres de l'Eglise Romaine et de tous les autres sans exception."[12] Catholic reaction, apart from the Papal anger at Wotton's distribution of the 1607 and 1608 editions, seems to have been quite favourable to Diodati's work. L.E.du Pin of the Sorbonne, in the history of the Canon, refers to it without animosity:- "About the beginning of our Age, *John Diodati* Minister in *Geneva*, gave us a New *Italian* Translation of the whole Bible, very conformable to the French Edition of *Geneva*."[13] Father Simon found both good and bad to say of Diodati's work, but he is far from being wholly unfavourable:- "I wish those who have a fancy to read Jo. Adeodates his Translation that they make use of the Italian Edition, which is more Elegant than the French; and I only advise them to read the Contents of the Chapters, whereby they may attain unto a full Compendium of the Bible."[14] He accused Diodati of making a paraphrase of Scripture:- "Neither were the Reasons slender why his translations should be so much cryed up and applauded, since every passage in it is so plain and easie, since the Author plays the Parapharist, and tickles the fancy of his Brother Sectaries."[15] Another of Simon's criticisms would not have displeased Diodati, since he accused Diodati of making the Scriptural text simple for the uneducated:- "this Gentleman, who acting according to his good will, not much minds the proper sense of words, so the vulgar may by any means understand him. Neither is he so much a Critick as an Orator and Divine making it his only business to please the Vulgar, and work upon their passions. His Notes generally are pretty plausible, serviceable to the Interpretation of Several *Texts* of *Scripture*."[16]

The few eighteenth century editions of Diodati's Italian version of the Bible reveal the continuing importance of his translation. Some of these editions, list nos. 4 etc. are "riveduto di nuovo" by Giovanni David Muller. This was the first of many attempts, typical of the nineteenth century as will be seen below, to modernise the Diodati text. Muller, in his introduction to the 1744 Leipzig edition of *La Sacra Bibbia* referred to the :- "Traduzzione del celebre GIOVANNI DIODATI, la quale, e per l'accuratezza del testo, e per la bellezza dello stille, fu sempre approuata, ed applaudita da tutti i letterati."[17] Darlow and Moule, in their *Catalogue of Printed Bibles*, state that the 1712 Nuremberg *La Sacro-Santa Biblia* was also modified by Mattia d'Erberg.[18] The 1702 Leipzig *Il Nuovo Testamento* dedicated to the Duke of Saxony is also a revision based on Diodati's translation.[19] Thus eighteenth century scholars and publishers were prepared to accept Diodati's version as standard, but with a modernisation of his language which had already become desirable only a century after the 1640/41 Bible.

The history of the Diodati translation in the nineteenth century is a most complex matter, it being printed many times. This has really little to do with the theology of the Genevan Academy at the time of the Synod of Dort. It is, however, a clearly related subject which deserves notice in this thesis. The work of Diodati lived for centuries after his death.

Diodati and earlier Italian translations

Despite Diodati's claim to Divine inspiration and despite much criticism of his French translation, it would be unwise to consider that his translations are entirely original. He relied on earlier versions from which he, like most translators, was incapable of disssociating himself.

Diodati's debts lie in various directions and this is most clearly seen when a series of texts are selected from his translations and compared with earlier versions. It was decided that Diodati's Italian translation might well be compared with the Bezan Greek New Testament, (the version used being the fourth major edition of 1588), the Rusticio edition of Brucciolini's translation published at Geneva in 1562, the French and Latin texts used by Calvin, the Junius/Tremellius Latin version (the 1673 Zurich edition being the one actually used) and, finally, the Genevan French and English versions dating from the sixteenth century. It was felt that this selection of versions might reveal something of the background to his translations. In order to limit the scope of what could become a whole thesis in itself, a series of texts was selected that would, it was hoped, show Diodati's methods in so far as they related to three series of relevant problems. Two sets of texts were selected because of well known textual problems: Mark 1/1-2 from the New Testament with the variants on whether Isaiah is mentioned in verse 2 and the still obscure and, to an extent, controversial text from Numbers 24/3 where difficulties in the Hebrew have confused translators as to whether the eyes mentioned are open or shut. Two further examples were used for their importance in contemporary disputes about the astronomy in which Geneva was much interested as is revealed by the study of the library contents, Ecclesiastes 1/4-5 and the *locus classicus* of astronomical disputes, the text of Joshua 10/12-13 where the sun and moon stand still. Two texts were chosen for their dogmatic interest to orthodox reformed circles, Deuteronomy 10/16, the most often quoted Old Textament text at Dort and the well known verses from John 20/22-3.

Diodati translates Mark 1/1-2 in a generally similar manner in the 1607:-

> *Il principio dell'Euangelio di Iesu Christo, Figliuol di Dio. Secondo che e scritto ne'profeti, Ecco io mando il mio messo dauanti alla tua fascia, ilquale preparera la tua via dinanzi a te.*[20]

and the 1640/41 versions:-

> *Il principio dell'Euangelio di Iesu Christo, Figliuol di Dio. Secondo ch'egli e scritto ne'profeti, Ecco io mando il mio Angelo dauanti alla tua faccia, ilqual preparera la tua via dinanzi a te.*

the only major difference from the 1607 version, apart from minor changes in style is that "Angelo" has replaced "messo" used in 1607, but since "messo" is noted as an alternative reading, this is also of minor importance. When the Rusticio version of Brucciolini is compared there is a general similarity in that the same Greek text is being translated, but while there are considerable differences in verse 2, the translation of verse 1 is exactly the same. Diodati is copying the earlier Genevan printed version. This will be noted elsewhere. *In toto* Diodati uses perhaps one third of the earlier work. Presumably he only re-translated texts where he was dissatisfied with Rusticio's work. This leads on to the question as to why texts were re-translated - the main possibilities being the use of different Greek or Hebrew texts, the updating of an antique style, or that the translation was in itself unsatisfactory. In this case the main differences seem to be stylistic:-

> *Il principio de l'Euangelio di Iesu Christo Figliuol di Dio si come e scritto ne i Profeti, Ecco io mando il mio messagiero dinanzi a la tua faccia il quale apparechiara la tua via innanzi a te.[21]*

the "messagiero" becomes "messo" in 1607 and the 1640/41 version used "Angelo" which presumably comes from the Bezan Greek *angelou*, though the Bezan Latin uses "nuncium."[22] Calvin in 1546 used "nuntium" and "messager" in French.[23] Thus the variant of "angel" would seem to hint at an expected Bezan influence, though "messager" had also appeared in the 1588 French version.[24] The verse 2 identification of "Isaiah" is nowhere mentioned except in the old Latin version quoted by Beza, and so all these versions have a basic similarity centred on the Greek text of Beza.[25]

The study of Numbers 24/3 reveals two somewhat dissimilar Diodatine versions in 1607:-

> *Et egli imprese il suo sermone profetico, e disse; Cosi dice Balaam, figliuolo di Beor; cosi dice l'huomo che ha gli occhi ferrati,[26]* and 1641:-

> *Ed egli prese a proferir la sua sententia: e disse Cosi dice Balaam figliuolo di Bexor: cosi dice l'huomo c'ha l'occhio chiuso.[27]*

which presumably reveals the translators struggle to make sense of an obscure passage. These two are, not surprisingly, quite different from the Brucciolini/ Rustici version with the major difference that while Diodati has the eyes shut, the earlier version had them open:-

> *Allhora riprese la sua parabola, e disse, Balaam figliuolo di Beor disse, disse, dico, l'huomo che he l'occhio aperto.[28]*

Who is Diodati following here? It is difficult to say. The only major reformed version that has the eyes closed is the English "Geneva" Bible (which has them "shut up")[29], but the Genevan French version[30], Calvin in his 1564 commentary[31] and Junius and Tremellius[32] all translate the eyes as "open." In this, we can see a measure of Diodati's independance in translation based on his own knowledge of Hebrew, and, one presumes, his intellectual integrity. It is not a point of dogmatic importance, but it is interesting to note that the English translators of the Breeches Bible and Diodati do not feel compelled to follow a clearly defined tradition in reformed Bible translation. The difference between Diodati and Junius and Tremellious is the most interesting since the latter work would appear to be an obvious source for Diodati. In this case the change from Brucciolini and Rustici is clearly due to a belief that the earlier translation misinterprets the Hebrew

Diodati's two translations of Joshua 10/12,13 are generally similar:-

Allhora Iosue parlo al Signore, nel giorno che'l Signore diede gli Amorrei in mano de' figliuoli d'Israel: e disse in presenza d'Israel, Sole, fermati in Gabaon: e tu Luna, nella valle d'Aialon.

E'l Sole si formo, e la Luna s'arresto, sin che'l popolo si fu verdicato de' suoi nimici.

Il sole adumque s'arresto in mezzo del cielo, e non s'affretto di tramontare, per lo spatio d'intorno ad un giorno intiero.[33]

and particularly in the later part, closely resemble the Brucciolini/Rustici version:-

Perilche Iosue in quel giorno che'l Signore dette gli Amorrhei dinanzi a figliuoli d'Israel, parlo al Signore. Et havea detto dinanzi a Isreal. Sole fermati in Gabaon, e tu Luna ne la valle di Aialon. Et il sole si fermo, e la luna si fermo, per fin che il popola si vendicasse de suoi nimici....Il sole dunque si fermo nel mezzo del cielo, e non si affretto di colcarsi circa a un giorno intero.[34]

which he was presumably conscious of following. The other versions were examined to see if there was any obvious model, other than the stylistic demands of seventeenth century Italian, for the changes. All versions considered begin with the statement that Joshua spoke to God and so no clear inference can be drawn, though it is interesting that Diodati is following the sixteenth century reformed usage in the vernacular by translating "Signore" like the Genevan French Bible's "l'Eternel"[35] and the Breeches Bible's "Lorde"[36] rather than either of the two Latin versions which both, Calvin and Junius/Tremellius,[37] refer to Jehovah.

There are some difficulties, none of great significance, in the two Diodatine translations of Ecclesiastes 1/4-5:-

Una eta va, & una altra eta viene: e la terra sta ferma in perpetuo. Il sole si leva anch'esso, e tramontana; &, ansando, trae verso'l luogo suo, ove egli si leva.[38]

and, from the 1640/41 Bible:-

Una eta va via, ed una altra eta viene: e la terra resta in perpetuo. Il sole si leva anch'esso, e poi tramontana: ed, ansando, trae verso'l luogo suo, ove egli si dee levare.[39]

Such differences as exist may be accounted for by the careful re-working of the translation of the texts used in then contemporary disputes. Both differ from the Brucciolini/Rustici version:-

> *Une generatione passa, e l'altra generatione viene, ma la terra sta in eterno. Et il sole nasce, e va sotto, e ritorno al suo luogo dove si leua.* [40]

The main difference is the translation of "eta" rather than "generation" and in this Diodati is independent of the English:-

> *(One) generacion passeth, and (another) generacion succedeth, but the earth remaineth for ever. The sunne riseth, and the sunne goeth downe, and draweth to his place, where he riseth.* [41]

and French versions:-

> *Une generation passe, et l'autre generation vient, mais la terre demeure tousiours ferme. Le soleil aussi se leve, et le soleil se couche, et ahane (sic) vers son lieu, dont il se leve.* [42]

as well as Junius and Tremellius:-

> *Generatio una abit, et altera advenit: quamvis terra in seculum permaneat. Oritur Sol, et occidit sol: iterumque ad locum suum aspirat, ubi oriatur.* [43]

which all refer to generation. The differences do not appear to make any major change in the sense that it is the sun which moves. The earlier Italian translation is perhaps more stylish than Diodati.

The text of Deuteronomy 10/16 presents no great problems in Hebrew, and Diodati uses the same translation in 1607 and 1640:-

> *Circumcidete adunque il preputio del vostro cuore, e non indurate piu il vostro collo.* [44]

which is practically identical to the Brucciolini/Rustici version:-

> *Circoncidete dunque il preputio del vostro cuore, e non indurate piu il vostro collo.* [45]

The only difference between the versions to be noted here is that while Diodati translates "neck" as singular, the English translators used "necks"[46] and Tremellius also uses a plural.[47] Diodati agrees with Brucciolini/Rustici and with Calvin:-

> *Circoncisez doncques le prepuce de vostre coeur, et n'endurcisiez plus vostre col.* [48]

Once again we see both an independence from earlier translators, and a reliance on the Brucciolini/Rustici version.

John 20/22 is translated in a similar manner by Diodati in both of his versions;-

> *E detto questo, alito loro nel viso, e disse loro, Ricevete lo spirito santo.* [49]

though verse 23 changes from 1607:-

> *I peccati di coloro, a cui gli haurete rimessi, saranno lor rimessi; e di coloro, a cui haurete retenuti, saranno ritenuti.* [50]

to 1640;-

> *A cui voi haurete rimessi i peccati saran rimessi, ed a cui gli haurete ritenuti saran ritenuti.* [51]

Both versions differ from the Brucciolini/Rustici version:-

> *E detto questo, soffio in essi, e disse loro, Pigliate lo spirito santo. A chiunque voi perdonarete i peccati, son perdonati loro, & a chiunque voi li riterrere, son retenuti.* [52]

In verse 22, Diodati has changed the translation for stylistic reasons, but in verse 23 it would seem that the later Diodatine version is, if anything, closer to Brucciolini/Rustici than that of 1607. Here again we may see the re-working of disputed texts - if anything the 1607 text is more difficult to reconcile with other reformed interpretations. It is hard to draw definite conclusions here, the nuances are too slight, but the 1640/41 translation is probably closer to the Bezan Greek and Latin texts[53] and the Genevan French:-

> *Et quand il eut dit cela, il souffla sur eux, et leur dit, Recevez le sainct Esprit. A quiconque vous pardonnerez les peches, ils seront pardonnes: et a quiconque vous les retiendrez, ils seront retenus.* [54]

and English texts:-

> *And when he had sayd that, he breathed on them, and said unto them, Receive the holie Gost.*
> *Whosoevers sinnes ye remit, they are remitted unto them: (and) whosoevers sinnes ye reteine, they are reteined.* [55]

- than that of 1607. The differences are not great and here we would see Diodati refining his own work.

A number of conclusions can be drawn from this brief comparison of Diodati's translations with those of likely sources for his work. The 1607 and 1640/41 translations are different, but their differences are mainly stylistic within the medium of a rapidly changing Tuscan dialect of Italian rather than changed Greek and Hebrew texts or changed dogmatic considerations. There is much less debt to the Bible of Tremellius and Junius than might have been expected but there is a great debt to the Brucciolini/Rustici version and where this is set aside by Diodati it can either be for reasons of style or reasons of re-interpretation of Hebrew. Diodati is also capable of being independent of all other reformed translations noted in this survey. Under the influence of God, as he saw himself as being, he had confidence in his own judgment. He certainly did not allow his work to be circumscribed by earlier reformed efforts in the same field.

The French translation of the Bible.

The publication of the complete Italian translation of the Bible with annotations during 1607 being completed when Diodati was still relatively young, it was not surprising that he should afterwards be tempted to consider the preparation of a French translation. Diodati's knowledge of French must have beem very considerable, due to his long residence in Geneva. He was, no doubt, encouraged by the fact that his Italian translation proved to be a considerable success.

Diodati's intention to prepare and publish a French translation of the Bible was first announced during 1618. His attempts to publish his French translation occupy a period of some twenty-six years, and there is a considerable amount of manuscript evidence relevant to this in the Archives d'Etat in Geneva, and elsewhere. The development of the conflict associated with his French translation within the Genevan Company of Pastors led Diodati to explain his reasons for undertaking Bible translation, his objects in doing so and his method of Scriptural interpretation. The controversy revealed the man. The struggle to publish the French Bible revealed the complete dedication of Giovanni Diodati to his self-appointed task.

Giovanni Diodati first announced his intention of preparing a French translation of the Bible to the Genevan Compagnie des pasteurs on the 2nd January 1618. He not only wanted to translate the Bible but to add extensive annotations:- "pour l'eclaircissement des passages les plus difficiles." He was encouraged to do so because of unsatisfactory French phrases:- "rudes et malpropres" - to be found in the Genevan French version then currently in use. Diodati was not discouraged, but was asked to publish nothing without the knowledge of the Compagnie des pasteurs.[56] By the end of the month, Diodati had begun his work on Genesis and asked the Compagnie to appoint several of its members to examine his work.[57] However, in April of that year, Diodati was asked to suspend his work for:- "beaucoup des raisons."[58] There were no explicit statements to suggest that this request was stimulated by any defects which were to be found in the work which he had begun.

No more was heard of Giovanni Diodati's proposed French translation until early in 1620. During the interval, Diodati could have had little time free for this work since he was present at the Synod of Dort and afterwards visited England. In January 1620 Diodati reminded the Compagnie that he had:- "longtemps travaille" at the French translation and that he was qualified to do so by the fourteen years which he had spent working at his Italian translation. He believed that he could explain certain somewhat obscure passages of the Old Testament - particularly among the prophetic books. He was already well advanced with the Old Testament and was considering a folio edition, but wished to have the advice of a French Reformed Synod as well as of the Compagnie des pasteurs before attempting publication. Diodati was asked to leave a copy to be examined by members of the Compagnie.[59] He was soon to be bitterly disappointed for the important French pastor Pierre du Moulin, writing after the Synod of Alais in 1620 expressed disapproval. He said in a letter to the Genevan Church that there were already too many protestant versions:- "et que les Jesuites et autres tels organes de mensonge, produisans en leurs sermons et es conferences plusieurs Bibles differentes, ont trouble plusieurs consciences debiles. Cela nous fait craindre que la Version Francoise, sur laquelle nous apprenons que Monsieur Diodati travaille, et y change plusieurs passages....donne nouvelle matiere de triompher a nos adversaires, qui iettent cette poussiere aux yeux des ignorans."[60] It was made quite plain that this unfavourable reception was not intended to cast any doubts on Diodati's ability or scholarship, and du Moulin suggested that a new Latin version might be more necessary:- "Ce n'est pas que nous n'estimions beaucoup le savoir de nostre dit frere, et son intelligence es saintes escritures et es langues Greque et Hebraique, et la dexterite de son esprit; que si la version estoit Latine nous l'exhorterions plustost a ce travail."[61] This letter, which was discussed by the Genevan Compagnie des pasteurs on 8 May 1621,[62] must have been a severe blow to Diodati. During March 1624 Diodati himself told the Compagnie that he was setting aside his work on the French translation:- "attendant que Dieu face naistre quelque autre occasion," and that:- "maintenant il entreprenoit, moyennant l'aide de Dieu, quelque chose en la version Latine."[63] There was no obvious necessity for a new Latin version - the reformed theologians already had others including those of Beza, Junius and Tremellius. Presumably its attraction was that it allowed Diodati an outlet for his desire to use his energies in Bible translation in a way that might lead to academic but not popular controversy. There is no trace of this Latin version - if it ever existed - to be found today.

Diodati's resolution to abandon his work on a French translation was short lived. In 1626 his *Le Livre de Iob tradvit et annote Par Iean Diodati* (s.a., s.l.) was printed and there were rumours in Geneva that his complete translation was to be published at Sedan.[64] When Diodati was ordered to explain this by the Compagnie des pasteurs, he protested that not only had he no plans to publish it at Sedan, but that his work was still incomplete.[65] It was not until seven years had passed that Diodati announced that his work was complete during 1634.[66] He then said that he feared that there were those in the Compagnie des pasteurs who wanted to suppress his work whether it was good or bad. Following this accusation it was decided that a full discussion should be held.[67] The most distressing part of Diodati's struggle was about to begin.

Preparations were made to discuss Diodati's French translation in the Compagnie des pastuers during January 1635,[68] but Diodati was not prepared to do so at that time and the debate within the Compagnie des pasteurs eventually began in May of that year.[69] However, the situation had altered by May, for Diodati had gone beyond the Compagnie des pasteurs and had presented his case to the Conseil of Geneva. He had told the Conseil that the present French Bible had faults in its language and in its annotations and was:-"pleine d'obscuritez et scabrositez."[70] Because of this, pupils found it difficult to read.

Diodati pointed out that there was no disadvantage in having more than one French translation since there were six Roman Catholic versions, and two German versions. His work had taken him ten years, but nevertheless he would submit to any valid criticisms. He also claimed that foreign scholars eagerly awaited the publication of this work and that even du Moulin had changed his opinion. Diodati explained away the decision of the Synod of Alais by pointing out that the decision had been taken suddenly, without preparation, and that the Synod had not examined his work.[71] Diodati warned the Conseil that if the Catholics were to find that his work had been criticised, they could well use this for propaganda. He was quite correct, for Francois Veron S.J., writing some years later made this very point.[72] The Compagnie des pasteurs ignored the possible consequences of their actions and the debate took place on 22nd and 26th May 1635. Diodati repeated many of the arguments which he had made to the Conseil, he claimed that the version in print was unsatisfactory, that it had already been criticised by Beza and others, and pointed out that there was more than one version to be found in various other languages and he criticised the judgment of the Synod of Alais. Diodati pointed out that if his work were to be suppressed, Catholic propagandists would think that it had contained material prejudicial to the Reformed Churches. His defence revealed the malice and pettiness of the Genevan Compagnie des pasteurs at that time for he claimed that his work had been pre-judged and that he was accused of trying to use bribery to further his ends. His statement also revealed the deep piety which led him to undertake his work:- "il avoit travaille longuement en la susd. version et pouvoit dire en sincerite qu'il avoit senti une singuliere assistance, et tres claire lumiere de l'Esprit de Dieu, dont il estoit venu a bout heureusement de cest oeuvre ayant mis l'Escriture Ste en une grande clarte avec perpetuelles annotations, qu'il esperoit que l'Eglise en recevroit grand fruict."[73] Diodati's insistence on human application with Divine assistance may well have had a Melanchthonian basis. When the Compagnie des pasteurs began to discuss Diodati's defense of his work, some were favourable and others not, but they agreed to refute scandalous rumours - such as the accusation of bribery - and all agreed that Giovanni Diodati possessed great gifts for the work which he had undertaken:- "Qu'on ne pouvoit pas nier que notre susd. frere n'eust une addresse singuliere a detailler la parole de Dieu, et a tirer les sens de l'Escriture Sainte."[74] The main arguments used against the publication of Diodati's work were the judgment of the Synod of Alais and the fact that he had been instructed to stop by the Compagnie des pasteurs. The underlying fear of the Compagnie des pasteurs was quite understandable. The French speaking Reformed Churches were under considerable pressure from Catholic controversialists at that time. Since the Reformed Churches claimed to base their doctrines on the correct interpretation of Scripture, on the text of the Bible as inspired Word of God, any apparent willingness to change their vernacular translations could be interpreted either as an uncertainty about the content of Scripture or as a willingness to accommodate their translations to satisfy the demands of Reformed dogmatics. The fear of arousing criticism was typical of French Reformed orthodoxy throughout much of the seventeenth century and revealed the effectiveness of Catholic polemics at that time. The Reformed Churches by that time seem to have lost much of the initiative in controversy and to have been preoccupied with a defence of their doctrinal positions. This attempt by Diodati to publish his French translation of the Scriptures reveals one facet of this large and complex subject.

The Genevan Compagnie des pasteurs expressed this attitude quite explicitly:- "qu'il n'estoit point expedient surtout en ces temps d'ouvrir la bouche aux adversaires pour nous reprocher que nous n'avons rien de ferme, et stabile que nous changeons a tous coups." The meeting did not end badly for Diodati, since a number of members of the Compagnie were to be appointed to examine his work.

Giovanni Diodati's book on Job was criticised by some of the members of the Compagnie des pasteurs. There were two criticisms, that the work was unnecessary, and that it was not well done:- "en l'essai qu'il avoit fait du livre de Job on avoit veu qu'il n'y avoit point de subject d'une nouvelle version. Qu'on n'y avoit reconu que des changemens fort legers et en choses et mots indifferens en quelques particuliers. qu'on avoit remarque des changemens non-seulement non-nesessaires mais mesmes des termes qui ne sonnoyent si bien que ceux qui sont en notre version."[75] For the first time, there was a suggestion that Diodati's command of the French language was not perfect. The appearance of the translation and annotation of Job had caused some interest in Europe during 1626 when Hottinger in Zurich wrote to Benedict Turrettini in Geneva to send him:- "Le Liure de Job de la version de Monsr Diodati avec ses anotations, qui est imprime nouuellement, come m'aduertit Mr Leger."[76] An examination of translations shows that of 1638, *Les livres de Iob Pseaumes Proverbes Ecclesiastes* etc. to be much more polished as is shown by the following passages of Job 1/1-4. Significant changes have been put in bold letters.

1626	1638
Il y auoit vn homme au pais d"Vs, nomme Iob lequel estoit entier, & droit, & craignant Dieu, & se retirant du mal. Et lui nasquirent sept fils & trois filles. Et son bestail estoit de sept mille brebis, trois mille chameaux, cinq cens coulpes de beufs, & cinq cens asnesses, auec vn fort grand labourage. Et cet homme estoit le plus grand d'entre tous les Orientaux Or ses fils alloyent, & banquetoyent en la maison d'vn chacun d'eux a son iour: & enuoyoyent appeler leur trois soeurs, pour manger et boire auec eux.	Il y auoit vn homme au pais d'Vs nomme Iob: **& cet homme-**la estoit entier, & droit, & craignant Dieu & se retirant **arriere** du mal. Et lui nasquirent sept fils, & trois filles. Et son bestail estoit de sept mille brebis, & de trois mille chameaus, **& de** cinq cens couples de beufs, **& de** cinq cens asnesses: auec vn fort grand labourage. Et cet homme-la estoit le plus grand de tous les Orientaux Or ses fils aloyent, & faisoyent des banquets en la maison d'vn chacun d'eux a son iour: & enuoyoyent **conuier** leurs trois soeurs, pour manger, & boire auec eux.

It is evident that the later text is written in more polished French, but even in 1626 Diodati was using more modern spelling than many of his contemporaries, e.g. he used "lui" and not "luy". The final 1644 text of *La Sainte Bible* (bibliography p. 14 no 15) follows the 1638 text almost entirely, the only significant change being:- "inuiter leurs trois soeurs" in the fourth verse being substituted for:- "conuier leurs trois soeurs." This is, of course, a period when the French language was undergoing rapid change. Diodati is obviously trying to keep pace with developments which would seem to indicate that he was by no means averse to revision of his work. The development of a written language having far less importance in his eyes than his basic inspiration.

There was a brief lull in the public discussion of Diodati's French Bible after the debates within the Compagnie des pasteurs and the Conseil in the May of 1635. In November Diodati appealed to the Conseil for a hearing and pleaded that his French Bible might be published. He claimed, as before, that other languages had more than one translation of the Bible. For the first time, however, there was an appeal to the pity of the Conseil, he spoke of his age, and begged that:- "il plaise a les Seigneurs le delivera de ceste angoisse en laquelle on l'a si long temps detenu."[77] The Conseil then examined a number of documents relevant to the case. If Diodati's arguments were by now familiar, so were those of the faction opposed to his work. A fresh French translation, they claimed, would give good arguments to those opposed to the Reformed faith:- "non qu'ils doutassent de son scavoir & grande addresse mais pour eviter scandale & re-donner de nouveau bouche ouverte a nos ennemis."[78] Letters were produced from the important French Huguenot pastor Mestrezat and from du Moulin which supported this view:- "L'impression de la dz. nouvelle version occasion du scandale qui en peut arriver par le moyen des blasmes qu'a ce subiect nous seront donnes par nos adversaires."[79] Three weeks later, on 28th November, Diodati claimed that despite the letters from Mestrezat and du Moulin, he could produce other letters from other French Huguenot pastors which supported his work.[80] Two days later the Conseil again discussed the matter and considered the previous progress of the debate, and decided that Diodati's work was to be examined by three pastors and that he should present his work to the next national synod of the French Reformed Church.[81] Three days later, on 1 December 1635 Diodati told the Conseil that he would show his work to the next French synod. He also defended himself against accusations that he was senile and that he worked mainly because of personal ambition:-"il dit de luy qu'il est porte a presser l'impression de sa version par avarice et ambition et en termes desguises, l'auroit appelle simoniaque."[82] Diodati asked permission of the Conseil to publish two or three books of the Bible in his French translation and with his annotations. The Conseil deferred its decision on the publication of the whole Bible until after the next national synod of the French Church.[83] Diodati's last public appearance in 1635 provided a sombre close to this troubled year when he went before the Compagnie des pasteurs on 11 December. He spoke of the conflict in embittered terms:- "qu'on l'avoit indirectement taxe de simonie...l'un l'appellant fol, l'autre glorieux, l'autre pape, et semblables outrages."[84] Diodati protested that there were many French protestants who wanted his work, that he would never refuse to consider the advice of his colleagues and that even the great Prince de Conde knew of the protracted dispute. Yet even after all the troubles which he had experienced, Diodati's faith was still equal to the challenge of adversity and his personal dedication was as great as ever:- "il protestoit devant Dieu qu'il y avoit travaille (apres une ardente invocãon du nom de Dieu avoir implore sa grace) en toute fidelite et bonne conscience, et y avoir senti une particuliere assistance de l'Esprit de Dieu."[85]

Diodati's next step was to publish the translation and annotations of *l'Ecclesiaste et le Cantique des cantiques* which he had mentioned to the Conseil on 1 December 1635. This is an extremely rare, only one copy having been traced. This copy is dedicated, in Diodati's hand:- "Pour Monsieur Laurent," This must have been Jacob Laurent, 1597-1665, who later became secretary to the Conseil.[86] Another hand, presumably Laurent's, has added:- "Ce Liure m'a este donne de la propre main de Monsieur Diodati, le Ieudi 4 May 1637. Et en mets icy le Memoire pour m'en recognistre tant plu(...) estroitement oblige enuers cet Excellent Theologien (.....)." The rest of the inscription is lost since the book must have been trimmed. This inscription is important since it reveals that there was support for Diodati and his view among influential Genevans. If such evidence were not forthcoming, there would be suspicions that some of the accusations made against Diodati were justified. The text of these books, as translated by Diodati, is much closer to the 1638 *Les livres de Iob Pseaumes Prouerbes* etc., than is the 1626 translation of Job, as is seen by a comparison of Ecclesiastes 9/14-18 in the two editions. The text has been improved, but the 1636-7 text was written in more stylish French than the translation of Job. Significant changes have been put in bold letters.

1636-7	1638
Il y auoit vne petite ville, & peu de gens dedans; & vn grand roi vint contr'elle, & bastit de grands forts contr' elle	Il y auoit vne petite ville, & peu de gens dedans: & vn grand roi vint contr'elle, & **bastir** de grands forts contr' elle
Et il se trouua en elle vn povre homme sage, qui deliura sa ville par sa sagesse: quoi que nul ne se souuinst de ce povre homme la	Et il se trouua en elle vn **poure** homme sage, qui deliura sa ville par sa sagesse: quoi que nul ne se souuinst de ce **poure** homme-la.
Adonc ie di, Mieux vaut sagesse que force: combien que la sagesse du povre soit mesprisee & que ses paroles ne soyent point escoutees.	Adonc ie di, Mieux vaut sagesse que force: combien que la sagesse du **poure** soit mesprisee, & que ses paroles ne soyent point escoutees.
Les paroles des sages doivent estre plus coyement escoutees, que le cri d'vn seigneur entre les fols.	Les paroles des sages doivent estre plus **paisiblement** escoutees, que le cri d'vn seigneur entre les fols.
Mieux vaut sagesse qu'armes: mais vn pecheur fait perir beaucoup de bien.	Mieux vaut **la** sagesse **que les instruments de guerre** mais vn pecheur fait perir beaucoup de bien.

These extracts would seem to reveal Diodati's ability to accept criticism. It is to be noted that bastir is a misprint.

There is no evidence of serious trouble concerning Diodati's French Bible-translation in Geneva during 1637, but it was in this year that a French national synod was held at Alencon. There is a text - albeit in English - of Diodati's letter to that synod.[87] It is long, but reveals Diodati's aims and personality more clearly than any of the evidence considered above. Diodati wrote that he would have attended the synod himself if he were not old[88] and ill.[89] He only had one manuscript copy of his French Bible translation and so did not send it to the synod since it might have been lost,[90] but recommended the members of the synod to examine the two volumes already published.[91] Diodati devoted much of this letter to a refutation of criticism which may be divided into three classes, viz., arguments for the desirability of a new translation, the damage it might do to the weak in faith and the possible trouble with adversaries. Diodati criticised the judgment of the synod of Alais. He pointed out that there could be no final, perfect Bible translation, for one translation supplied the defects in another, that there had always been more than one version, and that a new French translation was badly needed. Diodati also referred to the freedom of the translator:-"to Translate the Letter of the Text according to the Sense he hath conceived"[92] and assured the synod that the Church must never stop translating the Bible:- "or else one version becomes gradually harmful".[93] If the Church were:- "too captivated by one translation," then:- "we should at last meet with all those Defects, Obscurities, and Wanderings from the Scripture-Sence, and take upon us to forge Mysteries at our own wills, which we have justly condemned in the *Church* of *Rome*."[94] Diodati denied the suggestion that his translation would give:- "offence to the weak" since the poor in spirit:- "will never be so much Scandalised at those flights, easiness and new sweetness they shall find in God's Word, as they may be distasted with the Difficulties and Obscurities they have so long conflicted with."[95] Diodati assured the synod that his adversaries:- "shall never alledge one Text in which I have varied from the substance of Doctrine, or of the Dogmatical Passages."[96] His work was, he declared, theologically orthodox,[97] he had worked on it for a long time with the help of God[98] and if the synod should approve his French text, then he might be encouraged to complete his Latin translation.[99] The most important aspect of Diodati's letter to the synod was that he described in some detail how he came to translate the Bible:- "I shall therefore tell you, That the Providence of God having inclined me in the first years of my Theological Profession; yea, and almost from my very Youth upward, to Translate and Explain the Italian Bible, I was therein so successful...and the greatest Persons of this our Age, had my Poor Labours in singular recommendation, which I mention not without blushing; it is the Truth which I publish to the Glory of God only. I was from that very time, excited by a most vehement inward impulse, to Consecrate my Studies wholly unto this self-same Work in two other Languages the *French* and *Latin*, in which I was equally skill'd, and they were, as to their use, both alike, and as it were natural to me; and Learned Men, with whom I conversed, advised me unanimously hereunto, because there were very many things to be added, and amended, notwithstanding the pains and diligence of our Fathers; and that I should reserve the *Latin* Version unto my later years, because it demanded a more Consummate Judgment."[100] He claimed that:- "I have it imprinted powerfully upon my Conscience before God, so is it much more easie to verifie and make it good before Men, because I have Laboured without wages, I have Wrought without any Thanks or Favour, my Works have not gotten me any Honour. I aim'd only at this mark, to make clear and limpid this Fountain of truth".[101]

The Synod of Alencon appointed five commissioners to study Diodati's work and these were not able to agree upon its value, for two supported Diodati while three criticised his work.[102] The consideration of his work by the French

Reformed Church would not seem to have helped matters in Geneva, for in October 1637, the Conseil of Geneva asked and advised Diodati and another pastor of the opposing faction, Pierre Prevost, to forget the past and to live without strife.[103]

The year 1638 proved decisive for Diodati's struggle to publish his French translation of the Bible. On the 23rd March, Diodati informed the Conseil that he had delivered a manuscript to the printer Jean de Tournes containing the French translation of the books of Job, Ecclesiastes, Canticles, Psalms and Proverbs. He was interested in having them published at his own expense and asked that permission might be granted.[104] On 9th April the Conseil decided to permit the publication.[105] This did not, however, bring the dispute to a close. The Compagnie des pasteurs were irritated because they had not examined the passages to be published.[106] Diodati pointed out that three of the books had already been published:- "qui n'avoyent apporte aucun scandale."[107] The Compagnie decided to permit publication on the condition that Diodati would publish nothing without the knowledge of those whom the Compagnie would deputise.[108] Diodati agreed to this on condition:- "que la reveue et examen s'est limite dans ces deux points de la verite du text ou fidelite de la version: et de la purete de la foi."[109] The chosen representatives were Theodore Tronchin and Frederich Spanhein[110] who appeared before the Conseil with other pastors on 14th April, still not completely convinced of the wisdom of permitting publication.[111] The personal aspect of the affair was still bad, and Diodati complained to the Conseil on 20th April of accusations:- "soit contre sa personne soit contre oeuvre,"[112] but Diodati was again publicly reconciled

with Prevost in front of the Conseil on 21st April 1638[113] and things probably improved after that, though the two men were again opposed to one another during 1639.[114] The Conseil honourably discharged its responsibility for taking the decision to permit publication. Diodati complained that his book was still not published on 7th July[115] and the Conseil received a report, giving reasons for this delay from Tronchin and Spanheim on 13th July.[116] When Diodati made a similar complaint on 11 September, the Conseil ordered Spanheim and Tronchin to complete their work and to report.[117] They reported on 6th October and advised that the book should be published and that a decision to publish the complete translation might be taken on a consideration of the public reaction.[118] The Conseil took their formal, final decision to permit publication on the 8th October 1638.[119]

Diodati's French translation of Job, Psalms, Proverbs, Ecclesiastes and Canticles was published in the autumn of 1638. In his preface, he wrote an apology for his work. He stated that there could be no:- "Version canonique de la Bible"[120] and that if he believed his work would harm the Church, he would be the first to suppress it:- "Ie proteste devant Dieu que s'il paroist qu'il en naisse aucun preiudice a sa verite, ou trouble aux consciences des fideles, ou blessure & scandale a l'Eglise de Christ, ie serai le premier a le condanner a une eternele suppression."[121] Diodati could not avoid reference to his critics, and wrote of:- "un seul puissant ennemi"[122] presumably either Prevost or - more probably - du Moulin. Yet his preface ends on a pious and irenic note:- "ie n'ai point entrepris de donner un paragon de la langue Francoise...mais bien de faire clairement et netement entendre celle du S.Esprit."[123]

Diodati's great complete French translation of the Bible with annotations was not published until 1644, six years after the 1638 edition. In 1641 Diodati appeared before the Conseil of Geneva and asked them that he might have two years in which to prepare the complete translation in its final form. He asked to be allowed to do this because of his advancing years and because the 1638 edition and the 1640/41 Italian edition had been accorded a favourable reception. The Conseil permitted him to continue with his work on condition that he would submit any preface to them for examination.[124] This last point may explain why the 1644 French Bible has no preface, unlike the 1638 edition which has been discussed above. Diodati occupied himself in completing his work during the next two years, and it was complete by January 1643 when he again asked the Conseil for permission to publish.[125] He was prepared to meet the cost out of his own pocket and was, as always, concerned to counter malicious and incorrect rumours, for by this time the Dutch theologians were aware of the protracted dispute. In November 1644 Diodati wrote to a French Reformed synod for the last time, asking for their approval of his work. It was a sad letter, for he wrote that:- "mes incommodites anciennes redoublees, et mes dernieres heures precipites leur course."[126] He had, as always, complete confidence in Divine support for his work:- "ayant en mon ame une pleine certitude de un innocence, purete, et fidelite: et un seau indubitable de la vocation de Dieu au fort mouuement qui m'auoit porte a l'entreprendre et en la continuelle assistance de Son Esprit."[127] This letter was never answered by the French synod at Charenton in 1645, for it was delivered to the Royal Commissioner while still sealed. He opened it, read it, permitted that it be read to the synod, and then retained it and stated that it was Louis XIV's pleasure that no reply should be sent.[128] It would seem that the complete French translation had already been published.

La Sainte Bible of 1644 created very little controversy after its publication. There was little of the much predicted Catholic opposition, and there is no evidence that its publication harmed the standing of the French speaking Reformed Churches in any way. The only contemporary Catholic criticism which has been found is a tract of F.Veron S.J., *Grand trouble* etc., (bibliography p. 27 no. 53) of 1646 in which he actually makes use of the controversies within the Reformed Churches:- "long tēe y a que i'attendois ce gros Volume de Diodati, a la publication duquel on tenoit cy-deuant que les Ministres de Geneue s'opposoient." The translation was widely circulated, as is revealed by the Provenance List (pp. 27-32). Diodati lived long enough - he died in 1649 - to see his cherished work widely circulated, but apart from a few editions (bibliography pp. 14-15) it quickly fell into oblivion after his death when the most widely read version of the Bible in French remained the 'Genevan' version which was reprinted a number of times in the seventeenth and eighteenth centuries, sometimes with Des Marets' notes and increasingly in David Martin's version which first appeared at Amsterdam in 1707. Osterwald's version was first published at Rotterdam in 1724.

Translations of contemporary works.

This section must primarily be concerned with two major translations which Diodati made from Italian and English into French during the earlier part of his career. These translations were of Paolo Sarpi's *History of the Council* of Trent and Sir Edwin Sandys' *European Speculum*. The little "De miraficis pueri undecennis extasibus" is from the Breitinger correspondence and was published in the *Miscellanea Tigurina* during 1722 long after Diodati was dead.

Diodati's translation of Sarpi's history was first published in 1621 as *Histoire du Concile de Trente, Traduite de Pierre Soave Polan. Par Iean Diodati* (bibliography p. 20). "Pierre Soave Polan" was, of course, a pseudonym for Paolo Sarpi. The translation achieved a wider circulation than any of Diodati's other works excepting only the Italian translation of the Bible. It was reprinted in 1627, 1635, 1650, 1655 and in 1665 it was published simultaneously by a number of Parisian booksellers who all used the same folio edition, see bibliography, pp. 14-17.

Diodati had met Sarpi during his visits to Venice early in the seventeenth century. The English ambassador at Venice, Sir Henry Wotton, had written to Diodati as early as 1606 asking him to send a protestant preacher,[129] Diodati himself went to Venice during 1608 taking Benedict Turrettini with him.[130] This journey was quite dangerous for there was fear that Diodati might be assassinated by Papal agents and so he travelled under the assumed name of "Giovanni da Coreglia."[131] Diodati had long interviews with Sarpi at Venice:- "It was told him by Mro Paulo, that not so few as 12,000 in this city were more or less enlightened with the truth, and alienated from Rome."[132] Yet Diodati found Sarpi somewhat frustrating in that he would not directly encourage any attempt to introduce the forms of protestantism, believing that the inner spiritual life of man was more important than external matters such as ecclesiastical discipline. Diodati wrote that:- "Sarpi is rooted in that most dangerous maxim that God cares nothing for externals, provided the mind and heart are in pure and direct relation with Himself. And so fortified is he in this opinion by reason and examples, ancient and modern, that it is vain to combat with him."[133] Sarpi also irritated Diodati by his slowness. One of Sarpi's sayings, according to Sir Henry Wotton, was:- "non bisogna far salti"[134] and Diodati said that Sarpi was:- "huomo cubiculare, on what side soever he fell stood still."[135] Sarpi apologised to Diodati for his slowness and said that:- "God had not given him a nature that would act by spirit and zeal and fervour, but only by reason."[136] Despite these points, Diodati seems to have had a very high opinion of Sarpi, the translation of the history of the Council of Trent is surely proof of that, but he graciously said that Sarpi was saved from all excitement by the "dolcezza e maturita" of his soul.[137] William Bedell's son, writing about his father's stay in Venice as chaplin to Sir Henry Wotton, wrote that:- "Mr. Deodati travelled with Mro Paulo to put more spirit and courage in him; and to stir him up to availe himself both of those great graces that God had given him, and that favour and authority which he hath with these Seigniors, to the glory of God in the advancement of the truth."[138]

The translation of Sir Edwin Sandys' *Europae Speculum* may also be related to Diodati's association with Venice. Sir Henry Wotton had found this a most suitable book for influencing the Venetian nobility with protestant religious principles in the form of political discourses.[139] Oddly enough, Sandys' work was not generally available in English until 1629.[140] An edition of this tolerant work, Sarpi himself had helped Sandys to write it, was published without the author's consent from a stolen manuscript copy during 1605.[141] An Italian translation was unnecessary, for one had already been made[142] by William Bedell, aided by Sarpi. Bedell (1571-1642) later became bishop of Ardagh and Kilmore in Ireland where he himself engaged in Bible translation, producing the Scriptures in the Irish language, a version which Bedell constantly checked with Diodati's translation. Bedell's rescue from obscurity by Diodati is another aspect of this interesting relationship. In producing his French translation, Diodati probably hoped that it might influence the French nobility as Wotton had found that it influenced the Venetian. This translation of Diodati was also reprinted (see bibliography p. 12) but does not seem to have had as much success as the translation of Sarpi.

In a letter of Bedell's dated 30 November 1613, written to Dr. Samuel Ward, the friend of Archbishop Ussher of Armagh, there is a suggestion that Diodati might well have had other works for translation into Italian. Bedell mentions:- "those slender services I endeavoured to perform at Venice, in Translating the Booke of Common Prayer, his Majesty's Booke, Sir Edwin Sands his booke, The third Homily of Chrysostome touching Lazarus, and some other thinges into the Italian tongue; part whereof are there and part at Geneva in Sir Diodati his hands."[143] This reference seems to imply that Diodati has some of Bedell's translations at Geneva and cannot be taken as an indication that there remain undiscovered Diodati translations. There is no real evidence that any such now exist, if published they must be anonymous, and if in manuscript they remain lost.

This brief consideration of the minor printed works of Diodati serves to demonstrate that he was very much at the centre of European intellectual movements during part of his life. It is perhaps a pity that he made only a visit to Venice and did not remain there as a protestant pastor, considering the bitter struggle he had to publish his French translation of the Bible.

English material.

The English language material may be divided into the two classes of translations of the Biblical annotations and of royalist propaganda.

Diodati's Biblical annotations were translated into English and printed several times in the years 1643-64, during the period of the English Civil War and restoration of the monarchy. As early as 1641 Diodati was able to inform the Conseil of Geneva that:- "un grand personnage d'Angleterre nomme Monsieur Styl ayant represente que sa version Italienne estoit remplie de tres bonnes notes, on a donne charge a Monsr. Gentilis de travailler a la traduction des la Notes en langage Anglois."[144] Thus the English translation of the *Annotations* was carried out under parliamentary direction. No Member of Parliament called "Styl" can be traced, but this was probably the distinguished legal author Wm. Style, 1603-79.[145] "Monsr. Gentilis" was almost certainly Robert Gentili, 1590-1654(?), a professional translator who rendered Sarpi's history of the Council of Trent into

English. This information helps to set in perspective the considerable reputation which Diodati enjoyed in England.

The parliamentary approval for Diodati's Biblical Annotations might be regarded as evidence of English puritan interest in Diodati's work as might John Milton's not unfavourable reference to him in the *Pro Populo Anglicano Defensio secunda* (London 1645 etc.). Diodati was the kind of orthodox Reformed theologian whom the English puritans liked to regard as being favourable to their cause. With this in view, it at first seems odd that Diodati's name should have been used for the royalist *An answer sent to the Ecclesiasticall Assembly* at London. This work has a complicated printing history and has frequently been regarded as spurious.[146] In fact, Diodati's sentiments were quite definitely royalist and he was horrified by the execution of Charles I. There was considerable concern in the Counseil of Geneva on 14th March 1649 because of a sermon which Diodati had preached in the Cathedral of St Pierre in which he denounced the regicides in strong terms:- "que spect Jean Deodati en son sermon faict le iour du ieusne dernier non obstant les defenses a luy faictes de la part du Conseil de parler en chaire des affaires d'Angleterre et de la mort dy Roy, auroit parle de son execution fort avant declamant contre les auteurs de l'arrest de condamnation a mort contre luy rendu usant de ces termes un diable ces esprits infernaux fanatiques Anabaptistiques, ceste vermoulure, le bon Roy iuste, mort au lit d'honneur non pas des Rois mais de Dieu, Roy mort martyr."[147]

Diodati's own opinions do not help in forming a decision concerning the question of who wrote the tract, supposedly a letter sent to the Westminster Assembly. There is, quite simply, a total lack of evidence and it is impossible, unless new material is revealed, to state certainly whether Diodati did write the tract or whether he did not.[148] Because it has been impossible to resolve this uncertainty, all traced copies of the various editions of the tract have been included in the Diodati bibliography. Luke Harruney, in a preface, warned readers that:- "I have perused it: and must censure them very simple that will be seduced with such a notorious fiction, invented by some prophane Atheist: for none else durst so often to blaspheme the Name of God to countenance such abominable lies. A stranger hee is indeed, but so unlike Doctor Deodate, that the good old man will be full of sorrow to heare that a Presse should be conveyed to Newcastle to the King, to surprize him with such a scandall."[149] In *The King's Possessions*, it is stated in "The Copy of a Certificate from one of the Scribes of the Assembly to a minister in London", that:- "the whole letter now printed at *Newcastle* is an abominable forgery, I find that we did receive a letter from the Church of *Geneva* in *answer* unto ours sent unto them, but not signed by *Deodate*."[150] None of this evidence actually invalidates any claim that Diodati might have written the tract.

In conclusion, it may be seen that Diodati's reputation in England was considerable, and that this reputation extended beyond the bounds of any single faction. If Diodati's name was falsely added to polemical works, this would, in fact, tend to reveal the respect in which his works were held.

Work hitherto devoted to the study of Diodati.

There has not been any considerable amount of work devoted to Diodati, and not all that has been published can be regarded as satisfactory.

The seventeenth century work lies outside the rise of modern historiography, and mostly references to Diodati are polemical rather than objective assessments, such as Veron's *Grand trouble arrive de nouveau a Geneve*, which is an attempt to discredit Diodati's French Bible. Veron's work is considered in the sections on the translation of the Bible as is that of another Catholic divine, Father Simon, who wrote that Diodati:- "not much mind's the proper sense of the words, so the vulgar may by any means understand them."[151] Diodati's reputation was naturally more secure among the protestants of Europe, and John Milton in his *Pro Populo Anglicano Defensio secunda* (London 1645 etc.) wrote that while at Geneva he held daily conferences with John Diodati, the learned professor of Theology.

The eighteenth century seems to have been a period when there was little interest in Diodati. There were few Diodati Bibles published and little study devoted to his work with the exception of a very few classic bibliographies such as Jean Senebier's *Histoire litteraire de Geneve*, (Geneva 1786 etc.).

The first half of the nineteenth century reveals continuation of the eighteenth century's lack of interest in Diodati and his work, but there was a developing interest after 1840 stimulated by the evangelical revival, the use of Diodati's Italian Bible by the Bible societies and a general nineteenth century interest in the period of protestant orthodoxy. In 1844 G.D.J.Schotel published his life *Jean Diodati* at The Hague. By 1850 theologians were beginning to question the value of Diodati's Italian Bible. C.Cavedoni had already written:- "Osservazioni critiche sopra la Bibbia del Diodati" in the Modenese periodical *Memorie di religione, de morale e di letteratura*,[152] and another attack on the Diodati Bible was the *Intorno Alla traduzione della Bibbia del Diodati dialogo Fra Don Eusebio e un Letterato*, and although this was published anonymously and *sine anno*, it appears to have been written about 1850 by P.Francesco Vandoni, Barnabita, of the S.Allessandro Church in Milan.[153] Vandoni preferred the Martini translation of the Bible and criticised that of Diodati:- "L'essere il Diodati apostata da sospetta che la sua traduzione sia di mala fede," and:- "Essi l'hanno mutilata, non che mal tradotta."[154] In England a writer using the pseudonym "Clericus" wrote about Diodati's Italian Bible:- "Viewed as the work of a pious individual about two hundred and fifty years since, its accuracy may be sufficient to elicit much commendation", however, he continues:- "let any one moderately skilled in Greek, read carefully through Diodati's *New Testament*, comparing it verse by verse with the original, and he will, without doubt, see considerable reason for a growing opinion in Italy and elsewhere, that the time is come when a wise and scholarlike revision of the Italian Bible should be prayerfully undertaken."[155] Clericus supports his argument by a discussion of Diodati's translation of the Greek word λογος. M.A.Sayous mentioned Diodati's work in his *Histoire de la litterature francaise a l'etranger* (Paris 1853).[156] There were more biographical works printed during the nineteenth century following the unsatisfactory work of Schotel, one was *Brevi introduzioni al Libri Sacri dell' Antico e Nuovo Testamento per*

Giovanni Diodati traduttore della Bibbia proceduti dalla vita dell'Autore (Turin 1854) and the most widely circulated was the *Vie de Jean Diodati* by E.de Bude, published in French during 1869, Italian during 1870 and English during 1905. Another article of biographical interest was Ch.Dardier's "Jean Diodati a Nimes 1614."[157] Another polemical work was the *Commentaria sulla Sacra Bibbia tradotta da Giovanni Diodati* by Efisio Scotto-Pintor, published at Cagliari in 1857. Diodati's work was also mentioned in *L'Evolution Theologique a Geneve au XVIIe siecle* (these presentee a la faculte de theologie protestante de Paris) (Le Cateau, 1894) by Albert Montandon. This work is not to be recommended as being valuable for the study of Diodati.

The twentieth century has, fortunately, shown an improvement in the quality of the work devoted to Diodati, though the survey of the nineteenth century reveals little to the credit of either protestant historians or Catholic controversialists. A Genevan undergraduate theses by E.Sauty, "Calvin et Diodati essai de comparaison portant sur la predestination.", is a very competent work but its value is less than it might have been since it attempts to deduce dogmatic propositions from Diodati's Biblical annotations which would seem to be primarily pietistic. Victor Baroni gives a poor account of Diodati's work in *La Contre-Reforme devant La Bible* (Lausanne 1943). More recently, B.Lescaze has revealed some of Diodati's later activity in Genevan Church affairs in an unpublished theses:- "Un itineraire spirituel au XVIIe siecle, Nicolas Antoine 1602(?) - 1632." Madame Elisabeth Labrousse has also considered Diodati's responsibility for some possibly spurious tracts, as is mentioned in the section on English material. There has also been some Italian interest in the life and work of Diodati. In 1908 A.Milli wrote *Giovanni Diodati il traduttore della Bibbia* etc. (Lausanne) and in 1944 R.Coisson wrote an unpublished undergraduate theses on "Giovanni Diodati e la sua attivita ecclesiastica" for the Facolta Valdese di Theologia at Rome. Italian scholars have also been preoccupied by the use and revision of the Diodati Italian translation of the Bible. In 1907, E.Teza wrote an article concerning:- "Del Nuovo Testamento tradotto da G.Diodati nelle tre piu vecchie edizioni etc."[158] One useful work was the *La Versione Riveduta del Nuovo Testamenta* (Rome 1916, also published in English), which gave an account of textual changes made in Diodati's Italian Bible up to 1915. These revisions stimulated Francesco di Silvestri-Falconieri to write critically of them in *La versione della Bibbia di Giovanni Diodati* (Rome 1919). In 1942, Giovanni Luzzi wrote an account of Diodati's work in *La Bibbia in Italia* (Torre Pellice) and in 1967 Professor Dr. J. Alberto Soggin, dean of the Facolta Valdese di Teologia in Rome wrote an account of the:- "Problemi di una traduzione biblica in Italiano" which inevitably involved discussion of Diodati's work and included a brief bibliography.[159]

Thus it may be seen that a certain amount of academic consideration has been devoted to Diodati and his work. Yet it is obvious that there is room for a major work concerning Diodati, or at least, a series of specialised articles. Some of the work which has been done is quite satisfactory, but too much of it has been too polemical or too biographical to provide any valuable insights. It is with this background that this study must still be presented as a prolegomenon to future study. The shortcomings of previous work reveal the justification for writing and indeed, the necessity, of this present work.

The exegesis of Diodati compared with that of Calvin and with seventeenth century Reformed theologians.

From Calvin's death until after the Synod of Dort, there was no major work of systematic theology written by a professor serving on the staff of the Genevan Academy, with the exception of the treatises of Beza. No works of systematic theology were written by the Epigones. Since Calvin's *Institutes* were built up point by point on a great series of interpretations of Biblical texts, and may still have been used for teaching in the Genevan Academy, it seemed that the exegesis of his successors should provide some evidence of their systematic theology. Thus the search for evidence of the theology of the Epigones came to be concentrated not on explicit works of systematic theology, but on another field of study - that of the exegesis of Biblical texts. Since seventeenth century theologians generally belonged to well-defined exegetical traditions, it appeared that an examination of their interpretation of Calvin's proof-texts would demonstrate whether or not their exegesis conformed to this. One example of this is the similarity of student theses on Hebrews noted by Fraenkel and dated from 1566-7; they seem to have been taught how to use the *Institutes* as a tool rather than encouraged to comment upon its contents.[160] Here we have a list made of the proof-texts of those chapters of the *Institutes* which corresponded to the doctrinal disputes of the Arminian controversy at the time of the Synod of Dort.[161] Calvin's interpretation was noted and compared to that of his successors. Stated simply, the fundamental problem was to see if Calvin's own theology could be built up from the exegetical interpretation of his successors. As will be seen, it could not.

The texts chosen for this discussion were mostly taken from among those for which Calvin had found a place in his discussion of book three of the *Institutes* :- "The way in which we receive the grace of Christ: what benefits come to us from it, and what effects follow."

The main source of evidence for the exegesis of the Epigones is the Biblical annotations of Diodati from the 1640/41[162] Italian Bible which was published rather later than the period under discussion. One reason for this was the fact that the 1640/41 Bible represented Diodati's mature opinions in a way which his youthful translation and annotation of the Bible in Italian - published in 1607 - did not. Another and more important reason is that the 1640/41 Italian Bible of Diodati has very similar annotations to the various French versions which he produced. Since it is known that Diodati was already working on his French Bible by 1618, it would seem that this version represents the norm of Diodati's exegesis at the period of the Synod of Dort. It may well be that Diodati, who published the first edition of his translation of Sarpi in 1621 and the first edition of the Sandys translation in 1626, had a rather less productive period after the early twenties and it might not be unwise to suggest that he had largely ceased to develop intellectually by that time. The appearance of the various Diodati Bibles can be seen from the bibliography but it was decided to quote his work in

Italian rather than Franch, as it is this language in which he would appear to be most at home and, probably, that in which he thought.

Thus in this section, Diodati's exegesis will be compared to that of Calvin in order to see how "orthodox" was Diodati's interpretation of Scripture. This is one method of answering the question, fundamental to this thesis, of how "Calvinist" was Diodati, and in what sense. The chapter also contains an attempt to place Diodati in the context of other seventeenth century reformed theologians and exegetes.

Five Old Testament proof texts, used by Calvin were examined with reference to Diodati. The study of these revealed little evidence of interpretations noticeably similar to those of Calvin.

Deuteronomy 7/7-8

> It was not because you were more in number than any other people that the Lord set his love upon you and chose you, for you were the fewest of all peoples; but it is because the Lord loves you and is keeping the oath which he swore to your fathers, that the Lord has brought you out with a mightly hand, and redeemed you from the house of bondage, from the hand of Pharoah king of Egypt. [163]

Calvin does not really interpret these verses in the *Institutes*, but quotes from them verbatim, obviously believing them to be explicit enough without comment.[164] However, in the commentaries, he does interpret them, but simply by putting them into his own words:- "Indeed Moses says often, Not because you excelled other nations, or were more numerous, did God honour you with so many kindnesses, but because he loved your fathers (Deut VII, 7). The Jews were continually warned not to look for the reason for their adoption elsewhere than in God's free favor. He had seen fit to choose them; this alone was the source of their security."[165] Giovanni Diodati completely ignores this and interprets the phrase "piu grandi" as a moral platitude. In this case, he is certainly not following Calvin's interpretation:- "secondo che ne' regni mondani piu e bramata la dominatione sopra una grande e potente natione, che sopra una picciola, e debole: essendo da sperar da quella piu gloria, piu utile, e piu servigio. E sotto questo qualita deesi intendere ogni altra, che fra gli huomini puo incitare altrui ad amare, o disiderare."[166] It is important to note that Diodati is not the first reformed exegete to ignore Calvin's theological interpretations. Much had, in fact, already been lost in the increasingly secular nature of the exegesis of Junius and Beza. Junius in his notes for the translation of Tremellius may well be the source of Diodati omissions. This is the case with Deuteronomy 7/7 which Junius does not interpret as relevant to election, and also with Deuteronomy 10/14.[167]

Deuteronomy 10/14-5 .

> Behold, to the Lord your God belong heaven and the heaven of heavens, the earth with all that is in it; yet the Lord set his heart in love upon your fathers and chose their descendants after them, you above all peoples as at this day.

191

In the *Institutes*,[177] Calvin interprets this verse as having a relevance to a discussion of human and divine justice:-"the will of God is not only free of all fault but is the highest rule of perfection, and even the law of all laws. But we deny that he is liable to render an account; we also deny that we are competent judges to pronounce judgment in this cause according to our own understanding. Accordingly, if we attempt more than is permitted, let that threat of the psalm strike us with fear: God will be the victor whenever he is judged by mortal man."[178] Diodati gives a different interpretation which bears no resemblance to that of Calvin, and simply discusses David's sin. In this instance we see clearly the independence of Diodati's thought from that of Calvin as expressed in the *Institutes*:-

> "Dauid haue ben peccato etiando contr'agli huomini, cosi per ingiuria priuata, come per iscandalo publico: ma, per piu aggrauare il suo fallo, ed anche per ricercarne il perdono, e'l rimedio, la doue solo si puo trouare, egli si costituisce colpeuole appo Dio solo, come l'offesa degli huomini non essendo nulla appo quella di lui, la cui maesta e offesa, e la Legge violata in ogni peccato: ed anche, per mostrare che niuma scusa, perdono, accettione dipersone, o mancamento dipotere, dalla parte degli juomini, non lo poteuano scampare dal guidicio di Dio: benche, in qualita di re, egli fosse esente della punitione degli huomini."[179]

Junius is not a direct source here as he says little about this verse, though he does refer to Genesis 12/8, the exegesis of which could have been a source for Diodati.[180] While Diodati ignores the interpretations from the *Institutes*, he is, in fact, partly dependent on Calvin in that he is using part - but only part - of Calvin's commentary on this text.[181]

Psalm 78/67-8

> *He rejected the tent of Joseph,*
> *he did not choose the tribe of Ephraim;*
> *but he chose the tribe of Judah,*
> *Mount Zion, which he loves.*

Calvin uses these verses in the Institutes to show that within the spiritual covenant accorded to the race of Abraham, God still reserved the right to reject whom he wished, be it Esau, Ishmael, Saul, or the greater part of the nation of Israel.[182] In his works, Diodati interprets a number of phrases, but without relating them to God's election or rejection:- *"de Ioseph le lieu de Silo, qui estoit en la tribu d'Ephraim, issue de Ioseph: v 60. Il choisit ass pour le siege de son Arche."*[183] Here also, Diodati is following Junius,[184] This text provides us with the most striking contrast with Calvin.

    Thus, to conclude briefly, it may be stated that there is less evidence of a Calvinist tradition of textual interpretation in Diodati's Old Testament exegesis than there is evidence of the influence of Junius. However, when the main doctrinal books of the New Testament are considered, the Gospel according to St. John and the Epistle of Paul the Apostle to the Romans, it becomes obvious that in them Diodati is much more careful to approximate his interpretation to that of Calvin. Diodati's lack of interest in the Psalms is peculiar considering that he was not only professor of Hebrew at the Academy of Geneva, but that he produced metrical editions of the Psalms (see bibliography). It is, however, interesting and relevant to note that his attitudes may very well have been based on those of Junius in his annotation of the Bible of Tremellius.

John 1/13

> who were born, not of blood nor of the will of the flesh nor of the will
> of man, but of God.

Calvin quotes this text in the *Institutes* and interprets it to mean that man cannot concieve of God unless his understanding is illuminated by the Holy Spirit.[185] He adopts a similar argument in the Commentaries,[186] where he writes:- "However closely men examine themselves, they will find nothing worthy of the children of God except what Christ has bestowed upon them"

Diodati's exegesis is quite in accord with this. He sees that the believers do not owe their acceptability to either their race or to the effort of their own wills, but to the power of the Spirit of God.[187] It has already been seen how the interpretations of Junius in the Bible of Tremellius form a kind of missing link between Calvin and Diodati. It is therefore desirable to investigate whether Beza, as another representative of the intervening generation might be a more significant source than Calvin. This could not be asserted on the evidence of the exegesis of this verse. Both Calvin[192] and Diodati relate "will" to the personal, individual wills of the men involved, but Beza interestingly relates "will" to the desire of others that a particular person might be saved.[188]

John 6/37

> All that the Father gives me will come to me; and him who comes to
> me I will not cast out.

In the Institutes, Calvin includes this text in his discussion of Christ's own attitude to election.[189] He notes that the Father's gift is the beginning of our reception into Christ. In the Commentaries, Calvin again emphasizes that faith is not at men's disposal. God's purpose ensures that none in whom his Spirit works will fall away. The latter part of the verse is a consolation for the godly, to reassure them that they will be kindly received.[190]

In his annotations, Diodati emphasizes once more the power and initiative of the Holy Spirit:- "tutti gli eletti del Padre mio, inquali egli m'ha dati a quelli saluare, e donati per esser miei, come membra del mio corpo: quelli, tratti per la virtu del mio Spirito, si riducono ed aggiungono a me per viua fede; ed io gli accolgo benignamente, e gli guardo sicuramente."[191].

In this case also, there is little evidence to suggest that Diodati used Beza as a major source. Beza ignores this text in the annotations for the 1565 Bible but in the 1598 edition there is a note. This is in general accord with the ideas of Calvin and Diodati but includes a syllogistic argument to the effect that all is grace, and grace being permanent then there can be certainty of election, for even if those endowed with grace fall away, they will rediscover saving faith. This is the kind of argument much used at Dort in discussing the fifth article *De perseverante sanctorum* and it might be noted in passing that the Dutch theological professors and the Emden delegation both use this text in their discussion of this topic.[193]

Romans 8/29

> *For those whom he foreknew he also predestined to be conformed to the image of his Son, in order that he might be the first-born among many brethren.*

Calvin discusses this text at a number of places in the *Institutes* and draws various points from it. He interprets it as[194] a method of distinguishing the elect; they are those whom God has foreknown and predestined to be conformed to the image of his Son. Calvin includes the passage in discussions of the elect elsewhere in the *Institutes*.[195] In the commentaries, he notes that God did not simply elect those whom he foresaw would be worthy of His grace, but simply selected those whom he purposed to elect.[196] The text was also used by the Genevan theologians at the Synod of Dort in such a way that it reveals their belief in its relevance to a doctrine of election.[197] Diodati also accepts this idea in his annotations to the 1640/41 Italian Bible.[198] Similar ideas are to be found in Bezan exegesis.[199]

Calvin also drew a second line of argument from this text when he pointed out that those who are freely elected are also appointed to bear the cross - that they must suffer.[200] This is an idea that was taken up by Diodati:- "ordinati al sine della conformita, in vita e gloria celeste, al auo Figliuolo, lor Capo: e cio, per l'ordine e seguito dolla somiglianza d'esso in molte cose in questo mondo: ma particolarmente nell' afflittioni."[201]

A third idea derived from the text by Calvin is the association of 'firstborn' with Christ, something not made entirely clear by the various translations. This interpretation occurs elsewhere in the Institutes,[202] and in Diodati.[203]

Thus Calvin's own interpretation of this text is supported by Diodati in detail. In this instance one might suggest that Diodati is in a Calvinist exegetical tradition which does not exclude Beza.

Romans 9/6

> *But it is not as though the word of God had failed. For not all who are descended by Israel belong to Israel.*

In the Institutes,[204] Calvin takes this text as an illustration of the fact that while all Jews were blessed by hereditary right, the succession did not pass equally. In another place he uses this text to infer that God is not bound by persons, places or institutions, neither by the temple in Jerusalem nor by the 'Romanists'. To Calvin, there is no temple of the Lord, save that in which his word is heard.[205] Diodati takes up two of Calvin's points, which he discusses. Firstly, he notes that God's covenant has not failed even though the greater part of the Jewish nation can no longer be counted among God's people; and secondly, that the seed of Abraham are not the mere physical descendants, but rather those who have faith who are similar in spiritual matters.[206] The idea that it is not a mere carnal descent from Abraham - but rather a spiritual similarity - is also found in the Dort proof texts, in the first thesis of the section "De reprobatione",[207] "ex gratia et potente Dei operatione nati per fidem."[208] Beza uses more obvious academic sources when discussing this text in both Tractationes and annotations than does either Diodati or Calvin[209] but his conclusions follow the same pattern - that election comes through God's will as applied to an individual and not through race.

Thus, in this case, a definite exegetical tradition may be traced from Calvin through to his successors. The interpretation becomes more limited, but the most important elements remain basically unchanged.

Yet, even after this evidence of Diodati's attention to Calvin's interpretation of Scripture, it cannot be said that his New Testament analysis is completely similar to that of Calvin.

Romans 11/35

> *Or who has given a gift to him*
> *that he might be repaid?*

In the *Institutes*, Calvin states that Paul's intention is to show that:- "God's goodness so anticipates men that among them he finds nothing either past or future to win them his favour."[210] He cites this text as proof of the fact that God is debtor to no one.[211] He writes that Paul infers that:- "let us not suppose that we bring anything to the Lord but the sheer disgrace of need and emptiness."[212]

In the commentaries, Calvin writes that this is an argument by which Paul defends God against the accusations of the ungodly. God cannot be accused of unrighteousness since he is under obligation to none." Who can boast of any work of his own by which he has merited God's favour?"[214] God owes us nothing, since we have a corrupt and depraved nature, and therefore we cannot force God to bestow salvation upon us because of our good works. We cannot:- "deprive God of his right to do freely what he pleases with the creatures whom he has made."[214]

Diodati writes along the same lines as Calvin. With sublime confidence and considerable lack of feeling, he states:- "questo e aggiunto, per turar la bocca alle querele di quelli ch'Iddio tralascia."[215], thus losing all the sensitivity and much of the theology of Calvin.

Beza does not discuss this text in the *Tractationes*, but in the annotations he gives a note referring to patristic arguments to refute the idea that election might depend on works.[216]

Thus, it may be concluded that Diodati does interpret some texts in a way which might be described as Calvinist, notably those which have doctrinal significance, but it is obvious that he is not dominated by a purely Calvinist or Bezan tradition. It must be noted that there is a very considerable difference between the exegesis of Calvin and of Diodati. There are constant and considerable differences in the interpretation of texts. Diodati gives a number of Calvinist textual interpretations, but from whence come the others that are not to be found in Calvin? Some, as have been seen, come from Tremellius and Junius, though rarely from Beza, but it would seem that Diodati had a principle of exegesis that was quite alien to that of Calvin. Diodati was not so completely immersed in dogmatic theology as were the Reformed theologians of the sixteenth century. His exegesis is aimed at a less academic audience, and the information that he gives is partly picaresque and partly pietistic as well as having an orthodox dogmatic base. Yet the fundamental problem remains. In what lies Diodati's orthodoxy? In what way were the epigones following Calvin's teaching? Calvin's system of theology included the careful use of large numbers of Biblical proof texts. If, therefore, his successors failed to interpret texts used by Calvin in an exactly similar fashion, it is not immediately obvious how they accepted Calvin's systematic theology.

Diodati and other then contemporary Reformed exegetes.

This is no attempt at an exhaustive treatment of the subject in question, but a brief test based on the exegesis of 1 Peter 1/1-9. The problem to be resolved was that of the Calvinism of Diodati as compared with other European Reformed theologians of the day. It has been shown above that Diodati's exegesis is quite different from that of Calvin. Before posing the question of Diodati's principle of exegesis, a question which will be examined below, it is first necessary to determine whether or not this lack of conformity with Calvin was typical of Reformed exegesis of the earlier seventeenth century. Two theologians were selected, one was the "orthodox" William Ames, and the other was the "liberal" Moise Amyraut.

If it were obvious that both Ames and Amyraut were similarly different to Calvin, then it would be necessary to seek for a common source for this non-Calvinistic form of exegesis. In fact, as will be demonstrated, Diodati's form of non-Calvinist exegesis was untypical of his generation of Reformed exegetes.

William Ames (1576-1633) was an English "orthodox" reformed theologian who taught at the Dutch university of Franeker. The work by Ames which was considered was:- *An Analytical Exposition Of both the Epistles of the Apostle Peter, Illustrated by Doctrines out of every text. And applyed by their Uses, for a further progresse in Holinesse*, published at London in 1641. In this work, Ames is dominated by a desire to deduce "doctrine" from the Biblical text. His exegesis consists of the statement of a number of doctrines based on each group of texts considered. His basic interest is in systematic theology. It was noticed that Ames' grouping of texts for analysis in the first chapter of the first Epistle, i.e., 1 Peter 1/1-2, 3-5, 6-9 and 10-12, was the same as that used by Calvin in his *Commentarius in Epistolas Catholicas*, printed in volume fifty-five of the *Calvini Opera*, being volume eighty-three of the *Corpus Reformatorum*. Further study revealed that almost all of Ames' doctrines could be easily reconciled with statements made by Calvin. Thus it became obvious that Ames' exegesis was based, to some extent, on that of Calvin, though the form used to convey his interpretation was very different, employing a very rigid classification, typical of Ames, that appears somewhat crude when compared with Calvin's work.

The better known Moise Amyraut was a French Huguenot theologian who lived from 1596 until 1664. He was a near contemporary of Ames and taught at the French protestant college of Saumur. With the expatriate Scot, John Cameron, he is usually regarded as being the exponent of a more liberal form of Calvinism than that, for instance, which is generally thought to have been taught by Diodati at Geneva. It has recently been suggested that Amyraut's theology was more akin to that of Calvin than were the writings of then contemporary "orthodox" Calvinists such as, presumably, Ames and Diodati. In a modern work, *Calvinism and the Amyraut Heresy*, Dr. B.G. Armstrong[217] has written that:- "Both the methodololgy and content of the teaching of Calvin and Amyraut were found to contrast sharply with those of orthodox Calvinists of the seventeenth century."[218] Dr. Armstrong does not consider exegesis in his work on Amyraut, and so, with the evidence of a certain correspondence between the thought of Calvin and Ames, it was considered that a further comparative study of these two theologians and Amyraut's *Paraphrase sur les Epistres Catholiques* printed at Saumur by Lesnier in 1646, might well prove to be most interesting. Ames was most certainly a representative of what Armstrong calls an "orthodox Calvinist", being appointed to a chair of theology in the Dutch University of Franeker only three years after the Synod of Dort[219] at a time when it would have been unwise to question the decisions of that synod and when the orthodoxy of applicants for theological chairs must have been rigorously questioned. A man whose fidelity to the doctrines of Dort could be questioned, would certainly not have been an acceptable candidate. The work by Amyraut is quite accurately entitled "Paraphrase", being composed of a rewriting of the epistle by Amyraut, in French, with the original Biblical text being printed in the margin. In each case, the interpretation of these two exegetes is compared to Calvin and to Diodati.

Each group of texts is discussed separately, and each group is preceded by a quotation of the Biblical text from the *Common Bible* in English.

1 Peter 1/1-2

> *Peter, an apostle of Jesus Christ, To the exiles of the Dispersion in Pontus, Galatia, Cappadocia, Asia, and Bithynia, chosen and destined by God the Father and sanctified by the Spirit for obedience of Jesus Christ and for sprinkling with his blood: May grace and peace by multiplied to you.*

William Ames draws five "doctrines" from these two verses, all of which can be related to passages in Calvin's commentary. Ames' first and second doctrines:- "The beginning and fountaine of all our happinesse and consolation consists in this, that we are the elect of God," and :- "There is no other cause or reason to be given of our election unto salvation, but only the good pleasure of God,"[220] can easily be reconciled with Calvin:- "Quemadmodum tamen in electione nostra primas gratuito Dei beneplacito assignat"[221] and with Amyraut:- "Car Dieu vous a eleus et distingues d'avec les autres hommes en son eternelle prescience."[222]

Similarly, the third and fourth doctrines of Ames:- "True sanctification is a certain fruit of election" and :- "The mediation of Christ, and reconcilation made for us in him, is the only meanes whereby the force of our election is derived unto us, and our sanctification and salvation is propagated",[223] can be reconciled with statements in Calvin:- "mox tamen ad effectum nos revocat...Effectus ille est spiritus sanctificatis...",[224] and:- "Sancitificat ergo nos Deus, efficaciter nos vocando. Id autem fit, dum renovamur in obedientiam iustitiae eius, et Christi sanguine adspersi mundamur a peccatis."[225] Diodati emphasizes the role of the Spirit in sanctification:- "sancificandovi realmente per lo suo Spirito, a 'cui s'appartiene di render la vocatione di Dio ferma, ed efficace,"[226] while Amyraut writes that God has:- "vous consacrant d'une sanctification interieure et spirituelle." However, although the fifth doctrine of Ames:- "In that chaine of our salvation, the beginning is from God the Father, the dispensation of it is through his Sonne Jesus Christ, the application of it is through the Holy Ghost,"[227] containing the idea of the utility of Divine personality can be reconciled with Calvin:- "salutem nostram manare ex gratuita electione Dei: sed eam simul considerandam esse fidei experientia in eo quod spiritu suo nos santificat,"[228] it can be reconciled with neither Amyraut - who does not mention the Spirit - nor with Diodati.

There is one considerable difference to be noted between the exegesis of Ames and Diodati. Ames[229] writes that his second doctrine:- "may serve to refute those, that make God's election to depend upon our faith and perseverance, as a cause or condition requisite." Yet Diodati in his interpretation of the works "unto obedience" would seem to put faith in a primary position:- "accioche rendovi ubbidienti per fede all' Evangelio, voi partecipiate al beneficio della morte del Signore, alla rimessione de' vostri peccati. Overo, dichiara i due fini della vocatione de'fideli: che sono, la giustificatione nel sangue di Christo: e la nuova ubbidienza, per la santificatione dello Spirito."

There are also two points mentioned by Amyraut, Diodati and Calvin, which are ignored by Ames. Diodati writes about separation:- "cioe separati dal mondo, per la vocatione efficace di Dio: il che e l'esecutione dell' eterna elettione."[230] Similarly, Amyraut writes:- "Puis en executant ce sien misericordieux propos en son temps, il vous a separes effectivement d'avec ceux."[231] On the subject of obedience, Amyraut writes that God:- "vous a amenes a l'obeissance de son Evangile" while Diodati writes that faith makes men obedient to the Gospel.

Thus, to conclude, this first group of two verses shows Ames and Calvin to have a considerable similarity of exegesis. The interpretations of Amyraut and Diodati cannot be completely reconciled with this exegesis, and Diodati may be seen to be further removed from it than Amyraut. An examination of Beza on these texts would not seem to show a greater level of dependance on him than was demonstrated by the previously studied texts from John and Romans.[232]

Furthermore, although it is not directly germane to this thesis, the paraphrase of Amyraut would not seem to depend overmuch on that of Erasmus.[233]

1 Peter 1/3-5

> *Blessed be the God and Father of our Lord Jesus Christ! By his great mercy we have been born anew to a living hope through the resurrection of Jesus Christ from the dead, and to an inheritance which is imperishable, undefiled, and unfading, kept in heaven for you, who by God's power are guarded through faith for a salvation ready to be revealed in the last time.*

The second group of texts discussed by Ames and Calvin, consists of verses three to five of the first chapter. Ames draws eight points from these three verses, of which seven can be related to statements by Calvin.

Ames' first doctrine is:- "The state of grace depends upon the flowes from effectual calling." This can be related to a statement of Calvin:- "Hac de causa magnifice his extollit ingentem Dei gratiam in Christo, ne molestum nobis sit nos ipsos et mundum abnegare, ut potiamur inaestimabili vitae futurae thesauro" but it is to be noticed that the idea of rejection, employed by Calvin, is mentioned neither by Ames nor by Amyraut. There is no real equivalent of this doctrine in the writings of Diodati.

Ames' second doctrine:- "God regenerates us as the Father of our Lord Jesus Christ" can be related to an idea of Calvin's:- "Proinde quisquis verum Deum vere cognoscere cupit, hoc patris Christi titulo vestiat."[234] It is interesting that this idea of divine personality acting specifically as the Father of Christ, found in both Ames and Calvin, is alien to both Diodati and Amyraut.

In his third and fourth points, Ames emphasises the mercy of God and our hope of eternal life as opposed to eternal death:- "A wonderfull great mercy of God appears in our regeneration" and :- "Regeneration brings men a lively hope of eternal life." These two ideas are to be found in Calvin:- "Docet itaque Petrus nos qui natura morti aeternae eramus destinati, in vitam Dei misericordia restitutos esse."[235] The idea of hope is to be found in Diodati, but not the idea of mercy:- "cioe per concepere una viva, sempre crescente, ed operante speranza de'beni celesti: mediante la rigeneratione spirituale, che e la vera sementa, a caparra dell'eterna gloria".[236] Amyraut includes both ideas:- "il a este si riche en misericorde pour nous, qu'au lieu que nous naissons tous assujettes a la malediction de la mort, il nous a par l'avantage d'une nouvelle naissance, eleves en une vive esperance de la bien heureuse immortalite."

The fifth doctrine of Ames:- "The liveliness of our hope depends upon the resurrection of Jesus Christ from the dead" can be related to statements of Calvin:- "Spes viva pro spe vitae capitur" and "resurrectionem vero potius adduxit, quia de nova vita agebat." Similar ideas are to be found in Diodati:- "cioe in virtu della risurrettione di Christo, laquale e la fonte della rigeneratione" and Amyraut:- "en ce que ressusciat son Fils nostre Seigneur Jesus Christ d'entre les morts, il nous a donne cette asseurance que sa justice est contentee par satisfaction."

The sixth doctrine of Ames:- "That salvation we hope for is a celestiall and incorruptible inheritance," is to be found in Calvin:- "Haereditas dicitur in coelis conservata, ut sciamus eam esse extra periculum."[237] These two texts are so similar that Ames' may be seen as a paraphrase or even a translation of Calvin. These ideas can also be related to Amyraut:- "A ce que nous soyons un jour rendus jouissans de son heritage, qui doit estre incorruptible, exempt de toute tache de peche, et de toute tare d'incommodite, et tout lumineux d'une gloire dont le lustre et la splendour ne se fletrira jamais." Diodati also has similar ideas:- "Per questi titoli dimostra che, come i beni celesti sono eterni, e senza impurita di peccato; tali debbono altresi essere i fideli, per lo dono dello Spirito santo, che gli spoglia di queste due qualita: cioe peccato, ed infine anchora delle conditioni inferme della vita animale," but his exegesis has a slightly different character, since he reveals an interest in believers that is alien to the "doctrines"of Ames.

The seventh doctrine:- "The exceeding great power of God, his fidelity and constance, doth make this inheritance firme and sure unto us," reveals Ames' belief in the power of God, and in its utility for our protection. Similar ideas are to be found in Calvin:- "Quamlibet igitur infirmi simus, salus tamen nostra non est instabilis, quia Dei virtute fulcitur,"[238] and Diodati:- "cioe per la suo potenza, laquale sola opera efficacemente in questa guardia, contr'a tutti gli assalti, ed infidie de' nimici: Gio.10.29 ed e prestata all'huomo per lo mezzo della vera e viva fede." and:- "cioe preservati contr'a tutti i pericoli di perdere la salute," and " cioe per esser fatti possessori dell' ultimo fine, e perfetto compimento d'essa." Amyraut writes:- "Pource que Dieu nous ayant premierement convertis par sa puissance il deploye continuellement la mesme vertu pour nous garder." Whereas Ames mentions God's power to convert men, this idea of conversion is not to be found in Amyraut.

The eighth doctrine of Ames:- "These spirituall blessings of God, should never bee mentioned or thought upon by us, without a pious desire to blesse God for them," is not to be found in Calvin, nor in the work by Amyraut, nor in the Italian Bible of Diodati. It is, one presumes, an idea that is inherent in all four.

There are no significant theological ideas expressed by Amyraut that are not to be found in Ames. There is, however, one idea of Diodati's, the idea of a right to salvation:- "per acquistarcene la ragione, e rendercene capaci, come fatti figliouli di Dio," that would appear to be unique.

Thus this second group of texts reveals a very great similarity between all four exegetes. Ames and Diodati each produce ideas unique to themselves, while Diodati and Amyraut each, on occasion, interpret doctrine in a slightly different manner to Ames and Calvin. Ames' first doctrine is not to be found in Diodati's exegesis, nor is Ames' second doctrine to be found in the writings of Diodati and Amyraut.

1 Peter 1/6-9

> *In this you rejoice, though now for a little while you may have to suffer various trials, so that the genuineness of your faith, more precious than gold which though perishable is tested by fire, may redound to praise and glory and honour at the revelation of Jesus Christ.*

Without having seen him you love him; though you do not now see
him you believe in him and rejoice with unutterable and exalted joy.
As the outcome of your faith you obtain the salvation of your souls.

The third set of Texts examined by Ames and Calvin consists of 1 Peter 1/6-9. In this group there is a very considerable similarity to be seen in the exegesis of Ames, Calvin and Amyraut.

Ames' first doctrine:- "Joy and spirituall rejoycing ariseth from the sense and participation of spirituall grace," is similar to a statement by Amyraut:-"Et c'est pour ce que vous estes participans de cette bien heureuse esperance, que vous sentes en vos ames ces emotions de joye." Here Amyraut gives the same meaning to the text as does Ames, the emphasis being on subjective experience. Calvin, on the other hand, is objective:- "Consilium enim est docere quisquam ex spe salutis fructus nobis proveniat: nempe spirituale gaudium..."

Ames second doctrine:- "Manifold afflictions may well stand with this joy," can be related to texts in Calvin:- "Sed hoc nonnullam habet repugnantiae speciem, dum fideles, qui gaudio exsultant, simul tristes esse dicit...Verum melius experimento norunt fideles, illos simul consistere, quam verbis exprimi queat," and in Amyraut:- "vous sentes pour un peu de temps quelques atteintes d'affliction et de tristesse."

The third doctrine of Ames:- "Afflictions are turned into matter of rejoycing, when there is such use made of them as that our faith and every grace is stirred up and increased by them," is similar to ideas found in the exegesis of Amyraut:- "Car c'est la la condition des fideles en la terre, dure et facheuse a la verite, si vous la regardes en elle mesme, mais qui neantmoins n'est pas capable de beaucoup alterer la tranquilite de leur joye," Calvin:- "Tristitiam ergo ex malis sentiunt: sed quae ita lenitur fide, ut gaudere propterea non desinant. Ita non impedit tristitia ipsorum gaudium, sed potius locum illi cedit," and also Diodati:- la vostra fede ben prouata, e stando ad ogni cimento."

The fourth doctrine of Ames:- "This joy doth not depend upon the sight or visible presence of Christ" is similar to ideas of Calvin:- "Atque hoc prius ordine membrum est, non metiendam esse fidem adspectu. Nam quum misera in speciem sit Christianorum vita, nisi felicitas eorum in spe sita esset, protinus conciderent. Habet quidem et fides suos oculos, sed qui in regnum Dei invisibile penetrant, et qui speculo verbi contenti sunt...Quare verum est illud Pauli nos peregrinari a Domino quamdiu hac carne sumus circumdati, quia per fidem ambulamus, et non per adspectum." And also of Amyraut:- "Pour vous qui estes enseignes et illumines d'ailleurs, bien que vous ne l'oyes jamais veu des yeux de vos corps, vous l'aimes pourtant, et bien que vous ne le voyies point encore, si est-ce que vous croyes en luy."

The fifth doctrine:- "This joy is unspeakable and full of glory," can be reconciled between Ames and Amyraut:- "et de vostre foy naist en vos ames une si grande et si incomparable joye," and also with Calvin:- "Vocat autem gaudium inenarrabile, quia pax Dei sensum omnem exsuperat."

The sixth, and final, doctrine of Ames:- "By the joy we begin to looke for the end of our faith, even the salvation of our soules," can be related to Calvin:-

The Epigones

"Admonet quorsum sensum suos dirigere fideles debeant, nempe in salutem aeternam," Amyraut:- "et que vous anticipes deja dans la joye que produit en vous la certitude de vostre esperance," and with Diodati:- "cioe fin da questo mondo stesso havendo le primitie del godimento della salute, lequali anchora saranno indubitatamente seguite dalla pienezza."

Thus, in this case, the "orthodox" Ames and the "liberal" Amyraut are both writing exegesis that is similar to Calvin. However, the other "orthodox" theologian whose work is being considered, Diodati, writes an exegesis that is radically different from the other three. For instance, the word "joy" in various forms, is to be found in all of Ames' six doctrines. It is not found once in Diodati's exegesis. Apart from the two statements quoted above, that relate to the third and sixth doctrines, there is no clear link to be found between Diodati's work and that of the other three. On the other hand, Diodati expressed an idea that is unique to himself in this context, the idea of obedience:- "onde la necessita della volonta di Dio vi dee importe la legge di volontaria ubbidenza."

As has already been stated, this is no exhaustive consideration of the exegetical history of 1 Peter 1/1-9. Important problems such as the possibility of common influences upon Ames, Amyraut and even Diodati, other than Calvin himself, have been neglected. Possible sources for common influences might be sought in the writings of Vermigli, Bullinger, Musculus and, of course Zanchius. This problem has not been considered as it is really irrelevant to the basic problem of this thesis which is the description of the theology of the Genevan Academy at the time of the Synod of Dort and of its relation to Calvin's thought. It became clear from the study of Diodati and Calvin alone, that the exegesis of Diodati was quite different to that of Calvin. It had to be seen whether this divergence from Calvin was typical of Reformed exegesis in the early seventeenth century. Thus the test was made to compare Diodati with "orthodox" and "liberal" Calvinists. The test has been made and the result is clear. Not only is Diodati seen to be exegetically independent of Calvin, but this test would tend to show that other reformed theologians of his period, both "orthodox" and "liberal" were exegetically much more dependant on Calvin than was Diodati. From this it may be deduced that Diodati, and therefore the Genevan Academy at which he taught for so long, was propounding an exegesis that was not akin to Calvin and untypical of other reformed academies at the time of the Synod of Dort. Since Calvin's theology was based on the interpretation of a great series of proof texts, any change, by his successors, of Calvin's exegesis, could naturally tend to lead to changes in Genevan doctrine. This is a problem that has been discussed elsewhere in this thesis, with reference to the doctrines of salvation. Yet one conclusion can be drawn from what has already been said, which is, that if Diodati's theological position were to be described solely on the basis of his exegesis, that it would then be quite irresponsible to classify him as an "orthodox Calvinist."

In considering the exegesis of 1 Peter 1/1-9, one would appear to be faced with the problem of two "orthodox Calvinists," Ames and Diodati, whose exegesis of the same Biblical texts are quite different. It is hardly necessary to add that the verses 1 Peter 1/1-9 are of doctrinal significance if the Bible is to be examined on the basis of a propositional view of revelation. Yet this is no problem at all.

There is only one problem and that is a problem of terminology, the problem of the use of terms like "orthodox Calvinist" and "liberal Calvinist". The picture is infinitely more complex. These terms have been too often used in an undefined or underdefined sense as if they related to a uniform climate of reformed theological opinion. Their institution would not appear to have been based on a sound foundation of detailed research. The fact is that the intellectual and theological traditions and climates of the seventeenth century are still very imperfectly known, especially those relating to orthodox dogmatic systems whether Lutheran or reformed. What would appear to have happened is that modern historians of seventeenth century reformed protestantism have inherited the legacy of general terms which do not stand up to detailed analysis, because they were coined in the eighteenth and nineteenth centuries in polemical situations when modern historiographical methods were unknown. The present writer wishes to suggest, therefore, on the basis of this slight study, that it is impossible to use terms such as "orthodox Calvinist" since they seem to be incapable of exact definition. The initial verdict of this study, based on exegetical analysis, would seem to suggest that these terms are unacceptable in scientific works on historical theology. Inexactitude leads to obscurity, and obscurity to ignorance.

NOTES

[1] W.Schwarz *Principles and Problems of Biblical translation* (Cambridge 1955) p. 195 etc.

[2] Letter from Diodati to J.A. de Thou, dated 13 July, 1607. Ms in the Bibliotheque nationale, Paris, ms Collection Dupuy 806f 195.

[3] Logan Perrsall Smith, *The Life and Letters of Sir Henry Wotton* (Oxford, 2 vols., 1907) vol I, p. 90.

[4] Logan Pearsall Smith, *op. cit*, vol I, p. 90.

[5] *Ibid*. p. 462.

[6] Geneva, Archives d'Etat, RCP copy p. 334.

[7] Quick, *Synodicon in Gallia Reformata*, vol II, p. 413.

[8] Geneva, Archives d'Etat, RC (1641) pp. 151-2, 13 Nov 1641.

[9] G.Diodati, *Pious Annotations upon the Holy Bible* (London 1643) p. a4r.

[10] *Ibid*.

[11] *Ibid*.

[12] Geneva, Bibliotheque publique et universitaire, ms fr. 427, Correspondence Esslesiastique 1637-44, fol 183-5.

[13] L.E.du Pin *A Compleat History of the Canon and Writers of the Books of the Old and New Testament* (London 1699), part I, p. 119.

[14] Father Simon *Critical Enquiries into the Various Editions of the Bible Printed In Divers Places and at several Times* (London 1684) p. 238.

[15] Simon, *op.cit*. pp. 237-8.

[16] *Ibid*.

[17] *La Sacra Bibbia* (Leipzig 1744), Diodati edited Muller, p. 3v.

[18] Darlow and Moule, *Catalogue of Printed Bibles*, III/814.

[19] *Ibid*. p. 813.

[20] Diodati *Bibbia* 1607, p. 41, 3flr.

[21] *La Bibia* (Geneva 1562) Brucciolini/Rustici, D3r, p. 15.

[22] *Iesu Christi D.N.Novum Testamentum* (Geneva 1588) M6r, p. 143.

[23] *CR* XLV/107 and LVII/85.

[24] *La Bible* (Geneva 1588) 2Clv, p. 17.

[25] As note (2) supra.

[26] Diodati *Bibbia* (ed) 1607, R2r, p. 147.

[27] Diodati *Bibbia* (ed) 1640/41, N4v, p. 152.

[28] *La Bibia* (Geneva 1562) Brucciolini/Rustici, f3r, p. 71.

[29] *Holy Bible* ("Geneva Bible" or "Breeches Bible") (Geneva 1562) m6r, p. 72.

[30] *La Bible* (Geneva 1588) K3r, p. 75.

[31] *CR* LVI/241.

[32] *Biblia Sacra* (Zurich 1673) tr Tremellius, ed Junius, H2v.

[33] Diodati *Bibbia* (ed) S2v, p. 208.

[34] *La Bibia (Geneva 1562) Brucciolini/Rustici, B1v, p. 97.*

[35] *La Bible* (Geneva 1588) n8v, p. 104.

[36] *Holy Bible* (Geneva 1562) r2r, p. 98.

[37] *CR* XXV/496 and *Biblia Sacra* (Zurich 1673) tr Tremellius, ed Junius, L1r.

[38] Diodati *Bibbia* (ed) (1607) 2Cr. p. 585.

[39] Diodati *Bibbia* (ed) (1640/41) 3B6r, p. 575.

[40] *La Bibia* (Geneva 1562) Brucciolini/Rustici, 2X2r, p. 268.

[41] *Holy Bible* (Geneva 1562) 2X5r, p. 247.

[42] *La Bible* (Geneva 1588) O6r, p. 294.

[43] *Biblia Sacra* (Zurich 1673) tr Tremellius ed Junius, 2D5r.

[44] Diodati *Bibbia* (ed) (1607) V2r, p. 171; *Bibbia* (ed) (1640/41) p. 4v.

[45] *La Bibia* (Geneva 1562) Brucciolini/Rustici, X2v, p. 82.

[46] *Holy Bible* (Geneva 1562) O5v, p. 83v.

[47] *Biblia Sacra* op. cit. I4v.

[48] *CR* LVI/282.

[49] Diodati *Bibbia* (ed) (1607) 3Q2v, p. 124 and *Bibbia* (ed) (1640/41) L1v, p. 122

[50] Diodati *Bibbia* (ed) (1607) 3Q2v, p. 124.

[51] Diodati *Bibbia* (ed) (1640/41) L1v. p. 122

[52] *La Bibia* (Geneva 1562) Brucciolini/Rustici, 4M1r, p. 48.

[53] *Novum Test*. etc. (Geneva 1598) 202v, p. 444.

[54] *La Bible* (Geneva 1588) 2G8v, p. 56.

[55] *Holy Bible* (Geneva 1562) 2X5r.

[56] Geneva, Archives d'Etat (AEG), Registres de la compagnie des pasteurs, copy, E, p. 282, 2 Jan 1618.

[57] AEG E RCP copy p. 286, 30 Jan 1618.

[58] AEG E RCP copy p. 295, 3 April 1618.

[59] AEG F RCP copy pp. 7-8, 21 Jan 1620.

[60] Geneva, Bibliotheque publique et universitaire, ms Ami Lullin 53 folia 77-80.

[61] BPU ms Ami Lullin 53 folia 77-80.

[62] AEG F RCP copy p. 56, 8 May 1621.

[63] AEG F RCP copy p. 214, 26 March 1624.

[64] AEG G RCP copy p. 80, 27 April 1627.

[65] AEG G RCP copy p. 81, 11 May 1627.

[66] AEG G RCP copy p. 321, 19 December 1634.

[67] AEC G RCP copy p. 321, 19 December 1634.

[68] AEG G RCP copy p. 324, 16 Jan 1635.

[69] AEG G RCP copy pp. 332-40, 22 May 1635.

[70] AEG RC 134 (1635) pp. 122-5, 14 April 1635.

[71] AEG RC 134 (1635) p. 124, 14 April 1635.

[72] F.Veron S.J., *Grand Trouble* etc., bibliography no. 53, p. 34.

[73] AEG G RCP copy pp. 332-40, 22 & 26 May 1635.

[74] AEG G RCP copy pp. 332-40, 22 & 26 May 1635.

[75] AEG G RCP copy pp. 332-40, 22, 26 May 1635.

[76] Private Genevan Archives in possession of Dominice family, packet marked:- "Benedict Turrettini", letter of G.B.Hottinger to B.Turrettini.

[77] AEG RC 134 (1635) pp. 339-43, 3 Nov 1635.

[78] AEG RC 134 (1635) pp. 339-43, 3 Nov 1635.

[79] AEG RC 134 (1635) pp. 339-43, 3 Nov 1635.

[80] AEG RC 134 (1635) pp. 372-3, 28 Nov 1635.

[81] AEG RC 134 (1635) pp. 375-8, 30 Nov 1635.

[82] AEG RC 134 (1635) pp. 381-3, 1 Dec 1635.

[83] AEG RC 134 (1635) pp. 385-6, 2 Dec 1635.

[84] AEG G RCP copy pp. 363-4, 11 Dec 1635.

[85] AEG G RCP copy pp. 363-4, 11 Dec 1635.

[86] E. & E. Haag, *La France Protestante* etc., IV/433; *Dictionnaire Historique et biographique de la Suisse* etc., IV/465 (Neuchatel 1928).

[87] J.Quick, *Synodicon in Gallia Reformata*, (London 1692) II/412-22.

[88] *Ibid.*, II/421-2.

[89] *Ibid* p. 412 "a very long and dangerous illness".

[90] *Ibid* p. 412.

[91] Ibid p. 412:- "I have confined my self to a small Specimen of *Annotations* on the Books of *Ecclesiastes* and *Canticles*, which I have chosen from among the rest because of their obscurities and perplexing difficulties, both in the Original Text and Sense of it."

[92] Ibid p. 419.

[93] Ibid pp. 419-20.

[94] Ibid pp. 419-20.

[95] Quick, *Synodicon in Gallia Reformata*, vol II, p. 421.

[96] *Ibid* p. 421.

[97] *Ibid* p. 412.

[98] *Ibid* p. 412.

[99] *Ibid* pp. 421-2.

[100] Quick, *Synodicon in Gallia Reformata*, vol II, p. 413.

[101] *Ibid*, pp. 414-5.

[102] AEG RC 140 (1641) pp. 151-2, 13 Nov 1641.

[103] AEG RC 136 (1637) p. 430, 17 Oct 1637.

[104] AEG RC 137 (1638) p. 193, 23 March 1638.

[105] AEG RC 137 (1638) pp. 227-9, 9 April 1638.

[106] AEG G RCP copy p. 443, 13 April 1638

[107] AEG G RCP copy p. 444, 13 April 1638.

[108] AEG G RCP copy p. 445, 13 April 1638.

[109] AEG. Manuscript in Diodati's handwriting:-"Memoire des principaux points, que ie representai Mardi passe, a Vos Seigneurs du Conseil."

[110] AEG RC 137 (1638) pp. 484-5, 13 July 1638.

[111] AEG RC 137 (1638) p. 245, 14 April 1638.

[112] AEG RC 137 (1638) p. 255, 20 April 1638.

[113] AEG RC 137 (1638) p. 266, 21 April 1638.

[114] AEG RC 138 (1639) p. 452.

[115] AEG RC 137 (1638) p. 469, 7 July 1638.

[116] AEG RC 137 (1638) pp. 484-5, 13 July 1638.

[117] AEG RC 137 (1638) pp. 667-8, 11 September 1638.

[118] AEG RC 137 (1638) pp. 723-6, 6 October 1638.

[119] AEG RC 137 (1638) p. 728, 8 October 1638.

[120] G.Diodati, *Les livres du Iob Pseaumes Proverbes* etc., p. 4.

The Epigones

[121] G.Diodati, *Les livres de Iob Pseaumes Proverbes* etc. p. 3.

[122] *Ibid* p. 3.

[123] *Ibid* p. 7.

[124] AEG RC 140 (1641) pp. 151-2, 13 Nov 1641.

[125] AEG RC 142 (1643) pp. 32-3, 27 Jan 1643.

[126] Bibliotheque publique et universitaire, Geneva, ms Fr 427, Correspondence Ecclesiastique 1637-44, folia 183-5.

[127] *Ibid*, folia 183-5.

[128] Quick, *op.cit.*, II/441.

[129] Logan Pearsall Smith *The Life and Letters of Sir Henry Wotton*, (Oxford, 2 vols., 1907), vol I, p. 86.

[130] E.S.Shuckburgh, *Two biographies of William Bedell* (Cambridge 1902) p. 248.

[131] Smith, *op.cit.*, vol I, p. 91.

[132] Shuckburgh, *op. cit.*, p. 248.

[133] Smith, *op. cit.*, vol I, p. 89 *apud* H.Brown, *Studies in European Literature*, pp. 223-4; and M.Ritter *Briefe und Acten zur de Geschichte des dreissigjahrigen Krieges*, vol II, p. 131.

[134] Smith *op. cit.*, vol I, p. 400.

[135] *Ibid*, vol II, p. 496.

[136] *Ibid*, vol I, p. 400n.

[137] Smith, *op. cit.*, vol I, p. 400n

[138] Shuckburgh, *op. cit.*, p. 249.

[139] Smith, *op. cit.*, vol I, p. 91.

[140] *British Museum General Catalogue of Printed Books* (1960), vol CCXII, col 732.

[141] *Dictionary of National Biography*, vol L, p. 286.

[142] Smith, *op. cit.*, vol I, p. 91.

[143] Shuckburgh, *op. cit.*, p. 254.

[144] Geneva, Archives d'Etat, RC 140 (1641) pp. 151-2, 13 Nov 1641.

[145] *Dictionary of National Biography*, vol LV, p. 140.

[146] Baron de Schickler, *Les Eglises du Refuge en Angleterre*, vol II, pp. 91-3.

[147] Geneva, Archives d'Etat, RC 148 (1649), pp. 123-5, 14 March 1649. A shorter and slightly different account of Diodati's sermon is to be found in the Genevan Archives d'Etat, Archives de familles, II/33.

[148] Elisabeth R.Labrousse, "Rapport sur les Conferences de l'annee 1969-70", p. 603, in *Annuaire de l'Ecole Pratique des Hautes Etudes*, IVe Section, (1971).

[149] Diodati Bibliography, p. 32, no. 42, p. A1v.

[150] Diodati Bibliography, p. 32, no. 44, p(C)2v.

[151] Father Simon, *Critical Enquiries into the Various Editions of the Bible* (London 1684) pp. 237-8. See bibliography.

[152] *Ibid*, vol I, pp. 69-89.

[153] The authorship is mentioned in a bibliographical note by C.Cavedone in the *Memoire di religione, di morale e di letteratura*, third series, vol XI, (1850), pp. 322-4.

[154] (P.F.Vandoni) *Intorno alla traduzione della Bibbia del Diodati dialogo Fra Don Eusebio e un letterato* (c1850) pp. 1-2.

[155] "Clericus", The Supremacy of Truth etc. (London 1851) p. 12.

[156] See: *Bulletin de la Societe de l'histoire du Protestantisme francais*, vol I, (1853) p. 491.

[157] See: *Bulletin de la Societe de l'hostoire du Protestantisme francais*, vol XXXI, (1882) pp. 481-94. This article is incorrectly described in Piero Chiminelli, *Bibliografia della storia della Riforma Religiosa in Italia* (Biblioteca di studi religiosi, N 10) Rome 1921) p. 101.

[158] See *Atti e memorie della R. Academia di Scienze, Lettere ed Arte in Padova*. Nuova serie, vol XXIII (1907).

[159] In *Protestantesimo*, vol XXII, (1967), pp. 1-23.

[160] P.Fraenkel, *De l'Ecriture a la dispute* p. 14 etc.

[161] The edition of the *Institutes* used throughout was the edition of J.T.McNeill and F.L.Battles, London, S.C.M. Press, 1961. In references such as:- "3.21.5", the first number refers to the book, the second to the chapter within the book, and the third to the section within the chapter.

[162] See Diodati bibliography, p. 14, no. 15.

[163] The text of the English Bible quoted here, and throughout the thesis is that of The Revised Standard Version *Common Bible*, 1973, the first English version of the Scriptures to have received both protestant and Catholic approval.

[164] *Institutes* 3.21.5.

[165] Calvin *Commentaries* translated and edited by J.Haroutunian and Louise Pettibone Smith, (London 1958) (S.C.M. Press), p. 291.

[166] Diodati *La Sacra Bibbia* (1640/41) p. 173n.

[167] *Biblia Sacra* (Geneva 1630) tr Tremellius, ed Junius, p. 156.

[168] *Institutes* 3.21.5.

[169] *Institutes* 2.11.11.

[170] *Ibid* 4.16.3.

[171] Diodati *La Sacra Bibbia* (1640/41) p. 176n.

[172] *Biblia Sacra* (Geneva 1630) tr Tremellius, ed Junius, p. 159.

[173] *Institutes* 3.21.5.

[174] J.Calvin, opera in *Corpus Reformatorum* (ed Baum,Cunitz & Reuss) LIX/437.

[175] Diodati, *Las livres de Iob, Pseavmes* etc., (1638), p. 155n.

[176] *Biblia Sacra* (Geneva 1630) tr Tremellius ed Junius, part 2, p. 131.

[177] *Institutes* 3.23.2.

[178] *Institutes* 3.23.2.

[179] Diodati numbers it as verse 6. See *La Sacra Bibbia* (1640/41) p 500n; and *Les livres de Iob, Pseavmes* etc., (1638) p. 178n.

[180] *Biblia Sacra* (Geneva 1630) tr Tremellius, ed Junius, part 2, p. 133 and part 1, p. 16.

[181] J.Calvin, opera in *Corpus Reformatorum* (Ed Baum,Cunitz & Reuss) LIX/510.

[182] *Institutes* 3.21.6.

[183] Diodati, *Les livres de Iob, Pseavmes* etc., pp. 228n & 229n.

[184] Tremellius & Junius op.cit. part 2, p. 139.

[185] *Institutes* 3.22.10, 2.2.9 and 2.13.2.

[186] J.Calvin, *The Gospel according to St. John 1-10*, tr T.H.L.Parker, ed D.W.Torrance and T.F.Torrance, p. 19.

[187] Diodati *LaSacra Bibbia* (ed) (1640/41, p. 94n.

[188] Diodati *La Sacra Bibbia* (ed) (1640/41), p. 94n.

[189] *Institutes* 3.22.7.

[190] J.Calvin, *The Gospel according to St John 1-10*, tr T.H.L.Parker ed D.W. & T.F.Torrance, p. 161.

[191] Diodati *op.cit.*, p. 102n, part 2.

[192] As note (3) and T. de Beze, *Iesu Christi D.N.Novum Testamentum* (1565 Geneva) p. 86 etc.

[193] *Acta* 2/265 and 3/244. Also *Iesu Christi D.N.Novum Testamentum* (Geneva 1565) ed Th. Beza pp. 386-7 and *Iesu Christi Domini Nostri Novum Testamentum* (Geneva 1598), ed Th. Beza p. 380 (*sic*).

[194] *Institutes* 3.22.10.

[195] *Ibid* 3.8.1., 3.18.7., 3.24.1.

[196] J.Calvin, *The Epistles of Paul the Apostle to the Romans and to the Thessalonians*, tr R.Mackenzie, ed T.F. & D.W.Torrance, pp. 180-181.

[197] *Acta Synodi Nationalis...Dordrechti*, pp. 47, 101 etc.

[198] Diodati (ed) *La Sacra Bibbia* (1640/41), p. 173n.

[199] *Iesu Christi D.N.Novum testamentum* (Geneva 1565) ed Th. Beza, part 2 p. 186.

[200] Calvin *op.cit*., p. 180.

[201] Diodati *op.cit*., p. 173n.

[202] *Institutes* 3.1.1.

[203] As note 6.

[204] *Institutes* 3.22.4.

[205] *Institutes* 4.2.3.

[206] Diodati (ed) *La Sacra Bibbia*, (1640/41), part 2, p. 174n.

[207] *Acta Synodi Nationalis...Dordrechti*, p. 51.

[208] *Ibid* p. 52.

[209] *Iesu Christi D.N.Novum testamentum* (Geneva 1565) ed Th. Beza part 2, p. 189 and *Theodori Bezae Vezalii Tractationum Theologicarum*, vol 1, (Geneva 1582) p. 468.

[210] *Institutes* 3.22.3.

[211] *Ibid* 3.23.11.

[212] *Ibid* 3.14.5.

[213] J.Calvin, *The Epistles of Paul The Apostle to the Romans and to the Thessalonians*, tr R.Mackenzie, et T.F. & D.W.Torrance, p. 261.

[214] *Ibid*.

[215] G.Diodati (ed) *La Sacra Bibbia* (1640/41) part 2, p. 178n.

[216] *Iesu Christi D.N.Novum Testamentum* (Geneva 1565) ed Th. Beza p. 207.

[217] Published by The Universtiy of Wisconsin Press; Madison, Milwaukee, and London, 1969.

[218] Armstrong, *op.cit*., p. XIX.

[219] *D.N.B*., I/355-7.

[220] Ames, *Epistles of Peter* p. 3.

[221] *CR* LV/208.

[222] Amyraut *Paraphrase sur les Epistres Catholiques* p. 2.

[223] Ames *op.cit*., pp. 4-5.

[224] *CR* LV/208.

[225] *CR* LV/209.

[226] Diodati (ed) *La Bibbia*, (1640/41) p. 294.

[227] Ames *op.cit*., p. 5.

[228] *CR* LV/209.

[229] Ames *op.cit*., p. 4.

[230] Diodati *op.cit*. p. 294.

[231] Amyraut *op.cit*. pp. 2-3.

[232] *Iesu Christi Domini Nostri Novum Testamentum* (Geneva 1565) ed Th.Beza, part 2, pp. 457ff.

[233] D.Erasmus, *Paraphrases in N.Testamentum* in *Opera Omnia* (Leyden 1766), 7/1142ff.

[234] *CR* LV/210.

[235] *CR* LV/210.

[236] Diodati *op.cit*., p. 294.

[237] *CR* LV/211.

[238] *CR* LV/211.

Chapter 6
The Academy Library.

One final method that was attempted in order to investigate the intellectual and theological background of the epigones in the period of the Dordrecht synod, was that of examining the books acquired by the library of the Academy in the first twenty years of the seventeenth century. This study is made possible by the existence of two library catalogues from this period, the BPU Ms Bi f 29-74, the:- "Catalogus librorum Bibliothecae Genevansis scriptus anno domini mdcxii" and the 1620 catalogue, the BPU Ms B3. The 1620 catalogue contains a more complete description of the books than does that of 1612, almost invariably giving date and place of publication. Both are shelf catalogues and contain much overlapping of information and of book lists. The 1620 catalogue remained in use throughout the seventeenth century and contains many late additions in a number of hands. The 1620 catalogue eventually contained some 3723 distinct entries for books, multi-volume works, bound manuscripts and bundles of manuscript material. Of these 3723 items, at least 1082 dated from the seventeenth century. However, due to the inclusion of later items, these seventeenth century items were sorted for the purpose of this study so that only those dating from 1600-20 (inclusive) were retained for consideration, there being 596 items from this period.

The 596 items that were found to relate to this period were then sorted in the hope that they might reveal some information concerning the intellectual climate of the Academy at the period of Dort. There were a number of serious difficulties involved in this. In toto, these difficulties might well invalidate many specific assertions that might be based on a study of Genevan library acquisitions at this period. The difficulties fall into two classes. Firstly, there are problems concerning the acquisition of material. It is not possible to know how individual items were acquired. Was there a definite policy of purchasing? We do not know. Nor is it possible to state whether such a policy, if it were in existence, was strictly adhered to. Was it left to each professor to compile a periodical list of requisites? And, if so, were such requisites for the benefit of the professors or for the students. Who, in fact, was to use this library and how free was students' access? These questions are partly resolved by a study of the books included in the collection. Bellarmine's Hebrew grammar, for instance, must have been included for the benefit of students - Diodati, a better hebraist than Bellarmine would hardly have required it. Yet these points could all be invalidated by the simple matter of donations of books from sympathetic sources that were not necessarily in accord with any set policy of purchasing. Also, it is necessary to consider the position of the private libraries of professors. In the sixteenth century, particularly with the practice of students lodging with professors, such libraries were of very considerable importance in the education of theological students. In the early years, such private libraries were probably more important than the central Academy library. By the seventeenth century the position is less well defined, but it is unlikely that the private book collections of the professors had lost all significance. These problems amount to a formidable obstacle in interpreting data from the catalogues of 1612 and 1620. They are insufficient to invalidate all study of the catalogue contents but they are significant enough to lead to an elimination of all but the most general theses.

The library in 1620 still contained more works on theology than on any other subject, but the remainder related to a wide variety of academic disciplines. Some matters are notable by their absence. The library appears to have been limited by culture, interest and geography. The geographical limitation may be seen in the fact that very few books printed in England were included and even fewer from Scandinavia, Spain and northern Europe. The main centres of publication for the books in the Academy library were France, Germany, the Low Countries - especially Antwerp and Leyden - Italy, and above all, Geneva itself. The works available at the Frankfurt book market may also have contributed to this geographical selection.[1] The great number of Genevan printings contained within the library is due to the fact that the Academy library acted as a sort of copyright for Genevan printers who, from 1580, were required to present one copy of each printed book to the library. From 1582, this only applied to new works, not to new editions.[2] However, this places yet more difficulties in the path of any attempt to suggest that the contents of the library represent in any simple form those works considered as desirable by the epigones. It would seem to be erroneous to suggest that the library contents resulted from any single purchasing policy. However, the exclusion of books printed in more distant countries does seem to suggest that the scope of interest of the Genevan Academy in the non-French and non-German reformed churches had greatly decreased from the opening years of Calvin's direction. There is no reason to suggest much or any interest in or knowledge of the reformed churches of Hungary or Scotland from a study of this list. Compared, for instance, to the world wide interest of the Gregoriana at the same period, it would seem that this is yet more evidence of the Genevan Academy's steadily waning influence on and interest in the European reformed churches. Scots, English and Hungarian theologians might be interested in the Genevan's opinions, but from the evidence available in the 1620 catalogue, the Academy had little interest in them. Two contributory factors for this apparent parochialism would have been the books available at Frankfurt and the financial difficulties which Geneva experienced in the early seventeenth century.

The limitation as regards the interest of the Academy library is clearly definable. Some subjects are adequately catered for apart from theology, especially classics and law, though the collections representing these areas of study are not always predictable. Yet some disciplines are almost entirely absent. There appears to have been scant attention paid to music and the arts. No books concerning music appear on the catalogue for these years, nor are there any which concern the visual arts. There are none of the contemporary English works on exploration or cartography, though there are a few examples of Spanish work in this field. There is little contemporary or renaissance literature, though there was a German edition of Rabelais and an edition of Petrarch's letters *Epistolarum familiarum libri XIV* (Lyons 1601). There is no poetry apart from a few predictable works such as the poems of the Huguenot poet Guillaume de Salluste, seigneur du Bartas (1544-90), *Les Tragiques* by Agrippa d'Aubigne and the *Geneva liberata* of Antoine de la Faye.

The largest section of non-theological literature is related to the study of law. Again, this reflected an apparent parochialism on the Academy's interests. The great majority of books on this subject reflected an interest in French law. Apart from works of more general interest such as the 1620 Venice edition of Justinian's *Institutiones* almost all the legal volumes - at least 90% - emanated from Paris or Lyons. These works include customary law from different regions of France:- *Conference de la coustume de Paris* (Paris 1611), *Coustume de Paris* (Paris 1613), *Coustumes de Berry* (Paris 1615) and *Coustume de Normandie* (Rouen 1620) as well as more general informational works:- *Ordonnances Royaux par le faict de la justice des rois Francois I, Henri II, Francois II, Charles IX, Henri III et Henri IV* (Paris 1606) and *Edicts et Ordonnances des Eaux et Forests* (Paris 1610). These works on French law fulfilled a very practical purpose in the training of ministers to serve in the French Reformed Church in the period of the Edict of Nantes when a knowledge of law was of the utmost importance. By this period, France would have formed the main source of Genevan theological students, rivalled only by the Vaudois.

Another large section is related to classical studies. Perhaps half of these works had been published in Geneva. Yet the inclusion of works by Cutullus printed in Paris, Horace printed in Bale, Tacitus in Frankfurt and Virgil in Paris and Leyden suggest that the Genevan Academy had not entirely lost the humanist spirit with which it had been founded. Genevan printings included works by Aristophanes, Horace, Homer and Virgil.

Smaller sections considered a range of other subjects. Concerning architecture there is a 1618 edition of Vitruvius and the 1612 commentary on Vitruvius:- *De Verborum Vitruvianorum significatione . . . Accedit vita Vitruvii* by Bernardini Paldi (1553-1617) the polymathic friend of Charles Borromeo. Geography is represented by a 1605 Frankfort edition of Ptolemy and the 1611 revision of Ortelius (1527-98). There is also the *Historia natural y moral de las Indias* by the poet and cosmographer Joseph de Acosta S.J. (1539-1600). Mathematics are represented by several works on arithmetic and algebra including a late (1613) edition of the *Arithmeticae libri duo. Geometriae septem et viginti* by Pierre de la Ramee which had originally been published as long ago as 1569. There are also a few works on scientific matters such as the important work on optics by Francois Aguilon S.J. (1566-1617) *Opticorum libri sex philosophis juxta ac mathematicis utiles* and the German alchemist Henry Nolle's *Sanctuarium naturae. quod est physica hermetica* (Frankfort 1619). There were also a number of works on anatomy and medicine such as Jacques Fontaine's *Opera medica* published at Geneva in 1612 and a late edition of the *Opera* (Leyden 1604) by Jean Fernel (1496-1558) as well as two works of Peter Paaw (1564-1617) the early dissectionist and founder of the anatomical school of the University of Leyden where he was a professor:- *Primitiae anatomicae de humani corporis ossibus* (Leyden 1615) and *Succenturiatus Anatomicus continens commentaria in Hippocratem* (Leyden 1616). All these works would tend to show that the Genevan Academy was interested in a considerable range of academic work that was being carried out in various disciplines at the period of Dort. Their interest was by no means limited to theology. The collection of works relating to politics certainly relates to then contemporary controversy since it included the *De Rege et Regis institutione* by Juan de Mariana S.J. (1536-1623) in which he argued that tyrannicide was justifiable under certain circumstances.

Perhaps the most significant of the non-theological sections is, surprisingly, that concerning astronomy. The period of Dort coincides with much of the dispute about the Copernican revolution. It is interesting to note that the Genevan Academy had a good collection of recent astronomical works. This could have been because they were concerned about the most modern thought in this field for its relationship to the Aristotelianism in which they were still interested though this was being replaced by presocratic ideas well before the time of J.R.Chouet. Galileo had already fallen foul of the Aristotelians because of his work on falling bodies carried out by empirical observation at Pisa as long ago as 1589-91. The interest might also have been stimulated by a concern for the accurate computation of the age of creation. This type of chronology became a subject of passionate interest in the seventeenth century involving such diverse scholars as Spanheim, Ussher and Newton. It certainly helped stimulate cosmographical studies. The inclusion of books on the new astronomy might simply relate to a genuine interest in the subject for its own sake, but these other considerations are hardly likely to be entirely absent. It is most interesting, however, that the Genevan Academy library included the books at a time when there was such general ecclesiastical condemnation of copernicanism. Galileo had been forbidden to hold, teach or defend copernicanism at Rome in 1616. Kepler had been subjected to bitter Lutheran attacks for his defence of the Gregorian calendar reforms at the Diet of Ratisbon in 1613. In the absence of firm evidence, it would be impossible to state that the Genevans actually favoured the dissemination of the new astronomy. However, they do not appear to condemn it and the inclusion of these works in the Academy library hardly suggests an apathetic or an ultra-conservative approach. The Academy library contained the *Historia e dimostrazioni intorno alle macchie solari e loro accidenti* (Rome 1613) of Galileo which was the work that first brought him into conflict with the Holy Office. Another and less controversial Italian work was the 1609 Venice edition of the *Problematorum Astronomicorum* of Guidobaldo Ubaldi, Marquis del Monte (1540-1601). There are further works emanating from northern Europe, the earliest astronomer represented being Michael Mastlin, a professor at Tubingen and the teacher of Kepler who was almost alone in his day in that he accepted the copernican astronomical system as being basically correct. His *Epitome Astronomiae* (Tubingen 1610) is included in this collection. It is interesting to note that in his annotations on the Bible, Diodati refuses to be drawn into anti-copernican statements on texts such as Ecclesiastes 1/4-5, or Psalm 103/5. Diodati's position is even more clearly seen by his careful interpretation of the much disputed Joshua 10/12-13:-

Then spoke Joshua to the Lord...and he said in the sight of Israel, "Sun, stand thou still at Gibeon, and thou Moon in the Valley of Aijalon." And the sun stood still, and the moon stayed, until the nation took vengeance on their enemies . . . . The sun stayed in the midst of heaven, and did not hasten to go down for about a whole day.

where he says nothing that could be interpreted as being critical of copernicanism. Also represented by one work is the Danish astronomer Tycho Brahe, the
Academy had a 1604 Nuremberg edition of his *Astronomiae instauratae mechanica*
which had first been published at Hamburg in 1598. Brahe was certainly an
astronomer whose method and conclusions probably appealed more to the
Genevans than did those of the more extreme copernicans. There is increasing
doubt that distinctions between scholastic and cartesian can be drawn as simply
as has often been supposed by ecclesiastical historians. Brahe, because of his
own combination of modern and conservative elements, and with his insistence
on observation, seems to have had an appeal for the French protestant mind,
including scientists such as Derodon at Nimes and, significantly, Wyss, who was
Chouet's predecessor as philosophy professor at Geneva.[3] This catalogue provides evidence of an earlier interest in tychonianism. As with other aspects of
orthodoxy discussed in this thesis, the picture becomes increasingly complex
and increasingly interesting. There are three works by Kepler himself. There is
the *Epitome Astronomiae Copernicanae usitata forma questionum et responsionum* (Linz
1618) which, because of its title, was a complement to Mastlin and, indeed, a
provocation of further controversy because of the use of the name of Copernicus.
There is also his work on Archimedes;- *Ausszug auss der uralten Messekunst
Archimedis und deroselben newlich in Latein auszgangenen Ergentzung . . . Gestelt
durch J. Kepplern* (Linz 1616), and also the important treatise on optics *Ad Vitel-
lionem Paralipomena, Quibus Astronomiae Pars Optica Traditur* (Frankfort 1604).
Kepler dedicated this last to the Polish scientist Witelo or Vitellio (c1225-c75) who
had written on optics in his "Perspectiva" towards the end of his life. These works
form a very important corpus of the new astronomy. It might be mentioned that
there are some important works that are not here such as Kepler's *Astronomia
Nova* of 1609 which contained his first two laws of planetary motion or his *De Jesu
Christi Servatoris Nostri Vero Anno Natalito* of 1606, which would surely have been
an essential if the main Genevan interest had been chronological. The library also
had a copy of the 1602 Wittenberg edition of Matthias Hafenreffer's *Loci Theologici*. Hafenreffer, a Lutheran professor of theology at Tubingen was a teacher
and friend of Kepler, who would send him all his works for comment with, of
course, a view to polemics before publication. This is the second (revised) edition
of this work, written at the request of the Duke of Wurttemberg and is a simply
written handbook of theological science which retained an important place in
Lutheran academies for many years. It would be interesting to know if it were
also used for teaching at Geneva. Its inclusion is probably important because of
the small number of Lutheran works that the library was acquiring at this time.

In considering all sections of the library, the difficulty is always to judge not
only what is included in this collection but what is omitted. The lacunae are, in
some important ways, more interesting. This is nowhere more true than in the
collection of Bibles. There are some obvious inclusions such as the Diodati Bible
of 1607, and certain surprising omissions such as the Diodati New Testament of
1608. There is a copy of the second (but first complete) 1602 Amsterdam edition
of Cypriano de Valera's Spanish Bible, but other contemporary European languages are simply not represented. The 1605 Danish revision and versification of

Resen, the third edition of the Kralitz and the 1613 Prague edition of the Kralitz
Bible intended for members of reformed churches other than the United
Brethren, the 1602/3 Nuremberg reprint of Hutter's 1599 Polyglot, the 1602 Irish
New Testament, the 1609 Molnar Bible in Hungarian and the 1609 Icelandic New
Testament are all absent. There are no copies of Dutch, French, German or
English Bibles. This was not a period of great significance in Dutch or French
Biblical translation but in Germany the Piscator version was appearing from 1602
and there were the important Bibles of Amandus Polanus von Polansdorf of 1603
and the Heidelberg Bible of Paul Tossanus from 1617-18 which came under
Lutheran attack because of its Calvinist tendencies by the Giessen theologian
Winckelmann. Darlow and Moule list ninety-two English printings from this
period including not only reprints of the Bishop's Bible (thirteen) and the Geneva
Bible (forty-two) but the first thirty-two editions of the King James Authorised
Version, the Catholic Douai Bible of 1609/10 and Cartwright's important refutation of the Rheims translation *A Confutation of the Rhemists translation* of 1618. The
absence of this great volume of protestant biblical scholarship certainly begs
many questions about the epigones' involvement with contemporary scholarship. It is, of course, impossible to state that the Epigones knew any contemporary languages other than French and Italian - though Diodati probably knew
English - and so such translations might be useless to them, but this must surely
be yet another sign that the student population had become far less cosmopolitan
than in the sixteenth century. Perhaps the Academy was not expected to recover
the attraction it had in the days of Calvin and Beza to international students of
theology. One important version which does appear is Erpenius' *editio princeps*
of the Arabic New Testament printed at Leyden in 1616. There is only one Greek
testament, an edition of 1620 with Scaliger's notes. There are at least eleven
editions of the Greek text printed in this period, none of particular importance
except that of Stoer from 1609. There is one Latin version, a Plantin printing of
the Clementine Bible from 1603 with notes on the text and Francois Lucas of
Louvain's references to variant readings. The library did not have other important Latin Bibles of these two decades such as Osiander's first Bible of 1600 which
had an emended and annotated Vulgate text supplemented by paraphrastic
comments, the fourth edition of the Tremellius/Junius text of 1603, the 1609
Vulgate with Osiander's corrections or the important 1614 commentary on the
Apocalypse by Patris Ludovici ab Alcasar Hispalensis. The Genevan collection of
then contemporary biblical scholarship can hardly be claimed to be impressive.
They did, however, have three Hebrew Bibles, two editions of 1619 including the
sixth "Biblia Rabbinica" printed by Konig at Bale in four volumes with the revisions of the elder Buxtorf (1564-1629) then professor of Hebrew at Bale:- *Biblia
Sacra Hebraica & Chaldaica cum Masora*. There is also a 1613 Genevan edition
printed by Pierre de la Bouviere. It would normally be presumed that exegetical
teaching in the Genevan Academy at this period would have been carried out on
the Greek text using Latin as an interpretative medium. However, from this
period we have no lecture notes from any of the epigones, nor any student
manuscripts. What we do have is the unexpected remark of Diodati to the
Conseil of Geneva in 1635 that he believed[4] the old French translation of the Bible
should be replaced because students found it difficult to read. Translations may

have been more important than has been presumed and a limited collection of
them might be another means of monitoring the decreasing cosmopolitan mix-
ture of students at-the Genevan Academy.

The collection of scriptural commentaries, like that of the editions of the
Bible, is disappointingly brief. However, unlike the study of the Bible editions,
it does reveal a great deal about the epigones interests. It would appear that they
had two favourite exegetes, Drusius, represented by commentaries on Joshua,
Judges, Samuel (1618), the New Testament (1616) and the Pentateuch (1617), and
Pareus, represented by commentaries on Genesis (1614, #15), I Corinthians
(1613,14), Galatians (1613,14), Hebrews (1613,14) and the Apocalypse (1618).
Johannes Drusius (1550-1616) was a Dutch exegete who was professor of oriental
languages at Oxford from 1572-6, Leyden 1576-85 and Hebrew professor at
Franeker from 1585 until his death. His exegesis was greatly respected and
frequently attacked for its independence of judgment and lack of dogmatic
prejudice. In this we may suspect a basis for Diodati's non-dogmatic exegesis.
David Pareus (1548-1622) was an even more obviously interesting theologian to
the Genevans, being professor in Old Testament and New Testament at Heidelberg from 1598. A prolific and greatly respected orthodox theologian, he was
only prevented from attending Dort by old age, though he wrote a long letter to
the Synod that was read by Altingius on 4th, 5th and 6th March in the 98th, 99th
and 101st sessions. Other reformed commentaries included were those on the
Psalms by Stephen Fabricius of Bern, the Heidelberg professor Abraham Scultetus (1566-1624) on Isaiah, Polanus on Daniel, Cartwright on Ecclesiastes, the
Zuricher Rudolph Gualter (1519-86), assistant and successor to Bullinger on the
Psalms (1601), and Luke/Acts (1601) as well as the Genevan Antoine de la Faye
on Psalms, Ecclesiastes (1609), Romans (1608), I Timothy and Psalm 87 (1609).
Yet the library was not limited to reformed exegesis, there were Lutheran works
such as the Moller already mentioned, the Wittenberg professor Solomon Gesner
on the Psalms and the Tubingen professor Matthias Haffenreffer on Ezechiel, a
work that was more admired by his contemporaries than his *Loci Theologici*
although it may be less important. A number of distinguished Catholic commentaries were also included, such as the *Commentarii in quatuor Evangelica* by Juan
Maldonado S.J. (1534-83) who was a professor at Salamanca, Paris and the
Roman College. Maldonado was anti-Gallican and anti-Calvinist as was Thomas
Beauxamis, represented by his *Commentarium in Evangelicam harmoniam*. The
Genevans also had the commentary on the Psalms by the distinguished Theatin
bishop of Acerno, Antonius Agellius (1532-1608), the commentaries on Luke
1-12, Romans and Psalms by the Spanish papal diplomat Francis Tolet S.J.
(1532-96) and the commentary on II Peter by the anti-Calvinist writer Francois
Feuardent. From this survey, it would certainly seem that the epigones were
more interested in Catholic than in Lutheran exegesis. This is a pattern that will
be noted again when more general theological works are considered.

The Academy, on the basis of the works in its library, would appear to have
retained an interest in Aristotelian studies perhaps greater than that of many
other institutions of learning in the seventeenth century. Editions of Aristotle's
work were few in number during the seventeenth century compared with the
vast output of the sixteenth century. Apart from an annotated Boethius, their

interest in older studies of Aristotle is revealed by the presence of a 1604 edition of the *Physics* and *Metaphysics* by Aegidius de Columna (c1245-1316). They also had the third (Geneva 1605) edition of the *Organum* with the contents of Julius Pacius, the 1619 Toulouse reprint of Scaliger's edition of the *Historia de Animalibus*, a commentary on the pseudo-Aristotelian *Problemata* from 1602 & 1607 and the "Commentarii Collegii Conimbricencis" on the *Dialectics* (Cologne 1607). Anti-Aristotelian writings are represented by the *Prodromus* of the Dominican Thomas Campanella (Frankfort 1617). Having stated that the collection of Aristotelian works might demonstrate a particular interest in this subject, it is not really possible to go farther. Aristotolian interests in theology were still widespread in the seventeenth century and need not be sought in seventeenth century editions of Aristotle since it was so much part of the traditional systematic and exegetical framework. Another aspect might be to question how far an interest in Aristotelianism conflicted with acceptance of the new astronomy.

The Academy was still adding patristic works to its already considerable collection. From this period dates the third edition of *Bibliotheca Patrum* published at Paris in 1609. There are a number of editions collected printed outside Geneva which suggests a strong continuing interest in this subject. There is a 1604 edition of Aristides' orations which obviously antedates those of the Mechitarists. There is an edition of Athanasius' Greek and Latin works from 1600, an annotated version of Boethius' *De Consolation Philosophiae* printed at Antwerp in 1607, the opera of Cassiodorus printed at Geneva in 1609, the Easter sermons of Cyril of Alexandria printed at Antwerp in 1618, the opera of Gregory of Nazianzus printed at Antwerp in 1612, the Erpenius edition of Josephus from Leyden in 1617, a Genevan edition of Josephus from 1611, the 1604 Paris and 1602 Augsburg and 1603 editions of Chrysostom, the Nomocanon with the usual incorrect attribution to Photius, printed at Paris in 1615, a Genevan edition of Philo dating from 1613 and a Genevan edition of Salvian's *De Gubernatione Dei* from 1600. Members of the staff of the Genevan Academy were presumably involved in the preparation of the Genevan patristic editions of the period but none of the epigones were distinguished patristicians, though Diodati probably had a competence in patristic exegesis and both Turrettini and Tronchin used many patristic references in their refutations of Coton. Calvin would have approved of their continuing interest in Chrysostom. There are, of course, many gaps in their collection. In Pierre Petitmengin's list of Tertullian editions for this period there are some seventeen printings, none of which are included in this library. However, the library was at this time acquiring old books as well as new printings. This becomes clear from an examination of some lists of gifts and other acquisitions included at the end of the 1612 catalogue. The 1572 catalogue included 45 patristic items which had risen to 88 by 1612. Additions were still being made. In 1605/6 the library purchased 16 volumes, all Greek and Latin literature. In 1606 Simon Goulart gave fourteen volumes, including two patristic items, one being a work of Tertullian. Another volume of Tertullian was added about 1613 through a gift from one of the Lombard family, though most of the 35 other items then donated were historical. Patristic works were still being added but there seems to have been more urgency in the acquisition of historical works as well as the writings of medieval and reformation period theologians.

Associated with biblical and patristic studies are a number of linguistic text books such as the *Thesaurus Temporum Eusebii* printed at Leyden in 1606, a Genevan reprint of Pagninus' *Thesaurus Linguae Sanctae* from 1614, a *Grammatica Syro Chaldaice* printed at Geneva in 1619, Ballarmines little Hebrew grammar printed by Plantin in 1606 and the *Thesaurus* of scripture by Marlorat (c1506-62) reprinted at Geneva in 1613.

The seventeenth century for the reformed churches was a time of rediscovery of many medieval authors who had been dismissed as being erroneous, lacking in authority or outdated in the earlier years of the protestant reformation. The works of medieval mystical and spiritual authors played some part in the development of seventeenth century reformed pietism. Certainly, theologians later in the century such as Gisbert Voet (1589-1676) and Pierre Poiret (1646-1719) were influenced by works such as *The Imitation of Christ*. It is interesting to note, therefore, that the Genevan Academy had a copy of this book printed in the 1601 Antwerp edition of Thomas a Kempis' works. Other medieval authors whose works were acquired in this period had fewer pietist overtones such as the 1612 two volume Genevan edition of Bede, works of Duns Scotus, Bruno the Carthusian, Abelard and the Masson edition of Agobard printed at Paris in 1605.

The developing interest in medieval texts would seem to suggest that the Genevans, like the other reformed protestants of their day were perhaps unconsciously, involved in changing their concepts of Church history and their own sense of identity. It is possible, though unlikely, that the medieval texts were acquired solely for work in Polemics. The Academy library certainly had works of importance to church history including a number of contemporary interest such as the various editions of the Dort *Acta* printed at Leyden, the Hague and Dordrecht and two Catholic works on the Council of Trent. They also had Catholic works such as the *Annales* of Baronius as well as protestant works such as the continuation of Sleiden published in two volumes at Frankfort in 1614 and 15 and the Bucer *Constans defensio ex S.Scriptura, et vera Catholica doctrina atque observatione universalis christianae Ecclesiae Deliberationis de christiana reformatione* etc., actually published at Geneva in 1613. It is possible that the declining influence of the reformed churches at this time had helped to institute a mood of self questioning among their theologians but there is not really enough evidence here to support such a view and these are matters which would require basic studies of reformed historiography which have yet to be undertaken.

There were a number of Lutheran works included in the library. They include such standard contemporary items as a complete set of Gerhard's *Loci comunes*. There is also an anti-Socinian work by the naturalised German, Otho Casmannus (d1607) and Joachim Wehner's *Adagia sacra, sive proverbia Scripturae* (Leipzig 1601).

These hardly constitute a major collection when compared with the volume of catholic works in the library. This may partly be explained by the large quantity of Brenz which was already there, but does seem to suggest a lack of interest in Lutheran opinions especially considering the absence of works by noted anti-calvinists such as Aegidius Hunnius, Leonhard Hutterus, Jacobus Martini and Balthasar Meisner. This would again suggest that the Academy by this period was insulated from many of the disputes affecting reformed churches in other parts of Europe. Fewer students were now coming from areas where Lutheranism was active. Again, there is an indication that the Genevan Academy was losing if it had not already lost the intellectual leadership of the reformed churches.

A larger number of works related to contemporary Catholicism. These included reprints of works by some of the Catholic theologians of the reformations such as the Paris works of Cassander (1513-66), the opuscula of Edmund Campion (Paris 1618), opera and *Orationes Academiae* of Thomas Stapleton (Paris 1620 Antwerp 1600 respectively) as well as earlier works such as the 1607 Venice edition of the *Directorium Inquisitionum* of Nicolaus Hymericus (1320-99) which was first published at Rome in 1578-9 and the *De divinis Catholicae Ecclasiae officiis et mysteriis* (Paris 1610) of Melchior Hittorp (1525-84), bishop of Vercelli, which is a reprint of an ancient Roman ordinal. There are the printed indices of prohibited works produced at Geneva in 1619 and Cologne in 1620. William Barclay's work on the papacy, *De Regno et Regali Protestate* (1604) was included as was a *Traite des droicts et libertes de l'Eglise Galicane* (Paris 1609) that antedated Claude Robert's *Gallia Christiana* by fifteen years. There is Thomas Campanella's anti-Aristotelian *Prodromus Philosophia,* one of his more important works, printed at Frankfort in 1617. There are some direct attacks on protestantism such as Coton's *Geneve plagiaire* and the *Bibliotheca Catholica contra Institutiones Calvini et locos comunes* published at Cologne in 1602. There was also that essential of reformed libraries, the complete edition of Bellarmine's works in the 1617-20 Cologne edition. The Genevans would appear to have had a special interest in Martin Becanus S.J. (1563-1624)[5]and they have four of his works that are not biblical commentaries, the *Theologiae scholasticae* (Mainz 1612 & 14), the *Practatus de libero arbitrio* (Mainz 1613), *De Ecclesia Christi* (Mainz 1615) and the *Libellus de invocatione sanctorum* (Mainz 1616). However, they do not have his more notorious *Quaestiones de fide haereticis* of 1609 or the *Controversia Anglicana* of 1613 in which he asserted the moral rectitude of the regicide of heretics. It would seem from these brief surveys of Lutheran and Catholic works included in the library that the latter was a more considerable interest than the former. However, there is still a great deal of important Catholic work missing and the amount of Lutheran material is certainly inadequate for the library of a major academy of the period.

There was a collection of anti-Catholic works. This of course included the writings against Coton by Tronchin and Turrettini as well as the rabidly anti-papal *De excommunicate papae* by Gregorius de Heimburg printed at Frankfort in 1607 and the 1602 reprint of Stephen Kis Szegedini's *Speculum pontificam Romanem es traditiones.* Genevan anti-Catholic polemics are represented by the 1620 *Recueil de l'ordre de Jesuites* and the 1609 *Antithese de Jesus . . traitte des indulgences contre le decree du concile de Trente.* There are also unspecified treatises written against the Jesuits from 1610-12. There are also early examples of the seventeenth century Huguenot obsession with conversion to and from Catholicism such as *Le Reveille matin des Apostats* by Jean Valeton (1608), *Response a la Messe de Jaques Villaire Apostat* (1608) and the *Declaration du St Soulas sur la suite et sa conversion a la foy Catholique* (1613). On a more intellectual level there is the *Antibellarminus* of Conrad Vorstius (1569-1622) printed at Hanover in 1610. There are more anti-Bellarmine tracts, printed at Geneva and written by the temporarily expatriate Scot,

John Sharpe, who regained the favour of his king by this method, James VI (of Scotland, James I of England) having a horror of Bellarmine.

Inevitably, the library had a greater collection of reformed theological works than it had of Lutheran or Catholic material. There were works from the period of the reformation such as a 1605 edition of Zanchius' works and some symbolics such as a collection of Dutch catechisms by Johannes Kuchlin dating from 1612, a *Syntagma Confessionum fidei* from the same year printed at Geneva, the *Consensus orthodoxas de sententia et veritate . . . Coena Domine* from 1605 and printed in Zurich as well as a 1608 Genevan edition of Ursinius' catechism, presumably the Heidelberg Catechism. The library certainly had books from writers representing most of the main areas, from Geneva there was the *Enchiridion* of Antoine de la Faye, the *Anthologie Morale* and *Meditationes Chrestiennes* (several copies) of Simon Goulart the elder. Swiss reformed theologians represented by their works were the Zuricher Rudolf Hospinian (1547-1626) whose *Historia Jesuitica* was included as was the *Lectori Memorabilium* of his compatriot Johannes Wolphius, the *Tiberias sive commentarius masoreticus* of the elder Buxtorf and *Syntagma Theologiae Christionae* of Polanus. English material included works by Perkins, James VI & I, William Whitaker and the Irish archbishop Ussher's *Antiquitates Ecclesiae Britannicae*. German material included more works by Pareus, a miscellany of 1608 and a work on the eucharist from 1612 with the complete works of the reformed theologian Keckermann (1573-1607) from Danzig who, and this may be significant, considering the Genevans interest in Aristotelianism mentioned above, treated all theological and philosophical questions in an Aristotelian manner.

Dutch thought is represented by the obscure *Antidotum errerum* of Frederik Broecker and the more widely known works of Du Jon and Arminius. The epigones collection obviously included works by reformed theologians whose orthodoxy was being questioned. They had the *De Republica ecclesiastica libri* written by De Dominis in his London period, he did not return to Italy until 1622, and a number of Huguenot works by Jacques Cappelle, Claude le Faucheur, Pierre Charron and Philippe Du Plessis-Mornay. There are works by a number of participants in the Synod of Dort including Andre Rivet, Chamier, Cornelius Schultingius, Sibrandus Lubertus, Du Moulin and Scultetus. One of the works by Lubertus (1556-1625) *De Jesu Christo Salvator* is of interest because it is the only reformed polemic against socinianism to be found in the library.

The Academy may well have had an interest in the Philippist controversies, though the only two Lutheran works included that might bear on this would be the *Consilia sive Judici theologica* of Melanchthon produced in Neustad during 1600 by Christoph Pezel (1539-1604) a professor in Wittenberg and a leading figure in the earlier adiaphoristic controversies, and the *Enarratio in Psalmos* by Heinrich Moller, (Geneva 1619), a Philippist who had been professor of Hebrew at Wittenberg from 1560-74. They also had the Reformed theologian J.R.Lavaterus' *Quaestio ubi vera et catholica Jesu Christi ecclesia inuenienda sit* (Hanau 1610) which was largely based on work by Wolphius and Beza.

It is interesting to note that there had also been much development of the library in the period between 1572 and 1612. Interestingly, many of the authors included in Ganoczy's list of "grands absents" have now made their appearance.

Eck is there as are Anselm and Holcot as well as Gerson. The library in 1612 possesed the *Opus super tertium Sententiarum* by Alexander of Hale. (Venice 1475 fol.), Bonaventure's disputations on the sentences, Occam's *Super IV libros sententiarum subtilissimae questiones earumdemque decisiones* etc.(Lyon 1495 fol) and the *Propugnaculum ecclesiae adversus Lutheranos* of Clicthovius (Paris 1526 fol). Other departments of the library had developed in a similar manner.

A number of theses may be drawn from this consideration of the acquisitions to the Academy library in the period of the epigones. This is not to suggest that the caveats mentioned earlier are to be disregarded, but some suggested conclusions might be made. That there were many subjects excluded from the library at this time - notably music and the arts. That the largest section of the library concerned theology. That other large sections concerned French law, classics and astronomy. That those directing acquisitions had a considerable interest in the new astronomy. That there was an interest in Aristotelianism. That reformed theology formed a greater volume of the collection than the combined volume of Lutheran and Catholic work. That their most favoured theologian would appear to be Pareus. That no Anabaptist, Orthodox[6] or Socinian works were added in this period. That there was a much larger collection of Catholic than of Lutheran works. That there was a poor collection of Bibles. That there was a continuing interest in patristic works and a developing interest in medieval authors. There is an overall impression of incompleteness, this is marked not only in the Lutheran and Catholic sections but in the collections of reformed authors. They have only one work out of five published by Chamier in the period, one out of eighty-eight published by Du Moulin, one of fourteen published by Rivet and only one each out of the many published by Jacques Capelle, the older Buxtorf and Rudolf Hospinian. Thus it may well be stated that in the period 1600-20 the library of the Genevan Academy was not collecting books on the scale necessary to maintain a position of pre-eminence among the reformed academies. This again reflects on the decline of the Academy in the period of the epigones. Considering the wide range of subjects covered, it seems unlikely that the epigones would have failed to collect more books if they had been given the opportunity - though it is very hard to explain why such important theological works as those on the contemporary dispute on the Hebrew vowel points are ignored at the expense of works on the new astronomy. The changes in interests of the epigones from those of Beza and Calvin would seem to be even more complex than has been suggested elsewhere in this thesis because we are dealing partly with non-theological matters at this point. However, on the theological side, the conclusions generally complement those found elsewhere in this thesis. It is probable that the collections discussed here was poor because of lack of money rather than lack of interest on the part of the teaching staff. Geneva's debts had risen towards the end of the sixteenth century and did not improve to any great extent until the establishment of the "Chambre des bles" in 1628.[7] Genevan financial activities had also affected the Genevan delegation to Dort.[8]

The shortcomings mentioned above cannot be used to support the idea that Geneva was a theological backwater by 1620 for there is still the question of the epigone's own libraries. We know nothing of the size of these private collections nor the access to them that was permitted by the staff to the students.

Notes

[1] H.J. Martin and L. Fevre, *Apparition du livre* pp. 353ff.

[2] H.J.Bremme, *Buchdruckcr und Buchhandler zur Zeit der Glaubenskampfe Studien zur Genfer Druckgeschichte 1565-1580*, pp. 68ff.

[3] C. Wyss, *Logica quae est Cursus Philosophici* etc. (Geneva 1669) passim. On this whole subject, see the paper presented to the Institut d'Histoire de la Reformation, Geneva, by Michael Heyd in February 1973: "Between Scholasticism and Science J.R.Chouet and the Introduction of Cartesianism in the Geneva Academy."

[4] AEG RC 134 (1635) pp. 122-3, 14 April 1635.

[5] Probably because he, like Bellarmine, took note of Reformed positions.

[6] There are no printed works relating to the Orthodox Churches despite contemporary relations with the Patriarch Cyril Lucaris. Of Lucaris' own works, the earliest which are to be found in the B.P.U. are the Confession of Faith (1633 & 1645) and the Greek New Testament (ed by A. Leger Sr.) from 1638. Diodati was interested in this confession, but this was first published in 1629 (see K.Rozemond, "De eerste uitgave van de belijdenis van Cyrillus Lucaris" in *Nederland: Archief voor Kerkgeschiedenis*, N.S. vol 51, pp. 202-3, 1970.

[7] W. Monter, *Studies in Genevan Government*, p. 52ff.

[8] See Chapter 2, pp. 54-56.

Conclusion

It is a reflection on the state of seventeenth century studies that this thesis began as an attempt to outline the theological interests of the Genevan Academy in a kind of vacuum. So little research has been undertaken on this period of reformed history that there are no real theses to examine except the vague premiss that this was a period of orthodoxy. On many important matters such as the thought of Daniel Chamier, the only available works were written in the mid-nineteenth century. It has proved therefore to be a kind of theological voyage into the unknown faced with few acceptable terms of reference and peculiarly difficult problems of evidence. In my preface, I wrote that the best reccomendation for this thesis is not that it resolves many issues, for it clears up very little, but it poses many questions. I believe that my attempts to study the theology of the Genevan Academy in the period of Dort suggest that future study be carried out on topics such as the composition of the Genevan library in 1612 and 1620, the proof texts used at Dort, the theses written by students, the relation of the Dort *Acta* to Calvin and Beza, the influence of the Diodati Italian Bible, the contemporary Jesuit attacks on reformed theologians, the decline of reformed protestantism in the seventeenth century, the interpretation of predestination, the rediscovery of medieval authors by the reformed, the growth of reformed academies, the acceptance of copernicanism and tychonianism, reformed attitudes to the adiaphoristic controversies, justifications for persecution, tradition in the composition of catenae, awareness of disputes between Jesuits and Dominicans, the growth of pietism and many others. Each of these subjects could provide scope for doctoral dissertations and there are few terms of reference for Church historians working in this period, so this thesis is constantly hindered by the non-existence of reputable secondary works. Yet some points have been made a little more clear and this thesis can attempt to justify the time spent on it through a number of tendancies that can be observed from the research carried out, though it is with considerable reservations that I have the temerity to call them "conclusions."

The thesis provided evidence to support Monter's belief that this was a period of severe financial stringency in Geneva. In 1611, Diodati was sent to see if he could get help from the French and Benedict Turrettini was sent on a similar mission to Holland during the Thirty Years War. It was noted that one task of Diodati and Tronchin at Dort was to request the Dutch government to cancel debts incurred by the Genevan government. This financial stringency may have curtailed the intellectual independence of these Genevan delegates to the synod. Thus the financial troubles reflected on the intellectual level of the Academy at this period. This can also be seen in the limitations of the Academy library and may even be seen in the extreme youth of the epigones when they were appointed to their chairs, Tronchin at 24, Turrettini at 23 and Diodati at 20. Perhaps the government was unable to find the funds to attract distinguished strangers.

The particular weakness of the Genevan Academy in the first quarter of the seventeenth century is reflected by and is one concomitant of a more general weakness of the reformed churches at this period. This weakness may be seen in the failure to win new areas to the reformed faith and Diodati's part in the Venetian fiasco was part of this. The reformed areas were not only failing to expand, they were in decline. One of the ways this may be seen is that all three epigones were members of exiled families. Also, there were now no students from eastern Europe at the Academy and the library no longer collected works written and printed in the east. Disputes within the reformed Churches were another obvious source of weakness and evidence of decline. Dort was the first great public rift in the orthodox system which was at best a temporary concensus developed out of political rather than theological expediency. The letter to the synod by Goulart (Sr), Prevost, Turrettini and Chabrey recognises the weakening effect of violent internal controversy. Another illustration of the effects of weakness could be the unpleasantness of internal disputes revealed by the struggle of Diodati to publish his French Bible. Reformed orthodoxy was also acquiring its less favourable image in general historical works, for it has been noted that the antagonistic historiography of Dort has seventeenth century roots with Brandt and Heylyn and it is clear that even seventeenth century reformed historians like Fuller were already defending the synod from calumny.

It would also appear that the Academy was changing away from the character it had in the early years of Beza's direction. Not only was the student population less cosmopolitan, but there were disturbances between French and German students. The method of teaching some subjects, such as Hebrew was becoming more theological and less humanist. New subjects, such as astronomy were being introduced. If Diodati lectured at Geneva as he did at Dort, then his approach was more like a preacher than a schoolman. Thus the Academy was, in the way of most institutions, developing and changing. On the evidence of the students theses, the Academy was operating successfully as a teaching institution, and still attracting the children of illustrious parents, such as Hottinger and Primerose. The influence of the epigones on their students was no doubt considerable and the correspondence of Diodati would suggest that the epigones were well enough known throughout Europe. Turrettini's attendance at Alais is another aspect of this, as is the participation at Dort, though the negative side is not to be ignored, the evidence of Carleton that the Genevans were invited late.

The best measure of the influence of the epigones lies in the dissemination of their writings, the widespread and long lasting use of the Diodati Italian Bible, the English and Hungarian translations of the annotations, the translations of Sandys and Sarpi, Tronchin's introduction to the works of Keckermann and the use of Diodati's name by English royalist propagandists. This forms a considerable achievement, yet despite other evidence such as Milton's approval of Diodati or Du Moulin's desire to have Turrettini as a pastor, there has been revealed a failure in the most important area for the epigones, the failure to convince the members of the Synod of Dort of their interpretation of the second article.

It has been noted that the epigones are no slavish imitators of their distinguished predecessors in Geneva. Unlike the Hessian delegation at Dort, they do not use a Bezan version of the New Testament. They seem to prefer Beza to Calvin when considering the first article at Dort and this rejection of Calvin is seen in a number of important areas. Diodati, unlike other seventeenth century reformed exegetes, fails to interpret texts in the same manner as Calvin, the epigones at Dort state a doctrine of *perseverantia sanctorum* that is quite different to that of Calvin and some students prefer Diodati's exegesis to that of Calvin. The main exegetical influence on Diodati may have been Pareus and it would seem that Diodati's exegesis forms part of the growing pietism within the European churches.

The epigones have a limited share in the inter-church polemics of the period. The refutation of Coton was seen as an urgent matter which required much time and state support. Further evidence of Jesuit attacks was noted in Veron's criticism of the Diodoti French Bible of 1644. Nor is the figure of Bellarmine entirely absent, we find him mentioned in a set of student theses and it was at this period that Sharpe was writing anti-Bellarmine propaganda, probably with the support of the epigones. The struggle with catholicism continued long after the epigone's deaths, with the struggle to distribute the Diodati Bible translation in Italy, it being condemned by Cardinal Antonelli as late as 1871. It is never possible to judge accurately the effectiveness of polemics, but it has been seen that the Jesuit attacks were effective in causing the dispute between Du Moulin and Diodati over the decision of the Synod of Alez in 1620. It is also to be noted that Geneva was not engaging in any anti-Lutheran polemics at this time, there are few Lutheran works being collected by the library when compared with the mass of Catholic controversy and there is only the slightest hint of an interest in socinianism. The scope of Genevan interest had shrunk since the days of Calvin.

It is now time to return to the central topic of the orthodoxy of the Academy at this period. This has often been assumed without sufficient investigation. The unexpected Genevan treatment of the heritage of Beza and Calvin has been noted above. At Dort the Genevans preserve a fundamental resemblance to the other delegations, they insist upon absolute grace, and the incidence of Genevan proof texts within the Dort catenae give a generally similar Melanchthonian scheme to that of the other delegations when taken as a whole, but they prefer a doctrine of trinitarian providence to the more general emphasis on the divine decrees and they propound a doctrine of the death of Christ that is quite different different to the prevailing Anselmianism and on the second article the Genevans will accept the idea of the Son satisfying the Father but not the resultant idea of a reservoir of grace. These are important points and, combined with much of what has been said above, provide strong evidence that the Genevans were by no means entirely typical representatives of reformed orthodoxy.

But is it not perhaps our concept of reformed orthodoxy that is wrong? Was orthodoxy ever more than a general acceptance of basic dogma, allowing scope, as at Dort, for its expression through different theologies? The study of the historiography of Dort suggested that a new appraisal was long overdue, especially since this thesis contains the first study of the Dort theology based on the *Acta* that has been undertaken since the synod closed in 1619. Is it not our concept of "orthodoxy" that must be examined? If concensus was only achieved with much difficulty at Dort, when then was there concensus? How real was the "spread of Calvinism"? Was it the spread of Calvinism? What other sixteenth century theologians made major contributions to orthodoxy? How real an intellectual system was seventeenth century orthodoxy? Or has it existed mainly in the minds of Church historians as a useful generalisation? Whatever this orthodoxy may have been, it would appear from this thesis that it was a richer, more complex and infinitely more interesting thing than has been assumed. There is much to be done.

Bibliography

Lord Acton, *Lectures on modern history* (London, etc.)

B. Altaner and A. Stuiber *Patrologie* (Freiburg, Basel, 1966.)

J. Altensteig, *Lexicon theologium complectens vocabulorum descriptiones et interpretationes, omnibus sacrae theologiae studiosis* (Antwerp, 1576 8).

W. Ames, *Exposition of both the Epistles of the Apostle Peter* etc. (London 1641).

M. Amyraut, *Paraphrase sur les Epistres Catholiques* (Saumur 1646 8o).

Anselm, *Cur Deus Homo* (ed. R. Roques, Sources Chretiennes, Paris 1963).

G. Aulen, *Christus Victor* (London 1931, 8o)

B.G. Armstrong, *Calvinism and the Amyraut Heresy* (Madison and London 1969).

de Backer - See under Sommervogel.

J.H. Barkley, *The Antichrist* (Belfast 1967).

R. Baxter, *Grotian Religion* etc. (London 1658 8o).

R. Bellarmine *Disputationes de controversiis Christianae fidei Adversus Huius temporis haeretico* (Ingolstat 1596).

H. Bettenson, *Documents of the Christian Church* (London 1943 8o).

T. de Bèze, *Iesu Christi D.N. Nova Testamentu* (Geneva, 1567 fol.).

T. de Bèze, *De praedestinatione* (Geneva 1585).

T. de Bèze, *Theses Theologiae in Schola Genevensis* Geneva 1586).

T. de Bèze, *Questions et Responses Chrestiennes* (Geneva 1586).

T. de Bèze, *Ad acta colloquii Montisbelgardensis* (Geneva 1578).

T. de Bèze, *Tractationum Theologicarum* (Geneva 1582).

T. de Bèze, *Iesu Christ D.N. Novum Testamentum* (Geneva 1598).

Biblia Vulgata, different editions.

Bibliotheque nationale, Paris, *Catalogue,* (Paris 1897-1980, 229 vols.).

M. Blondel, *Geneve plagiaire; Jerusalem et Rome au secours de Geneve* (Geneve 1621).

C. Borgeaud, *Histoire de l'Université de Genève* (Geneva 1900 4o)

W. Bouwsma, *Venice and the Defense of Republican Liberty* (Berkeley 1968 8o).

G. Brandt, *Historie der Reformatie, en andre Kerkelyke geschiedenissen in en ontrent de Nederlanden* (Amsterdam 1671).

J.S. Bray *Theodore Beza's doctrine of predestination* (Nieuwkoop, 1975).

H.J. Bremme, *Buchdrucker und Buchhandler zur Zeit der Glaubenskampfe* (Geneva 1969)

British and Foreign Bible Society, 67th report (London 1871).

British and Foreign Bible Society, 68th report (London 1872).

British Museum General Catalogue of Printed Books (London 1965-6, 263 vols.).

E. de Budè, *Brieve relation de mon boyage a Venise* (Geneva, 1863).

E. de Budè, *Life of Giovanni Diodati Genevese Theologian* (London 1905 4o)

E. de Budè, *Vie de Jean Diodati* (Lausanne, 1869 4o).

E. de Budè, *Vita di Giovanni Diodati* (Lausanne, 1870 4o).

J. Buxtorf, *Tiberias sui commentarius massorethicus* (Basel, 1620 4o).

J. Buxtorf, *Tractatus de punctorum origino* (Basel, 1648).

J. Calvin, works edited by H.W. Baum, E. Cunitz, E. Reuss, P Lobstein and A. Erichson, *Corpus Reformatorum*, XXIX-LXXVII; 59 vols. (Brunswick 1863-1900). Also: "Petit supplement aux bibliographies calviniennes 1901-63" par une equipe de l'Institut d'Histoire de la Reformation in *Bibliotheque d'humanisme et renaissance,* travaux et documents, vol XXXIII, 1971, pp. 406-7.

The edition of the *Institutes* used throughout was that of McNeill and Battles (London, 1961) and some use was made of the translations of the commentaries by T.H.L. Parker, edited byD.W. andT.F. Torrance.

J. Cappel, *Plagianus vapulans* (1620, Geneva).

J. Cappel, *Arcanus punctationis revelatum (1623, Sedan, 4o).*

Sir Dudley Carleton, Letters from and to Sir Dudley Carleton, Knt., during his embassy in Holland (London, 1775).

O. Chadwick, *The Reformation* (London, 1965 8o).

A. de la Roche Chandieu, *La confirmation de la discipline ecclesiastique* (s.l. 1516, 8o).

C. Chiminelli, *Bibliografia della storia della Riforma Religiosa in Italia* (Rome, 1921).

N. Colladon, *Methodus . . . . ad explicationem . . . Apocalypsos* (Morges, 1584).

P. Coton, *Geneve plagiaire ou verification des depravations de la parole de Dieu* (1618, Paris, fol.).

P. Coton, *Recheute de Geneve plagiaire* (1619 Lyon, 4o).

M. Cottiere, *Traitez . . . servant de reponse a la Geneve Plagiaire du P. Coton* (1619, Saumur 8o).

B. Cresson, *Responses aux allegations* (1599 Geneva, 8o).

F.L. Cross, *Oxford Dictionary of the Christian Church* (London, 1968).

C. Dardier, *Une page inedite de l'histoire de Nimes, Sejour du pasteur et professeur genevois Benedict Turrettini* (Nimes, 1885).

J. Dantine, *Die Pradestinationslehre bei Calvin und Beza (Gottingen, 1965 8o).*

"Das christologische Problem im Rahmen der Pradestinationslehre von Theodor Beza" *in Zeitschrift fur Kirchengeschichte* 77, (1966) pp. 81-96.

"Les Tabelles sur la Doctrine de la Prédestinationslehre von Theodore de Bèze" *Revue de Théologie et de Philosophie* 3rd Series, vol. 16, (1966) pp. 365-77.

T.H. Darlow and H.F. Moule, *Historical Catalogue of Printed Bibles* (London, 1905-11).

P. Dibon, *La philosophie neerlandaise au siecle d'or,* vol. I (Amsterdam, etc. 1954).

Dictionary of National Biography (63 vols., London, 1885-1900 etc.).

Dictionnaire historique et biographique de la suisse (Neuchâtel, 1921-33).

Diodati - see special bibliography.

Dort - See special bibliography.

A. Dufour, *Bibliographie . . de Théodore de Bèze* (Geneva 1960).

D. Erasmus, *Opera Omnia* (Leyden, 1766).

G. Fatio, *Geneve et les Pays Bas* (Geneva, 1928).

O. Fatio, *Methode et théologie, Lambert Daneau et les debuts de la scholastique reformée* (Geneva, 1976).

Formula Concensus Helvetica (Zurich, 1675).

P. Fraenkel, "De l'Ecriture a la dispute" *Cahiers de la Revue de theologie et de philosophie,* (Lausanne, 1977).

T. Fuller, *Church History of Britain* (London, 1655).

J.A. Gautier, *Histoire de Genève* (Geneva, 1909).

J. Glazik, see E. Iserloh.

E. & E. Haag, *La France Protestante* (Paris, 1846-58 8o).

J. Hales, *Golden Remains of the ever memorable John Hales* (London, 1659).

A.H.W. Harrison, *The beginnings of Arminianism to the Synod of Dort* (London, 1926).

H. Hauser, *La préponderance Espagnole 1559-1660* (Paris, 1933 8o).

H. de Vries de Heeckelingen, *Genève Pépiniere du Calvinisme Hollondais* (The Hague, 1924).

H. Heppe, *Die Dogmatik der evangelisch-reformierten Kirche* (Neukirchen, 1935 8o).

G. Herlyn "Die Lehre von der Pradestination in Genfer und Heidelberger Katechismus" in *Reformierte Kirchenzeitung,* vol. 88, 1938, cols. 460-4.

M. Heyd, "From a rationalist theology to Cartesian voluntarism: David Derodon and Jean Robert Chouet" *Journal of the History of Ideas* vol. 40 no. 4, oct-dec 1979, pp. 527-42.

P. Heylyn, *Aerius Redivivus or the History of the Presbyterians* (Oxford, 1672 fo) *Historia Quinqu-Articularis* (London 1660 fo).

H. Jedin, *Geschichte des Konzils von Trient.*

F. Junius and I. Tremellius, *Sacra Biblia* (Zurich, 1703, Zurich 1673 and Geneva, 1630).

W. Kickel, *Vernunft und Offenbarung bei Theodor Beza.*

B. Keckermann, *Operum omnium Quae Extant* (Geneva 1614).

E. Labrousse, 'Rapport sur les Conferences de l'annes 1969-70" in *Annuaire de l'Ecole Pratique des Hautes Etudes* (1971 Paris).

E. LaVisse, *Histoire de France.*

L. Lefevre, see under H.J. Martin.

G. Leonard, *Histoire generale du protestantisme* (Paris, 1961 etc.).

Lexicon fur Theologie und Kirche (Freiburg, 1957-67).

Peter Lombard, *Sentences* (different editions).

J. Lecler, *Histoire de la tolérance au siecle de la Réforme.*

H. Meylan and others, *Correspondance de Théodore de Bèze.*

J. Morély, *Traicté de la discipline et police chrestienne* (Lyons, 1561).

L. Moréri, *Le Grand Dictionnaire etc . . . . Commencé en 1674.* (2nd ed., Basel, 1733).

P. du Moulin *Du Juge des controverses* etc. (Sedan, 1630).

P. du Moulin *Oppositions de la parole de Dieu avec la doctrine de l'Eglise romaine* (Geneva, 1637).

P. du Moulin *Des traditions et de la perfection et suffisance de l'Escriture saincte* (Sedan, 1631).

P. du Moulin *Anticoton, ou Refutation de la Lettre du P. Cotton.*

R.B. McKerrow, *Introduction to Bibliography* (Oxfore, 1928).

J.T. McNeill, *History and Character of Calvinism* (1967 edition).

H.J. Martin and L. Lefebvre, *Apparition du Livre.*

W. Monter, *Studies in Genevan Government.*

J.L. Motley, *The Life and Death of John of Bearneveld* (1874).

H.F. Moule, see under Darlow.

Nieuw Nederlandsch Biografisch Woordenboek

W. Niesel, *Bekenntnisschriften und Kirchenordnungen.*

Oxford Dictionary of the Christian Church.

L.D. Petit, *Bibliographische Lijst den werken van de Leidsche Hoogleeraren (1575-1619)* (Leyden 1894).

A. Polanus von Polansdorf *Syntagma theologiae christianae* (Hanover, 1625).

H. Perkins, *A golden chaine* (Cambridge, 1597).

L.E. Du Pin, *History of the Canon* etc. (London, 1699).

P.P. Plan, *Pages inedites de Theodore - Agrippa D'Aubigne* (Geneva, 1945).

I Pollin, *Theses Theologiae de Dei Providentia* (Geneva, 1619).

J. Quick, *Synodicon in Gallia Reformata.*

C. Read, *Daniel Chamier* (Paris, 1858).

C. Read, "Le Grimoire du R. P. Coton," in *Bulletin de la societe de l'histoire du protestantisme francais,* vol. XXXIX, (1890).

Die Religion in Geschichte und Gegenwart (Tubingen, 1957-65).

W. Rex, *Essays on Pierre Bayle and religious controversy* (The Hague, 1965).

M. Ritter, *Briefe und Acten sur du Neschichte des Dreissigjschrigen Krieges.*

O. Ritschl, *Dogmengeschichte des Protestantismus.*

K. Rozemond "De eerste uitgave van de belijdenis van Cyrillus Lucaris" in *Nederlands Archief voor Kerkgeschiedenis,* N.S., vol. 51, 1970.

W. Schwarz, *Principles and Problems of Biblical translation* (Cambridge, 1955).

P. Schaff, *Creeds of Christendom* (The Hague, 1844).

G.D.G. Schotel, *Jean Diodati* (The Hague, 1844).

J. Senébier, *Histoire Litteraire de Genève* (Geneva, 1790).

W. Schuckburgh, *Two biographies of William Bedell* (Cambridge, 1902).

Fr. Simon, *Critical enquiries* (London, 1684).

L.P. Smith, *The life and letters of Sir Henry Wotton* (Oxford, 1907).

Society for the Promotion of Christian Knowledge, Annual reports for 1849, 1852, 1855, 1858, 1862. (London).

A. & A. de Backer and C. Sommervogel, *Bibliothèque de la Compagnie de Jesus* (Brussels and Paris, 1890-99).

S. Stelling, Michaud, *Le Livre du Recteur de l'Academie de Geneve 1559-1878* (Geneva 1959 etc.)

A.M. Toplady, *The History of the Doctrinal Calvinism of the Church of England* (London, 1774).

Tremellius, see under Junius.

Tronchin, see special bibliography.

Turrettini, see special bibliography.

F. Turrettini, *Notice Biographique sur Bénédict Turrettini* (Geneva, 1871).

F. Turrettini, *Institutio Theologiae Electicae* (Geneva, 1680).

W. Tyndale, *The Exposition of the Fyrste Epistle of Seynt Jhon* (1531) et. T.H.L. Parker (Philadelphia and London, 1966).

J. Ussher, *Irish Articles* (1615).

F. Vandoni, *Intorno alla traduzione . . de Diodati* (c 1850 s.l.).

F. Véron, *L'Escriture saincte et toute la religion chrestienne combatue par Mestrezat, ministre de Charenton* etc. (Paris, 1633).

F. Véron, *La Saincte Bible abandonne par les ministres du Languedoc et des Sevenes* (Paris, 1625).

F. Véron, *Tous les ministres de France convaincus d'estre faussaires de l'escriture saincte* etc. (Paris, 1623).

F. Véron, *Adrien Hucher ministre d'Amyen, mis a l'inquisition des passages de la Bible de Genève* (La Flèche, 1615).

F. Véron, *Grand trouble arrivé de nouveau a Genéve* etc. (s.l. s.a.)

Westminster Confession of Faith (London, 1648).

C. Wyss, *Logica quae est Cursus Philosophici* (Geneva, 1669).

Appendix 1

Analysis of Biblical catenae used by delegations at the Synod of Dort.

Incidence of Texts

Abbreviations: B - Bremen
   D - Three Dutch Professors, Polyander, Thysius and Wallaeus
      for the first article, joined by Gomarus for consideration of
      the 2nd, 3rd and 4th articles.
   E - Great Britian
   G - Geneva
   H - Hesse
   M - Emden
   P - Palatinate
   1 - First article
   2 - Second article
   3 - Third and Fourth articles
   5 - Fifth article.

Genesis
1/31 D3
3/15 E2 H2
6/3 G3
6/5 E3 P3 H3 H3
6/8 H3 H3 M3
6/18 E5
6/21 H3 H3
8/20 B5
8/21 P3 D3
17/7 H2 B1 B1 D1
17/14 M3
19/30 B5
22/17 H2
22/18 H2
25/15 H2
28/10 H2
28/13 H2
28/14 H2
31/2 P3
32/32 M1
33/19 B1 B1 M1
35/32 M3 M3

Leviticus
10/1 M3
26/3 B5

Numbers
23/23 D3
24/3 G3
26/16 G3

Deuteronomy
4/1 M5
4/2 M5
4/7 M1 M5
4/8 M1
4/12 M5
4/32 M1
4/33 M1
4/34 B1 M1
4/37 M1
6/5 D3
7/6 G1 H1 M1
7/7 H1 M1 M1
7/8 H1 M1 M1
7/9 M1
7/10 M1
7/14 M1
9/4 E1
9/5 E1 M1
9/6 M1
9/7 M1
10/12 B1

231

The Epigones

10/14 G1	27/8 G3
29/2 G3	27/13 G1
29/3 M1 M3	30/6 G5
29/4 M1 M3	31/28 D1
30/2 M3	31/32 E5
30/6 P5 B5 M3 D3 D5	32/3 E5
30/17 M3	32/11 E3 M5
32/8 M1	33/1 M5
36/6 E5	33/11 H1 H5
	36/7 P2
2 Samuel	37/23 M5 D5
2/13 M5	37/24 H5 B5 M5 M5 M5 M5
7/12 H2	37/28 D5
7/13 H2	40/7 M3
7/14 H2 B5	40/9 H2
11/4 M5	47/5 G1
11/15 M5	51/3 M5
12/9 B5	51/10 E5
12/13 M5	51/12 G3 P3 H3 M3 D1
12/49 M5	53/3 H3
	58/5 E3
1 Kings	65/5 G1
8/58 M3	69/21 M1
21/27 E5	84/6 G5
21/29 E5	86/11 G3
	89/31 E5
2 Chronicles	89/33 B5
24/20 E3	89/34 B5 B5
32/31 G3	89/35 B5
	107/10 G3
Job	112/6 G5
3/2 E5	115/1 G5
6/3 D1	119/32 M1
13/15 D5	119/36 M3
15/16 E3	119/72 E5
21/13 G3	125/1 M5
22/13 G1	130/3 G5
	138/8 G1
Psalms	143/10 M3
1/3 H5 M5	147/6 P1
6/38 M3	147/8 E2
11/4 M3	147/19 G1 P1 H1 M1 M3 D1
12/7 M3	147/20 G1 H1 H1 M3
14/3 H3	
16/7 G1	Proverbs
18/24 G3	1/24 E3 M3
23/4 D5	2/14 E3
25/14 G1	16/4 H1 M1 M1

16/6 M1
19/21 D3
21/1 E3
24/16 H5

Song of Songs
1/3 M3
3/4 D1
3/5 D1

Isaiah
1/16 M3
1/17 M3
1/24 P2
5/3 M3
5/4 M3
6/9 H1 M3 M3
6/10 M1
6/13 G5
9/5 G1
14/1 G1
14/27 M3 D1
29/13 M3
33/15 G5
38/5 E5
41/9 G1
43/17 B1 B1
46/3 P5
46/4 P5 H5 M5 M5
46/9 B1 B1
46/10 E1 H1 H5 B1 B1 M3
47/14 E1
48/8 P3
53/5 D2
53/10 G2 E2 M2
53/11 P2
53/12 G2
53/22 G5
54/7 G5
54/8 G5
54/10 H5 M5 M5 D5
55/7 M3
59/21 G5 E2 P5 B5
61/10 M5
63/10 G3 M3
65/22 G1

Jeremiah
6//30 M1
13/23 E3 P3 H3 M3 M3
14/7 E3
14/32 E3
14/39 E3
17/5 G5
17/7 P5
17/8 P5
17/9 G3 P3
17/10 P3
17/14 E3
24/6 G5
24/7 M3 M3
30/40 M1
31/18 G3 M3
31/31 G3
31/32 M2
31/33 G5 P3 M3 M5 M5 D3
31/34 P3 M3 M5
31/39 M3
31/39 M3
31/40 P5
32/29 P5
32/39 M5
32/39 G3 P5
32/40 G5 G5 E5 P3 P3 P5 H5 H5 B5 M3
M3 M3 M5 M5 M5 D5 D5
39/40 M5
41/9 M1
46/9 D3
46/10 M1 D3

Ezekiel
2/19 G3 M3
3/5 H1
11/9 H3 M3
11/19 H5 M3
11/36 M3
16/4 E1
16/6 E1
18/27 E5
32/36 P3
33/31 G3
36/16 G3 M3
36/26 E3 P3 P3 H5 M3 D5

2

36/27 H3 B5 M3 M3 M3 D3 D5
36/36 H3
36/37 M3
38/26 P5
38/27 P5

Daniel
12/1 M1

Hosea
2/19 D5
9/12 G5
11/7 G5
13/9 G1
13/14 M1 M5
14/2 G3

Joel
2/12 M3
2/38 G2

Jonah
2/5 E5

Micah
6/8 B1

Zechariah
3/2 G5
10/12 M5 M5
11/12 G1
12/10 G3 P3 P5 B5 M5

Malachi
1/2 G1 M1 M1
1/3 M1 M1
1/6 P5
3/6 E1 H1 H5 B1 B1 M1

Matthew
1/21 H2 M5
3/2 P5
5/6 E5 P3 H3
5/8 E3
5/13 E5
5/20 H3
5/21 H3
5/26 D2

5/45 P2
6/10 P5
6/24 E5
7/18 P3 P3 H3 M3 M3
7/21 H5
7/22 H5
7/23 G1 P1 H5 B1
7/24 M5
8/11 G1
10/7 E5
10/9 E5
10/12 B5
10/15 E2
10/24 M3
11/15 M1
11/21 G1 H1
11/23 G1
11/25 G1 P1 P1 P1 P2 H1 H1 M1 D1
11/26 P1 P1 P1 P1 P2 H1 H1 M1
11/27 D1
11/29 P3
12/20 M5
12/23 M5
12/24 H3
12/31 M5
12/32 M5
12/33 P3
12/43 E5
13/6 H5 H5 H5
13/8 H5
13/9 M3
13/10 G1 M1
13/11 G1 E1 P1 P1 P1 P1 P2 P5 H1 H3 M1
13/12 G5 P3
13/13 G1 E5 M1
13/19 E3 D1
13/20 G3 P5 P5
13/21 P5 H5 H5 H5 H5 M5
13/22 H5
13/27 H5
13/37 M3
13/38 G1
14/24 P5
15/12 G5
15/13 G1
16/15 P5
16/16 P5
16/17 G3 P3

16/18 G5 E2 M5 M5 D5
17/10 G5
17/20 G5
18/34 D2
19/13 B1
19/14 B1 B1 D1
19/28 M3
20/15 E1 E2 P1
20/16 E1 P2 H1 H1 M1 D1
20/23 P1
20/28 P2
21/19 G5
22/14 G1 H1 H1 M1
22/32 G1
22/37 P3
22/38 P3
23/27 M3
23/37 M3
23/38 M3
24/11 P5
24/13 P1 P5 B5
24/24 G1 E1 E5 P5 P5 H1 H1 H5 B5
    M5 M5 M5 M5
24/31 G1
24/40 M2
25/3 G5
25/22 P2
25/28 E3
25/30 G5
25/32 H1
25/34 D1
25/40 M3
25/41 H1
25/42 E3 P1
25/46 H1
26/30 B5
26/70 M5
26/75 M5 M5
28/19 G2
28/20 E1

Mark
1/15 P5
3/29 M5
6/20 E3 E5
7/21 H3
10/14 B1
11/14 G5

13/20 P1
16/15 E2 E2
16/16 P1 P1 H2 H2
16/28 E5

Luke
1/33 E1
2/24 G1
8/8 M3
8/10 H1
8/13 E5 P5 P5 P5 M5 M5
8/15 E3 P5 M5
8/18 P5 M3
10/9 E2
10/11 E2
10/16 M3
10/20 G1 P1 H1 M1 D1
10/21 G1
10/27 D3
10/28 M1
11/21 E3
12/32 E1 M1 D1
13/2 E5
15/18 G5
16/24 P2
16/25 P2
17/5 P5 M5
18/16 E1
21/15 P3
21/36 H5
22/31 G5 E5 H5
22/32 G5 E5 P5 P5 P5 H5 H5 H5 M5 M5
22/61 M5
24/45 H3

John
1/2 D1
1/5 H3 D5
1/12 E5 P1 P2 H1 M1 M1
1/13 E3 D3
1/15 G1
1/16 E1 E1
1/22 E1
3/3 P2 P3 M3 M3 M3
3/5 E2 P3 P5 M3
3/8 G1 M3 D2
3/16 P2 H1 H2 M1 D2

3/17 E2 P2
3/18 E2 P1 P1 H2
3/27 G5
3/36 E2 P1 H1 H1 H2 D3
4/10 P2
4/14 E5 E5 E5 D1 D5
5/11 B5
5/21 P3
5/24 H1 H2 H5
5/25 G3 P3 P3 M3 M3
5/30 D2
5/31 B5
5/34 E3
5/35 G3 D5
5/38 G3
5/40 E3
6/22 E5
6/29 H1 H5
6/35 M5 M5 D1
6/37 E1 E3 P3 P3 H2 M1 M5 D3 D5
6/40 P1 H2 M1 M1
6/43 D1
6/44 P3 H2 M3 M3 M3 M3 M5
6/45 G1 G2 H2 M1 M3 M3 D3
6/47 H2
6/59 H5
6/63 M3
6/65 G1 H2 D1
6/66 E3
6/68 P3
8/21 G1
8/31 G5
8/35 G5
8/36 E3
9/39 G1
9/44 G3
10/3 P1 H1
10/11 D2
10/12 D2
10/14 G2 M5 D2
10/15 P2 P2 M2 M5
10/16 G1 E1 E1 P1 H1
10/16 G5
10/18 G3 P2
10/20 G1
10/26 E5 P1 P1
10/27 G1 B5 D1 D1
10/28 E1 E5 H1 B5 B5 B5 M1 M3 M5
    D1 D5

10/29 E1 P5 P5 H1 B5 D1
10/35 D3
10/37 G1
10/38 M5
11/26 G5
11/42 P5
11/51 G2 E2 D2
11/52 P1
12/12 P1
12/14 G1
12/32 G2
12/39 G1 P1 H1
12/40 G1 P1
12/42 E5
13/1 D3
13/10 G5
13/17 G5 P1 P1 P1 M5
13/18 G1 P1 P1 P1 H1 M1
13/41 D5
14/6 M3
14/15 H5
14/16 G5 G5 P5 H2 H5 M5
14/17 G1 P5
14/23 H5
14/31 D2
15/2 G5
15/3 M5
15/4 B5
15/5 G5
15/7 B5
15/13 H1 M2
15/15 E3 D1
15/16 G1 E1 P1 H1
15/22 E2 E5
16/8 G3
16/22 P5
17/2 M1
17/6 G1 G2 P1 P1 H2 M5
17/7 H2
17/8 H2
17/9 G1 G2 P1 P2 P2 H2 M2 M5
17/10 G1
17/11 D1
17/12 G5 G5 E5 P1 P1 P2 M1
17/13 G5
17/15 H5
17/16 G2
17/17 H5
17/19 P2 D5

17/20 E5 H2 H5 D5
17/21 P2
17/24 G2 P5 M1 M1 M5
17/25 G1
17/26 M5
17/32 G2

Acts
2/8 M3
2/9 M3 M3
2/10 M3 M3 M3
2/16 M3 M3 M3
2/36 E1
2/37 E3
2/39 B1 B1 D1
4/18 M1
4/31 P5
7/51 G3 M3 M3
8/12 E5
8/13 M5
9/5 G3
10/37 P5
10/43 E2 E2 P2
11/17 P3
11/18 E5 P5
11/20 D2
11/21 D2
11/33 P3
12/7 D3
13/9 H1
13/38 E2 D2
13/39 E2 D2
13/46 E3
13/48 G1 E1 E1 P1 P1 P1 P1 P5 P5
    H1 H1 H1 H5 B1 B1 M1 M1 M5
    D1 D3
14/6 G1
14/16 E2 P1 P1 H1 M3 D1
15/8 D3 D3
15/9 H1 D5
15/11 H2 M1
15/16 H1
15/18 M2
16/6 H1 M1 D1
16/7 H1 M1 D1
16/8 H1
16/9 M1 M3
16/10 M1 M3

16/14 H1 M1 M3 M3 D3
16/18 M3
17/8 M3
17/12 M3
17/18 P3
17/25 P2 M3
17/28 M3
17/30 M3 D1
17/31 M1
17/32 P3
18/9 M3
18/10 G1 H1 M3
20/18 D2
20/28 D2
26/18 M3 M3
27/31 E5
28/24 D1
28/25 D1
28/26 H1
28/27 E3 H1

Romans
1/5 G2
1/7 E5 M1
1/16 P2 P3
1/18 H1 D1
1/19 H3
1/20 H3 M3 M3 M3 M3
1/21 H3 M3
1/22 M3
1/24 M5 D1
1/28 M3 D1
1/32 M5
2/4 P2 P3 M3
2/9 E1 E5
2/12 P1
2/14 E2
2/15 E2
3/4 E2 H5 H5
3/5 P2
3/8 P2
3/9 G1 G1 E1 D1
3/10 H3
3/11 H3 H5
3/12 P3 H3
3/14 G1
3/19 E1 D3

The Epigones

3/20 D3
3/22 G1 G1 P2 H2 D2
3/23 P1 D1 B1 B1
3/24 E2 E5 P2 P2 H2 H2 B1
3/25 E5 E5 P2 H2 H2 B1 B1
3/27 D2
3/29 H2
4/4 P2
4/6 G2
4/7 G1
4/12 M1
4/16 G1
4/21 G1 D2
4/25 P2 D2
5/1 E2 E5 H5 B1 B1 B1 D5
5/2 E1 E5 H5 D1
5/3 P5
5/5 E1 M2 D1 D5 D5
5/6 E3 P2 P2 P3 P5 M2 D2
5/7 D2
5/8 P2 H1 M2 D1 D2
5/10 G1 H2 H2
5/12 G1 E1 M5
5/19 M1
6/1 G5
6/4 G3
6/6 P3
6/8 G3
6/12 H3 H5 M5 M5
6/14 E3
6/17 G3 G3 E3 D1
6/18 E3
6/21 E1
6/22 B1
6/23 E1 M5
7/4 G3
7/7 D3
7/9 D3
7/15 M5 M5
7/17 G3
7/19 B5 M5
7/22 B5 M5
7/23 G3 B5
7/24 E5 B5
8/1 E3 E5 E5 H5 M5 M5
8/2 G3 P2
8/4 H5 M1
8/5 G3 H5 M5
8/6 M3

8/7 G3 P3 H3 M5
8/8 H5 M5 M5
8/9 G1 G5 M5 M5
8/11 M5
8/12 H5 B1
8/13 G3 G3 E5 H5 M5
8/14 M5 D1
8/15 E1 P5 B1 B1 M5 M5 M5
8/16 G1 E5 H5 M5 M5 M5
8/17 E5 E5 H5
8/23 G3
8/27 G1
8/28 G1 P1 P2 P3 M1 D2
8/29 G1 G2 G5 P1 P1 P1 P1 P1 P1 P1 P1
       P1 P1 P2 P2 P3 P5 P5 H1 H1 H1
       H1 H1 H1 B1 B1 B1 B1 M1 M1 M5
       D1 D1 D1 D1 D5
8/30 G1 G1 E1 E1 E1 E5 P1 P1 P1 P1
       P1 P1 P2 P3 P5 P5 H1 H1 H1
       H1 H1 H1 H5 H5 B1 B1 B1 B1
       B1 B1 B1 B1 B5 M1 M1 M1 M1
       M3 M5 D1 D1 D1 D1 D1 D1 D5 D5
8/31 B5 D5
8/32 G2 G2 E2 E5 P2 P5 H1 H2 M1 M2
       D2 D5
8/33 G1 G5 E2 P1 H1 H5 M5 M5
8/34 E2 P2 H1 M2 M5 M5 D2
8/35 E5 P1 P5 H1 H5 H5 B5 M5 D1 D1
8/36 G1 H1
8/37 H1 D5
8/38 G1 H1 B1 B1 M5
8/39 G1 G5 E5 P1 P5 P5 H1 M5
9/6 G1 P2 M1 D1
9/7 P2 D2
9/8 M1 D2
9/9 E2
9/11 G1 G1 E1 E1 E1 P1 P1 P1 P1 P5
       H1 H1 H1 B1 B1 B1 B1 B1 B1 M1
       M1 M1 M1 M1 D1 D1 D1 D1 D1
9/12 P1 H1 H1 B1 D1
9/13 G1 G2 P1 H1 H1 M1 M1 M1 D1 D1
9/14 B1
9/15 E1 E1 P1 B1 B1 M1 M1 D1 D1 D1
9/16 P1 P1 H1 B1 B1 B1 D1 D1 D1
9/17 P1 P1 H1 M1 M1
9/18 G1 G1 E1 E3 P1 P1 P1 P1 P1 P1 P2
       H1 B1 M1 M1 M1 M1 M1 D1 D1 D1
       D3
9/19 G1 B1 B1

9/20 E1 B1 M3
9/21 E1 B1 M1 M1 M1 M1 M1 D1
9/22 G1 E1 P1 H1 H1 H1 B1 M1 M1
   M1 M1 M1 M1 D1
9/23 E1 E1 P1 P3 B1 B1 B1 M1 M1
   D1 D1 D1
9/24 P3 D1 D1
9/25 G1 B1
9/26 B1
9/27 D1
9/29 B1 M1 D1
9/30 P1
9/31 H1
10/3 H2
10/4 H2
10/5 H2
10/9 P5 H2 H5 D2
10/10 E3 P5 H2 H5
10/11 H2
10/14 E3 H2 M3
10/17 P3 M3
10/19 G1 M3
10/20 P1 P3
11/1 G1 M1 D1
11/2 D1
11/5 G1 E1 E55 M1 M1 D1 D1 D1
11/6 M1 D1 D1
11/7 G1 G5 E1 P1 P1 P1 P5 M1 D1
   D1 D1 D1 D5
11/8 P1 P1 D1
11/9 G1
11/11 P5
11/12 G5
11/16 G1
11/21 G1
11/22 G1
11/25 P1
11/28 G1 E1 H5 D1
11/29 G1 E1 P1 P1 H1 H5 M5 M5 D1
11/33 E1
11/35 E3
12/2 G3
14/17 H5
14/23 H3
15/4 M3
15/8 M3
16/20 E5
16/25 P3 M5

16/26 G2 P3

I Corinthians
1/2 E5 M1
1/3 G3
1/7 G5 E5
1/8 E5 P3 P5 H5 B5 M3 M3 D1
1/21 M1 M1
1/23 P3
1/26 P3 B1 B1
1/27 P3
1/30 P2 P2 P3 B1 M1 D5
2/2 P2
2/4 M3
2/7 G3 G5 P3 M1
2/9 G1 D1
2/10 G5 D1
2/11 P5
2/12 E5 P5
2/14 G3 P3 P3 H3 M3 M3
3/6 M3 D2
3/7 P3
3/9 E2
3/17 H5 M5
4/7 G1 E5
4/15 E3
5/5 G5
5/7 G5
5/13 D1
6/9 E5
6/11 M5 D2
6/17 G3
6/19 M5
6/20 M2
7/14 B1 B1 D1
9/24 D5
9/27 G1 E5
10/2 G1
10/3 G1
10/13 E5 E5 P1 H5 H5 D5
11/12 P1
11/29 M3
11/32 E5
12/3 G3
12/4 H5
12/5 H5
12/6 G1 H5

The Epigones

12/7 H5
12/8 P5 H5
12/9 P5 H5
12/10 P5 H5
12/11 H5 H5
13/1 P5
13/2 H5
13/11 G3
14/24 G3
15/10 P3 M1
15/14 D2
15/17 D2
15/22 P1 M1
16/15 B5

2 Corinthians
1/20 B1 B1
1/21 G1 M5 D1 D5
1/22 H1 H5 M5 D5
2/2 E5
3/5 G1 G3 E3 P3 H3 M3
3/6 E2
3/9 G2 E2 P5
3/17 E3
3/18 G3
4/4 M5
4/5 G1
4/6 G3
4/9 H5
4/13 G1 G2 G5 E3 P3
4/16 M5
5/2 E3
5/4 G3
5/11 M3
5/15 P2 D2
5/17 P3 P3 M3 M3 D3
5/18 P2 P3 D3
5/19 E2 P3
5/20 P3 D2
5/21 H2 D2
6/1 E3 M3
6/16 H5 B5
7/1 G5
7/10 E5 P3
12/9 E5
13/5 G1 H1

Galatians
1/6 E3

1/15 M1
2/3 H5 H5
2/14 B5
2/15 D1
2/16 E2
2/20 G3 M5
3/13 E2 P2
3/14 P3
3/15 D2
3/16 H2
3/17 D2
3/22 G1
3/26 M1
3/27 E5
4/4 G2
4/5 M5
4/6 G2 E1
4/7 E5 E5 M5
4/9 G1
5/6 H5
5/12 M5
5/16 G3 E3 H3 M5
5/17 E3 H3 M5
5/19 E3
5/21 E5
5/22 H5 H5 D3
5/23 H5 H5
5/25 G3 E5

Ephesians
1/1 E5
1/3 E1 P1 P5
1/4 G1 G2 G2 E1 E1 E1 P1 P1 P1 P1
    P1 P1 P2 P2 P2 H1 H1 H1 H1 H1
    H1 H1 H1 H1 H5 B1 B1 B1 B1 B1
    M1 M1 M1 M1 M1 D1 D1 D1 D1
1/5 E1 E1 E5 P1 P1 P1 P1 P1 P1 P2 P2
    H1 H1 H1 B1 B1 B1 M1 M1 M1
    M1 M1 M1 M1 M5 M5 M5 D1 D1
    D1 D1 D1
1/6 P1 P2 H1 B1 B1 M1 M1 M1 D1
1/7 E1 P1 P2 H1 H1 B1 B1 D1
1/8 H1 D1
1/9 P1 P1 H1 D1
1/10 H1
1/11 G1 G1 E1 E1 E1 P3 H1 H1 H1 H5
    M1 M1 M1 D1 D1 D3
1/12 H1 M1
1/13 G1 G5 E1 H1 H1 H5 M5 M5 D1 D5

1/14 E1 E3 E5 D1
1/16 H3
1/17 G3 H3
1/18 E3 H3
1/19 G3 P3 H3
1/20 H3
1/22 G2 G2 G3 E1
1/23 G1 G2
2/1 P1 P3 P3 P3 D1 D1 D3 D3
2/2 E3 M5 D1 D3 D3
2/3 G1 P1 P2 P3 P3 M3 D1 D1 D3
2/5 H3 M3 M3
2/8 G1 P1 P3 P5 H1 H1 M1 M5 D1
2/10 G3 G3 E3 H3 B1 M1 M3
2/11 M3
2/12 G1 G3 D1 D1
2/14 G2
2/20 E2
3/7 D3
3/10 G1
3/13 G2
3/17 P5 H5 M5
3/18 M5 M5
4/7 H5
4/10 G2
4/12 M5 M5
4/13 M5
4/14 M5
4/15 G3 G5
4/16 E2
4/17 D1
4/18 H3 D1 D3
4/19 G5
4/22 G3 H3 M3 M5
4/24 E3 P3 H3 D3 D3 D3
4/29 G3
4/30 G5 E3 H5 M5 M5 D5
4/33 G3
5/8 P3 H3 D3 D3 D3
5/9 D3 D3
5/14 P3
5/23 G2 E2
5/25 H1 H2 D2
5/26 H2
5/27 H2
6/10 H5
6/11 H5 M1
6/23 G1

Philippians
1/1 E5
1/6 G5 E3 E5 1 P3 P3 P5 P5 P5 P5 H5 B5
    M3 M3 M3 M3 M5 M5 M5 D5 D5
1/16 M5
1/19 G5 E5 H1
1/25 P5
1/29 G1 G2 E3 P3 M5 M5 D1
2/12 G5 P1 H3 H5
2/13 G1 G3 E3 P3 P3 P3 P3 P5 H3 H3 H3
    H5 M3 M3 M3 M3 M3 M3 M5 M5
    M5 M5 M5 M5 D3 D5
3/8 E5
3/10 M3
3/12 G5
3/18 D2
4/3 H1
4/13 H5 B5

Colossians
1/12 E5
1/17 G2
1/19 P2
1/20 P2
1/21 G3
1/22 G5
2/3 E1
2/5 D3
2/7 E1 P5 P5 M5 M5 M5
2/10 E1
2/11 D3
2/12 G3 G3
2/13 P3 M3
3/1 D2
3/6 E5
3/7 G3
3/9 G3 M5
3/10 G3
3/11 G2 G3

1 Thessalonians
1/4 G1 P1
3/12 G5
5/9 H1 M1 M5
5/23 P3

The Epigones

2 Thessalonians
1/3 M5
1/8 D1
1/11 G3 G3
2/2 H1
2/11 G1 D1
2/12 D1
2/13 G1 G1 E1 H1 H1 H5 B1 D1 D1
    D5 D5
2/14 B1 D1
2/15 B5
2/16 B1 B1
2/17 G5 B1 B1
3/2 G1 P1 H5
3/3 E5

1 Timothy
1/5 P5
1/9 B1
1/15 E1
3/14 B5
4/5 G5
4/10 P2
6/11 G5
6/17 G5

2 Timothy
1/5 E5
1/9 G1 G1 E1 E1 E1 P1 P2 P2 P2 P3
    H1 B1 B1 M1 M1 M1 D1 D3
1/12 G1 E5 P5 H5 M5
2/9 E1
2/10 D1
2/12 M1
2/18 G5 P5
2/19 G1 E1 E5 P1 P1 P1 P1 P1 P1
    P5 P5 H1 H1 H1 H5 B1 B1 M1
    M5 M5 D5
2/20 M1
2/26 E3
2/28 M1
3/8 G3
4/7 E1 E5 D3
4/8 E5 E5
4/17 G5
4/18 E5

Titus
1/1 G1 E1 E1 E5 P5 H1 H5 M5

1/2 G1 P5
1/4 H1
1/9 H1
2/11 E2
2/13 G2 M3
3/3 G1 P3
3/5 P3 P3 M1 M1 M3 D3
3/6 P3 P5

Hebrews
1/5 H2
1/12 M1
2/3 E2
2/10 D2
2/13 E2 D2
3/6 G1 G5 B5
3/7 E3
3/12 G3
3/13 G5
3/14 G1
3/20 G3
4/13 D3
6/4 G3 E1 E2 E3 E5 E5 P5 P5 H5 M3
    M5 M5 M5 D5
6/5 P5 H5 M5 D1
6/6 G5 E5 M5 D1
6/11 G1
6/13 G1 G1
6/17 G1 E1 M1
6/18 M1
8/6 E2 H2
8/10 E2 E2 D3
9/10 H2
9/12 D2
9/13 M2
9/14 H2 M2 D2
9/15 H2 H2 H2 D2 D2
9/24 D2
9/26 D2
9/28 D2
10/9 H2
10/10 D2
10/14 D2
10/15 D2
10/26 E5 E5 H5 M5 D1
10/27 M5
10/29 E5 M5 M5
10/30 D5
10/38 G5 D5
10/39 P5

11/6 H3 M1 M1 D3
11/9 G1
11/16 G1
12/1 P5 D5
12/2 G5 P3
12/14 E5
12/22 P1
12/23 G1
12/24 H2
13/5 P5 D5
13/12 H2
13/20 G1
13/21 G5

James
1/2 G5
1/13 D3
1/14 D3
1/17 G1 M1 M1
1/18 G1 G3 M5
1/21 G3
2/9 M5
2/14 M5
2/17 M5
2/29 M5
3/2 E5

1 Peter
1/2 G1 G1 H1 H5 B1 B1 M1 M1 M3
    D1 D1
1/3 E5 H1 M5
1/4 G1
1/5 G5 E1 P5 P5 H1 H5 H5 H5 M5
    M5 D5 D5
1/6 B5
1/8 E5
1/9 P5
1/18 D2
1/20 G1 G1 G2 H1 M1
1/21 G2
1/22 G1 G1 G2
1/23 E3 E5 H5
2/4 M1
2/6 D5
2/7 M1
2/8 M1 M1 D1
2/9 G1
2/12 M1

5/8 H5
5/9 H5
5/10 M1 D5

2 Peter
1/5 E5
1/6 E5
1/10 G1 G1 G5 E5 P1 P3 D1 D5
1/11 E5
1/20 P1
2/1 M5
2/5 D3
2/20 E5 E5
2/21 E3 E5 M3
2/22 D5

1 John
1/5 D3
1/7 H2 D2
1/8 E5
1/12 M1
2/1 G5 P2 P2
2/2 P2 P2
2/3 E5 E5
2/9 E1
2/19 G1 G5 P5 P5 P5 P5 M5 D1 D5
2/20 G1
2/25 H5
2/27 H5 M5 M5
3/2 B1 B1 D1
3/3 E5
3/5 M5
3/8 E5
3/9 G5 G5 E5 E5 P5 P5 H5 H5 H5 H5
    H5 M5 M5 M5 D5 D5
3/12 G1
3/14 H1 H5 H5
3/16 H1
3/19 G1 G5 P5
3/21 E5 H5
3/24 G5 G5 D1
3/29 G1
4/4 G3
4/6 G1
4/7 E3
4/9 H1
4/10 G1 D3

The Epigones

4/12 B1 B1
4/13 G1 G5 B1 D5
4/14 G1
5/1 E3
5/4 E5 D5
5/5 G5
5/9 D1
5/10 E5 H5 D1
5/11 H5 D1
5/12 H5
5/13 H1 H5
5/14 H5
5/15 H5
5/16 E5
5/20 H3

2 John
3/9 E5

Jude
3 H1
4 P1 P1 P1 M1 D1 D5
12 G5 G5

Revelation
2/17 G1
3/3 E3
3/8 G5
3/20 G3 E3 M3 M3
5/8 D2
5/9 G2 D2
7/4 H1
7/9 D1
7/14 G1
13/8 G1 G1 M1
17/8 M1 M1
20/6 E5
20/12 E1
21/6 E5
21/27 G1 E1 E5 H1
22/11 G5

Appendix 2

A bibliography of the Synod of Dort, 1619-1969.

This bibliography is arranged in chronological order, by year of publication. A short title catalogue and an author catalogue will be found at the end, pp.

abbreviations
KBH - The Royal Library at The Hague.
TCD - The library of Trinity College Dublin.
BM - The British Museum Library.
BPU - Bibliotheque publique et universitaire, Geneva.
AC - The library of Assembly's College, Belfast.
BNS - Bibliotheque nationale, Strasbourg.
MHR - Musee historique de la Reformation, Geneva.
LLB - Linenhall Library, Belfast.
BSHPF - Bibliotheque de la societe de l'histoire du protestantisme francais,
    Paris.

The numbers that follow British Museum entries supply the volume and column number of the *General Catalogue of Printed Book*.

This must not be considered as a complete bibliography of the Synod of Dort. It is largely composed with the help of the published catalogues of the libraries mentioned above.

1618

(1) Optima Fides Festi Hommii, cuius specimen in citatione insignium locorum ex Thesibus provatis M.Simonis Episcopii SS. Theologiae Professoris demonstratur ex libro quem inscripitsit Specimen Controversiarum Belgiaarum. Lugduni Batavorum, Ex Officina Godefridi Basson, Anno 1618. - KBH

(2) Remonstrantie van Johannes Wtenbogaert ghepresenteert in Novembri deses Jaers 1618. Aen de...Staten Generael...Nopende het presenterem van sijne verantwoordinge tegens seeckere beschuldigen Festi Hommij, aen den Synodum Nationalem, mitsgaders ronde verclaringhe over verscheyden geruchten t'onrecht hem nagestroyt. Tot Leyden, By Govert Basson, 1618. - KBH

(3) Remonstrantie van Joannes Wtenbogaert...Eerst tot Leyden by Govert Basson, MDCXVIIJ. Ende nu Tot Amsterdam, By Broer Jansz. - KBH

(4) Ses vragen by de E, Heeren Burghermeesteren voorsbestelt, dienende tot naerder openinghe over het honden eens Nationalen Synodo. Met de antwoorde der Kercke. MDCXVIII. - KBH

(5) Eenighe Vraghen By de E, Heernen...MDCXVIII. - KBH

(6) Afbeeldinghe des Synodi Nationael... - KBH

(7) Des Eerw-Bishops van Landavien Oratie Gedaen inde vergaderinge van de...Staten-Generael, op den vijfden November 1618. Stylo nova. In 's Graven-Hage. By Aert Meuris...Anno 1618 - KBH

(8) Oratie Ghedaen vande Eerweerdighe Bischop Georgio Landavensi. Tot Amsterdam, By Broer Jansz, 1618. - KBH

(9) Specimen Controversiarum Belgicarum. Seu Confessio Ecclesiarum Reformatarum in Belgio, Cujus singulis Articulis subjuncti sunt Articuli Discrepantes, ...In usum futurae Synodi Nationalis Latine edidit, et collegit, Festus Hommius. Addita est in eundem usum Harmonia Synodorum Belgicarum. Lugduni Batavorum, Ex Officina Elzeviriana Anno 1618. - KBH

(10) Monster Vande Nederlantsche Verschillen Ofte Belydenisse der Ghereformeerde Kercken in Nederlant. Al waer onder elcken Artijckel lygevoecht zijn de verschillende artyckelen Inde welike hendensdaechs sommighe Leeraers der Nederlantsche Kerken, vande aengenome Leers schijnen te wijcken. Tot gherief vande aenstaende Nationale Synode...uytghegheven Van Festus Hommius. Bedienaer des H. Evaghelij tot Leyden Alwaer...bijgedaen is D'overeenstemminghe der Nederlantsche Synode. Alles...Door Johannes a Lodensteyn, Dranaer des Goddelijcken woorts tot Soeterwonde. Tot Leyden, By David Jansz van Ilpendam...1618. - KBH

(11) Naem-register. Van alle de ghecommitteerde, so Politike als Kerckelijcke, opt Nationael Synode van de Nederlantsche Ghereformeerde Kercken, twelcke ghehouden wert binnen der Stede van Dordrecht 1618. - KBH

(12) Copie van sekeren Brief uyt Dordrecht. Van een Goet Patriot, Aen een Lief-hebber gheschreven, waer in verhaelt wordt 'tghene op de inleydinghe van het Nationale Synode binnen Dordrecht ghehouden, den 13 Novembris 1618 ende op naervolghende daghen is ghepasseert... - KBH

(13) De namen der Staten Generael ghecommitteerden...tot desen nationael synodus te houden ghesonden, binnen Dordrecht 1618. Amsterdam 1618. - KBH TCD

(14) Afbeeldinghe des Synodi Nationael, met de sidt plaetsen der...Staten Generael...Professoren ende Predicanten...Binnen Dordrecht, An.1618. KBH BM54/ 924

(15) De namen der...Staten Generael Ghecommitteerden soo wel uytheemsche als in-landsche Theologanten...desen nationael Synodus te houden, gesonden binnen Dordrecht. KBH BM54/925

1619

(1) Carleton,G. An Oration made at the Hague before the Prince of Orange and the States Generall of the United Provinces. BM

(2) Antidotum ende naerder openinghe van het eyghenegehvoelen des nationalen synodi ghehouden binnen Dordrecht, 1618-19 (By S.Episcopius) KBH BM 54/925

(3) Belydenisse des gheloofs der ghereformeerde kerchen in Nederlant, overghesien in de synode nationael ghehouden tot Dordrecht. KBH TCD

(4) Verroogh (sic) ende supplicatie, by de Remonstranten gecitteerde...op hat synodes nationnael tot Dordrecht...den 26 Januarij 1619 afghesonden aen den...Prince van Oraignen, etc...In Druk uyt laten gaen door een liefhebber der Vrijheyt, etc. KBH BM54/926

(5) Vertoogh by de Remonstranten...ghedeputeert op het Synodes Nationnael tot Dordrecht, affghesonden...den 26 Januarij...1619, aen de...Staten Generael, etc. KBH BM54/926

(6) Judicium Synodi Nationalis Reformatus Ecclesiarum Belgiacarum etc. Subjunctae sunt sententiae, edicta, judicia lata in publicae pacis et ecclesiarum reformatorum perturbatores, Heidelberg 1619. BM54/923

(7) Oordeel des Synodi nationalis der gereformeerda kerchen van de vereenichde Nederlanden: ghehouden...inden Jare 1618. ende 1619. Welcke geassisteert is geweest met vele treflicke Theologen etc. Over bekende vijf Hoofstucken der Leere, daer van inde...Nederlanden verschil is gevallen uytgesproken op den 6 May 1619, uyt het Latijn ghetrouwelijk in't Nederduytsch overgheset (signed by S.Damman, F.Hommius etc.). Dordrecht 1619. - KBH BM

(8) A caricature of the Proceedings of the Synod of Dort, with an Explanation subjoined headed: "Erklarung uber diesen hochnotigen Tembst." 1619. - BM54/925

(9) Corte...ontdeckinghe vande Bedrieghelijckheydt des Dortschen Synodi in't smeden van seeckere Artijckelen van...Verdraegsaemheyt tusschen den Remonstranten ende Contra-Remonstranten, Ende syn hier noch bygevoeght 34 Artijckelen vervattende 'tgevoelen der Remonstranten (nopende de Goddelijcke Predestinatie...), etc. (By S.Episcopius) KBH BM54/925

(10) Een cort verhael van die principaelste puncten die in Hollandt tot D., in die Synode ghetrackteert worden, ghestelt in Rijme. Tot confucie van die selve Synode...gemaect door een Liefhebber der C.A.R.R. Gazette of Antwerp, January 1619. KBH BM54/925

The Epigones

(11) Onbillijcke wreetheyt der Dortsche Synode...teghen de Remonstranten etc. (by S.Episcopius) Leyden 1619. KBH BM54/925

(12) 'Themelsch Synodus ende rechtmatigh oordeel gehouden tot Zion 't Aerdsche Synodus Nationael ende onrechtveerdich Oordeel ghehouden binnen Dordrecht in de Dool-Cappelle Anno 1618 ende 1619 (By A.Neomagus, ed. H.Slatius). Antwerp 1619. BM54/925

(13) Vertroostinghe aen de remonstrantsche kerchen...over het...bonnissement van hare...predicanten, op het nationael synode gheeiteert. (By K.van Baarle). BM54/925

(14) Request aende...Staten Generael der Vereenichde Provintien van weghen de Remonstranten...gedeputeerde tot den Synodum Nationael binnen Dordrecht (versoeckende dat de selve gelieve de supplianten van arrest te outslaan). KBH BM54/926

(15) Iudicium synodi nationalis reformatarum ecclesiarum Belgicarum, habitae Dordrechti anno 1618 et 1619...de quinque Doctrinae capitibus in Ecclesiis Belgicis controversis. Promulgatorum. Dordrecht 1619. BM TCD

(16) The Judgment of the Synode holden at Dort concerning the Five Articles: as also their sentence touching C. Vorstius. London 1619. TCD BM54/924

(17) Nulliteyten, Mischandelingen, ende onbillijcke Proceduren des Nationalen Synodi, ghehouden binnen Dordrecht Anno 1618-1619 in 't korte ende rouwe afgheworpen, etc. (By B.Dwinglo?). Enkhuizen 1619, TCD BM54/925

(18) Ontdeckinghe vande bedrieghelijckheydt des Dortschen synodi in 't smeden van seeckere artijckelen van moderatie en onderlignhe verdraegsaemheyt. tusschen den remonstranten ende contra-remonstranten etc. TCD

(19) Oratie Davidis Parei Proffessor in de H Theologie tot Heydelbergh, van't Nationael Synodus tot Dordrecht Midtsgaders Des selven oordeel aengaende de vijf Remonstrantische Artijckelen. Ghedaen in't Latijn tot Heydelbergh den 1 Februarij Anno 1619, Wt de Latijnsche Tale ghetronwelijch over-gheset door Petrum Iacobi Austro Silvium, Dienaer Iesu Christi etc. Amsterdam 1619. KBH TCD

(20) Oordeel des nationalen Synodi van Dordrecht over de Theologie ofte Leere C.Vorstij...mitsgaders de Resolutie vande...Staten van Holland...daer opghevolght. KBH BM54/924

(21) Reqveste verduijtsch uyt de Latijnsche tale, aen de gecommitteerde vande staten generael; op den synode nationnael, binnen Dordrecht vergadert. KBH TCD

(22) Vale hondende verclaringe, In wat voeghen de sinodus Nationael tot Dordrecht, Den Remonstranten afscheyt heeft ghegheven. TCD KBH

(23) Dordrecht - dordeel des Synodi Nationalis Dordrecht 1619. TCD

(24) Jugement du Synode National 1619 Dordrecht. BSHPF KBH

(25) Hendrici Stromberg P.L. Meletma Epicum de Synodis ad Synodum Nationalem Solemniter celebratum Dordrechti An 1618/19...Dordrechti, Exscribebat typis Petrus Verhagius...An 1619. KBH

(26) Tractatus Synodicus ad Synodum Dordracenam In quo de Synodorum sive Conciliorum Institutione, Usu, Causis, Fumitate, Authoritate, et Praerogativa Authore Laurentio Beyerlinck Archipresbytero Ciuitatis Antuerpiensis, Antwerp 1619. KBH

(27) Een cort verhael, hoe ende in wat maniere die Gommarissen van Hollant, Hemel en eerde willen innemen met eenen slack, Nae die Leere ende Professije van plancius, soo sal Roomen en het gheheele Roomsche Rijck vergaen, ...En nae die Leere van Calvinus die no in die Synode benesticht wort soo is Godt die oorsaeck van alle sonden...Ghesteldt in Rijme, ende Ghemaeckt door een Lieflhebber t'Hantwerpen 1619. KBH

(28) Schandigh ende grouwelije Laster-dicht gheintituleert Ene Cort Verhael Vande Sententie...van die Joden over Christus..., en oock die schroomelijcke Sententie, van de Gommaristen, ghedaen in die Stadt van Dort, al daer inde Synode Wtghesproken over den Hemelschen Vader, ...Gestelt in Rijmme, door eenen Liefhebber. Alwaer tot Antwoort is by gevoecht een cort Verhael vande vermetententheyt des Paus van Roomen enz...Mitsgaders de grouwelicke abuysen die inde Roomsche...Kercke...geleert worden. Door een Lief-hebber. Eerst Ghedruct tot Hantwerpen by Anthoni Spirinex, ende daer na met de Ant woorde daer by, Ghedruckt tot Breda by Steven Wylicx, Anno 1619. KBH

(29) Naem-register Van alle de Ghecommitteerde, soo Politijcke als Kerckelijcke, opt Nationael Synode van de Nederlantsche Gepretendeerde Ghereformeerde Kercken, d'welcke ghehouden wordt binnen der Stede van Dordrecht int jaer 1618.   Naer de Coppije tot Dordrecht Ghedruckt by Pieter Verhaghen...t'Hantwerpen MDCXIX. KBH BM

(30) Auspicium Synodi Nationalis Ecclesiarum Reformatarum Belgicarum, quae celebratur Dordrecht, Ann 1618 et 1619 cum Nomenclature Deputatorem ad hanc Synodum. Dordrechti 1619. KBH

(31) Oratie Van...Mr Symon Episcopius...By hem inde Synode Nationael tot Dordrecht...gedaen, den 7 December Ao 1618, 1619. KBH

(32) Vertoogh ende Supplicatie...Ghedruct 1619. KBH

(33) Korte ende Klare Verantwoordinghe, Der Remonstranten: Tegens Verscheyden onwaere ende ongefundeerde blaemen, die hun over handel inde Synode Nationael hier ende daer, met groote misleydinghe der eenvoudigen nagestroyt ende te laste gheleyt werden Ghedruct MDCXIX. KBH

(34) Requeste Verduytscht uyt de Latijnsche Tale, Aen de...Gecommitteerde vande...Staten-Generael; op den Synode Nationnael, binnen de Stadt Dordrecht vergadert. MDCXIX. KBH

(35) Oordeel...(Na de Copye Ghedruckt tot Dordrecht) 1619. KBH

(36) The Judgement of the Nationall Synode of the Reformed Belgique Churches, assembled at Dort, Anno 1618 and 1619...Concerning the fiue Articles controverted in the Belgique Churches:...Englished out of the Latin copie. London 1619. KBH

(37) Confession de Foy Des Eglises Reformees Du Pays-Bas.Reveue au dernier Synode National de Dordrecht: Et au nom d'icelui mise en lumiere, ..Par Privilege de sept ans. 1619. Dordrecht 1619. KBH

(38) Kerken-ordeninge: Gestelt inden Nationalen Synode...Binnen Dordrecht, inden Jare 1618 ende 1619. Ende alsoo goet ghevonden ende gearresteert by de...Staten s'Landts van Vtrecht, Opden vj Augusti des voorsz Jaers 1619. KBH

1620
(1) Kercken-ordeninge, gestelt inde nationalen synode der ghereformeerde kercken, gehouden binnen Dordrecht in 1618 en '19, Utrecht 1620. TCD. Arnhem 1620. BM54/924

(2) Naemregister van alle de ghecommitteerde, soo Politijcke als Kerckelijcke, opt Nationael Synode...d'welcke ghehouden wordt binnen...Dordrecht int Jaer 1618 Naer de Coppije tot Dordrecht ghedruckt, etc. Antwerp 1620. BM

(3) Acta et scripta Synodalia Dordracena ministrorum Remonstrantium in foederato Belgio. Harder-wiici 1620. TCD BPU BM54/926

(4) Acta Synodi Nationalis, In nomine Domini nostri Iesu Christi, Autoritate illustr. et praepotentum DD ordinum generalium foederati Belgii Provinciarum, Dordrechti habitae Anno 1618 et 1619 Accedunt Plenissima, de Quinque Articulis, Theologorum Judicia. Lugduni Batavorum, Typis Isaaci Elzeviri, Academiae Typographi, Societatis Dordrechtanae sumptibus 1620 Cum privilegio Ill. Ord. Generalium. BPU TCD AC BM54/923

(5) Antidotum continens pressiorem declarationem propriae et genvinae sententiae quae in Synodo Nationali Dordracena asserta est et stabilita. Belgice primum in lucem editum, nunc vero non parum auctum et Latinitate donatum. Accersit duplex Index, tum rerum memorabilium, tum omnium Scripturae locorum, quae in nuper editis Actis et Scriptis Citatorum Remonstrantum Synodo exhibitis occurrunt...Herder-Wiici Ex Officina typographi synodalis Anno MDCXX. KBH BM54/925

(6) Acta Synodi Nationalis, In nomine Domini nostri Iesu Christi, Autoritate DD ordinum generalium foederati Belgii provinciarum, Dordrechti habitae Anno 1618 et 1619. Accedunt Plenissima, de Quinque Articulis, Theologorum Iudicia. Dordrechti, Typis Isaac Ioannidis Canini, et Sociorum ejusdem Urbis Typographorum 1620. Cum provilegio Ill. Ordd. Generalium. AC

(7) T'Hemelsch Synodus ende Rechtmatigh Oordeel gehouden tot Zion. Teghen 't Aerdtsche Synodus Nationael Ende Onrechtueerdich Oordeel, Ghehouden binnen Dordrecht in de Dool-Cappelle Anno 1618 en 1619. KBH

(8) Acta Synodi Nationalis, In nomine Domini nostri Iesu Christi, Autoritate illustr. et praepotentium DD. ordinum generalium foederati Belgii Provinciarum Dordrechti habitae Anno 1618 et 1619 Accedunt Plenissima, de Quinque Articulis, Theologorum Iudicia Dordrechti. Typis Isacci Ioannidis Canini et Sociorum, 1620 Cum Provilegio Illustr. Ordd. Generalium. MHR BM54/923

(9) Effigiatio Synodi Nationalis inchoatae Dordrechti anno 1519 (sic). In quo loca tam Delegatorum...Ordinum Generalium Foederatarum Provinciarum, quam exterorum Professorum...graphice delincatae exhibentur. Amsterdam? BM54/926

(10) Malderus, Johannes. Anti Synodica, sive animadversiones in decreta conventus Dordraceni, Quam vocant Synodum Nationalem, de quinque doctrinae capitibus, inter Remonstrantes et Contraremonstrantes controversis. Antverpiae, 1620.

(11) Acta Synodi Nationalis...Dordrechti habitae. Hanau 1620.

1621
(1) Openinghe der Synodale Canones begrepen in het eerste (Tweede) Hooftstuck. Waerin claerlijck bewesten wort hoe onghefondeert de selve zijn, ende strijdich met de Schriftur, etc. Leyden? BM54/926

(2) Oordeel...van het Synode Nationael...tot Alez...ever het Synode Nationael...tot Dordrecht in...1618 ende 1619 etc. TCD BM54/926

(3) Harangue ou Exhortation, prononcee en Latin, au Synode de Dordrecht en Hollande...1618...mise en Francois. Geneva. BM54/281

1622

(1) Bestorming van de burcht des Satans die hem de Dortsche nationale synode onder den schoonen naem van den berch zyon heelft ghearbeyt te herstellen en te beschermen. TCD

(2) Canones synodi Dordracenae cum notis et animadversionibus Dan. Tileni. Adjecta sunt ad calcem papalipomena ad amicam collationem quam cum Dan. Tileno ante biennium institutam nuper publicavit Jo. Camero. Paris, apud Nicolam Buon. BNS TCD BM54/924

(3) Gronwel der verwoestinghe staende in de Heylighe plaetse: dat is…Verhael vande…Nulliteyten des nationalen Synodi, ghehouden binnen Dordrecht, in de jaren 1618 ende 1619 (By D.Dwinglo) Enghuyssen. BM54/926

(4) Verhael vande mis-handelingen, …des nationalen synodi, ghehouden binnen Dordrecht, in 1618 en '19. 3 vols Enghuysen. TCD

1623

(1) Historisch Verhael van't ghene sich toeghedraeghen hefr binnen Dordrecht in de Jaeren 1618. ende 1619. tusschen de Nationale Synode der Contra-Remonstranten…ter eender, ende de Geciteerde Kercken-Dienaeren Remonstranten, ter ander zyden. Oorspronek . . . Der Nederlantsche Kerckelijcke verschillen, etc. BM54/926

1624

(1) Actes du Synode National Tenu a Dordrecht, l'An 1618 et 20. Ensemble les Jugemens tant des Pais Bas, sur les poincts de doctrine y debattus et controvers. Mis en Francois par Richard Iean de Neree. Ministre de la parole de Dieu. Avec des Tables et Indices des noms et des matieres generales qui y sont contenues. Leyden. BPU BM54/923

1626

(1) The Anatomy of Arminianisme or, the opening of the Controversies of these times (formerly handled in the Low-Countries) concerning the doctrine of Prouidence, of Predestination, of the death of Christ, of Nature and Grace etc. By Peter du Moulin, Minister of the Church at Paris,. London. AC

(2) An examination of those things wherein the author of the late appeale holdeth the doctrines of the Pelagians and Arminians to be the Doctrines of the Church of England. Written by Goerge Carleton, Dr of Divinitie and Bishop Chichester…Whereunto also there is annexed a joint Attestation, avowing that the Discipline of the Church of England was not impeached by the Synod of Dort. London. TCD

(3) Pelagius redivivus or Pelagius raked out of the ashes by Arminius and his Schollers. London TCD

(4) A Second Parallel Together with a Writ of Error sued against the Appealer. London TCD

1627

(1) Suffragium collegiale Theologorum Magnae Britanniae de quinque contro-versis Remonstrantium Articulis judicio Synodico praevium (signed by G.Carleton, J.Davenant, S.Ward, T.Goad and W.Balcanquall) Cui adjuncta est Concio de gratia discriminante...per S.Wardum, ab authore jam recognita. Lon-don. BM65/3014

1629

(1) Conciliabuli Dordraceni Ascia, by Dausquius, C. BM54/926

(2) Ondersoeck Vande Wettelijckheydt der Remonstrantiche Conventiculen. Dienstich Om te bethoonen dat de Remonstrantien inde Requesten die so aende Ed Mog.H.M.Staten, als aende E.Magistraet van Amstelredam, ende anders, tegen de selve Conventiculen sijn overgeven in goede redenen sijn gefondeert. etc. hiet achter is by gevaecht de propositie ghedaen by Mr Rouse in het Lagher-Huys van het Parlement. Haerlem. TCD

(3) The Collegiate Suffrage of the Divines of Great Britaine concerning the Five Articles controverted in the Low Countries...delivered at the Synod of Dort, March 6, Anno 1619 etc. London. BM65/3014

(4) J.Hall, the Reconciler, an Epistle Pacificatorie of the seeming Differences of Opinion concerning the trueness and Visibility of the Roman Church. London. BM96/283

1630

(1) WmPrynne, Anti-Arminianisme. Or the Church of England's old antithesis to the new Arminianism. Wherein seven Anti-Arminian Orthodox tenets, are evidently proved, their seven opposite Arminian (once Popish and Pelagian) Errours are manifestly disproved, to be the ancient, established, undoubted Doctrine of the primitive and moderne Church of England; (as also of the prim-itive and present Churches of Scotland and Ireland). By the concurrent testi-mony of sundry ancient Brittish, English, Scottish, Irish Authours and Records, from the yeare of our Lord 430 till about the yeare 1440: and by the severall Records and Writers of these Churches, from the beginning of the reformation to the present: By William Prynne, an utter-Barrester of Lincolnes Inne.

1633

(1) Guiliemi Amesii, Anti-synodalia scripta vel animadversionibus in Dogmatica illa, quae Remonstrantes in Synodo Dordracena, exhiberunt, postea divulgar-unt. Amsterdam. TCD

1642

(1) G.Carleton, His testimony concerning the Presbyterian Discipline in the Low Countries and Episcopall Government here in England. London.

(2) The opinion of the English Doctors and Divines at the Synod at Dort concerning episcopacy and lay-elders. BM54/924

1645

(1) Canones ecclesiastici conditi in Synodo nationali Dordracena. BM54/924

1650

(1) The Doctrine of the Synod of Dort and Arles reduced to the practice (By W.Twysse) London? BM54/925

1651

(1) ...Redemption Redeemed. Wherein the work of the Redemption of the world...is vindicated...against the incroachments of later times made upon it...Together with a sober...discussion of Election and reprobation etc. London BM88/910

1653

(1) The history of Great Britain, being the life and reign of King James the first, relating to what passed from his first Access to the Crown, till his Death, by Arthur Wilson. London

1658

(1) The Grotian religion discovered, At the Invitation of Mr Thomas Pierce in his vindication. With a Preface, vindicating the Synod of Dort from the calumnies of the New Tilenus, and David, Peter, etc., And the Puritanes, and Sequestrations, etc from the censures of Mr Pierce. By Richard Baxter. London. LLB

1659

(1) Golden Remains of the ever Memorable Mr Iohn Hales of Eton College etc. London.

(2) Arcana dogmatum Anti-Remonstrantium Or the Calvinists Cabinet unlock'd in An Apology for Tilenus against a pretended Vindication of the Synod of Dort. At the provocation of Master R.Baxter, held forth in the Preface to his Grotian Religion. Together, With a few soft Drops let fall upon the Papers of Master Hickman. London. AC BM6/446

1661

(1) A brief account of the Synod at Dort in Stimluus Orthodoxus, Sive Goadus Redivivus. A disputation Partly Theological, partly Metaphysical, concerning the Necessity and Contingency of Events in the World, in respect of God's Eternal Decree. Written above twenty years since by that Reverend and Learned Divine, Thomas Goad, Doctor of Divinity, and Rector of Hadleigh in Suffolk. London.

1663

(1) Post Acta ofte Nae-handelingen des Nationalen Synodi...Ghouden...tot Dordrecht Anno 1618 ende 1619. Hier...bij ennige Extracten uyt de Actis Synodi Provincialis Ultrajectinae, gehouden Anno 1619 den 10 Augusti en geeyndicht den 1 Septemb 1620 als mede een Extract van de...Staten...van Utrecht, wan wegen het Jus Patronatus. Noyt voor desen in druck geweest...Zutphen, voor Hieronymus van Willemsteyn... KBH TCD

1666

(1) The history of the Church of Scotland. Beginning the Year of our Lord 203, and continued to the end of the reign of King James the VI of ever blessed Memory etc etc. By John Spotswood, Lord Archbishop of Saint Andrews. London. LLB

1668

(1) Acta Synodi nationalis...Dordrechti Habitae. Anno 1618 et 19 etc. Apud Hillebrandum a Wouw. Hagae-Comitis 1668. BM (*BM Gen. Cat. Printed Books, Ten Year Supplement 1956-65*, vol 12, col 914)

1669

(1) Handelingen des Nationalen Synodi gehouden tot Dordrecht in de Jaren 1618 en 1619 etc, Jacobus Scheltus 's Graven-Hage. (*BM Gen. Cat. Printed Books, Ten Year Supplement 1956-65*, vol 12, col 914).

1670

(1) Korte Overweninge van het Synode van Dort. Gehaelt uyt de Brieven van Mr Hales en Mr Balcanqual, geschrieven uyt Dort aen...Dudley Carleton, als doen Ambassadeur in den Hage. In 't Engelsch beschreven door Dr Laurentius Womachius, ...Na de Engelse Copye, Gedrucket tot London by W.Leaske Anno 1661 Verstaelt in 't Nederduytsch. En gedruckt tot Amsterdam 1670. KBH

1671

G.Brandts Historie der Reformatie, en andre Kerkelyke geschiedenissen, in en ontrent de Nederlanden. Met eenige Aentekeningen en Aenmerkin-gen. Amsterdam, 4 vols MHR

1672

(1) Aerius Redivivus or the history of the Presbyterians containing The Beginning, Progresse, and successes of that active Sect. Their Oppositions to Monarchial and Episcopal Government. Their Innovations in the Church; and their Imbroilments of the Kingdoms and Estates of Christendom in the pursuit of their Designs from the Year 1536 to the Year 1647. By Peter Heylyn, DD. London.

1674

(1) The history of the Church of Great Britain from the Birth of our saviour; untill the Year of our Lord 1667. With an exact Succession of the Bishops, and the memorable Acts of many of them. Together with an Addition of all the English Cardinals; and the several Orders of English Monks, Friars, and Nuns, in former Ages. London. LLB

(2) H.Witte - Memoriae theologum nostri saeculi clarissimorum renovatae Dec I-VI.

1675

(1) The Marrow of Ecclesiastical History, divided into two parts: The First containing the Life of our Blessed Lord and Saviour Jesus Christ, with The Lives of the Ancient Fathers, School-Men First-Reformers, and Modern Divines. The Second, Containing The Lives of Christian Emperors, Kings, and Sovereign Princes. Whereunto are Added The lives of Inferiour Christians, who have lived in these latter centuries. And Lastly, are subjoyned the Lives of many of those, who by their Vertue and Valor obtained the Sirname of Great. Divers of which, give much light to sundry places of Scripture; especially to the Prophesies concerning the Four Monarchies. Together with the lively Effigies of the most Eminent of them cut in Copper. By Samuel Clarke. London. LLB

1676

(1) L.Moreri - Le Grand dictionnaire historique, ou le melange curieux de l'histoire sacree et profane etc. Bale 1731-2, 6 vol. fol.

1679

(1) Apologie pour le Synode de Dordrecht, ou Refutation du livre Intitule, L'Impiete de la Morale des Calvinistes, etc. Geneva. BPU BSHPF

1681

(1) ...the historical and miscellaneous tracts of the Reverend and Learned Peter Heylyn, D.D. Now collected into one Volume. (No. III) Historia Quinquarticularis: or, A Historical Declaration of the Judgment of the Western Churches, and more particularly of the Church of England, in the Five Controverted Points reproach'd in these last times with the Name of Arminianism. London.

1684

(1) Extract uyt de Hollandse rym-kronych aengaende het neemen van judicieele information, en het poortreght van Dordregt. Amsterdam. TCD

1688

(1) Golden Remains of the ever Memorable Mr John Hales of Eaton-Colledge, etc., ...With Additions from the Authors own copy...Letters and Expresses Concerning the Synod of Dort. London.

1697

(1) A Carolus, Memorabilia ecclesiastica saeculi a nato Xto 17 juxta annorum seriam. Tubingen.

(2) P.Bayle - Dictionnaire historique et critique. Rotterdam 1697 2 vol. fol.

1712

(1) Extracten, Getrokken uyt den Nationalen Synode, gehouden tot Dordrecht, in...1618 en 1619. Raakende Den Voet, ordre, en mainere van de Catechisatien: Mitsgaders Copien van de Extracten der nadder regelmenten uyt de Provinciale Synoden van Zuyt-Holland, op het poinct van de voorseyde Catechisatien: Gelyk ook Tegens de Conventiculen redert den voorseyden Jaare gearresteert, tot...1682 incluys. Mytgegeven door ordre van den E Kerkenraad van Leiden. En nu wederom...door ordre en resolutie van de...Classis van Zuyd-Holland (Junii 1712) Dordrecht, J. van Braam. KBH

1720-23

(1) The History of the Reformation and other Ecclesiastical Transactions in and about the Low-Countries From the Beginning of the Eighth Century, Down to the Famous Synod of Dort, inclusive. In which all the Revolutions that happen'd in Church and State, on Account of the Divisions between the Protestants and Papists, the Arminians and Calvinists Are fairly and fully represented By the Reverend and Learned Mr Gerard Brandt, late Professor of Divinity, and Minister to the Protestant Remonstrants at Amsterdam. Faithfully Translated from the Original Low-Dutch. London 1720-23.

1721

(1) Heidelberg Catechism. A Chatechism of the Christian Religion, with the Confession of Faith revised in the Nationall Synod...held at Dordrecht, etc. BM54/926

1723

(1) Synode de Dordrecht, cf. Miscellanea Cigurnica, 2nd part, III, 1723, BSHPF

1724

(1) J.Halesius, Historia concili Dordraceni, Latin translation and life of Hales by J.L.Mosheim. Hamburg.

1725

(1) De Heydelbergsch catechismus, met de schriftuur-texten; en het oordeel van de nationale synode van Dordrecht over de vyf stucken der leere. Dordrecht.

1726

(1) La Confession de foy des Eglises Reformees des Pais Bas, representee en deux colomnes, l'une portant la Confession ancienne; et l'autre, la revision qui en este faite au Synode National de Dordrecht, L'an 1619: avec le jugement du dit Synode sur les 5 articles et la discipline ecclesiastique, etc. BM

(2) G.Brandt, Histoire abregee de la reformation des Pays-Bas, translated from the Dutch. The Hague, BPU

1754

(1) de Burigny, The Life of the truly Eminent and Learned Hugo Grotius Containing A Copius and Circumstanced History of the several Important and Honourable Negotations In which he was employed; Together with a Critical Account of his Works. Tr. from the French. London.

1760

(1) La discipline ecclesiastique des eglises reformees de France et la discipline du Synode de Dordrecht. BSHPF

1774

(1) Historic proof of the doctrinal Calvinism of the Church of England Including, among other Particulars, I A Brief Account of some Eminent Persons, famous for their Adoption of that System, both before and since the Reformation; more especially, of our English Reformers, martyrs, prelates, and universitys: With Specimens of their testimonys. II An incidental review of the rise and progress of Arminiamism in England, Under the Patronage of Archbishop Laud. With a complete Index to the Whole. London. By Augustus Toplady.

1775

(1) Letters from and to Sir Dudley Carleton, Knt. during his embassy in Holland, From January 1615/16 to December 1620. London. TCD

1776

(1) Historie van de synode gehouden binnen Dordrecht, in 1618-19; door den procureur van de vaderlandsche kerke, Arnhem. TCD

1818

(1) The Articles of the Synod of Dort, and its rejection of errors: with the history of events which made way for that Synod, as published by the Authority of the States-General: and the documents confirming its decisions. By T.Scott. BM54/923

1825

(1) M.Graf - Beytrage zur Kenntniss der Geschichte der Synode von Dordrecht. Basel 1825. 8o.

1826

(1) Bishop Hall, his life and times or, Memoirs of the life, writings, and sufferings of the Right Rev Joseph Hall DD. successively Bishop of Exeter and Norwich; with a view of the times in which he lived; and an appendix, containing some of his unpublished writings, his funeral sermon, etc. By the Rev. John Jones. London.

1838

(1) Zeitschrift fur die Historische Theologie 1838, pp 39-105. Uber den in Heidelbergischen Katechismus ausgedruckten Lehrbegriff. Ein historisch-dogmatischen Versuch von D.Moritz Johann Heinrich Beckhaus, ordentlichem, Professor de Theologie zu Marburg.

1841

(1) The Articles of the Synod of Dort translated from the Latin, with notes, by the Rev. Thomas Scott DD to which is added an introductory essay by the Rev. Samuel Miller DD. Philadelphia. AC BM54/932

(2) Histoire du Synode de Dordrecht consideree sous ses rapports religieux et politiques, des 1609 a 1619 publiee par N.Chatelain. Paris and Amsterdam. BPU BSHPF MHR

1843

(1) The Decision of the National Synod, of the Dutch Reformed Churches, held at Dort in 1618 and 1619...Translated into the English language, by O.Jones. BM54/923

1844

(1) G.D.G.Schotel, Jean Diodati. BPU

1853

(1) Zeitschrift fur die Historische Theologie, 1853, pp 226-327. Historia Synodi nationalis Dordracenae, sive Literae delegatorum Hassiacorum de iis quae in synodo D. acta sunt ad landgravium Mauritium missae. Editae ab H.Heppe, SS.Theol. D. et Prof. P.E. in academia Marburgensi.

1854

(1) Zeitschrift fur die Historische Theologie, 1854 IV pp 645-8. Dordrechter Synode, die, und die Apokryphen, Von Dr A.Schweizer, Prof in Zurich.

1855

(1) Jean Gaberel, Histoire de l'Eglise de Geneve depuis Le commencement de la Reformation jusqu'en 1815. Geneva. II/284-9.

1856

(1) A.Schweizer, Die Protestantischen Centraldogmen. Zurich.

(2) The Articles of the Synod of Dort, and its rejection of errors: with the history of events which made way for that Synod, as published by the authority of the States-General: and the documents confirming its decisions. Philadelphia. BM54/923

1863

(1) The History and Literature of the Heidelberg Catechism and of its Introduction into the Netgerlands translated from the German of von Alpen by J.F.Berg. Philadelphia. AC

1864

(1) Zeitschrift fur die Historisch Theologie 1864, pp 362-3. Geschichte, Geist und Bedeutung des Heidelberger Katechismus. Ein Beitrag zur dreihundertjahrigen Jubelfeier. Von Dr Philipp Schaff.

1868

(1) Vereeniging tot Bevordering der Volksgezondheid. Verslag van de Vereeniging...1867, etc. Dordrecht. BM

(2) The Church History of Britain from The birth of Jesus Christ until the year MDCXLVIII endeavoured by Thomas Fuller DD Prebendary of Sarum Author of "The Worthies of England", "Pisgahsight of Palestine", "Abel Redivivus", etc etc. Ed. J.Nichols. ACetc

(3) Letters of Wtenbogaert, ed. H.C.Rogge. Utricht, III vols.

1869

E.de Bude, Vie de Jean Diodati Theologien Genevois. Lausanne.

1874

(1) J.L.Motley, The Life and Death of John of Barneveld, Advocate of Holland; with a view of the primary causes and movements of the Thirty Years War. London. LLBetc.

(2) H.C.Rogge, Johannes Wtenbogaert en zijn tijd. Amsterdam.

1877

(1) P.Schaff, A History of the Creeds of Christendom with translations. London. pp 502-23.

1881

(1) H.Blind, Le synode de Dordrecht. Geneva.

1884

(1) L.Ulbach and others. La Hollande et la liberte au xviie et au xviiie siecle.

1886

(1) G.Lewis. Life of Joseph Hall.

1887

(1) Acta of Handelingen der Nationale Synode...gehouden...te Dordrecht ten jare 1618 en 1619...In de tegenwoordige spelling naar de oorspionkelijke Nederduitsche uitgave onder toezicht van J.H.Donner en S.A.van den Hoorn. Leyden. BM54/923

1889

(1) C.Flour, Etude historique de l'Arminianisme. Nimes.

1897

(1) T.Fuller. Life of John Davenant.

1899

(1) H.H.Kuyper. Post-acta of nahandelingen van de Nat. Synode van Dordrecht in 1618 en 1619 gehouden, naar den authentieken tekat in het Latyn en Nererlandsch uitgegeven en met toelichtingen voorzien, voorafgegaan door de gerschiedenis van de acta, de autographa en de post-acta dier Synode...Een historische studie door H.H.Kuyper. Amsterdaman Pretoria. BM54/924

1900

(1) Die vijf artikelen tegen de Remonstranten - Canones of Leerregelsvastegesteld op de Nationale Synode, gehouden binnen Dordrecht in de jaren 1618 en 1619. Groningen. BM54/926

(2) Nederlandsch Archief voor Kerkgeschiedenis, new series, I, 1900-1901 pp 418-22, Twee brieven van Prins Maurits over Antonius Walaeus. Dr E.J.W.Posthumus Meyjes.

1903

(1) Nederlandsch Archief voor Kerkgeschiedenis, new series, II, 1903, pp 98-100, Eene verklaring van den Kerkeraad te 's-Gravenhage van 21 Sept 1618. Dr B.Tideman.

(2) ibid. pp 210-13, Twee brieven van Johannes Wtenbogaert. Dr H.C.Rogge.

(3) ibid. pp 276-9, De wording der Reformeerde gemeente te emmerik. W.Meijer.

(4) ibid. pp 309-12, Een onderteekeningsformuier voor predikanten. Dr P.A.Klap.

1904

(1) C.Harwick. A history of the Articles of Religion to which is added a series of documents from A.D.1536 to A.D.1615 together with illustrations from contemporary sources. London. AC

1908

(1) Nederlandsch Archief voor Kerkgeschiedenis, new series, V, 1908, pp 161-190. Kerkelijcke twisten omtrent d'Arminiaenschen tijt. J. de Vries Az.

(2) O.Ritschl - Dogmengeschichte des Protestantismus. Grundlagen und Grundzuga der theologischen Gedanken und Lehrbildung in dem protestantischen Kirchen. Leipzig 1908-27. 8o.

1909

(1) L.H.Wagenaar. Van Strijd en Overwinning. Utrecht.

1910

(1) P.Tschackert - Die Entstehung der lutherischen und der reformierten Kirchenlehre samt ihren innerportestantischen Gegensatzen. Gottingen 1910. 8o.

1913

(1) A.H.Haentjens. Remonstrantsche en calvinistische dogmatick. Leyden.

1914

(1) H.Kaajaan. De Pro-Acta der Dordtsche Synode in 1618. Rotterdam.

1915

(1) T.Bos. de Dordtsche Leerregelen. Kampen BM54/924

1918

(1) H.Kaajan. De Groote Synode van Dordrecht in 1618-19. Amsterdam.

(2) W.Meindersma. De Synode van Dordrecht. Zelt-Bommel.

1919

(1) G.Oorthuys. Anastasiuse "Wechwijzer", Bullingers "Huys Boeck" en Calvijn's "Institutie" vergeleken in hun leer van God en Mensch. Een bladzijde oit de vaderlandsche Theologie voor de Synode van Dordrecht. Leyden.

(2) De Remonstranten. Guedenkboeck bij het 300 jarig bestaan der Remonstrantsche Broederschap. Leyden.

1923

(1) Harvard Theological Review. The Remonstrants at the Synod of Dort in 1618. H.D.Foster.

1924

(1) M.Meijerling. De Dordtsche Leerregels. Groningen.

1926

(1) W.A.Harrison. The beginnings of Arminianism to the Synod of Dort. London.

1932

(1) Nederlandsch Archief voor Kerkegeschiedenis, new series, XXIV, pp 187-204, Koning Jacobus I en de Synode van Dordrecht. P. van Itterzoon.

(2) ibid, pp 1-24, Scotland and the Synod of Dort. G.D.Henderson.

1934

(1) Huntington Library Bulletin, 1934. Arminian versis Puritan in England c 1620-50. G.Davies.

1936

(1) Nederlandsch Archief voor Kerkgeschiedenis, new series, XXVIII, 1936, pp 3-20. Betrekkingen tusschen Roomsch-Katholien en Remonstranten inden tijd der Synode van Dordrecht. Dr J.Lindebloom.

1937

(1) Dr J.G.Feenstra. De Dordtsche leerregelen. Kampen BM54/924

(2) J.J.van der Schuit. De Dordtsche Synode en het supra-Lapsarisme. Dordrecht. BM

(3) A.W.Harrison. Arminianism. London AC TCD BM

1838

(1) D.Noble. Theocracy and Toleration. A study of the Disputes in Dutch Calvinism from 1600 to 1650. Cambridge.

1943

(1) Tijdschrift voor Geschiedenis, 1943, pp 6-21, Nederlandsch-Engelsche betiekkingen op den boden van Arminianismus. C.W.Rolandus.

1945

(1) P.H.Winkelman. Remonstranten en Katholieken in de eeuw van de Hugo de Groot. Nijmegen.

1946

(1) W.F.Dankbaar. Hoogtepunten uit het Nederlandsche Calvinisme in de zestiende eeuw. Haarlem.

1947

(1) J.H.van Aken. De Remonstrantsche Broederschap in verleden en heden. Arnhem.

(2) E. van Gelder. Vrijheid en onvrijheid in de Republiek. vol I. Haarlem.

(3) H.Smitskamp. Calvinistisch nationaal besef in Nederland voor het midden der XVIIe eeuw. The Hague.

1948

(1) W.J.MEysinga. Die internationale Synode van Dordrecht, in "Exuli amico Huizinga". Haarlem.

(2) Theology. The Church of England and non-Episcopal Churches in the seventeenth and eightteenth centuries. N.Sykes.

1950

(1) J.G.Feenstra. De Dordtse Leerregelen. Kampen 1950.

1951

(1) J.N.Bakhuizen Van den Brink, Controverse in de zestrende eeuw, in "Geloofsinhoud en geloofsbeleving". Utrecht.

1952

(1) Nederlandsch Archief voor Kerkgeschiedenis, new series, 1952, pp 132-46. Engelse kerkelijke in de Nederlanden in de eerste helft der XVII de eeuw. J.N.Bakhuizen Van den Brink

1956

(1) N.Sykes. Old Priest and New Presbyter. Cambridge.

1957

J.Veenhof. Het Remonstrantisme te Kampen tot de regeringsverandering in 1620, in "Kampen Almanak 1957-8", pp 255-72.

1958

(1) A.L.Drummond. The Kirk and the Continent. Edinburgh.

(2) K.Guggisberg. Bernische Kirchengeschichte. Bern. pp 299ff, 333, 415.

1961

(1) Nederlandsch Archief voor Kerkgeschiedenis, new series, vol 44, 1961, pp 45-64. Remonstrantse sympathieen en controversen in de Hervormde Gemeente van Breda, 1610-20. Een bejdrage tot de geschiedenis van de ondste Remonstrantse stromingen heer te lande. A.Hallema.

(2) Church History 1961, pp 155-70. Arminius and the Reformation. Carl Bangs.

1962

(1) Doctrinal Standards of the Christian Reformed Church. pp 44-66. Grand Rapids.

1964

(1) Studies in Church History, I, 1964, pp 20-34. Arminianism and Laudianism in Seventeenth Century England. T.M.Parker.

1965

(1) W.Rex. Essays on Pierre Bayle and religious controversy. The Hague, BPU Zt 2564/8.

1966

(1) The Churchman, vol 80, no 3, Autumn 1966, pp 194-200. Bishop Joseph Hall, 1574-1656: An Ecumenical Calvinist Churchman. M.W.Dewar.

1967

(1-) Nederlands Archief voor Kerkgeschiedenis, new series, 1967/8, pp 267-80. Englese belangstelling voor de Canones van Dordrecht. G.P.Itterzoh.

(2) Nederlands Theologisch Tijdschrift, December 1967. Daar moet veel stijds gestieden zijn. Het Cevan van Dirk. Rafaelsz Camphuysen 1586-1627.

(3) Proceedings of the Huguenot Society of London, vol 21, no 2, 1967 for 1966, pp 119-123. The Synod of Dort, the Westminster Assembly and the French Reformed Church, 1618-43. M.W.Dewar.

1968

(1) Calvin Theological Journal, vol 3, no 2, 1968, pp 133-62. A new English translation of the Canons of Dort. Anthony A. Hoekema.

(2) P.Y.De Yong, (ed), Crisis in the Reformed Churches. Essays in commemoration of the great Synod of Dort, 1618-19. Grand Rapids.

1969

(1) Nederlands Theologisch Tijdschrift, June 1969, pp 349-63. De kerkordelijke kant van de Dortse Synode. G.J.Hoenderdaal.

(12) ibid, pp 339-48. De Dortse Synode 1619-1969. S.van der Linde.

Short title catalogue.

The following short title catalogue is arranged in alphabetical order. The article has been ignored when listing the items in this fashion, i.e. "The Articles of the Synod of Dort" is listed as "Articles", etc. Where there is a relevant article which has been published in a periodical, the item is listed both under the title of the article and the name of the periodical. Where two items are listed under the same short title, e.g. 1619/22,25, this should not be regarded as an indication that the items are identical, but rather that they have a similar short title. Two abbreviations have been used in the compilation of this list, "SG" for States General and "SD" for Synod of Dort irrespective of language.

Acta SD 1620/4,6,8,11. 1668/1.
Actes du SD 1624/1
Acta et scripta SD 1620/3
Acta of Handelingen der SD 1887/1
Aerius Redivivus or the history of the Presbyterians 1672/1
Afbeeldinghe des SD 1618/6 1618/14
Anastasieuse...Een Baldzijde oit de vaderlandsche Theol. voor de SD 1919/1
Anatomy of Arminianism 1626/1
Anti-Arminianisme 1630/1

Antidotum continens pressiorem declarationem...in SD 1620/5

Antidotum ende naerden openinghe van het eygeneghevoelen des SD 1619/2

Anti-synodalia 1633/1

Anti Synodica 1620/10

Apologie pour le SD 1679/1

Arcans dogmatum Anti-Remonstrantum Or the Calvinists Cabinet unlock'd 1659/2

Arminianism 1937/3

Arminianism and Laudianism 1964/1

Arminius and the Reformation 1961/2

Auspicium SD 1619/30

The Articles of the SD 1818/1 1841/1 1856/2

The beginnings of Arminianism to the SD 1926/1

Belydenisse des gheloofs der ghereformeerde kercken in Nederlant, overghe-sien in de SD 1619/3

Bernische Kirchengeschichte 1958/2

Bestorming van de burcht des Satans 1622/1

Betrekkingen tusschen Roomsch-Katholieken en Remonstranten 1936/1

Beytrage...zur Kenntniss der...Synode von Dordrecht 1825/1

Bishop Hall, his life and times 1826/1

Bishop Joseph Hall 1966/1

A brief account of SD in Stimluus Orthodoxus 1661/1

Calvinistisch nationaal besef in Nederland 1947/3

Calvin Theological Journal 1968/1

Canones Ecclesiastici conditi 1645/1

Canones SD 1622/2

Caricature of the Proceedings of the SD 1619/8

The Church of England and non-Episcopal Churches 1948/2

Church History 1961/2

Church History of Britain 1868/2

The Churchman 1966/1

The Collegiate Suffrage of the Divines of Great Britain 1629/3

Conciliabuli Dordraceni Ascia 1629/1

Confession de Foy des Eglises Reformees du Pays-Bas 1619/37 1726/

Controverse in de zestrende eeuw 1951/1

Copie van sekeren Brief uyt Dordrecht. 1618/12

Corte...ontdeckinghe vande Bedrieghelijckheydt des SD 1619/9

Cort verhael van die principaelste puncten die in Hollandt 1619/10

Crisis in the Reformed Churches 1968/2

Daer moet veel stijds gestieden zijn 1967/1

The Decision of the SD 1843/1

Dictionnaire historique et critique 1897/2

La discipline ecclesiastique des eglises reformes de France et...du SD 1760/1

Doctrinal standards of the Christian Reformed Church 1962/1

The Doctrine of the SD and Arles 1650/1

Dogmengeschichte des Protestantismus 1908/2

Dordrecht, dordeel des SD 1619/23

Dordrechter Synode, die, und die Apokryphen 1854/1

De Dordtsche Leerregelen 1915/1 1937/1

De Dordtsche Leerregels 1924/1

De Dordtse Leerregelen 1950/1

De DS en het supra-lapsarisme 1937/2

De Dortse Synode 1969/2

Een cort verhael 1619/27 1619/28

Eenighe Vraghen 1618/5

Eerw-Bischops van Landavien Oratie...vijfden November 1618. 1618/7

Effigiatioj SD 1620/9

Engelse kerkelijke in de Nederlanden 1952/1

Engelese belangstelling voor de Canones van Dordrecht 1967/2

Die Entstehung der lutherischen and der reformierten kirchenlehre 1910/1

Essays on Pierre Bayle 1965/1

Etude historique de l'arminianisme 1889/1

An examination of...the doctrines of the Pelagians & Arminains to be the
    Doctrines of the Church of England 1626/2

Extracten, Getrokken uyt den SD 1712/1

Extract uyt de Hollandse rym-kronych...en het poortreght van Dordregt 1684/1

Exuli amico Huizinga 1948/1

Geloofsinhoud en geloofsbeleving 1951/1

Geschichte, Geist und Bedeutung des Heidelberger Katechismus 1864/1

Golden Remains 1659/1 1688/1

Le Grand Dictionnaire 1676/1

Gronwel der Verwoestinghe staende in de Heylighe plaetse 1622/3

De Groote Synode van Dordrecht 1918/1

The Grotian religion discovered 1658/1

Handelingen des SD 1669/1

Harangue ou Exhortation, prononcee in Latin au SD 1621/3

Harvard Theological Review 1923/1

Heidelberg Catechism...revised in the SD 1721/1

De Heydelbergsch catechismus 1725/1

Historii concili Dordraceni 1724/1

Historia SD sive Literae delegatorum Hassiacorum 1853/1

Histoire abregee de la reformation des Pays-Bas 1726/2

Histoire de l'Eglise de Geneve 1855/1

Histoire du SD 1841/2

Historic proof of the doctrinal Calvinism of the Church of England 1774/1

historical and miscellaneous tracts...of Peter Heylyn 1681/1

Historie der Reformatie 1671/1

Historie van de SD 1776/1

Historisch Verhael 1623/1

The History and Literature of the Heidelberg Catechism 1863/1

History of Great Britain 1653/1

A history of the Articles of Religion 1904/1

The history of the Church of Great Britain 1674/1

History of the Church of Scotland 1666/1

A History of the Creeds of Christendom 1877/1

Oratie Davidis Parei 1619/19

Oratie Ghedaen vande...Bischop...Landavensi 1618/8

Oratie...Symon Episcopius 1619/31

Oration made at the Hague 1619/1

Ordeel des Synodi nationalis 1619/7

Pelagius redivivus or Pelagius raked out of the ashes 1626/3

Post Acta of nahandelingen van de SD 1899/1

Post-Acta ofte Nae-handelingen des SD 1663/1

De Pro-Acta der Dordtsche Synode in 1618 1914/1

Proceedings of the Huguenot Society of London 1967/3

Die Protestantischen Centraldogmen 1856/1

The Reconciler 1629/4

Redemption Redeemed 1651/1

De Remonstranten 1919/2

Remonstranten en Katholieken in de eeuw van de Hugo de Groot 1945/1

Remonstrantie van Joannes Wtenbogaert 1618/2 1618/3

Het Remonstrantisme te Kampen 1957/1

The Remonstrants at the SD in 1618 1923/1

De Remonstrantsche Broederschap 1947/1

Remonstrantsche en calvinistische dogmatick 1913/1

Remonstrantse sympathieen...in...Breda 1961/1

Request aende...der Vereenichde Provintien van weghen de Remonstranten 1619/14

Reqveste verduijtsch...aen de gecommitteerde SG; op SD 1619/21,34

Scotland and the SD 1932/2

Schandigh ende grouwelije Larter-dicht gheintituleert Een Cort Verhael 1619/28

A Second Parallel 1626/4

Ses vragen...dienende tot naerder openinghe...SD 1618/4

Specimen Controversiarum Belgicarum 1618/9

Van Strijd en Overwinning 1909/1

Studies in Church History 1964/1

Suffragium collegiale Theologorum Magnae Britanniae 1627/1

Synode de Dordrecht 1723/1 1881/1

The Synod of Dort etc. 1967/3

De Synode van Dordrecht 1918/2

Testimony concerning the Presbyterian Discipline 1642/1

'Thelmelsch Synodus 1619/12 1620/7

Theocracy and Toleration 1938/1

Theology 1948

Tijdschrift voor Geschiedenis 1943/1

Tractatus Synodicus 1619/26

Twee brieven van Johannes Wtenbogaert 1903/2

Twee brieven van Prins Maurits over Antonius Walaeus 1900/2

Uber den in Heidelbergischen Katechismus ausgedruckten lehrbegriff 1838/1

Vale hondende verclaringe 1619/22

Vereeniging tot Bevordering der Volksgezondheid 1868/1

Verhael vande mis-handelingen, ...SD 1622/4

Eene Verklaring van de Kerkeraad...van...1618 1903/1

Veroogh (*sic*) ende supplicatie, by de Remonstranten 1619/4,32
Vertoogh by de Remonstranten 1619/5
Vertroostinghe aen de remonstrantsche Kercken 1619/13
Vie de Jean Diodati 1869/1
Die vijf artikelen tegen de Remonstranten 1900/1
Vrijheid en onvrijheid in de Republiek 1947/2
De wording de Reformeerde gemeente te emmerik 1903/3
Zeitschrift fur die Historische Theologie 1838/1 1853/1 1854/1 1864/1

Author Index

The following list is, in fact, much more than an author index for it lists any personal name which appears in the titles of the works listed above. It is arranged in alphabetical order, and in doing so prefixes such as "von" or "de" have been ignored; e.g. Pierre du Moulin is entered as:- "Moulin, P. de".

Aken, J.N. van 1947/1
Alpen, von. 1863/1
Ames, Wm. 1633/1
Arminius 1626/4
Baarle, K. van 1619/13
Balcanqual, W. 1627/1 1670/1
Bangs,C. 1961/2
Barneveld, John of 1874/1
Baxter, R. 1658/1 1659/2
Bayle,P. 1697/2
Beckhaus, M.J.H. 1838/1
Berg, J.F. 1863/1
Beyerlinck,L. 1619/26
Blind,H. 1881/1
Bos,T. 1915/1
Brandt,G. 1671/1 1720-23/1 1726/2
Brink, Bakhuizen van den 1951/1 1952/1
Bude, E. de, 1869/1
Burigny, de. 1754/1
Calvin, J. 1619/27
Cameron,J. 1622/2
Camphuysen,R. 1967/1
Carleton,D. 1670/1 1775/1
Carleton,G. see Llandaff, Bishop of.
Carolus,A. 1697/1
Chatelain,N. 1841/2
Clarke,S. 1675/1
Damman,S. 1619/7
Dankbaar,W.F. 1946/1
Dausquius,C. 1629/1
Davenant,J. 1627/1 1897/1
Davies,G. 1934/1

Dewar,M.W. 1966/1 1967/2

Diodati,J. 1844/1 1869/1

Donner,J.M. 1887/1

Drummond,A.L. 1958/1

Dwinglo,B. 1619/17

Episcopius,S. 1618/1 1619/2,9,11,17,31

Eysinga,W.J.M. 1948/1

Feenstra,J.G. 1937/1 1950/1

Flour,C. 1859/1

Foster,M.D. 1923/1

Fuller,T. 1868/2 1897/1

Gaberel,J. 1855/1

Gelder,E. van 1947/2

Goad,T. 1627/1 1661/1

Goet Patriot 1618/12

Gomarus 1619/10

Graf,M. 1825/1

Grotius 1754/1 1945/1

Guggisberg,K. 1958/2

Haentjens,A.H. 1913/1

Hales,J. 1659/1 1670/1 1688/1 1724/1

Hall,J. 1629/4 1826/1 1886/1

Hallema,A. 1961/1

Hardwick,C. 1904/1

Harrison,W.A. 1926/1 1937/3

Henderson,G.D. 1932/2

Heppe,H. 1853/1

Heylyn,P. 1672/1 1681/1

Hickman,H. 1659/2

Hoekema,A.A. 1968/1

Hoenderdaal,G.J. 1969/1

Hommius,F. 1618/1,2,9,10. 1619/8

Hoorn,S.A. van den 1887/1

Huizinga,M. 1948/1

Itterzoh,G.P. 1967/2

Itterzoon,P. van 1932/1

Jones,J. 1826/1

Jones,O. 1843/1

Kaajaan,H. 1914/1 1918/1

Klap,P.A. 1903/4

Kuyper,H.H. 1899/1

Lewis,G. 1886/1

Linde,S. van der. 1969/2

Lindebloom,J. 1936/1

Llandaff, Bishop of. 1618/7,8 1619/1 1626/2 1627/1 1642/1

Lodensteyn,J. 1618/10

Malderus,J. 1620/10

Meijer,W. 1903/3

The Epigones

Meijerling,M. 1924/1
Meindersma,W. 1918/2
Meyjes,E.J.W. Posthumus 1900/1
Miller,S. 1841/1 1856/2
Moreri,L. 1676/1
Motley,J.L. 1874/1
Moulin,P. du 1626/1
Neomagus,A. 1619/12
Neree,R.J. de. 1624/1
Nobe,D. 1938/1
Dorthuys,G. 1919/1
Orange, Prince of. 1619/1 1619/4 1900/2
Pereius,D. 1619/19
Parker,T.M. 1964/1
Plancius 1619/27
Prynne,Wm. 1630/1
Rex,W. 1965/1
Ritschl,O. 1908/2
Rogge,H.C. 1868/3 1874/2 1903/2
Rolandus,C.W. 1943/1
Rouse 1629/2
Schaff,P. 1864/1 1877/1
Schotel,G.D.C. 1844/1
Schuit,J.J. van der. 1937/2
Schweizer,A. 1854/1 1856/1
Scott,T. 1818/1 1841/1 1856/2
Slatius,H. 1619/12
Smitskamp,H. 1947/3
Spotswood,J. 1666/1
Stromberg,H. 1619/25
Skyes,N. 1948/2 1956/1
Tideman,B. 1903/1
Toplady,A.M. 1774/1
Tschackert,P. 1910/1
Twysse,Wm. 1650/1
Ulbach,L. 1884/1
Utenbogaert, see Wtenbogaert.
Veenhof,J. 1957/1
Vorstius,C. 1619/16,20
Vries,J. de. 1908/1
Wagenaar,L.H. 1909/1
Walaeus,A. 1900/2
Ward,S. 1627/1
Wilson,A. 1653/1
Winkelman,P.H. 1945/1
Witte,H. 1674/2
Womack,L. 1659/2
Wtenbogaert,J. 1618/2,3 1868/3 1874/2 1903/2
Yong,P.Y. de. 1968/2